Economic Development in Latin America

Economic Development

in

Latin America

An Introduction to the

Economic Problems of Latin America

Simon G. Gabriel Hanson

Editor, Inter-American Economic Affairs

Washington ● The Inter-American Affairs Press ● *1951*

Preface

The author who has the temerity to undertake to describe and analyze the economies of the twenty Latin American republics in a single short volume deliberately invites a barrage of criticism—for the inevitable decisions on omission and inclusion of material, for the sketchiness of much of the analysis, for the emphasis, in fact for having the temerity to embark upon such an undertaking. The university instructor who has been given only a semester, or at best two, in which to cover the broad field of Latin American economic problems will readily appreciate both the motives which prompt one to take on such a task and the influence of space limitations. He will have had experience with rushing from descriptions of soil to analyses of internal money markets to discussions of international trade all within a period of weeks. His classes will have participated in discussions of the more advanced countries for which reading assignments have been relatively adequate and in classroom work on a country on which the paucity of data is explained by the fact that up to 1940 it had "not one trained statistician, not one trained economic analyst, not one trained economist." While the quality and quantity of research on the various Latin American economic problems have been very uneven, the characteristic feature of the field has been the lack of adequate monographic material on which to base a survey course or from which to produce a satisfactory interpretation of the pattern of economic development.

In his own university teaching, the writer has found it useful to link the course to the central theme of acceleration of economic development which is a focus of public policy in the economic field in Latin America and is the core of Latin American relationships with the United States. In many respects the twenty countries of Latin America do not constitute a homogeneous region for an economic survey. But the area of similarity in the pattern of economic behavior and in the character of policy problems involved in the acceleration of economic development is sufficient to warrant or-

v

ganization of a course on a functional basis rather than on a country-by-country basis. Supplementary reading and problem-assignments can serve to bring the student closer to the distinctive problems of individual countries.

The author acknowledges with appreciation the assistance of the students who have been exposed for some years to many of the chapters now published in this book and who have compelled modification of many sections by their intelligent criticism and discussion in the classroom. Acknowledgment is made gratefully of the permission granted by many publishers to cite passages from works published by them.

Contents

Tables

Tables

(Continued)

ix

Tables

Tables

(Continued)

Figures

Economic Development in Latin America

Chapter 1

The Approach to Economic Development

Latin America is a relatively unproductive area. Production is commonly estimated to be less than one-sixth that of the United States of America, although the populations of the two regions are roughly the same.[1] The increase in productivity in recent years has been less rapid than that of the United States. While the United States was able to boost its production some 75% from 1939 to the peak year of the second world war, Latin America had difficulty in achieving a 25% gain, and it has made no significant progress in closing the gap since that time. Correction of the maldistribution of national income has proceeded so slowly that the initial reaction of observers of the Latin American scene still reduces to the findings of Humboldt almost 150 years ago that "nowhere does there exist such a fearful difference in the distribution of fortune, civilization, cultivation of the soil, and population."

---

[1] Data on national income and productivity of the Latin American countries are generally unsatisfactory. In most cases the fragmentary data permit little more than very rough approximations. In 1940 it was estimated that Latin America had total national incomes only one-sixth that of the United States. Its position relative to the United States deteriorated during the 1940's. See National Bureau of Economic Research, *Studies in Income and Wealth*, Volume X (New York, 1947), pp. 160-244, especially pp. 240-244.

The reader should bear in mind that Latin America includes twenty countries which differ widely in resources, standard of living, stage of development, economic potential. For instance, the study cited above lists two countries (Argentina and Uruguay) as having per capita national incomes 30 to 50% that of the United States, 3 countries (Chile, Cuba, Panama) 20 to 30%, four countries (Peru, Colombia, Venezuela, Brazil) 10 to 20%, the remaining countries under 10%. The relationship among the countries changes but great differences in conditions remain.

1

The low level of consumption and the increasingly unfavorable comparison with the standard of living in the United States combine with optimistic (too frequently overoptimistic) appraisals of the physical endowment of the area to provide a challenge to political leadership in Latin America, to exert steady pressure for radical modifications in the system of economic organization, and to condition the atmosphere of relations with the United States. The startling contrast between fabulous dream and meager reality has prompted a continuing search for a formula for accelerating economic development. In studying the structures of the economies of the Latin American countries, we shall keep in mind one central question: *Why have the Latin American economies failed to function at higher levels of efficiency?*

Development Formulas. In 1824, the Treasurer of the Geological Society in London puzzled over the fact that "with the richest mines in the world, with a splendid college for instructing miners, and with a code of laws which pretended to encourage them, Mexico made no advances in the science of working its mineral treasures; while England, with only metals of inferior value, without any public institution for instruction of this kind, and even without books upon the subject, has within a few years raised the art of mining to a perfection hitherto unknown, and has carried it on in spite of difficulties not to be met with elsewhere." After suitable cogitation, he came up with the opinion that "if the skill and experience in mining which we possess and the use of our engines could ever be applied to the mines of Mexico, the result would be that of extraordinary profit." [2] The flow of some $15 billion of foreign capital to Latin America, and the importation of advanced techniques, ranging from the complicated marketing mechanism of the banana empire of Middle America to the constantly improved methods of exploring and exploiting petroleum resources, from the building of the Argentine railways to the establishment of the great Volta

---

[2] John Taylor, *Selections from the Works of the Baron de Humboldt, Relating to the Climate, Inhabitants, Production and Mines of Mexico* (Longman, London, 1824). Introductory remarks by Taylor.

Redonda steel mill, testify to the use of the formula in the past century. Change Taylor's "skill and experience" to "know-how" and his "engines" to American capital, and you have the most popular prescription of our times for the development of Latin America. The formula is particularly well suited to the prevailing diagnosis of under-development which stresses industrialization as the key to larger per-capita incomes. Whether it is a politician like Ezequiel Padilla, formerly Mexico's Secretary for Foreign Affairs, emphasizing the "lack of stability and the inequality which envelop agricultural life confronted with industrial life," [3] or a technician like Josué Sáenz, director of statistics in the Mexican Ministry of National Economy, urging that a shift of 300,000 workers from agriculture to industry would mean a half billion dollar rise in Mexico's national income, *the thinking of makers of public policy in Latin America generally is in terms of accelerating development by a shift in the labor force from primary occupations (agriculture, forestry, and fishing) to secondary (manufacturing, mining and construction) and tertiary (trade and services) occupations.*[4] Given the fact that (a) capital is the short-supply factor of production in Latin America, (b) $1,000 to $2,000 per person is required as the average investment for shifting a worker from less productive agriculture to more productive activity, much of it for expenditure on imported goods, and (c) the need for modern technology if the shift is to prove successful, it is easy to account for the emphasis on the import of "know-how" and capital.

Unfortunately, the ways and means of achieving this flow of technological competence and capital are matters of controversy. For some Latin Americans there is a simple inevitability about the process. Thus, shortly after the outbreak

---

[3] Ezequiel Padilla, *Free Men of America* (Ziff-Davis, Chicago, 1943), p. 119.

[4] Gilberto Loyo told the Economic Commission for Latin America (United Nations) in June, 1948, that in Mexico primary activities absorb two-thirds of the employed population, secondary activities one-sixth, and yet the contribution of primary activities to national income is one-fifth of the total, secondary one-third.

of World War II, Eduardo Villaseñor, a prominent Mexican banker-economist, stated that the choice rested with the United States whether it wanted to be linked to a poor Latin America or to a rich Latin America. He believed that the United States *must* export capital and that the natural outlet was Latin America. Accordingly he urged the United States to "get rid of your treasure—lend it, give it, throw it away— if you do not want to perish in the midst of plenty." [5] However, while Latin American problems have increasingly engaged the sympathies of the United States, there has been an understandable reluctance to act as an international fat boy—especially while the Latin Americans themselves lag in modifying domestic economic policies that tend to perpetuate and deepen the weaknesses of their economies. Private foreign capital has been increasingly reluctant to flow without assurance of a suitable climate for investment. And with respect to government-to-government lending, the multiple opportunities for constructive statesmanship in the various under-developed areas of the world and the primary responsibility to its own "ill-fed, ill-clad, and ill-housed one-third" have forced upon the United States increasingly realistic appraisals of the directions in which it is to act. For if Americans have been able to sense the political, ideological, and economic implications of uneven development among the other American republics, they have been equally capable of realizing the implications of irregular achievement of the American standard of living in their own country. The sort of mental stasis which has obstructed provision of suitably attractive conditions for investment combines with unwarranted complacency regarding the ease with which governments can mobilize risk-capital abroad to stand in the way of full realization of the "know-how and capital import" formula of development.

Fortunately, development does not hang on external assistance alone. *Great economic advances can be effected in Latin*

---

[5] Eduardo Villaseñor, *Inter-American Trade and Financial Problems* (Reprinted for private circulation from *Inter-American Solidarity*, Chicago, 1941), p. 94.

America without assistance or leadership or pressure from the United States. Latin American resources can be mobilized to support a much richer community without any expansion in external aid. Or they can continue to provide only a marginal livelihood for the masses despite more generous economic cooperation from abroad. The decisions on land policy, tax policy, the role of the government, investment policy, the mobilizing of domestic savings, tariff policy, armament policy, and the like, are all within the competence of the individual Latin American republics. As a former President of Panama has said: "We Latin Americans must realize the truth that we are the only ones to cure our own evils." [6]

Bases of Development Decisions. Any developmental formula which comes out of these decisions, however, must rest upon (a) an understanding of the limitations of the physical resources of the area, and (b) a realization that there is nothing inevitable about achieving a standard of living similar to that of the United States. While the myth of an El Dorado dies hard, intelligent Latin American analysts in recent years have come increasingly to appreciate the facts about the "untold riches" of their countries. "The legend of our pretended wealth has harmed us," said a competent Chilean Minister of Economy a few years ago. "Through four centuries we have fed the illusion of an unparalleled wealth and the hope of an easy life, and we have always had to admit without really being convinced that the only wealth of the country consists in work . . . applied to a land which is loathe to surrender its fruits. It is time we reacted and understood that we have a rough road before us." [7]

In the same vein, a Brazilian engineer with experience in working out government policy, after analyzing the limitations of Brazil's soil and mineral endowment, concluded that Brazilians have been "dazzled by the resounding uselessness

---

[6] Proceedings of the Seventeenth Institute under the Auspices of the Norman Wait Harris Memorial Foundation, *The Political and Economic Implications of Inter-American Solidarity* (Chicago, 1941), p. 57.

[7] Taken from a speech delivered at the convention of the Chilean Association of Manufacturers in December 1944.

of its wild waterfalls, the glittering of the butterfly's wings, the brilliant coloring of the flowers" to the point where they blinded themselves to economic realities.[8] If the Latin witticism that "Latin America is the land of tomorrow but tomorrow is always a holiday" is a bit harsh, it is nevertheless a healthy reaction to the traditional observer who has for centuries joined in Amerigo Vespucci's enthusiasm that "the terrestrial paradise cannot be very far from these shores."

An American scholar, studying the combination of land misuse and population increase, has not hesitated to conclude bluntly that "with the possible exception of Argentina and Brazil, the countries to the south of us are fundamentally and inescapably so poor that a living standard approaching that of the United States is unattainable." He has pointed out that "the land of Latin America has such a low carrying capacity and is able to produce so little wealth per thousand acres that the purchasing power of the people cannot be increased to a degree even comparable with that of European and North American countries." This inadequacy of internal markets, coupled with marked deficiencies in the supply of fuel and power and an inability to compete in foreign markets, brought from him a warning against misting the issue of development with over-emphasis on industrialization.[9]

The contrast between Cortes' description of the country that "contains the most vast and varied wealth ever bestowed upon a single people in a single area" and William Vogt's chilling analysis of a Mexico able to feed and shelter its citizens only by a "progressive and accelerating destruction of natural resources" points up the realistic present-day approach to Latin American development. There will doubtless continue to be misguided enthusiasts—so recently again become legion in the whooped-up campaign for good-neighborliness—who will confidently seek the trail to the land of Cinnamon and El Dorado. And many of our neighbors will somewhat pathetically expect miracles to follow the pronunciamentos on industrialization. But only when we under-

---

[8] *O Jornal*, Rio de Janeiro, January 7, 1945.

[9] William Vogt, "A Continent Slides to Ruin," *Harper's*, June 1948.

stand with Isaiah Bowman that "the leaders who dream of expansion in terms of the example of the United States find that realization never comes because the whole economic, social and physical setting is different," [10] only when we free ourselves of the myth of "untold riches," only when we realize that development does not stem exclusively from industrialization nor hang solely on the import of foreign capital and technology, only then can we hope to make any progress in the study of Latin American development.

The Issues Outlined

Immigration and Land. Against glib suggestions of expanded immigration for rural development, we shall have to weigh the consequences of a semi-feudal organization of land that has discouraged any concept of the social function of land in favor of the selfish interest in a few cash export crops, obstructed diversification in favor of mobility of adaptation to export markets, made it possible for prevailing standards of social security protection to be lowered deeply within the area dominated by the landowning group, enabled land to evade its share of the cost of government. Almost a century ago, Ponciano Arriaga during the drafting of a new constitution for Mexico put this problem well when he said that he had heard foreign colonization frequently discussed as a cure for the poverty of the country and he wondered whether *Mexican* colonization in the sense of redistribution of land among Mexicans and revision of domestic agricultural policy, might not be an even more successful formula.

Instead of the preoccupation with immigration which suits the politician who takes the easy way out by concluding that "sparse population and lack of capital have made our countries economically weak," [11] which excites the world citizen who finds that South America is the "only continent containing both a large temperate and a large tropical area capable of cultivation which still remains greatly underpeopled . . . and

---

[10] Isaiah Bowman (Editor), *Limits of Land Settlement* (New York, 1937), p. 300.
[11] Padilla, *op. cit.*, p. 98.

is therefore the chief resource to which the overpeopled countries may look as providing a field for their emigration," [12] which is stimulated by the statistician who flourishes data on the ability of "Brazil to carry a population of 1.2 billion" [13] and by the vested interests who want a cheap abundant labor supply, we need to go behind the sparseness of population to analyze the economic and social pattern which failed to produce the resources and drive necessary for full and effective exploitation of the physicial endowment and the stimulus to both immigration and a healthy natural increase in population. And finally we need to probe for remedies to the basic difficulties rather than multiply the problems by introducing population without modification of the underlying structure.

Government Function and Finance. Against the easy acceptance of the emergence of government as the dominant element in the economies and of the continuing practice of seeking funds abroad for public expenditures, we shall have to set up an analysis of the areas of expenditure, challenge the use of over five per cent of national incomes on military outlay, investigate whether by the steady expansion of their function these governments are warranted in hoping that they can improve everybody's economic status relative to and at the expense of everybody else, face boldly the tradition of government as a "control for special privilege without even the saving grace of a professed idealism," [14] make note of the many state-owned and operated enterprises which already stand as unprofitable monuments to government participation in commercial and industrial activity and which permit therefore an appraisal of the contribution to development that may be anticipated from the flood of new ventures being undertaken. From the time Bazaine wrote to Napoleon that

---

[12] James Bryce, *South America, Observations and Impressions* (Macmillan, New York, 1914), p. 555.

[13] Since Latin America has only about 6% of the world's population on an area one-sixth of the world's habitable area, the potential occupancy of the "empty spaces" challenges writers. In 1924, for instance, Albrecht Penck estimated Brazil could carry a population of 1.2 billion. In 1936 Freise thought in terms of 395 to 430 million.

[14] Bowman, *op. cit.*, p. 300.

"empleomania, that is to say, the monomania and craving to live at the expense of the government, is a malady inherent in Mexican character and education" to the recent rejection by a Costa Rican official of a budgetary cut because "government employment is our form of unemployment insurance," the peculiar philosophy of government has intruded decisively and adversely on the issue of economic development.

Scarcity of Capital. In the absence of adequate studies of capital formation in Latin America, we may have too readily accepted the idea that the primary difficulty lies in the volume of local savings rather than in their distribution and in the methods by which they are mobilized for optimum developmental purposes. We must determine whether domestic savings can be harnessed to the purposes of an expanding economy more effectively so as to reduce the concentration of incomes, reduce luxury consumption, raise the level of consumption of low-income groups, and yet make possible heavier investment for the most worthy lines of development. This will involve us in the argument that Latin Americans are not "psychologically suited" for high income taxes and that their governments must therefore show preference for getting financing out of the North American taxpayer when the alternative is to enact proper tax legislation at home.[15] It necessitates an examination of the regressive character of the tax system, the heavy reliance on taxes on consumption expenditures. In seeking an approach to developmental technique, we need to understand the limitations in such a public finance system as that which a study group found in Haiti during the 1940's: in a population where over half suffer from malnutrition, 90% are unable to pay for elementary medical care, laundry soap can be acquired only by serious sacrifice in other directions and kerosene for lighting is beyond the means of most of the peasants, the bulk of the government revenues were being derived from import duties on basic necessities paying 50% or more duties while liquor and other perquisites of the elite

---

[15] See Javier Marquez, "Notes on Balance of Payments Problems in Relation to Economic Development in Latin America," *Inter-American Economic Affairs*, September 1947, p. 116.

paid 20%. Or, to take another familiar case, the findings of the American Advisory Economic Mission to Venezuela in 1939 that low-cost foodstuffs were the most heavily burdened by tariffs, savings were being permitted to go substantially untaxed without the salutary effects on enterprise usually advanced as justification for such exemptions, taxes on necessities were in effect being paid not to the government but to a privileged group of domestic producers protected from competition of imports, and the three-fourths of all Venezuelan families who lived on less than $85 per month were carrying an excessive proportion of the total cost of government.[16]

Motive of Industrialization. Against the current overwhelming acceptance of the role of industrialization, we must pose the simple question whether in Latin America the primary motivation is more and cheaper goods or whether it is another attempt to create a privileged position for a small group rivaling that of the traditional landowning group. On the distribution side, the readiness to substitute a mass-consumption business philosophy for the prevailing philosophy of small volume and high unit profits must also be examined.

Historically, there is a strong tradition of effort to maintain monopoly positions in local markets to perpetuate the very high profit level which is considered normal for commercial and industrial activity. The post-war effort to boost import duties still more in order to prevent a tapering off from the fabulous war-time profits of 50 to 125% per year on investment does not augur well for the increase in availability of goods which is the final test of industrialization. Whether it is a country like Colombia, going ahead from pre-war import duties of 100% on wheat, 200% on refined sugar, 100% on lard, 30% on cotton, to build protection for deficit staples unsuited to Colombian conditions regardless of the cost to consumers; or Chile, giving its shoe industry customs duties roughly the equivalent of the existing retail price for low and medium-grade Chilean-made shoes, and finding questionable solace in balancing the hurt to the consumer in terms of the

---

[16] Report of the American Advisory Economic Mission to Venezuela (Washington, 1939), pp. 194-202.

fact that "close to the engine and the boiler a concept of social dignity has arisen"; or Brazil, subjected to the propaganda of the textile industry that by consuming more and more Brazilian cotton at home Brazil can clothe the world more cheaply, only to be confronted with the charge that "if there were not tariff protection our exported fiber could return to the national consumer made up into cloth at prices very much less than we pay for locally-woven cloth"; in every case the slogan "industry regardless of cost" holds out dangers of disappointment.

Before the drive for industrialization opened in Latin America, the cartoonist was perhaps correct who depicted a billboard reading: *Consume lo que el país produce,* with a text asking: *Y qué produce el país?*—and the devastating answer: *Políticos y Generales.* But from the standpoint of development, the test of the drive is not the fact that the country may thereafter be consuming what is produced at home, but whether it is consuming more than previously. For the six out of every ten persons in Latin America who suffer from the physical effects of hunger, for the majority of the Colombian urban workers who suffer from uncinariasis and tropical anemia for lack of elemental sanitation, for the average Latin American who suffers a life expectancy 15 to 30 years lower than that of the average North American, for the third of the workers in Mexico City who can afford only the simplest of shacks, for the peasants honored by a Quiché song which refers to them as *vestido de viento y de frío* (clothed in wind and cold), the motive and the justification of industrialization can only be more goods and cheaper goods. To such a simple formula do the grandiose pronouncements of development reduce.

The Varied Founts of Development. Again, in evaluating the big "show-case" developments like the steel mills and the international air and maritime lines which have so captured the imagination of the Latin Americans, we must not lose sight of the magnitude of the contribution to economic advancement that may be made by less flashy activity. In the aggregate pattern of development, the scientists, working to promote hybrid-corn-breeding programs in a country like Mexico where corn is a vital element in the dietary, may do more for Mexico than the loudly hailed industrialist who picks a commodity now being imported, goes off to the capital to get assurances of heavy tariff protection, wins the collaboration of opportunistic labor leaders,[17] and permanently replaces the cheaper and possibly better imported product with a product that may conceivably thereafter be less available than ever to the Mexican people. The refugee scientist, experimenting in Caracas with a vitamin-rich soybean which would taste and look like the common black bean that is the chief source of protein for millions of Latin Americans but which would be loaded with proteins and contain all the known vitamins except C and would be cheaper to grow and thus more available, may truly, as a Venezuelan Minister of Agriculture recognized, "change the national economy of our country." The educator, fighting for a piddling increase in the educational budget to bring advanced technical programs to his country, may in the long run add more to the national income than the new industrialist getting aboard the gravy train in the capital. In the same way, much greater importance relatively might attach to an effort to make drugs freely available to the tens of millions of Latin Americans suffering with malaria, which "continues to sow havoc among the poorer classes, reducing their life span, their solvency, and their working efficiency, increasing infant mortality, planting wretchedness and distress through three quarters of this hemisphere." [18]   Against the enthusiasm with which the Colombian government in the late 1940's embarked on an adventure in international merchant shipping as the first of a series of new activities, one soberly reflects that at the outbreak of the war it was estimated that only 60% of Colombia's potential school population attended primary schools, that

---

[17] The Mexican labor leader, Vicente Lombardo Toledano, for instance, was reported in April 1946 urging that workers pay higher prices for domestic products than for similar foreign goods if that be necessary to maintain home industries.

[18] Charles Morrow Wilson, *Ambassadors in White* (Henry Holt, New York, 1942), p. 311.

one-fourth of the students were seriously under-nourished, 40% were inadequately fed, one-fifth came to school without breakfast, that it then was proving financially impossible to bring the school lunch program up from $1.1 million to the $7 or $8 million which would have protected adequately these human resources of the nation. And yet, at war's end, the choice for new governmental activity falls into lines that may further restrict the availability of goods to the masses or at best involve a fruitless substitution of resources. Choices of this kind are admittedly decisions that must be made locally rather than abroad, but they inevitably condition and limit the extent to which foreign capital and know-how can promote development.

Demographic Position. Against the emphasis of such specialists as Raymond Pearl on the superior demographic position of Latin America, on the superior vigor in the biological sense indicated by its vital index, on the more favorable age-distribution for production of goods and for further growth and for health; against the emphasis of such authorities as Kingsley Davis on the good fortune demographically of the area to have a population increasing at a faster rate than that of any other major area, we shall have to weigh Vogt's insistence that with three or four exceptions, "biological bankruptcy hangs over their heads like a shaking avalanche." Against the impressive quantitative data, we shall need to appraise the fact that the "American continent has been undergoing a veritable tragedy due to under-nourishment," [19] that Afranio Peixoto, a Brazilian sociologist, has had to conclude that "we do nothing well because our people live in a permanent state of malnutrition," that Charles Morrow Wilson has found that 40% of the Latin American people are sick, that a Mexican doctor visiting war-torn Europe in 1945 could write home that

"... Never in these war-stricken lands have we seen anything to compare with the low hygienic conditions of our Mexican towns and our people. ... Here it is impossible

---

[19] Findings of the International Conference on Nutrition held in Buenos Aires in 1939.

to find the terrible food that our poor eat in our very capital. . . . Not in all of Europe, not even in bombed-out Holland, do we find one place as unhygienic as our beautiful Acapulco, where each visit is a game of death in the form of malaria, dysentery and typhoid. . . . When one thinks of sanitation and hygiene, one is convinced that the countries that really need help from the outside are not those in Europe, but our own Latin American countries . . ." [20]

Plural Economy. Against the popular diagnosis of the "plural economy" which disputes the existence of foreign economic communities as something distinct and apart from the native economies, which heralds the passing of the "Anglo-American spot of civilization in the wilderness," which continually condemns the foreign sector of the duality for alleged misuse of political power, for unreasonable insistence on a privileged economic position and for draining away of the resources of the country, we must put an analysis of what is the more vital cleavage in Latin America and the more important deterrent to development: the existence of a very small privileged class of native origin and a very broad marginal group condemned permanently to sub-standard consumption as hewers of wood and drawers of water.[21]

Just as new currents of foreign interest will have to achieve a successful integration with the local economy or fail, just as important is it that the gap be closed between the two sectors of the local duality if development is to proceed effectively. The very advocates of industrialization have often failed to understand that what is involved in the spread of industrialization, in the spread of the American technic as the key to economic advance, is a structural change which

---

[20] Published in *Excelsior*, Mexico City, December 28, 1945, and cited in Herbert Cerwin, *These are the Mexicans* (Reynal and Hitchcock, New York, 1947), pp. 244-245.

[21] A proper analysis of the "plural economy" would point to the discriminatory thoroughness with which social security legislation is implemented in the case of the foreign companies, the vigor with which tax legislation is directed against them, the relative superiority of the status of the local laborers in such enterprises as against native-controlled ventures, the willingness to assume risks as compared with the local practice of insisting on enormous profit margins without assumption of the function of taking risks.

means something more than an altered relationship for the foreign participant. As a leading American scholar has put it: "So far as our capitalistic culture can be transferred and is transferred to Latin America, it involves the introduction of mobility, of industrialism, of emphasis upon material achievement, the introduction to a degree of social and material insecurity — true, possibly also rising material standards of living. All of this involves something of a real threat to the exclusive position of the very wealthy, some narrowing of the gap, the horribly shocking gap between the social classes." [22] To bottle all this up in terms simply of an attack on foreign capital is utterly to confuse the issue.

And over-simplification, in terms of accepting the naive theory of exploitation which has dominated the thinking of many observers of the Latin American scene, is equally unwise. The findings of Mr. T. S. Simey for the West Indies bear generalization for a large part of Latin America. Simey points out that "although the West Indian peoples have on many occasions been exploited in the past, and although on some occasions they still are, the natural resources of the lands in which they live are poor, and little can be accomplished by a mere redistribution of existing wealth. Everything must depend in the long run on a considerable increase in the efficiency of the existing productive processes," and that requires first of all abandonment of the fantastic portrait which has often been painted of "the boundless fertility of the soil, of inexhaustible mineral wealth, and of seas teeming with fish, all of which goes, not to maintain the lives of the common people, but in the form of excessive profits to the sinister vested interests represented by 'international capitalism'." [23]

It is significant, perhaps, that the most widely advocated device for integrating foreign activity with the local economies has been the joint-capital enterprise, in which foreign entre-

---

[22] Leland H. Jenks, in *The Political and Economic Implications of Inter-American Solidarity*, p. 59.

[23] T. S. Simey, *Welfare and Planning in the West Indies* (Oxford, London, 1946), p. 126.

preneurs invite (in some Latin American countries are compelled by law to accept) local capital participation in the undertakings. Yet, the alliance in most instances is precisely with that group in the community whose position and practices must themselves fall under increasing challenge if the shocking gap between the classes is to be narrowed.[24]

Influence of Experience. Throughout the analysis it should be borne in mind that the readiness to accept sound developmental policies is conditioned by the particular experiences which the various countries have had in the past. Thus the unhappy experience with sharply fluctuating world markets, with the impact of foreign depressions, with prices of exported primary goods tending to fall more than those of imported manufactured products, conduces to the acceptance of more stable diversification even at the cost of some of the advantages of specialization. The Brazilian remembers doggedly building the coffee bonfires which "cancelled the work of a million people laboring from dawn to dusk six months a year in sweltering heat." [25] The Chilean has seen copper go from 18 cents to 5 cents per pound in the Great Depression, has seen copper production fall precipitately from 320,000 tons to 103,000 tons, has seen the value of exports fall in 1932 to 12% of the 1929 figure. The Cuban has known sugar at 22 cents a pound and has lived to see it below a cent per pound; he has seen sugar carry exports to a figure in excess of $700 million and seen a dismal turn in the market bring total Cuban exports below a hundred million dollars. Small wonder then that they are sometimes willing to pay an insurance premium in the form of less efficient production in order to

---

[24] It has been suggested that the practice of shortening the foreign capital commitment in order to "cut in" a local financier reduces the amount of capital available to under-developed countries and is thus open to criticism. The value of this sort of "insurance" against local difficulties has also been questioned since the local partners may themselves be under attack when the risk actually materializes. See Acierto, "A Marshall Plan for Latin America," *Inter-American Economic Affairs,* September 1947, p. 7.

[25] J. W. F. Rowe, *Markets and Men* (Macmillan, New York, 1936), p. 22.

free themselves from the drastic dependence on overseas markets over which they have little control.

It may be costly to worship at the altar of economic independence, but each interruption of commerce—whether by war or by economic mishap—feeds the political appeal of "economic independence." In his day, Humboldt saw the stimulus to local production that must proceed from the fact that although "the nation can procure by means of foreign commerce all the articles . . . in the midst of its great wealth, want is severely felt whenever the commerce has suffered any interruption, whenever a war throws obstacles in the way of maritime communications." In our day, two world wars have provided potent stimulus to the drive against reliance on overseas sources of supply and overseas markets, even against use of foreign bottoms to carry the traffic. The political usefulness of the appeal for "independence," however, is so great that a debauch of purposeful political oratory on the subject usually ends by blinding speaker and audience alike to the forbidding cost of such an achievement.

Litany of the Good Neighbor. In recent years the litany of the good neighbor has tended to stress only one side of the picture: Will the United States continue to buy heavily from Latin America? Will the United States make heavy loans? Will American investors share the gains with local interests more equably? Will the United States stabilize prices and markets for Latin American staples?

In a sense this has put the United States in a position of a man asked to protect from murder a person already engaged in committing suicide. From the viewpoint of development, the litany must be expanded to include: Will the Latin Americans revise their system of land control and land exploitation to remedy the evils of an insecure landless farming class, to accept the social function of land, to accelerate technological advances, to maximize productivity, to end the centuries of Latin American agricultural history written in terms of exploitation of native labor? Will local industrial management abandon the philosophy of small volume and large unit profits? Will tariff protection be used wisely to bring efficient industries into being or be used to perpetuate inefficient producers? Will social legislation be directed at foreign capital and other selected groups or be broadened in application to protect politically inarticulate rural populations and the mass of urban workers? Will steps be taken to incorporate effectively into the community such large sectors as the 30 million of Indian origin whom José Carlos Mariátegui has called the "extra social class"? Will the experience with state-owned enterprises be used meaningfully or will further unprofitable monuments to political policy be erected? Will abuse of foreign capital as a whipping boy suffice indefinitely to obscure the really significant cleavage that retards the Latin American economies? Will governments turn to the conservation of the human resources of their nations or accept deterioration as lands "where wealth accumulates and men decay?" Will the hollow opulence of the string of hospitable capitals continue to contrast so sharply with the poverty of the interior producing regions? Is the goal of self-sufficiency to be pursued regardless of cost?

Public policy finds its orientation in a multitude of factors of which strictly economic analysis is only one. We are now ready to examine the Latin American economies in more detail to find out at least what *might* be desirable bases of economic policy in the other American republics.

SUPPLEMENTARY READING

Harold G. Moulton, *Controlling Factors in Economic Development* (The Brookings Institution, Washington, 1949), Chapter 1, "Sources of Economic Development," pp. 3-38.

Colonial Office, *Report of the British Guiana and British Honduras Settlement Commission,* Cmd. 7533 (London, 1948), pp. 1-27.

Carlos Davila, *We of the Americas* (Ziff-Davis, Chicago, 1949), pp. 207-253.

Nathan L. Whetten, *Rural Mexico* (The University of Chicago Press, Chicago, 1948), pp. 563-572.

Chapter 2

The Human Resources

About 150 million people live in Latin America. *The population is growing faster than that of any other major region. The proportion of the population that is gainfully employed tends to be lower than that of the United States or of the western European countries, so that the production of the economically active people must support a larger number of persons. The productivity of the gainfully employed tends to be reduced by such qualitative population characteristics as widespread illiteracy, malnutrition, and generally poor health, and by less effective economic organization in terms of the equipment at the command of the worker and the conditions under which production proceeds.*

Rate of Growth of Population. The annual rate of growth of the population of Latin America is more than double the world rate and well above that of the United States.[1] In the decade ending 1946, Latin America accounted for one-seventh of the world's population increase, although it had only about 6% of the total world population. Although there are scattered indications that the temperate sections at least are achieving some control over the birth rate, a continued rapid rise in population is forecast from the prospect of continuation of relatively high birth rates and steadily declining death rates. Kingsley Davis, a noted authority in the field, looks for the peak rate of growth to be passed within three or four decades, and forecasts a Latin American population of 200

---

[1] Population data for Latin America, like much of the other statistical data for Latin America, are uneven in their usefulness. For some countries, there are good vital statistics, some provide fairly good census data, for a few countries both the vital statistics and the censuses are fairly satisfactory.

to 225 million in 1970 (compared with a high estimate of 170 million for the United States in that year), and a Latin American population of 300 to 375 million in the year 2000 (compared with a high estimate of some 200 million for the United States). He notes that

"Whenever an area has passed through the industrial revolution, it has manifested in the early stages a veritable crescendo of population increase, because industrial progress brings a drop in the death rate before it brings a drop in the birth rate. Later, as an urban-industrial milieu emerges, the birth rate begins to fall to the level of the lowered death rate and the population again approaches the same stationary condition it manifested before the great transition. . . . The Latin American countries find themselves in various intermediate stages of the industrial transition. Some have hardly begun the shift; others are far along. Everywhere in this region, however, we find urbanization accelerating, literacy increasing, health improving and communication expanding. It seems likely, then, that Latin America as a whole will make the transition from illiterate agriculturism to literate industrialism in a few decades, and that her population growth will taper off as the change is made." [2]

Table 1 shows the estimated average annual percentage increase of population in Latin America and other areas of the world since 1936. Since data for Latin America are more nearly an effort at intelligent guesses rather than scientific predictions, the forecasts shown in the table are more important for establishing in your mind the nature of the relationship among the areas rather than for fixing specific percentages as representing the actual prospective rate of growth.

Birth Rates and Death Rates. The high birth and death rates are costly in terms of standards of welfare and efficiency of economic activity. It has been estimated that the average

---

[2] Kingsley Davis, "Latin America's Multiplying Peoples," *Foreign Affairs*, July, 1947, pp. 645-46. It should be noted that in 1950 the view that the United States will reach a population peak and begin to decline before 2000 was being replaced by the view that substantial growth of unpredictable magnitude will continue. See Joseph S. Davis, "Fifty Million More Americans," *Foreign Affairs*, April, 1950, pp. 412-426.

TABLE 1

Population Growth

Average Annual Percentage Increase

	1936-45	1945-46	1946-50	1950-55
World	0.83	0.85	0.87	0.94
Africa	1.48	1.16	1.17	1.11
North America	1.02	1.51	0.89	0.66
Middle America	2.22	2.12	2.10	1.91
South America	1.96	1.84	1.84	1.74
Asia	0.89	0.64	0.76	0.91
Soviet Russia	−0.03	1.07	1.19	1.21
Europe	0.36	0.60	0.51	0.55
Oceania	1.00	0.52	0.95	0.93

Source: U. S. Department of State, *World Population Estimates* (O. I. R. Report No. 4192), March 1, 1947. Note that the figures for the Americas include not only the independent republics but also the colonies and dependencies.

birth rate per thousand is between 40 and 50 in Latin America, or more than double that of the United States.[3]   In the more advanced countries like Argentina declines appear to be well under way; the Argentine birth rate, for example, dropped from 38 to 24 per thousand in the years between the first and second World Wars.   In the tropical areas, however, as T. Lynn Smith has pointed out, "no precipitous decline in the birth rate was registered between 1911 and 1939 comparable to that occurring in England, the United States and other great nations of the temperate zone." [4]   The spreading tendency to greater literacy and more urbanization and the adoption of the cultural characteristics of modern western

---

[3] The wide variation among the Latin-American countries must be kept in mind.   In the 1940's, for instance, the Mexican birth rate was well over 40 per thousand, the Chilean rate in the lower part of the 30 to 40 range, the Argentine in the 20's.   Similarly the Mexican death rate was over 20 per thousand, while the Argentine rate was little over half that.   It should also be remembered that improvement in registration system often accounts for changes in rates, especially in the less advanced countries, to a degree that cannot be measured.

[4] T. Lynn Smith, "The Population Problems of the Tropics," *Proceedings of the Fourth International Congresses on Tropical Medicine and Malaria* (Washington, 1948), p. 1539.

civilization hold out a promise of lower birth rates generally in Latin America, since fertility has tended to decline under such conditions. Nevertheless, reproduction and subsistence activities are likely to continue long to absorb a larger share of the energy and time of the Latin-American population than in the United States. Table 2 provides a comparison of birth and death rates among the major regions of the world for the year 1937.

TABLE 2

Birth Rates and Death Rates

(Per thousand of population)

1937

	Birth Rate	Death Rate
World	36	26
Africa	40–45	35
Canada and U. S.	17	11
Latin America	40–45	20–25
Near East	40–45	25–30
Japan	28	17
South-Central Asia	40–45	30–35
North-west-central Europe	17	13
Southern Europe	23	16

Source: United Nations Department of Economic Affairs, *World Economic Report 1948* (Lake Success, 1949), p. 222.

The average death rate in Latin America has been estimated at 20 to 30 per thousand, again more than double that of the United States. The growing availability and ease of application of mass mortality controls, the increase in control over tropical diseases, the growing interest in public health, the tremendous improvement that can be effected in infant mortality rates by better medical attention and better child care, all promise sharp decreases in the death rates— in fact, have already brought results. As Smith points out, "the death rate has responded quickly to the scientific knowledge" even in the tropical areas.

The economic importance of such improvement can be appreciated better when it is realized that in Chile one out of every four children born alive had been dying in the first year and over half have failed to reach their ninth year; that early deaths among the adult male population in most of Latin America constitute a heavy drain on the economically active element of the population—for instance in such a city as Rio de Janeiro half of the male population has failed to reach the age of 29 and only one-fourth reached 59, while in Buenos Aires half failed to reach 39 and only one-fourth reached 59; that life expectancy of persons born and living in Latin America has ranged from one-half to three-fourths that of persons born and living in the United States. An Argentine scholar has estimated that Argentina could add perhaps 50% to its national income by stopping the waste of human resources involved in the early removals from the ranks of the gainfully employed.

Urbanization. The cities of Latin America are growing even faster than the population as a whole, and the larger cities are growing faster than the smaller ones. While only one-fourth of the Latin-American population lived in places of over 5,000 population in 1940 compared with a little over half in the United States, the speed at which urbanization is proceeding is great and concentration in the very large centers is especially notable. The area has at least 20 cities over 200,000 in population and about 45 over 100,000. Concentration is occurring in very large measure by migration from the rural areas, since the natural rate of increase in the cities is usually lower than the rural rate; the birth rates are generally lower and the urban death rate has failed to fall sufficiently fast to offset this. In fact, in some cases the urban mortality rate is higher. Davis estimates that half or more of the urban growth derives from migration.[5] With the lower birth rate and substantial flow of rural population, the cities benefit from a concentration of persons in the productive ages.

It should be noted, however, that urban concentration in Latin America frequently has run ahead of industrial develop-

---

[5] Davis, *op. cit.*, p. 653. See also Kingsley Davis and Ana Casis, "Urbanization in Latin America," *Milbank Memorial Fund Quarterly*, April 1946 and July 1946.

ment and stems rather from such factors as the centralization of government, the importance of ocean-borne commerce, and the lack of opportunity in the typical form of agricultural organization. Carl C. Taylor, writing on rural life in Argentina, a country which already in 1938 had half of its population in cities of over 10,000 population and which in a population of perhaps 16 million now has one city of over 3 million, seven of over 100,000, and six between 50,000 and 100,000, argues that it would be a great error to assume that urban growth is merely following the pattern of other great cities of the world. He points out that in key Latin American cities there is an abnormally large number of persons not engaged in basic economic enterprises such as occupy the populations of great cities elsewhere. "The city's population contains thousands of persons, members of landowning families, whose economic enterprises are largely on farms; a tremendous number of government employees; thousands of service persons, barbers, taxi drivers, etc.; and above all hundreds of thousands of domestic servants." [6] In the same vein, Whetten, writing on Mexico, notes that the proportion of the economically active population of Mexico City employed as domestic servants is three times that of New York City, although the figure for the country as a whole is lower than that for the United States.[7]

Schurz attributes the "unhealthily large" ratio of urban to rural population to the "weakness of the Spaniards for city life and their failure to make country life more attractive." [8] Preston James, noting that "the urban nucleus exerts such a strong attraction that the tendency is for people to move in toward that center rather than to expand the frontier into a new pioneer zone" and that the areas of concentration remain distinct from one another with little overlap, suggests that "urban development in Latin America, in the light

---

[6] Carl C. Taylor, *Rural Life in Argentina* (Louisiana State University Press, Baton Rouge, 1948), p. 123.

[7] Nathan L. Whetten, *Rural Mexico* (The University of Chicago Press, Chicago, 1948), p. 64.

[8] William Lytle Schurz, *Latin America* (E. P. Dutton, New York, 1941), p. 72.

of European or North American experience, seems to be out of proportion to the population density of the hinterlands which are served."[9]   In the Caribbean, Blanshard finds a distressing drift away from the land where the workers are needed to the cities where they are not needed, due partly to the stigma which attaches to country labor but more largely to the impoverished life of the rural laborer who "has always been exploited and now knows that he is being exploited."[10] It is clear that in Latin America the characteristic very big head on a small body cannot be identified as the typical urban concentration of productive activities.

Age Distribution. Latin America's population is younger than that of the United States. While the United States has about one-fourth of its population in the age category 0-14, about 53% in the category 15-49, and 22% in the category 50 and over, Latin American population probably runs closer to 40%, 50%, 10%, respectively.[11]   Table 3 compares age distribution under a different classification for certain major regions of the world.

Raymond Pearl has pointed out that the concentration in the younger brackets is a hopeful sign—in terms of further growth and a progressive youthful outlook on life and its problems.[12]   One important implication of the age distribution is that the area has a relatively flexible population in that

---

[9] Preston James, *Latin America* (Lothrop, Lee and Shepard, New York, 1942), p. 5.   T. Lynn Smith has pointed out that the Brazilian center of population since 1920 has actually moved to the south and in a slightly easterly direction so that population has become even more concentrated in this limited section of the country.   Taylor similarly notes that in Argentina the center has moved toward the coast rather than the interior.

[10] Paul Blanshard, *Democracy and Empire in the Caribbean* (Macmillan, New York, 1947), pp. 39-40.

[11] In Brazil, the distribution in these three age groups in 1920 was 42.7%, 48.3%, 9%, compared with 31.9%, 52.8%, 15.3% in the United States.   In Argentina in 1938 the distribution was 31.6%, 52.8%, 15.6%, compared with 1940 U. S. distribution of 25.0%, 54.6%, 20.4%.

[12] Raymond Pearl, "A Comparative Examination of Certain Aspects of the Populations of the New World," *Human Biology*, September, 1940, pp. 395-96.

TABLE 3

Age Distribution of Population

(Percentage of Total Population)

	Under 15 years	15-59 years	60 years and over
World	36	57	7
Africa	40	55	5
Canada and U. S.	25	64	11
Latin America	40	55	5
Near East	40	54	6
Japan	37	55	8
North-west-central Europe	24	62	14
Southern Europe	30	59	11

Source: United Nations Department of Economic Affairs, *World Economic Report*, 1948 (Lake Success, 1949), p. 224.

more workers are entering the labor market annually and can be channeled into new lines of activity and otherwise adjusted to the demands of a changing economic structure. But in immediate terms the age composition makes for a larger burden on the economically active section of the population. As Smith notes: "Every breadwinner has more mouths to feed . . . many youngsters, large numbers of them hardly more than babes in arms, are cast forth to make their own way in the world . . . and such a high proportion of woman's energy is going into the physiological process of reproduction that the care and feeding of the children, their training and education, are likely to be sadly neglected." [13]   For example, Smith estimates that counting persons under 15 and over 70 as dependents and those between 15 and 69 as producers, in 1920 there were 80 dependents for every 100 producers in Brazil, compared with only 53 dependents per 100 producers in the United States; and for later years the differential has been even greater.[14] The adverse effect on the standard of living and on the volume of production occasioned by this limitation on the proportion of the labor force is obvious. Clearly, here is one cause of low per capita income.

---

[13] Smith, *op. cit.*, pp. 1532-33.

[14] T. Lynn Smith, *Brazil: People and Institutions* (Louisiana State University Press, Baton Rouge, 1947), pp. 202-204.

Health. Another significant limitation on the labor force is the prevailing poor health and malnutrition. Charles Morrow Wilson a few years ago put it bluntly when he said that 50 million Latin Americans are sick at this very moment— "sick of everything, from sprue to leprosy." [15] Every study of health and diet in Latin America turns into a dismal report on the wasting away of human resources. Soule, Efron and Ness reported in 1945 that two-thirds or more of the Latin Americans are physically under-nourished, to the point of actual starvation in some regions, and that one-half are suffering from infectious or deficiency diseases.[16] Diets generally lacking in the protective elements and too often barely maintaining life at an uncertain and unproductive level; entire provinces in even such advanced countries as Argentina where the rural population is consumed by anemia resulting from lack of satisfactory diet, as well as by malaria and other diseases; Indian populations among which hunger is endemic; large sections of the population which are "more suitable as clinical materials than as workers"; tens of millions of people infected with malaria; half of the population in some of the relatively advanced countries lacking even the most elemental sanitation services; coefficients of infection with tuberculosis running 75% or more among persons age 20 and over in some countries; hookworm debilitating as much as 90% of the rural population in a number of countries. Reports of this kind can be multiplied many times over.

Similarly voluminous is the evidence of inadequate corrective action; the pitifully small budgets for public health expenditures; the fact that not more than three countries are supplied with as much as half as many hospital beds and doctors per thousand persons as the United States has; 404 out of 1,575 municípios in Brazil lacking medical service of any kind in 1942; only 445 out of 84,452 centers of population in Mexico possessing medical services as late as 1935. A

---

[15] Charles Morrow Wilson, "How Latin Americans Die," *Harper's*, July 1942.

[16] George Soule, David Efron and Norman T. Ness, *Latin America in the Future* (Farrar and Rinehart, New York, 1945), p. 4.

Chilean Minister of Public Health translated the situation into economic terms when he said that one-fifth of the Chilean potential in gainful activity is eliminated by illness, so that there is a running cut of 20% in national production, as though that share of the labor force were continually on strike.[17] And Chile has by no means the worst record in Latin America on this subject. Thus, Latin America gets off to a bad start in the number of persons it brings to the working of its physical endowment.

The Will to Work. The prevailing health standards account in part at least for the "natural indolence" characteristic with which Latin-American populations have frequently been branded. It is true that labor, especially manual labor, has generally been looked down upon in Latin America. Unlike the United States, where hard work has commanded respect, labor in Latin America has been a mark of social inferiority. The Brazilian saying "Trabalho é para cachorro" (manual labor is for the dog) illustrates this. And both outside critics and Latin Americans themselves have stressed the reluctance to work more than is required to meet simple wants. A Bolivian President, speaking of his own voters, noted that "they have no real feeling for progress so that any increase in wage rates results merely in reduction in hours of actual work, and a distortion of the output curve; the worker has no desire to raise his standard of living—and at best he is out to work less."[18]   Bazaine from Mexico worried Napoleon with the fact that "a people that considers itself dishonored by work and is always inclined to dissipation and idleness can find no incentive in any honest occupation." Leyburn has pointed out that "not even friendly authors have been able to refrain from comment on the inertia of the Haitian man."[19]

---

[17] Salvador Allende, *La Realidad Medico-Social Chilena* (Santiago, Chile, 1939), p. 197.

[18] Quoted in *The Political and Economic Implications of Inter-American Solidarity* (Chicago, 1941), p. 180.

[19] James G. Leyburn, *The Haitian People* (Yale University Press, New Haven, 1941), p. 203.

It is true, as Smith has pointed out for Brazil, that a mild climate and the generous gifts of nature often permit a vegetative existence with a minimum of effort. But to conclude, as did a British Commission in the West Indies, that "most people in moist, hot, tropical climates . . . seem to prefer to be satisfied with a lower standard of living and more leisure" [20] seems little more scientific than the findings of *Punch* in an amusing essay on mythical Galapagonia where "the uniformity of temperature induces a high rate of sleep and even in broad daylight insomnia is unknown. This is fortunate, as there are no sheep in Galapagonia." [21]

Brown writes more effectively when he finds that "the laziness and lack of economic ambition of the workers at first available in (such) areas are due partly to malnutrition and disease. . . . Much of the remaining laziness and lack of ambition is attributable to the traditional outlook engendered in other ways by the original social setting. . . . How important the residual and unalterable factors of climate and hereditary constitution are in determining the working capacity of a people, it is difficult to say, but it would appear wise in general to rate them low." [22]

It is clear that before subscribing so willingly to the "natural indolence" theory one must consider the full picture. For instance, in one Latin American country whose males are typically maligned for their laziness, 60% have yaws or syphilis, 50% have malaria, 90 to 95% are illiterate, 83% of the one out of six who do get to school do not advance beyond the second grade, and none of the stimuli to enterprise, such as the capacity to achieve land ownership, are present. Probably the most widely used illustration in the United States of the "unwillingness to work" arose from reports that when Henry Ford first tried to stimulate rubber production in Brazil, his high wage offers caused a loss of the working force, since one day's pay sufficed to meet the "needs"

---

[20] *Report of the Economic Policy Committee on Jamaica* (1945).

[21] *Punch*, March 14, 1945.

[22] A. J. Brown, *Industrialization and Trade* (Royal Institute of International Affairs, 1943), pp. 26-27.

of the men for a week or more. Yet, when Ford gave up on Brazilian rubber after the second world war and turned the operation over to the Brazilian Government, after proving among other things that health conditions could be controlled, the workers had reached the stage where they resented a cutback in wages and educational and housing and medical facilities, and were prepared to seek opportunities elsewhere to maintain their new standards.

When Morris Cooke, a famous management engineer, studied Brazil's economic potential in 1942-43, he sought specifically to answer the question whether "the Brazilian workman has the physical and mental capacity to meet the demands of modern scientifically-organized and invention-charged industry." Employers furnished him abundant testimony on the adverse effect on efficiency of the high frequency of malnutrition and disease, the poor educational facilities, and the social system. But they testified also that "with proper health and nutritional care and competent managerial direction the Brazilian worker gives a work performance that compares satisfactorily with that of workmen in the industrially more mature countries." [23]

Admittedly, the cultural pattern of a large section of the population has been far from the optimum for the requirements of a great rapid industrial advance. The Indian cultural pattern would be expected to resist swift sharp changes in Central America, Mexico, and much of the West Coast area. And in the Plate and southern Brazil where the population pattern more closely resembled that of western Europe, the limited physical endowment for industry's demands retarded.

At present, three-fourths of the Latin American countries have illiteracy ratios exceeding 50% and probably only two have cut the ratio below 20%. Most of the countries lack facilities for providing elementary schooling for every child of school age. In none of the countries has popular education been oriented to the scientific requirements of an industrial civilization. When educational opportunities have broadened,

---

[23] Morris L. Cooke, *Brazil on the March* (McGraw-Hill, New York, 1944), p. 64, 76.

when faulty diets and endemic disease have been brought under control, when opportunities for economic advancement have been provided by adjustments in the landowning system and by urban industrialization with its demonstration of the material benefits that can be forthcoming, we shall hear less of the "natural indolence" theory and its corollary that substantial rises in the standard of living cannot be expected.

Immigration. The same slowness to grasp the possibilities in improved health standards has contributed to confusion on the subject of immigration. Of some 60 million Europeans who migrated in the century before the second world war, about 11% went to Argentina, 7.4% to Brazil, 60% to the United States, 8.7% to Canada, 7.3% to Australia, New Zealand and South Africa.[24] Of the four leading destinations for emigrants, Argentina had the greatest annual intensity of immigration (proportion of immigrants to population of receiving country), with 22.2 for 1881-90 and 29.2 for 1901-10.[25] Of the 11 to 12 million immigrants into Latin America, over 4 million were of Spanish origin, over 4 million Italian, over 2 million Portuguese, with lesser numbers of German, French and other origins. The east coast of South America, which was the major beneficiary of the flow to Latin America, also received about a quarter of a million Asiatic immigrants.[26] In this area especially, lack of hands (*falta de braços*) has been a central theme of economic history. While it is true that in Argentina "the magnitude and influence of the foreign peoples who poured into Argentina after 1853 has been so great as literally to remake the ethnic composition of the population," *most of the population growth of Latin America has come from natural increase rather than from immigration.*

---

[24] Julius Isaac, *Economics of Migration* (Oxford University Press, New York, 1947), p. 62. Note that not all immigrants settled permanently in the receiving countries. Isaac reports that 47% of the immigrants into Argentina 1857-1924, for instance, returned home.

[25] Isaac, *op. cit.*, p. 65.

[26] Asiatic immigration into Latin America included about half a million Indians, who settled largely in British and Dutch possessions, less than a half million Chinese, and over a quarter million Japanese, who settled largely in Brazil and Peru.

In planning for acceleration of economic development, there has in recent years been considerable emphasis on immigration. In Argentina, for instance, analysts see in immigration the key to expanded markets for domestic industries which would bring outlets for industrial plants of a more economic size and lessen the dependence of traditional export industries on export markets. This is pretty much the other side of the coin which the mercantilists once used in Europe to oppose migration because "for every person who emigrated the country lost £6 through the decrease in the sale of home-produced goods." The Brazilians, as in times past, want cheap farm labor to perpetuate their large landed estates rather than independent farmers seeking an opportunity to intensify agriculture and make rapid economic advancement. Yet a two-point drop in the Brazilian death rate would add more to the population growth in a decade than Brazil ever added in the heaviest decade of immigration. And a one-point reduction in the death rate of Latin America generally would add about 150,000 annually to the population growth, which is more than is likely to be achieved over any sustained period through immigration. Both the necessity for and the likelihood of mass immigration must be questioned.

The operating reality of the situation is that Latin America "cannot attract the kind of immigrants it wants and does not want the kind it can attract." [27] Latin America typically seeks farm laborers of European origin, who are not articulate politically, who will remain content with very limited economic opportunity, who will accept increasingly discriminatory treatment as compared with the native population. On the other hand, an industrialized, urbanized Europe whose population growth has slowed down lacks the mass of peasant labor desired for such migration.

Density of Population. Mass immigration is not only unlikely and of questionable necessity, but the basic premise of the argument for immigration may require reexamination. Underlying the argument for population increase are the

---

[27] Kingsley Davis, "Future Migration into Latin America," *Milbank Memorial Fund Quarterly*, January, 1947, p. 62.

statistical presentations of density of population per square mile which have been given significance far beyond their merits. We learn that 6% of the world's population is in Latin America which contains one-sixth of the habitable area of the world. It has the lowest density of any major region except Africa and Australia. In the early 1940's density per square mile was 17 compared with a world figure of 43 and with European density (excluding USSR) of 195. In South America the density was only about 13, or less than one-third that of the United States. From such data flows the easy argument that a filling of the empty spaces is the key to economic development. (See Table 4).

TABLE 4

Estimates of Density of Population in 1940

(Per square mile)

Argentina	12	Costa Rica	34
Bolivia	8	Cuba	100
Brazil	13	Dominican Republic	100
Chile	18	El Salvador	136
Colombia	21	Guatemala	78
Ecuador	28	Haiti	260
Paraguay	6	Honduras	20
Peru	14	Mexico	26
Uruguay	29	Nicaragua	16
Venezuela	11	Panama	22

But in Middle America, such countries as Cuba, Dominican Republic, El Salvador, Haiti, have population densities running from 100 to 275 per square mile, and the colonial islands range up to some 1,200 per square mile in Barbados. In all such areas a serious downward movement of the death rate, unless speedily accompanied by parallel movement of the birth rate and rapid improvement in technique, equipment and skills of production, could mean further decline in the standard of living.

And throughout Latin America the significant comparison for population is with the resources to which the population can be effectively applied and with the manner of organization of production. For example, Taylor doubts that Argentina can "successfully absorb a much greater population than it now has unless it drastically changes its economic structure." This for the country considered generally among the more favorable outlets for emigrants. He points out:

It would be easy to conceive of Argentina adequately supporting a population of twenty million, the vast majority of whom could live on higher levels of consumption than at the present. This could be done if all those geographic areas adaptable to diversified farming were colonized by family-sized farms such as now prevail in the cereal belt and are developing in the cotton and fruit belts. Under such a system, even then, farm families would need to be highly self-sufficient, otherwise they would quickly overproduce their available markets. If relatively self-sufficient they could easily make a good living for themselves from the land, still supply adequate raw products for the domestic and foreign markets, and greatly expand the Argentine market for urban-made products. This could come only as a part of an entirely different economy and culture than now prevails.[28]

We would be getting ahead of our analysis if we undertook at this point to examine Taylor's view that the Argentine Republic cannot be developed industrially to support effectively a greatly expanded urban population. What is clear is that we cannot accept such widely-accepted statements as "Latin America's economic development is handicapped by a shortage of people," and "Latin America is still greatly underpopulated," until we examine the resources of the region and their organization, in order to find clues for development in the relationship of population, natural endowment, the character of organization for production, the obstacles in the path of altering that organization.

SUPPLEMENTARY READING

George Soule, David Efron and Norman T. Ness, *Latin America in the Future World* (Farrar and Rinehart, New York, 1945), pp. 14-58.

T. S. Simey, *Welfare and Planning in the West Indies* (Oxford at the Clarendon Press, 1946), pp. 1-30.

---

[28] Taylor, *op. cit.*, pp. 86-87.

W. L. Schurz, *Latin America* (E. P. Dutton & Company, New York, New Edition, 1949), pp. 64-100.

Kingsley Davis and Ana Casis, "Urbanization in Latin America," *Milbank Memorial Fund Quarterly,* April, 1946, July, 1946.

Kingsley Davis, "Future Migration and Latin America," *Milbank Memorial Fund Quarterly,* January, 1947.

Chapter 3

The Physical Resources

In natural resources Latin America is among the least favored of the major regions of the world.[1] It is the poorest of all the major regions in energy resources. The proportion of total land area that is adapted to agricultural production is far less than that of Europe and the United States and little higher than that of Africa. It has the least proportion of good soil in relation to total area. The relative extent, accessibility, and degree of juxtaposition of mineral resources make it likely that there are in the area no centers of potential industrial development of the magnitude of our Northeast-North Central concentrations or of those of the Ruhr, Midlands and Kuznetsk. And it is questionable whether the requirements even for important secondary industrial centers can be met anywhere in the area. While Latin America contains the largest reserves of unexploited forest reserves, the proportion of the "productive" forest estate that is accessible under existing technology is lower than that of Western Europe and North America, and the region is badly deficient in the softwoods whose increased consumption tends to be a fundamental of industrial development. The natural obstacles to the improvement and maintenance of the transportation facilities required for major economic advances are unusually great.

---

[1] See A. P. Usher, "The Resource Requirements of an Industrial Economy," *The Journal of Economic History*, Supplement VII, 1947, pp. 35-47; Frank A. Pearson and Floyd A. Harper, *The World's Hunger* (Cornell University Press, Ithaca, 1945), p. 50; Howard A. Meyerhoff, "Natural Resources in Most of the World," *Most of the World* (edited by Ralph Linton, Columbia University Press, New York, 1949), p. 91; S. B. Show, "The World Forest Situation," *Trees: The Yearbook of Agriculture* 1949 (U. S. Government Printing Office, Washington, 1949), pp. 742-753.

The Land. It is estimated that less than five per cent of the total land area of Latin America has the combination of climatic, topographical, and soil conditions necessary for agricultural production. This compares with an average for the world's land of over 7%, a high of 37% for Europe, and an estimate of over 10% for the United States and Canada. Analyses of isolated characteristics frequently distort the picture. For example, Latin America is credited with a proportion of well-watered land second only to that of Europe, although a considerable portion gets too much rain, which leaches the soil. No other continent except Europe has so small a proportion of desert as South America. The proportion of the land area with high enough temperature for plant growth is much greater than that of North America. But as Pearson and Harper have pointed out in their concise volume on *The World's Hunger,* what is required is the combination of favorable topography, adequate sunlight and carbon dioxide, favorable temperature, reliable and adequate rainfall, fertile soil. And Latin America has definitely fared less well in this endowment than have certain other areas. Table 5 shows a compilation of estimates on this subject. The ten countries of South America are used as a unit, while the other ten countries of Latin America are included in "North America." The essential character of the comparison is not significantly altered by that fact, however.

Attention has been called increasingly to the fact that Latin America has only limited regions with an agricultural value comparable with that of the corn and wheat belts of the United States and Canada and the Russian Ukraine. Emphasis has been placed realistically on the large volume of soils that are mediocre in quality, highly erosive under current usage, seriously damaged by past practices. Of Mexico, Manuel Gamio has written: "The mountainous nature of the country makes cultivation of more than half the land impossible. Lands that have regular and sufficient rainfall or are artificially irrigated are very scarce in the highlands. The tropical lands which have sufficient moisture are very fertile, but the presence of tropical diseases results in their

TABLE 5

Factors Relating to Endowment for Agricultural Production

	Total land area (Billions of acres)	Percentage adapted to agricultural production*	Percentage with adequate rainfall	Percentage with favorable topography**	Percentage with good soils	Percentage with sufficient temperature
Asia	10.4	6	29	56	47	90
Europe	2.4	37	79	63	79	96
North America	5.5	10	38	71	40	71
Africa	7.3	3	25	78	64	100
South America	4.6	5	70	70	26	98
Oceania	2.1	3	9	86	67	100
Antarctica	3.4	0	0	24	0	0
World	35.7	7	34	64	46	83

* Based on the combination of amount and reliability of rainfall, temperature, soil, and topography.

** Based on assumption that 5% of the mountains, 25% of the hills, 75% of the plateaus, 95% of the plains can be used. The distribution of South America's area among these types of land forms is 11%, 9%, 24%, 56%, compared with the European 4%, 21%, 8%, 67% and North American 13%, 11%, 24%, 52%.

Source: Frank A. Pearson and Floyd A. Harper, *The World's Hunger* (Cornell University Press, Ithaca, New York, 1945), pp. 27, 34, 41, 42, 46, 50. Note again that the table uses a figure for South America which covers only 10 countries of Latin America. The other ten appear in the group headed "North America." But the character of the comparison indicated by use of the South American figure does not seriously alter the character of the comparison which a classification "Latin America" would reveal.

having low agricultural productivity. The remaining lands, which occupy an enormous expanse, are semidesert or desert and consequently produce little or nothing." [2] Adolfo Orive Alba had to lower the standards for "favorable" topography and suitable soil to find as much as 57.5 million acres out of Mexico's 486 million acres of land area adapted to agriculture.[3] The Central American endowment provides sharp contrasts between (a) El Salvador's pitifully inadequate acre per capita of cultivable land—much of it not first-grade and needing advanced techniques for suitable utilization, the forests largely destroyed and the ground water level falling steadily, and (b) Costa Rica's substantial stands of timber, localized concentrations of erosion-resistant soils, some excellent soil and a quantity of fairly good unsettled farm land; but the endowment on the whole is quite unimpressive.

Reviewing the South American situation, Osborn noted that "land with a slope of less than 8 per cent—in other words, land that lends itself readily and safely to cultivation—is extremely scarce except in the Pampas of Argentina, in parts of Patagonia and in the Amazon basin. In turn, a study of the rainfall charts indicates the unfavorable situation of many of these level areas because climatic variations run to the extremes of either too much or too little precipitation. The deficient rainfall that characterizes the great Peruvian desert extends across the highlands of Bolivia into southern Argentina. In violent contrast, the vast Amazon basin lying

---

[2] In his Foreword to Whetten, *Rural Mexico*, p. xv.

[3] Adolfo Orive Alba, "Conservation and Multiple Use of Water in Mexico," *Proceedings of the Inter-American Conference on Conservation of Renewable Natural Resources*, Denver, Colorado, 1948 (Department of State, Washington, 1949), p. 111. He includes a low-quality of soil in his definition of adaptability to agriculture and uses a slope of 25% or less as suitable. In the United States, land with slope exceeding 5% usually claims special attention in the form of contour plowing, strip cropping, etc. It is true that Latin America by the character of its organization of agriculture and by population pressure has been forced to cultivate slopes far greater than 25%, even to 100% and more. Calkins, also in this volume of Proceedings, p. 389, discusses a Costa Rican farm which "proved on measurement to be cultivated on a slope of 137 per cent."

to the northeast of Brazil, extending southward from the equator, receives torrential rainfalls; most of the region is densely covered by tropical forests. When the tree canopy is removed the land suffers rapid leaching of the life-supporting mineral elements in the soil because of the violence of the tropical rains." [4] Vogt concludes his comments on the small proportion of level or near-level land with the remark that "except for the Argentine pampas, these lands have such low carrying capacity that farmers are largely restricted to small intermont basins or forced up the slopes. The intermont basins do not begin to support the populations they should. On the slopes, the land is being washed out from beneath the farmers' feet." He cites the *llanos* of Venezuela whose potential is damaged by poor soil and irregular rainfall; the coastal plains suffering excessive heat and rain; the level areas of the Amazon with poor soils and further deterioration when the heavy forest is removed; the drought-afflicted northeast of Brazil; the poor soil and rainfall deficiency of the near-level plateau northwest of Rio de Janeiro; the over-grazed semisteppe of Patagonia with only 13 inches of rain per year and poor grasses.[5] And erosion and misuse have compounded the weakness of the initial endowment. In South America alone, it has been estimated that around a fourth of the cultivated land (past and present) has either been ruined or seriously damaged for further practical cultivation.[6]

In avoiding the popular misconception regarding Latin America's "fabulous" natural endowment as it relates to agricultural production, we must nevertheless not lose sight of some more encouraging factors. Latin America is still using in food crops less than 40% of the land adapted to agricultural production, so that the prospect of substantial expansion by taking up new lands exists. By comparison,

---

4 Fairfield Osborn, *Our Plundered Planet* (Little, Brown and Company, Boston, 1948), pp. 174-175.

5 William Vogt, *Road to Survival* (William Sloane Associates, New York, 1948), pp. 153-154.

6 H. H. Bennett, "Soil Conservation," *Proceedings of the Inter-American Conference on Conservation of Renewable Natural Resources*, Denver, 1948, p. 353.

North America and the western European countries already have in food crops 55 to 60% of their suitable area, Asia over 80%. South America has more than four times as much cultivable land per capita as Asia, and 50% more per capita than Europe. And there are good lands as well as bad, as attested, for example, by some splendid unoccupied soil in Paraguay and eastern Bolivia and by the generous soil of the Argentine pampas which can take as much punishment as perhaps any region in the world; and even arable-land-poor Mexico still has some rich farming areas especially in the south which are undeveloped and capable of producing high-value tropical crops. Nor is it wise to over-emphasize the statistical limitations on arable land, since scientific advances continually necessitate re-definition of what is adapted to agricultural production. New crops, new seeds, new types of livestock, mechanization, more fertilizer, etc., all play a part in extending the limits of production. We can reason better, however, on how Latin America is likely to fare relatively in expanding its horizons by technical advances after we have studied the flexibility and character of its organization for production in Chapter 4.

The Forest. A great geographer has suggested that the forests of Latin America exerted disproportionate influence on the Spanish and Portuguese colonial activities. "For a people with the background, the attitudes, and the technical knowledge of the Spaniards and the Portuguese, a great significance is attached to the presence of dense woods—precisely the opposite significance which was attached to such woods by the English pioneers." Thus, while incentive on occasion was sufficiently great to bring the Portuguese through the belt of coastal forest to occupy the highlands and the Spaniards through the jungles of Panama and through the lowlands back of Veracruz, the forests of the Paraná Valley and of the Chaco and of the Amazon, the forests of the eastern Andes slopes and of the Guiana region did what distance, heat, cold, pestilence, steep mountainous slopes and warlike Indian tribes could not do in retarding colonial activity.[7]

---

[7] Preston E. James, *Latin America* (Lothrop, Lee and Shepard Company, New York, 1942), p. 814.

For later day Latin America, the challenge of the forests on the economic side also failed in large measure to provide the incentive that might have been expected from the oft-repeated statistics of the area's forest wealth. Latin America contains the largest reserve of unexploited forests. Brazil alone contains about one-tenth of the forest area of the world, some 22 acres per capita or almost five times the per capita forest area of the United States. And Latin America as a whole is endowed with far more forest area per capita than any other major region. The endowment loses some of its significance, however, when the statistical data are broken down and when the forests are considered in relation with other economic factors.

Examine Table 6, fixing in your mind the definition of the terms used there. The proportion of the forest area of Latin America that is "productive and accessible" is smaller than that of the United States and the western European countries. With 60% of its great forests inaccessible, Brazil actually has less "productive and accessible" forest area than the United States. Again, the distribution of forest resources among the twenty Latin-American countries is very uneven. For example, Brazil has 46% of its area in forests, while Argentina has only 18%, Chile 22%, Uruguay 2%; compared with Brazil's 22 acres per capita, Uruguay has less than half an acre. The qualitative appraisal is even more important. Since countries that have relatively abundant supplies of softwoods have a great competitive advantage in developing and maintaining an industrial economy, Latin America's relative scarcity of softwoods is particularly significant. While well over half of the productive forested area of the United States and three-fourths of the European area consist of softwoods, Latin America has only 2 to 3% in softwoods. It is true that hardwoods have great value, but so far they have been used more for specialty woods than for the general utility woods required in industry, construction, agriculture, and publishing. With about 70% of the wood used in construction, packaging, manufacture of wood pulp and other industrial purposes provided by the softwoods, it is not surprising that Stuart Show suggests that "native

TABLE 6

Forest Resources

(Millions of hectares unless otherwise indicated)

	Forest Area	Productive Forests	Productive and Accessible	% of total forest area that is Productive and Accessible	Productive Accessible Conifers	Productive Inaccessible Conifers	Forest Area Per Capita (hectares)
Europe	1046	727	424	41%	316	212	1.8
North America	728	507	334	46%	180	135	3.6
South America	755	664	307	41%	10	5	7.3
Africa	849	306	150	18%	2	—	4.4
Asia	520	358	174	33%	31	43	0.4
Pacific	80	50	24	30%	4	4	6.7
United States	252	192	171	68%	88	19	1.8
Brazil	396	377	153	38%	5	4	8.5
Canada	334	211	113	34%	73	83	27.2
Argentina	49	23	17	35%	0.1	0.1	3.1

Definitions: *Productive forests*—forested lands physically capable of producing crops of usable wood. Excludes forests incapable under existing technology of yielding forest products other than fuel.

Accessible forest—forested lands now within reach of economic exploitation as sources of forest products, including immature forests. Excludes forested lands of productive quality which are not yet economically accessible.

Coniferous (softwoods)—forests in which 75% or more of the volume of standing timber is of coniferous species.
Source: Compiled from Food and Agriculture Organization of the United Nations, *Forest Resources of the World* (Washington, 1948).

softwood supplies of Latin America are less than required for the long run for those regions." [8]

There are other qualifications, too, that must be considered with respect to the Latin-American forest endowment. In typical areas of the largest concentration of forests, as for example the Amazon stands, exploitation is handicapped by the characteristic intermingling of a large number of species in a given forest and by the erratic nature of the occurrence of the desired species, by physical conditions in the forest, by special difficulties of transportation. In the lower Amazon valley, for example, the number of merchantable trees of commercial size varies greatly among localities and is frequently very low; there may be fifteen or more merchantable trees per acre in some places, only one or two per acre in others. The problem of singling out and recovering the desired trees is so great that the operation often becomes impractical. Yet, when a reduction of logging costs is attempted by logging more species in a given area, new difficulties of manufacture arise in the problem of sawing and handling so many different kinds of timber, additional costs of seasoning, classifying, storing, and distributing.[9] "To

[8] *Op. cit.*, p. 751. World use of wood is about 48% for construction and industrial purposes, 52% for fuel. But of the use of softwoods, over 70% is for industrial and construction purposes and less than 30% for fuel; for the hardwoods, over 70% of usage is for fuel. While a little over a third of the productive forests of the world are in softwoods, over 70% of the demand for wood for industrial and construction purposes is for softwoods.

[9] Probably the most frequently cited obstacle to exploitation of the tropical hardwood forests is the intermingling of species. Each tree of desired species must be located after careful search. After felling, it is difficult to get the logs out if no other trees are cut down, and yet if other species are cut merely to make space, there is no return on the additional labor. Logging roads have to be cut, but again trees are involved which may be of no use and thus involve a loss of labor and forest. And the cost of roads is large in terms of volume transported because occurrence of the desired species is very scattered. Yet, use of other species, which would improve the cost structure, waits on study of their qualities, etc. See E. R. Reichard, *The Forest Resources of Paraguay and Their Possible Industrial Utilization*, (Inter-American Development Commission, Washington, 1946).

harvest 33 million cubic meters of timber over the area of 7 million hectares of almost virgin land is not an economic undertaking in any land," concluded Eugene Reichard in his survey of the Paraguayan forests in 1946, "especially when it is found scattered among 1,800,000,000 cubic meters of other timber." In Pará, Brazil, the cost-of-production picture is complicated by the wood of many trees being of such density that the logs will not float in water; practically none of the good timber trees are found in a solid stand over extensive areas; transportation facilities are entirely inadequate; the primitive character of the entire area is retarding in its influence; and an unsatisfactory barter system imposed on lumber extractors by the traders of the interior is discouraging. "In transportation dollars," wrote an officer of the United States Embassy in Caracas in 1949, "the Douglas fir forests of our Pacific Northwest are closer to the coastal consuming markets of Venezuela than are the forests of Amazonas." And "in a country where probably half the area is covered with trees, promoters from time to time have projected a match factory, looked confidently at the forests, and then concluded that it would be best to import the match sticks." [10] Individual attempts to accelerate the development of forest resources have frequently led to exaggerated generalizations. For instance, when the sawmill operations conducted by Ford on the Tapajóz River in the 1930's failed financially despite the importation of highly skilled technicians from the United States, the argument was advanced that this was proof that advanced techniques of exploitation simply could not be adapted to the mixed hardwood tropical rain forests. Yet, other factors—the fact that the technical properties of most

---

[10] Acceleration of development in each field has its own pattern of influencing factors. When Bethlehem Steel Company was building the railway to move ore from mine to ship in Venezuela, it offered $2.10 per tie at roadside in 1945, but although the supply of trees was adequate, ties were not forthcoming since the worker who could get $4.20 per day from an oil company was not inclined to cut, square, and transport ties of standard length for $2.10. Similarly, the availability of deck space for timber on incoming tankers returning in water ballast affects the economics of forestry development in Venezuela.

of the hardwoods were unknown and introduction into the United States had been attempted as general utility woods for which purposes they were unsuited; the mill was too large and operations had been out of line with world market conditions; the stands had not been heavy enough to warrant construction of the logging railways—could be cited as contributing to the particular experience. Nevertheless, the comparison with the more easily exploited resources of other major regions of the world necessitates reservations as to the relative potential of Latin America's forest endowment.

There is, of course, no finality in technique so that the existing softwood situation and the barriers to effective exploitation of the tropical hardwood forests do not fix rigid permanent limitations. There are still vast areas of forest for which there is no expert knowledge of the woods to be found there; few of the species of hardwoods have established a place in world markets as yet. At the present time Latin America devotes only one-fifth of its wood consumption to industrial purposes, compared with the more than three-fourths used for industrial purposes in the more advanced countries. The growth in industrial demand in Latin America seems certain to be accompanied by adaptation of some of the hardwoods to purposes served elsewhere by softwoods. Improved recovery of products from trees and from forests, technological advances in utilization of the tropical woods, the pressure of world demand on the economics of transportation improvement, changing definitions of "accessibility," can all alter the bare picture established by a statistical account of the endowment. Yet, serious changes in the pattern and economy of utilization come slowly.

The Complex of Power: Coal, Oil and Water Power. Latin America has less than 2.5% of the world's energy resources to provide for a region comprising one-sixth of the world's area. Since the resources in mechanical energy are the controlling factor in economic activity today, Abbott Payson Usher, a famous economic historian, concluded in 1947 that on the basis of present estimates, even in a fully developed world Latin America will remain the poorest of all the major

regions of the world. Usher did not suggest that this precluded some diversification of the Latin-American economies
and achievement of a measure of industrial expansion, but
rather stressed the fact that "the developments will be of local
importance and will not constitute major changes in the
pattern of the world economy." Study Table 7 carefully.
"Subject to some qualification for atomic energy, the resource
tables indicate the potentialities of the world for at least the
coming century and a half. Technical changes may alter
the proportions in which the resources are used, but the
power that can be produced by local resources is indicated
by the tables." [11]

"Where fuel is cheap," an American reminded the British
Parliament 140 years ago, "all the arts are carried on with a
corresponding thriftiness and ease." But while he could anticipate independence of English coal by pointing to Pennsylvania's coal "enough for the most remote posterity . . . the
exhaustless magazines of fuel," the Latin American endowment in coal permits no such comfort.[12] Less than 1% of
the world's estimated reserves of coal are in Latin America.[13]
Such coal as is available tends to be non-coking and poor in
quality, to occur in irregular seams, to be scattered in relatively
small quantities, is frequently inaccessible and lacks the favorable location near other resources, such as iron ore, which
would maximize its usefulness. Latin America has not been
able to produce 0.1 tons per capita per year, compared with
United States output of around 4.3 tons per capita. One

---

[11] Abbott Payson Usher, "The Steam and Steel Complex and International Relations," *Technology and International Relations* (Edited by
William Fielding Ogburn, The University of Chicago Press, Chicago,
1949), p. 68. See also Usher, "The Resource Requirements of an Industrial Economy." *The Journal of Economic History*, Supplement VII,
1947, pp. 35-46.

[12] Quoted in *Coal Through the Ages* (Second edition, American Institute of Mining and Metallurgical Engineers, 1939), p. 68.

[13] Based on estimates prepared by Elmer Walter Pehrson for a
discussion of "Estimates of Selected World Mineral Supplies by Cost
Range," at the United Nations Scientific Conference on the Conservation and Utilization of Resources, August 23, 1949.

TABLE 7

(Expressed as billions of tons of bituminous coal)

World Resources of Mechanical Energy

	Coal	Oil	Water Power	Total	% of world resources	% of world area	Thousands of tons per sq. kilometer
World	7,245	39	1,373	8,670	100.0%	100.0%	66
North America	2,860	14	214	3,087	35.6	16.9	138
South America	3	6	158	167	1.9	13.7	9
Europe excluding U.S.S.R.	653	1	145	800	9.2	4.1	147
U.S.S.R.	1,240	5	69	1,314	15.1	16.9	62
Asia excluding U.S.S.R.	2,143	13	191	2,348	27.1	18.4	96
Africa	206	–	559	765	8.8	22.6	26
Oceania	139	1	50	190	2.2	8.3	17
United States	2,378	12	123	2,513	29.0	5.9	321
Argentina	–	0.4	15	15	0.17	2.1	6
Brazil	–	–	73	73	0.84	6.4	9
Chile	2	–	7	9	0.11	0.6	13
Venezuela	–	4.3	9	13	0.15	0.7	14
Mexico	–	0.6	18	18	0.2	1.5	9
Central America	–	–	15	15	0.17	0.4	26
Colombia	–	0.5	12	12	0.14	0.9	11
Peru	1	0.3	13	14	0.17	0.9	12

Source: Abbott Payson Usher, "The Resource Requirements of an Industrial Economy," *Journal of Economic History,* Supplement VII, 1947, pp. 40-44. The student should consult this original work for fuller details and more satisfactory country-by-country presentations. The data here have been rounded off to simplify study and occasionally, as in the case of petroleum data for Latin American countries, may mislead the student into thinking that there is a complete absence of resources in some countries where actually petroleum does exist.

hundred years ago the United States production was only double that of present-day Latin America, but the resource potential which permitted the United States to more than double production each decade in the last half of the nineteenth century is absent in Latin America. Argentina doggedly pursues a hope of utilizing 200 million tons of reserves in the Patagonian coal fields, avoids weighing the feasibility of exploitation in economic terms lest it be discouraged by the cost, quality, and magnitude data. Small reserves, thin seams, low quality, high ash content, unfortunate mode of occurrence, have all plagued Argentina's attempt to meet this resource deficiency. Brazil glumly surveys the non-coking, high-ash, sulphur-bearing coal of Rio Grande do Sul and the high-ash coal reserves of Santa Catarina and seeks out costly methods of utilizing the available quality while searching into the depressing problem of boosting production. Mexico limps to record production by approaching 0.1 tons per capita and uncomfortably watches coal and coke remain a bottle-neck to expansion of steel and base metal production in smelters. Chile takes on purely local importance by sur-passing its neighbors when it hits a piddling two million tons per year. Peru looks optimistically to relatively inaccessible deposits of only fair quality and relatively small extent. Colombia is tied by economic inaccessibility. It is true that there has been a long-run world trend to supplement coal with other sources of fuel and energy, but the preponderant magnitude of coal reserves as compared with other elements of the power complex, which is well demonstrated in Table 7, the prospective adaptation of coal to more efficient methods of processing and utilization, and the relatively insignificant composite of Latin-American resources even with water power included, underline the basic weakness.

In petroleum, for example, the Latin American endowment compares much more favorably. It has been estimated that in ultimate potential reserves, there is less than 20% difference between the United States and Latin America, although the variations within the Latin-American area are immense. In proved resources, the margin is wider, with United States reserves possibly double those of Latin America. And far less of the ultimate potential reserves of Latin America have already been used.[14] Yet, the relationship of total resources of mechanical energy is little altered by this strength in petroleum. Usher notes that "in some of the Central and South American oil fields, gas and oil might become a source of power of considerable local importance, but costs would be high and would hamper any substantial industrial development." [15]

It is in water power that the ultimate future of Latin America lies. Morris Cooke concluded in his study of Brazil, for example, that "unless electricity produced from water power, hydroelectricity, can supplement Brazil's inadequate supply of low-grade coal, not enough metals can be smeltered, not enough railroads can be run, not enough machinery can be built, not enough cloth can be woven, not enough paper can be made, to carry out the plans for the necessities of peace." [16] In its water power potential, as Table 7 shows,

[14] L. G. Weeks in "Highlights on 1947 Developments in Foreign Petroleum Fields," *Bulletin of the American Association of Petroleum Geologists,* June, 1948, offers these estimates:

	% of world's proved reserves	% of world's ultimate potential reserves	% of ultimate produced
United States	31.6%	18.0%	32%
Rest of North America	1.7	6.6	6
South America	14.2	13.1	7
Eastern Hemisphere excluding Russia	45.1	37.7	2.5
Russia	7.4	24.6	3.8

See also E. De Golyer, "Global Oil Reserves as of January 1, 1949," *The Oil and Gas Journal,* December 30, 1948, p. 144.

[15] Usher, "The Steam and Steel Complex," p. 73.

[16] The energy supply pattern in a country like Brazil differs widely from that of the United States. For instance, in 1940, wood and miscellaneous fuels provided 71%, coal 11%, petroleum 11%, water power 7% (with much of the coal and oil imported); U. S. sources were: coal 48%, petroleum and natural gas 40%, water 9%, wood etc. 2%. There are differences in the use pattern, too. For instance, domestic heating requirements are relatively small for much of Latin America; and there is absent the great haul of coal so that transportation needs are reduced. In the United States, one-fifth of the coal used in the wartime peak year was used to operate the railroads which in turn depended on coal for one-third of their revenue freight.

the Latin American position is more satisfactory. Compared with about one-sixth of the world's oil and only an infinitesimal portion of its coal, Latin America has about 14% of the world's water-power resources. Even in this field, the endowment is inferior to that of the United States and western Europe. And the distribution among countries, particularly among those most conscious of the urge to industrialize, is very uneven. Industrially ambitious Argentina, for instance, looks wishfully at the far-off Iguazú Falls with all the transmission problems that would be involved, and at the southern mountains where its optimists envisage great industrial cities, and anticipates help for industrial Buenos Aires from the distant Salto Grande site on the Uruguay River; but the endowment in water power is smaller than is brought to bear on the average throughout the world per square kilometer of area, although it is better than Argentina's potential in coal and oil. Mexico, equally ambitious for industrial development, has a superior volume of mechanical energy resources in both water power and petroleum. Brazil similarly outdistances the Argentine potential, although here too the regional distribution of potential power resources is hardly ideal when the probable outlets for energy are considered.

Meanwhile, since the United States flashed the three-letter code message TVA around the world, the hopes of millions have been lifted to the potentialities of water power development, whether in the form of multiple-purpose river development such as is projected for the São Francisco in Brazil or in less ambitious advances. Yet, it is well to remember that hydroelectric installations involve tremendous investments including a heavy percentage of foreign exchange; their overhead costs require a huge and continuing demand; and as a source of heat energy they are not sufficiently economical for many purposes. The opinion is widely held that regions wholly dependent on water power are likely to enjoy less intensive industrialization than those which can avail themselves of both coal and water power, and are less likely to become major areas of primary industry which is characterized by heavy industries and those light industries dominated by power costs.

The Metals and Minerals. *"If* Argentina had coal, she could make steel, *if* she had iron," wrote a professor of geology somewhat unfeelingly in 1949.[17] This "iffyness" is not uncharacteristic of the Latin American endowment in minerals. Brazil, for instance, has probably the largest of the world's iron ore deposits in the fabulous iron mountain of Itabira, perhaps one-sixth to one-fifth of the iron ore reserves of the world, with an abundance of higher-grade ore. *If* it had been endowed with good coking coal that would provide the necessary close grouping of coal, iron ore and limestone flux, it might have had the makings of a major steel center; *if* the investment required for the necessary improvement of rail and port facilities and for maritime transport and mining equipment were not so enormous, and *if* there were not a tendency in iron production to adapt operating procedure to the available raw materials rather than to depend on raw materials adapted to existing techniques, and *if* there were not available alternative sources of ore in North America, there might already have been huge exploitation for export. *If* a very large part of the mineral wealth of Latin America were not concentrated in the high Andes and in the interior of the Brazilian plateau and perhaps north out of the Guiana Highlands, exploitation would have been less hampered by the inhospitable high average elevations, the extreme local heights, the unattractive physiography, the difficulties with water supply, the great distances. The most commonly repeated *"if"* refers to the acceleration of development which would have been possible *if* improvement of transportation facilities were not so often beyond the realm of economic feasibility. Sumner M. Anderson of the Bureau of Mines in the late 1940's wrote: [18]

"In most instances, full and profitable exploitation of these resources is more dependent on the expansion of transportation facilities than on any other single factor. The area (Latin America including the European possessions) in 1946 produced more than half the total world

---

[17] Meyerhoff, *op. cit.,* p. 87.

[18] Sumner M. Anderson, "Review of the Mineral Industries of Latin America," *Economic Geology,* May, 1948, p. 231.

output of natural nitrates, quartz crystal, beryllium ore, antimony, and silver; and more than a quarter of the bauxite, bismuth, tin, vanadium, arsenic, copper, and tantalite. The area also produced about one-fifth of the world's supply of tungsten, zirconium, and crude petroleum, and smaller but important portions of chromite, lead, zinc, platinum, diamonds, fluorspar, graphite and mica. The production potential is believed to be much higher than indicated by past performance for several strategic items: notably, bauxite, chromite, copper, iron ore, maganese, nickel, titanium, vanadium, diamonds, coal and petroleum." *If* transportation . . .

If the vast areas that have not yet been geologically mapped or intensively prospected were better known, new ore bodies might be added to the current appraisal of the mineral endowment. The great Pre-Cambrian shield of Brazil, for instance, is an area of considerable promise; within a few years important deposits of iron, manganese, and tungsten have been discovered there, and the task of prospecting and exploring this area is only in its early stages. Again, in the Cordilleran chain from Cape Horn to the Isthmus of Panama, where most of the known base metal deposits of South America have been located, there are believed to be many deposits yet undiscovered. *If* exploration were less hampered by nationalistic politics, there would be less reason to fear that some of the potential wealth of this region may never be exploited, for the constant improvement in technique of beneficiation, the progress in devising synthetic mineral products, the advances in extraction and processing, all compete actively with the development of new natural resources.

This works both ways, of course. Chile's lower-grade copper ores waited on improved technique for exploitation to become active resources as a result of scientific advances. On the other hand, the battle against depleting reserves of higher-grade iron ores may result in more and more dependence on the "formation materials" as a source of iron ore, to the disadvantage of higher-grade deposits in Latin America which may be found less feasible of exploitation. Similarly, progress in the development of the technique for utilization of low-grade domestic manganese ores in the United States might threaten the active exploitation of better ores in Latin America. Chile has seen its monopoly of natural nitrates broken by the development of processes for the manufacture of synthetic sodium nitrate and ammonium nitrate. On the other hand, the west coast countries have also seen improved techniques expand production of minerals. For instance, in the Cerro de Pasco district of Peru, mining progress was checked after the exhaustion of rich silver ores by difficulties of transportation, wet workings, lack of power and metallurgical facilities, only to be resumed when a group of mining men availed themselves of twentieth-century technique and made the necessary investment. The early success with rich copper ores was threatened by deterioration of resources, only to be followed by introduction of improved techniques that have actually enabled the corporation working the resources to maintain itself as the largest producer of copper in Peru, become a world leader in bismuth, top the gold, lead and silver producers in South America, and produce as well zinc, antimony, sulphuric acid, tin, cadmium, indium, calcium carbide, calcium arsenate, white arsenic. Skillful application of differential flotation; electrostatic precipitation of dust and fumes from roasters, reverberatory furnaces and converters; reduction of losses in smoke and slag; development of new uses for products like bismuth alloys which had been less appreciated previously; expansion of markets for insecticides so that the attack on the pests of the coastal valleys provided an outlet for arsenical compounds formerly regarded as annoying impurities; profitable mining of ores hitherto considered too low in grade: all meant larger production.

We are anticipating the discussion in a later chapter when we point out that the growing competition of the new technology has raised a policy question for every Latin American government: whether to delay in permitting exploitation of their resources out of political aversion to activity by foreign interests and thereby risk permanent failure to mobilize these resources to the benefit of the nations, since advanced techniques may make exploitation of such resources uneconomic. Confronted with (a) the example of synthetic nitrates, artificial crystals, artificial mica and artificial graphite, and artificial abrasives, silicon carbide and carborundum, (b) daily demonstrations of advances in metallurgy, ore separation, etc., that enable more and more refractory low-grade deposits to become "economically workable," (c) advances in industrial processes that bring hitherto valueless rocks and minerals to the status of useful materials, and (d) advances that permit working to greater depths in known deposits—confronted with technological change of this kind, the decision to accelerate development assumes proportions of a decision weighing carefully the cost of politically motivated viewpoints.

Data on mineral resources can be discussed in terms of current production or in terms of estimated reserves. Currently, Latin-American per capita consumption of the leading metals and minerals is less than 5 per cent that of the United States. The fact that most of the region's mineral output is exported tends to create an impression of Latin America as an unusually large producer of minerals among the major regions of the world—which is not exact. Tables 8 and 9 are of interest in this respect. Similarly, the importance of minerals as a "cash crop" creating foreign exchange draws disproportionate attention to the industry and tends to conceal the relatively small proportion of the population which is engaged in mineral production and the relatively small share of total production of Latin America which is accounted for by minerals. In fact, in two-thirds of the countries metal and mineral production plays little part in the economy; on the west coast of South America, in Venezuela and in Mexico, it assumes a larger role. It is probable that the value of production of metals and minerals in Latin America is well under one-sixth that of the United States.

Table 9 reflects the substantial reserves of iron ore in Brazil, Chile, and Venezuela and the lesser deposits of Mexico and Cuba; the relative absence of coal, accentuated by the fact that coal of coking quality is even more scarce; the excellent reserve position in copper, which includes the Chuquicamata mines of Chile which may be the world's richest copper deposit and which takes on added significance because of the tight balance between world supply and demand of copper;

TABLE 8

World Production-Consumption Position in 1948
Aluminum, Copper, Lead, Zinc

(thousands of metric tons)

	World	United States	Canada	Latin America	Europe*	Others
Aluminum:						
Consumption	1,591	975	40	11	396	169
Smelter production	1,546	830	335	0	217	164
Copper:						
Consumption	2,454	1,220	95	45	768	326
Mine production	2,295	752	218	559	443	323
Smelter production	2,471	974	198	548	480	311
Lead:						
Consumption	1,866	1,030	54	61	477	244
Mine production	1,375	345	170	285	149	426
Smelter production	1,841	850	135	217	240	399
Zinc:						
Consumption	1,730	780	46	19	623	262
Mine production	1,788	550	249	264	259	466
Smelter production	1,728	770	170	54	449	285

* Figures for Europe cover only countries participating in Marshall Plan operations of Economic Cooperation Administration and their territories.

Source: Economic Cooperation Administration, *Nonferrous Metals, World Production-Consumption Situation Background Analysis* (Washington, 1949).

the less satisfactory position in lead and zinc, which with copper form the Big Three of the metal world. The tin reserves shown in Table 9 are more notable for the strategic importance of the lack of reserves within the United States than for their quality, since there are more economic resources capable of more efficient utilization in the eastern hemisphere. The bauxite reserves are in large measure in European possessions rather than in the independent republics of Latin America. It should be emphasized again that there is no finality in mineral discovery, and that estimates of reserves are at best very very rough.

TABLE 9

Comparison of Recent Production Rates and Estimated Reserves of Various Metals and Minerals
(Percentage of world total)

	United States		Other Western Hemisphere*		Eastern Hemisphere	
	Production	Reserve	Production	Reserve	Production	Reserve
Iron ore, iron content:						
Actual	52%	12%	3%	35%	45%	53%
Potential	—	33	—	26	—	41
Manganese ore, 50% Mn ore equivalent	3	1	6	4	91	95
Chromite, metallurgical, chemical refractory	(a)	(a)	6	2	94	98
Tungsten, 60% WO_3	11	1	15	1	74	98
Copper, recoverable content	35	24	33	34	32	42
Lead, gross content	29	18	38	21	33	62
Zinc, gross content	32	27	29	23	65	98
Tin, recoverable content	—	—	25	8	36	46
Bauxite, crude ore	19	3	48	35	75	92
Potash, gross content K_2O	35	2	(a)	—	39	50
Phosphate rock	64	51	(a)	3	33	61
Petroleum, recoverable						
Proved and indicated	59	36	19	14	22	50
Ultimate	—	14	—	20	—	66
Coal, all types Coal equivalent	40	49	1	2	59	49

*Note well that this includes not only Latin America but also the great mineral activity of Canada, the European possessions in the hemisphere, etc.

(a) Less than half of 1 percent.

Source: Elmer Walter Pehrson, estimates used in a discussion at the UN Scientific Conference on the Conservation and Utilization of Resources, August 23, 1949.

Transportation. The physical obstacles to transportation in Latin America were probably more formidable than those which confronted any other major region. Coupled with economic factors arising in considerable measure from other characteristics of the endowment, they have been a continuing and decisive factor in retarding economic growth. For generations the problem of penetrating the interior with land transport facilities and of maintaining such facilities has revolved in a vicious circle: conditions in the interior which stem largely from the absence of suitable means of transportation are such as not to warrant the construction of the means, unless the countries were prepared (a) to grant to private promoters speculative concessions and special subsidies so broad in their scope as to be utterly impracticable politically and economically, or (b) to establish priorities on government funds which would absorb for transportation a wholly disproportionate share of the resources which the government could possibly mobilize without putting an intolerable and unacceptable burden on the more advanced sectors of the economies and retarding their progress.

No major region has greater navigable river systems. But while the Paraná-Paraguay system taps a significantly productive area, the other major river systems—the Amazon the Magdalena, the Orinoco—are characterized by sparsely populated tropical regions with a limited volume of cash crops and with all the physical barriers to effective exploitation. For instance, the vagaries of the Magdalena, its steady deterioration as a medium of transportation, and the persistent shortening of navigable waterways have been a central theme in Colombian economic history; the prolonged droughts with depressed water level, and the recurring problems of storage and shortage at different points, have occasioned a perennial demand for expanded rail facilities. Other examples are the thinly productive area of the Amazon system, with its six to nine feet of rainfall per year, immense variations in high and low water levels, its tributaries interrupted by rapids and falls. The Orinoco's meagerly populated and unproductive area. The Paraná's clogged channels at low water, sand bars, recurring flood torrents wiping out channels. The navigation difficulties on Mexico's internal waterways with their sand bars, overhanging trees, snags, submerged obstructions; the frequent absence of uniform conditions that necessitate frequent transshipments on even the more important commercial waterways; the less significant rivers, virtual mountain torrents, with their seasonal drying up and stubborn rapids. All such physical characteristics detract from the superficially impressive statements that point to the Amazon as a river with a dozen branches as long as, or longer than, the Rhine, that marvel at the Amazon as exceeding in volume of water any three of the world's other rivers combined and carrying one-fifth of all the world's running fresh water, that point to the Paraná River as alone greater than the Mississippi, and to the immense two and a half million square miles or more drained by the Amazon system and the million or more square miles drained by the Paraná-Paraguay river system.

The combination of obstinate tropical jungle with its dense and rapidly growing vegetation, torrential rains, recurring floods, perennial swamps, and the rugged mountain barrier provided by the Andes and the steepness of the edge of the Brazilian plateau has led geographers to remark that "man is here overburdened by nature as in no other major region in the construction and maintenance of effective land transportation facilities." Conditions for railway construction in the Argentine pampas were extremely favorable, except for the unavailability of stone and gravel for road bed and the imperfect drainage of the physiographically youthful region, and lines running hundreds of miles with hardly a curve or gradient testify to it. There were smaller areas in Cuba, Mexico, Chile, Uruguay, and southern Brazil which also had relatively favorable construction conditions. But the more characteristic feature of the Latin-American endowment was the topographical obstacles to railway construction that assured heavy per mile cost of construction, heavy maintenance burden, and marked the period of railway construction in Latin America as an era of brilliant feats of engineering rather than as one of the opening up of vast new territories by rapid expansion of railway mileage. In Latin America it usually took productive hinterlands demanding outlets to bring out the railways, in contrast with the North American experience of pushing lines out to precede and stimulate development.

There is much to marvel at in the Leopoldina Railway in Brazil, with the steepest ascent by adhesion (a 9% gradient) of any steam railway in the world; the La Guaira-Caracas electric railway climbing 3,000 feet in 22 miles without the use of racks; the Great Venezuelan passing through 86 tunnels in 110 miles; the world's longest cable system in the mountainous Caldas district in Colombia; the Peruvian Central, highest in the world, reaching 15,680 feet within 106 miles of the sea, by use of 65 tunnels, 67 bridges, 16 switchbacks. To ship freight from Buenaventura to Bogotá in Colombia, it has been estimated, requires the equivalent of elevating each ton three miles in the air.

But it is more significant that a region more than two and a half times the size of the United States was to end the great period of railway construction with less than a third the railway mileage of the United States; with four-fifths of South America more than twenty miles from a railway and most of it hundreds of miles off; with no genuinely national railway system and instead merely a number of routes leading from interior concentrations of specialized traffic to the nearest or most accessible port; with not only an absence of important international railway facilities among the countries but even an absence of suitable routes within the same country to connect the regions of concentrated settlement. The dominance of outgoing traffic in raw materials and foodstuffs, compared with the more limited volume of incoming traffic for sparse population with low living standards, was to impose pressure alike on rate structure and profitability of operation. Nowhere was there the reciprocal relationship between the development of fuel and the railways which in the case of the United States is demonstrated in the late 1940's by railways depending on coal for one-third of their revenue freight while one-fifth of coal production is used to operate the railroads. In fact, the scarcity of domestic fuel was a handicap to development of railway facilities, just as the need to import petroleum requirements for highway traffic impeded the development of this more flexible medium of transport, and the need to import equipment and materiel for both rail and road transport imposed the further barrier of inevitable shortages of foreign exchange.

For road construction and maintenance, the physical obstacles have again been determining factors: rugged terrain, large number of streams, jungle growth, constant strain of heavy rainfall on roadbeds and bridges, and the inevitable altitudes. True, man-made obstacles, in the form of political pressure to locate roads where they would compete with the railways rather than bring in feeder traffic, and the economic limitations of inadequate public budgets, have been retarding factors too.

The accessibility of the region by sea, again, has been handicapped by the paucity of good natural harbors. The west coast of South America lacks natural harbors, and while the east coast is better provided, there are few excellent natural harbors. While artificial facilities can and have been provided, they involve a substantial drain on limited financial resources. In Mexico, for instance, the harbors with the exception of Vera Cruz and Tampico handle little tonnage; port facilities are generally inadequate; in most harbors the water depths are too shallow, suitable protection is often lacking, bars are found at entrances, loading and unloading are slow and costly.

The growing importance of air traffic has revived the hope that some easier way around the physical obstacles to efficient transportation and communication might be found. It is true that as economic development proceeds, the topographical barriers tend to become less significant. Yet, the slowness with which Latin America achieves intensive coverage by cheaper transportation service is likely to continue to reflect the greater burden of the physical factors which it has had to assume relative to that of other areas.

Summary. It has been customary for writers on Latin America to unleash their most extravagant adjectives in describing the potential of Latin America. "For four hundred years," proclaimed Wallace Thompson in opening

Greater America in 1932, "one of the mightiest reservoirs of wealth in human history has lain, virtually untouched, in the midst of the world." "Latin American potential wealth," wrote Carlos Davila in *We of the Americas* in 1949, "is even greater than that which was put to such splendid use in the United States." We have seen in this chapter the need for caution in our appraisal of the resource potential of the area relative to that of other major regions of the world. Yet, we must remember that land, minerals, forests, climate, resources, are not alone the determinants of progress. They may conceivably determine limits, but the extent to which any group of people approach those theoretical limits will depend on the human factor, on the economic system and the political system adopted, on the method used to organize the resources, on their ability to profit from successive scientific discoveries and inventions and the engineering applications of the discoveries. We must now examine, therefore, some characteristics of the Latin-American organization for production.

SUPPLEMENTARY READING

H. Foster Bain and Thomas T. Read, *Ores and Industry in South America* (Council on Foreign Relations, Harper & Bros., New York, 1934), Chapter I, "The Problem."

Howard A. Meyerhoff, "Natural Resources in Most of the World," *Most of the World,* edited by Ralph Linton (Columbia University Press, New York, 1949), pp. 11-93.

Earl Parker Hanson, *New Worlds Emerging* (Duell, Sloan and Pearce, New York, 1949), pp. 101-151 (The Amazon— A New Frontier, Walls of Colonialism).

E. W. Shanahan, *South America* (E. P. Dutton & Company, New York, 1947, 7th edition, revised), pp. 1-36.

Preston E. James, *Latin America* (Lothrop, Lee and Shepard Company, New York, 1942), pp. 1-42.

U. S. Department of State, *Energy Resources of the World* (Washington, 1949), pp. 3-26.

Chapter 4

Organization for Production: The Land

More than two-thirds of the Latin Americans are directly dependent upon farming as a major source of income. They produce about one-tenth of the food and fiber output of the world. They provide about one-fifth to one-quarter of the food and fiber that enter into international trade. They account for more than two-thirds of Latin America's total exports and in several of the countries more than 90% of exports, and must continue to be the chief reliance for the foreign exchange needed to finance the capital equipment requirements of industrialization and the transportation network as well as the foreign manufactured goods that move into current consumption. They have managed to increase the per capita food supply inside Latin America slightly in the past decade, but extreme deficiencies in diet continue to characterize the area except for the River Plate countries, and the 2% per year growth in population exerts steady pressure upon productive capacity.

The productivity of the large amount of manpower in Latin-American agriculture is low. Productivity per man-hour worked in agriculture may have been as little as one-fifth that of the United States before World War II and the relationship has become even more unfavorable to Latin

---

[1] In 1949 Colin Clark estimated "real product per man-hour worked in 1940" as follows: U. S. A. 0.28, Canada 0.21, Argentina 0.43, Rest of Latin America 0.06, France 0.17, Great Britain 0.21. The unit used was "international unit," defined as "a measure of real wealth, not of money—defined as the quantity of goods and services exchangeable for $1 over the period 1925-34." See Colin Clark, "World Resources and World Population," a paper prepared for the United Nations Scientific Conference on the Conservation and Utilization of Resources (Lake Success, 1949).

America since that time.[1] Given the importance of farming
to the area, this low productivity would on economic grounds
alone become the primary challenge to development activity.
But it assumes even greater significance because it is associated popularly with a system of land tenure that has balked
a satisfactory adjustment between population and land resources. Thus the acceleration of economic development, so
far as it involves increasing agricultural productivity, is
inextricably immeshed in a movement for social reform and
political adjustment. In fact, the demands upon public policy
for correction of the social and political consequences of the
land system in most cases have taken priority over the technical requirements for economic expansion and may conceivably determine the pace at which developmental activity
can proceed.

The Standard Indictment. There is a standard indictment
of the character of the organization of Latin-American agriculture which has been as widely accepted as it has been slow
in producing effective substitutes. The substance of the
charge is that a small group of land monopolists has controlled the bulk of the productive land of Latin America,
has failed to accept the social responsibility that properly attaches to landownership, has prevented the state from align-
ing the exercise of this private power with the public welfare, has provided a base for the economy which is both
weak and unstable.

The landowner has failed to discharge effectively with a
long-range broad viewpoint the duties of estate management.
His preference for the immediate gains of commercial crops
keyed to foreign markets has prompted over-concentration on
a few crops, holding of land unproductively to permit quick
shifts into such crops as world markets indicate, development
of a transportation and marketing mechanism adjusted to the
demands of export markets rather than to the broadening of
the domestic market. His willingness to accept the particular
year's returns as a measure of success in exploitation of the
land—whether as is frequently the case he is an absentee
owner, or whether he is himself directing the operation of the

property — has militated against sound agricultural practices, such as maintenance of soil fertility, in favor of exploitative agriculture, soil mining, and the like.

The landowner has failed to provide the capital and managerial drive for a continuing expansion of production, for constant improvement of the competitive position of commercial crops in export markets, for broadening of domestic outlets through the larger purchasing power that might flow from greater productivity per man. His comfortable acceptance of the lush livelihood provided him by his estates, of the social prestige attaching to landownership, of the knowledge that land values might be expected to rise almost inevitably to reward speculative holding of idle lands, and his easy command of both the political and financial machinery of the country which lessened his concern over periodic fluctuations in international markets, reduced his interest in making adjustments to the economic and social needs of the community.

The landowner has not been disturbed by the lower carrying capacity of the land which was a consequence of the system. His tenants have been exposed to insecurity of occupancy and meagerness of opportunity to transfer capital into land ownership. His workers have been inadequately protected by the government, not provided with conditions that might furnish incentive to personal effort and education for eventual assumption of managerial responsibilities. His government has been discouraged from adequately taxing the rural properties, from penalizing the practice of withholding extensive tracts of land from productive use, from raising sufficient funds to provide the minimum of social services, from enforcing adequately such protective legislation as occasionally but increasingly filtered through the landowner's control of the political machinery. And far from attracting to the land the leadership which should have gravitated toward it in so overwhelmingly agricultural an economy, the educational and social system has tended to separate the ablest youth from the soil.

Many qualifications should accompany these generalizations. In some cases, for instance the Argentine pastoral industry, there was a high degree of product-adaptation to market involving a large and continuing degree of technical progress, and some notable economic advantages accruing from resistance to the proposals for fragmentation of holdings. Some landowners have exhibited a suitable sense of responsibility for the well-being of their workers. Where landowners accepted the sense of mutual obligations without which the commonly used label of "feudal relationship" is incorrectly applied, the population of the estates had a certain type of security—at least suffering no more from deep declines in world markets than they benefited from prosperity in other periods. In many cases the depressing "normality" of partial unemployment has lowered real income, but the impact of genuine unemployment has been less serious. Again, statistics showing the heavy concentration of ownership have frequently failed to distinguish between land immediately available for production and land for the time being economically inaccessible under any form of ownership, and many of the largest blocks of holdings in some countries have been of the latter type. In some instances technical developments dictated concentration on a crop and imposed their own rigidities —the sugar central, heavily dependent upon large volume, promoting regional concentration on a single crop and the full range of rigidities that accompany it. But generally, though unevenly, Simpson's findings for Mexico can be applied to Latin-American agriculture under the characteristic system of land tenure: "The fundamental failure was not only that it was politically unjust and socially unfair, but also that it was technologically inadequate and agronomically inefficient." [2]

The Problem Restated. The glib recitation of the glaring inadequacies of the system of land tenure has been so simple, the political call of protest so evocative of response from its victims, the appeal to the social conscience so great, that the difficulty of correcting the situation has been underestimated. Popular editorialists can write that "we are not so much

---

[2] E. N. Simpson, *The Ejido* (University of North Carolina Press, Chapel Hill, 1937), pp. 496-97.

poor as impoverished; the sources of public wealth are not exhausted but choked; as soon as the hand of power applies itself to releasing them, they will begin to flow bountifully." But whether it is Mexico with its revolutionary fragmentation of large holdings that redistributed some 76 million acres in 30 years or Brazil relying on an evolutionary process of colonization and subdivision by inheritance; whether it is Haiti with its excessively parcelled peasant holdings covering 90% of the total cultivated area or Chile with two-thirds of the land in the hands of less than one-half of one per cent of the landowners; whether the technique is Cuba's legislative compulsion for subsistence-crop activity in the dead season and a structure of minimum wages or Chile's throwing open of lands on the frontier; whether the soil is Mexico's earning Waldo Frank's label of "an earth unwieldy to man's pleasure" or Argentina's incomparable endowment; whether the population consists of the millions of Brazilian rural workers who are resigned to not owning land or the Andean Indian who clings to his aspiration with dogged affection for a piece of land of his own: *the common denominator is bad farming. And the key to the problem is better farming.* But as Dr. Tomás Amadeo has preached to the Argentine people for forty years, agricultural reform is not merely land reform; it is "practical and vocational education, agricultural experimentation, long-term agricultural credit, co-operatives, professional organizations, home-demonstration work, legislation;" it is "a union of the whole agricultural system and a complete understanding of the rural economy—land, labor and capital in all of their manifestations." [3]   And this must take place in an area where the relationships growing out of the large estates have matured into deep inflexibility, where productive capacity is at best straining to stay up and ahead of a rapidly increasing population, where government finances permit little experimentation; an area where the technological position, far from providing a cushion for solution of social strains, is still so backward that even the assistance of the

---

[3] Quoted in Carl C. Taylor, *Rural Life in Argentina* (Louisiana State University Press, Baton Rouge, 1948), p. 382.

less privileged at the expense of the more fortunate would fail to conceal the utter inadequacy of the total product of the community. Some cases and some recent prescriptions may be examined at this point.

The Mexican Experience. Agrarian reform has been the cornerstone of the Mexican Revolution, which has been hailed as the "most significant phenomenon in the modern history of Latin America." [4] Up to 1910 rural Mexico was dominated economically, politically and socially by the system of large landed estates. Ninety per cent of the rural population had no land whatever. By the end of 1945, the government had distributed 76 million acres to 1.7 million individuals — an area constituting 15.5% of the total area of the country and 23.3% of the area included in the agricultural census of 1940. In addition to the land provided for the agrarian communities known as *ejidos*,[5] a number of minor colonization projects had received 3 million acres from 1916 to 1943 (two-thirds

---

[4] Robin A. Humphreys, *The Evolution of Modern Latin America* (Oxford University Press, New York and London, 1946), p. 122.

[5] The *ejidos* are the agrarian communities that received and hold land in accordance with the agrarian laws stemming from the Revolution. Land accrued to them in various ways: (a) By outright grant from the government. (b) As restitution of land formerly owned by the community and adjudged to have been illegally taken by others. (c) In confirmation of titles to land long in their possession. The ordinary *ejido* has at least 20 individuals, usually family heads, eligible to receive land under the rules of the agrarian code. The pasture lands and wood lands are used in common and cannot be divided among individuals unless opened for cultivation. But the crop lands of about 95% of the *ejidos* have been divided into parcels and each family farms its own section in its own fashion. Thus a very small portion of the activity is collective farming in the sense of farming crop lands by and for the group as a whole rather than by and for the family.

There are some collective farms mostly in highly commercialized activity where irrigation is practiced or where the land is otherwise sufficiently moist. They have had difficulties with a lack of discipline, lack of appreciation of the managerial function, absence of sufficiently trained local leadership. Their task is made the more difficult because they must advance efficiency without laying themselves open to the charge that they are so restricting the freedom of the individual that he is practically back to serving a new master.

from private holdings and one-third from government lands),
irrigation projects had yielded up 2 million acres from 1928
to 1944 for distribution to small farmers, and some voluntary
division of estates by large landowners to avoid government
action had occurred. It is true that a considerable concentration of landownership continued to be indicated by statistical
summaries. In 1940, for instance, 301 holdings each exceeding 100,000 acres, comprised one-fourth of the land covered
in the census. Holdings of over 2,470 acres comprised 0.3%
of the landholders but 61.9% of the land. But a considerable
proportion of the land in the larger holdings was of questionable value agriculturally; it was concentrated mostly in semi-
arid regions where land was not suitable for cultivation and
at best was usable for grazing and an extensive form of agriculture. A great diffusion of ownership of land suitable for
cultivation had clearly been achieved in Mexico. About half
of the crop land of Mexico was held by the agrarian communities; the large estates were fighting for survival; and
some stimulus had been given the development of small private
holdings.

The political requirements of a Revolution based on a program of "Land and Freedom" had compelled rapid distribution of land without adequate preparation of a plan to maximize the economic efficiency of distribution. Thus, lands were
expropriated without regard for the relative efficiency with
which they were being farmed; many properties that had
finally come to be organized efficiently along modern lines
were broken up, when the alternative indicated on strictly
economic grounds was to subject them to legislative controls
looking to payment of better wages, under better working
conditions and with suitable welfare services. The speed
dictated by political exigencies caused expropriation in some
cases to proceed without regard for the distinction between
lands properly acquired and those acquired by illegal means,
and often without regard for the specific provisions of the law
as to exemptions. The economic demands of community
planning were ignored in the hit-or-miss fashion in which
new communities were established. There was neglect of
economic criteria for the size of the holding required on

different types of land for suitable subsistence exploitation, for economic production of particular crops, for the organization of economic producing units. And there was considerable leakage as tribute to the prevailing political morality.

When, in the late 1940's, Nathan L. Whetten wrote his superb analysis of *Rural Mexico*,[6] he concluded: (1) The agrarian reform had sought to confer responsible proprietorship on a large segment of the population which had previously experienced little more than serfdom, and the development of initiative, self-reliance, and sound judgment on the part of an illiterate population long and deeply steeped in the peon-patron tradition must necessarily be a long-range adjustment. (2) The masses were probably better off than they would have been under the previous feudal type of organization, assuming that the landowners would otherwise have continued to blind themselves to the need to adjust their power to the public welfare. Yet, he noted carefully, the chief gain thus far appeared to be not economic but rather in the greater measure of personal freedom. (3) The *ejidos* provided employment for two-thirds of all the persons gainfully employed in Mexican agriculture, comprised about half of total crop land, over half the irrigated land, and over one-fifth of all the land covered in the Census of 1940, and numbered 57% of all rural landholders. But the problem of efficient agricultural production in the *ejido* had not been solved. Most of these production units were on a subsistance basis. For the most part, the peasant had been given land without equipment for working it and without managerial experience. The parcelling out of land had been excessive so that the available land per farmer often was too small or too poor in quality to yield him a satisfactory livelihood under prevailing techniques of production. And where the land was of good quality, efficiency was frequently checked by the lack of competent management and by the lack of discipline. The cry for cheap and adequate credit was an old one in Mexico, but the agrarian communities had yet to find the answer.

---

[6] Nathan L. Whetten, *Rural Mexico* (The University of Chicago Press, Chicago, 1948).

Unable to mortgage their lands and offering therefore only their crops as security, farmers found the special credit facilities set up for the communities to be inadequate. And the financial institutions in turn complained that administrative costs were high, delinquent accounts numerous, banking on sound principles difficult; they sought to operate in well-defined restricted areas where they could provide technical supervision that might help develop efficient producing units; but they soon found themselves criticized because they were making credit available to only about one-sixth of the farmers, with no other credit facilities available except at appalling rates of interest for the others.

(4) Soil erosion had been rampant before the Revolution, but the situation deteriorated further under the impact of the agrarian program. The farmer, given an inadequate (perhaps 10 acres) tract of land for the family, found that he must squeeze every possible bit of food from the soil. There was no place for rotations, fallowing, grazing, fertilizing, none of the room within which to shift production in the fashion of a large-scale efficient operation. Inexperienced in efficient land usage, he overgrazed, cut down timber on steep slopes and replaced it with row crops—farmed for the day. From 1930 to 1940 the proportion of crop land left fallow decreased from 51% to 27%. One-eighth of the plains and one-third of the steep lands already were made totally unproductive by erosion—a grim picture on which to impose the continuance of the prevailing techniques. (5) Still, Whetten concluded, it was probable that total agricultural production had risen since 1910, despite the fact that production on the *ejidos* was probably not more efficient than it had been on the much-criticized large estates. Land had been brought into production through irrigation; there was more intensive use of lands that formerly lay idle on the estates, there had been a shift to products better adapted to the soil; farming was more efficient on the small private holdings that had resulted from the breakup of the large estates. Although the climate and a major part of Mexican land had not been especially well adapted to corn, the pressure for subsistence crops had kept two-thirds of the crop land in corn, one-

twelfth in wheat, despite the fact that yields were low on these crops. While the production of some staples like corn suffered under the new program, the agricultural base was broadened by substantially increased production of other crops better suited to the land—which in itself represented a sign of progress—and exports had risen despite the rapid increase in population.

Jesús Silva Hérzog has pointed out that it was necessary under the political pressure of the Revolution "to give land to the peasants, to give it to them rapidly, without a definite plan, without a program and subordinating the distribution more to the political requirements of the moment than to what science would have counselled in such a complicated problem. . . . What was done, rightly or wrongly, is done, and the important thing now is to improve it, to adjust the *ejidos* to the economic needs of the country, to educate the peasant socially and politically, to improve and increase the extension of credit, and perhaps at least in some regions to rectify the size of the parcel, enlarging it so that the peasant may obtain not only the indispensable to keep him alive but also what he needs to live with decorum and be a positive and progress-ive factor in this grave historical moment." [7] Granting the priority which was attached to the political phase, however, it does not follow that an enumeration of the many tasks which must be accomplished before the desired improvement in material standards of living is achieved warrants optimism. *Mejor diablo conocido que desconocido,* but even recognition of the real economic issues is still faulty.

The antiquated methods of production of the *ejidos* offer scant hope for meeting the food requirements of a rapidly growing population. There is little surplus crop land avail-able; enough land cannot be irrigated fast enough; many plots are already too small to support a family. And at best the opportunities for rural employment for a natural increase in rural population are limited.[8] Accordingly the cry for land

---

[7] Jesús Silva Hérzog, *La Revolución Mexicana en Crisis* (Mexico City, 1944), pp. 21-22.

is likely to persist and to be unanswered. The program of technical guidance to good farming is not quickly imposed on a backward people; it is expensive in the extension work and research and experimentation required, and it does not often have the necessary appeal to political policy-makers in a government whose finances are already strained. The critics who assailed the "blood-sucking" tactics of the creditors of the previous system of land organization have quickly turned their attack on the bankers of the new system who would expose the farmer to "balance-sheet technique" and "repayment in money rather than in general welfare." Yet, well-meaning as have been the guardians of the political accomplishment, they have been slow to find any enduring basis for financing agriculture merely as "agents for social reform." And if it was difficult to win over a few thousand owners to the merits of a long-range soil policy, it is proving even more difficult to teach tens of thousands of even less competent farmers the merit, the method, and the obligation to future generations, of farming in scientific fashion.

Consolidation of the political triumph over the traditional system of landownership would require on the economic side an improvement in living standards. But with two-thirds of the Mexican people making their living from agriculture and another 10% from rural arts and crafts, population growth presses prevailing resources even to hold to current levels. It is not surprising, therefore, that the difficult-to-attain goal of "good farming" has been joined with and even subordinated to a new political appeal—this time for industrialization. When Eyler N. Simpson published his great book on *The Ejido* in 1937, he subtitled it "Mexico's Way Out." Within a decade emphasis—even hope and prayer—was being laid on the fact that this was not the only way out. Of industrialization, the new "way out," more later.

---

[8] There are some minor prospects for sharecropping privately owned lands, some limited opportunites for farm-labor on the *ejidos*, the suggestion of a shift into rural arts and crafts directed at urban and tourist markets, employment in gathering wild products, and migratory work in the United States. But discussions of this subject inevitably turn to the prospect of migration to the cities for work in Mexican industry.

The Brazilian Experience. In 1822 a Brazilian writer warned that "our lands are already almost all divided and there are few left to distribute except those subject to Indian invasion. The monopolists control up to twenty leagues of land individually but even when they consent to a family establishing itself on their land it is only a temporary concession and never by contract that would permit the family security of occupancy for several years. Many poor families wander from place to place at the favor and caprice of the landowners and can never obtain any land for permanent residence. Our agriculture is as backward and unprogressive as is possible among any agricultural people, even the least advanced in civilization." [9]   The inferior quality of farming, the withholding of extensive areas of land from productive use encouraged by among other devices the absence of a land tax, the concentration of ownership, the evils of absentee ownership, the lack of a homesteading law, were recurring plaints in the century that followed. The clerical issue did not insinuate itself as it did in Mexico since church participation in landownership was not heavy. Although there were some sizable foreign-owned holdings, they were sufficiently limited to prevent a nationalistic attack being made the core of the dissatisfaction with the system. And the general resignation of millions of politically inarticulate rural workers to the hopelessness of any aspiration to landownership added to the rather inflexible adherence to the prevailing cultural practices and techniques of production.

By the mid-1940's, when an eminent North American rural sociologist studied Brazilian institutions,[10] he could report: (1) The slowness of the diffusion of improved farm practices was shown by the long-continued dominance of fire agriculture as the characteristic system of agriculture in Brazil. "Whether in the north, as in the state of Maranhão or Ceará; in the west as in Mato Grosso; in long-settled mountainous

---

[9] Quoted in Ruy Cirne Lima, *Terras Devolutas* (Porto Alegre, 1935), pp. 43-44.

[10] T. Lynn Smith, *Brazil: People and Institutions* (Louisiana State University Press, Baton Rouge, 1947).

parts of the most advanced state of São Paulo; or even in parts of Santa Catarina and Rio Grande do Sul, where peasant immigrants from Europe recently have introduced a well-rounded pattern of small-farming practices": fire-agriculture was the system almost exclusively used to produce the food for the nation.[11]   (2) Evolutionary processes were definitely under way to reduce the concentration of landownership, but these were not always associated with better farming practices.   In the south the colonizing activities had resulted in establishment of a class of small farmers, heavily reliant on European cultural background and with the skills, aptitudes, and attitudes for good farming, whose energies were making themselves felt not only in a more progressive agriculture but also in industry and commerce.   A second process tending to decrease the size of the average holding consisted of the high rate of reproduction among the landowning class and the absence of a system of primogeniture, with the resultant necessity of dividing estates among many heirs, especially since alternative outlets outside of agriculture were usually inadequate to satisfy children of the owner.   This process did not assure better farming, however, since it was entirely possible to sacrifice such advantages as might have accrued from large-scale operation and still suffer the deficiencies of the old agricultural techniques and attitudes.   Other factors—legal restrictions on the amount of public land that could be sold to one person (frequently evaded), trouble with the labor supply, deterioration of the market position of some highly commercialized crops formerly grown on the larger estates, were also contributing to reduction in the size of the

---

[11] In fire-agriculture, land is prepared for planting by clearing underbrush with a machete, hacking down larger trees with an axe, burning off vegetation; the soil then being pliable, seed is planted; implements used in planting are the hoe or digging stick; further attention to growing crop is limited to use of hoe or swinging knife; a few crops— the number depending on local conditions—are taken from the clearing; then with fertility waning and noxious growths reappearing, the tract is abandoned and the firing process repeated farther on.   Smith notes exceptions to the system in the rice areas of Rio Grande do Sul, the diversified farming section found elsewhere in the south and São Paulo, and in small zones around the large centers.

average holding. Between 1920 and 1940 the number of rural establishments had risen from 0.65 to 1.9 million (partly accounted for by better statistical technique), and the area in properties of 480 acres or less had risen from 15% to 27%. It is true that nearly half of the rural area was still constituted of properties exceeding 2,500 acres, but a considerable portion of this acreage was in less economically accessible land. (3) The relative lessening of the importance of the large landed estates had not yet fundamentally altered the basic Brazilian conception of immigration policy—as a means of supplying more farm workers for the large estates rather than supplying small landowners for opening of sparsely populated areas.

(4) A significant increase in farm tenancy was developing both on a cash rent basis and on a share basis, with tenants furnishing equipment and part of the capital requirements. In São Paulo, Smith was encouraged to find that the tenants were not dispossessed owners bringing their backward technique down the ladder to tenancy status, but rather rural workers moving up to tenancy with an eye to managerial responsibility and ownership. In some of the areas whose specialized crops were suffering a decline, farmers were staying on the land as more or less independent renters, sharing with the owners the yields from backward farming methods. In Rio Grande do Sul, Santa Catarina, and Paraná there was an increase in tenancy with owners tending to drop down the ladder.

If Brazil thus far has escaped the violence of the adjustment of population to soil resources through which Mexico has been passing, it is exposed, with no less urgency, to the central issue: How to make better farmers out of a population deeply steeped in traditional methods—to attack successfully and simultaneously the problems of general education, specialized education for better farming, soil conservation in the face of rapid soil erosion, under the burden of a population that promises to grow at least 10 million in a decade, with little economically accessible public land for distribution, and with unutilized crop land resources far below those with which this vast territory is credited in the popular mythology.

Wythe, for instance, has estimated that with an actual farm population approximately as large as that of the United States, the cultivated area in all important crops is less than a tenth that of the cropland harvested in the United States and the amount of new agricultural land available for settlement is so limited that if brought fully into use it would give the Brazilians a total of not more than 15% of cropland harvested in the United States.[12] Crop yields in the basic subsistence staples, such as corn, compare unfavorably with those of North America. Mechanization has been retarded by the character of the crops many of which require much hand labor, by the low economic and cultural level of the bulk of the rural population, by the topography of much of the arable area, and by the costliness of imported equipment. In 1949 it was estimated that only about one-fourth of the farms had machinery other than hoes and simple hand tools, that only 99,326 plows were in use in 1947, that there were about 3,500 tractors on Brazilian farms.[13] The use of commercial fertilizer has been slow to expand, although the increase that was becoming apparent at the outbreak of World War II has been resumed. And diversification has lagged behind need, despite the stimulus of successive crises in the major export crops since the time of the coffee crisis of 1907.

In 1948 the Brazilian Minister of Agriculture warned Brazilians that they were witnessing the end of a cycle in Brazil-

---

[12] Wythe puts cultivated area in all important crops as 37.3 million acres in 1945 and 1946 compared with cropland harvested in the U. S. in 1945 totaling 352.9 million acres. He estimates new agricultural land, available for settlement, chiefly in Goias, northern Paraná and western São Paulo, at 16 million acres. This does not allow for certain small areas that might be brought into cultivation as population and transportation facilities expand, some coastal lands potential by drainage, some strips of alluvial soil in the São Francisco Valley suitable for irrigation, some additional acreage suited for tree crops in the north, and such abandoned lands as might be brought back by changing price-and-fertilizer price relationships. On the other hand, exhaustion and erosion claim a toll also. George Wythe, Royce A. Wight, Harold M. Midkiff, *Brazil: An Expanding Economy* (The Twentieth Century Fund, New York, 1949), pp. 62-63.

ian agriculture—the final phase of extensive agriculture characterized by the search for new lands for coffee plantations and the destruction of virgin forests by semi-nomadic farmers who left exhausted and eroded lands behind them. It was true that Brazil had been able to achieve an increase in production of crops grown chiefly for domestic consumption of some 40% in the decade ending 1947, that the food supply for local use had therefore outdistanced the population increase to provide a per capita supply in 1946-47 perhaps nine to ten per cent above that of 1934-36. But the Abbink Mission in 1949 pointed out that farm population was not increasing as rapidly as the total population and that unless the population shift were accompanied by expanded efficiency in agricultural production, there would be new difficulties ahead for Brazil.[14] But there were not lacking in Brazil, as in Mexico, those who studied the varied and abundant components of the "way out" through agriculture—special and adequate financing facilities for small farmers and long-term mortgage credit of a type little developed in Brazil; integrated research and extension services; technical guidance in use of machines, fertilizer, in soil and water conservation, in insect and disease control; better agricultural technique for control of erosion, reforestation, use of soil-building crops, spread of mixed farming, and all the other elements that make up the

---

[13] *Report of the Joint Brazil-United States Technical Commission* (Department of State, Washington, 1949), p. 202. This is the report of the so-called Abbink Mission. When the great cotton growing and exporting firm, Anderson Clayton Company, set up an experimental demonstration farm in western São Paulo in 1949, was reported that the firm had about concluded that animals and hand labor were better suited to Brazilian production for the time being than advanced mechanical aids; the cotton picking machine had been tried without very favorable results—the cotton does not mature uniformly which is a great hindrance to current use of the machines. The firm laid out experimental plots to demonstrate the need for fertilizing cotton land, for combatting insects which were curtailing yields by use of new insecticides, etc. In some cases the common practice of interplanting and the custom of leaving stumps and logs in the fields impose obstacles to mechanization in Brazil.

[14] *Report of the Joint Brazil-United States Technical Commission,* p. 68.

complement of good farming—and asked whether there was not an easier "way out"—industrialization perhaps?

The Haitian Problem. In Haiti the pattern of agricultural production consists of a very large number of very small individual holdings devoted primarily to subsistence farming. Only about 10% of the cultivated area is taken up by large estates—a few sizable plantations, mostly foreign-managed, devoted to sugar, bananas, sisal, and some extensive individual holdings that are an exception to the general pattern. The typical peasant cultivates his land with a hoe and machete and little else in the form of tools; he uses no fertilizer and usually burns his crop residue instead of adding it to the soil; his seed is frequently poor, his yield low; he plants the same crop year after year—perhaps two or three crops per year. Not surprisingly, much of the land is worn out and produces only inferior crops of inadequate nutritive value. The relentless search for land has led the peasant up the slopes to strip the mountain tops and steep slopes of protective forest cover; the forest cover cut and burned, the thin layer of fertile soil is exposed to rains which carry it into the valleys and to the sea; the land grows less productive and the destructive process of denuding once-extensive well-wooded areas continues under even greater pressure. His forest resources have been sadly reduced and the loss of forest cover has precipitated erosion and brought him disastrous floods. His land is excessively subdivided, and since the division proceeded without adequate survey and registration of titles there is insecurity and uncertainty in tenure. The peasant is a victim of usurious credit practices, his marketing costs are high, export taxes on leading products weigh heavily on primary producers, net yields are low.

For this case, a United Nations Mission made out a prescription in 1949.[15] Confronted with the challenge of devising ways of raising the standard of living of a backward growing population which is pressing relentlessly on limited and shrinking land resources, the Mission recognized that the

---

[15] *Report of the United Nations Mission of Technical Assistance to the Republic of Haiti* (Lake Success, 1949).

first problem actually is to prevent a decline in the standard of living. It recommended that emigration be encouraged since the process by which resources could be organized so that they might catch up with the population would be long and costly. The production of the farms was not large enough to provide the population, directly or through imports arising out of its export capacity, with the goods needed for a satisfactory minimum standard of living. Impoverished land must be reclaimed, and unproductive tracts opened to agriculture by irrigation, drainage, flood control, and reforestation. The cultural background of the population did not lend itself to rapid reorganization, yet patterns of land use must be revised, better implements and seed adopted, governmental services improved and vastly expanded. As the Mission enumerated it: Rehabilitation through a series of projects planned comprehensively, financed to secure repayment from those benefited; rural credit service for small farmers; training of agronomists as the core of a research and extension-work program; encouragement of coffee plantations on state lands at high elevations where the quality of the output tended to be best; enlargement of crop area by irrigation; encouragement of cocoa plantations on suitable lowland slopes; and simultaneously a program of health, education, public works, as well as general fiscal reorganization.

The prescription—make the Haitians better farmers—was a familiar one. But unlike some of the Latin-American countries where an initial advance of some magnitude might be achieved by a leveling out of inequalities in distribution of current product, this economy was so unproductive that the program from the start must wait for any considerable success on enlargement of the total national product, and this in turn required heavy assistance from outside the country.

Andean Indian Agriculture. In the sierra of Peru several million Indians, eking out as meager an existence as is imaginable, are a continuing challenge to the social cohesion of a nation. More than 90% illiterate, given the lowest of priorities as a "problem" by the government, continually on the verge of starvation, the Indians live largely outside the money economy, with little progress toward effective incorporation in the Peruvian economy. Population mounts steadily, pressing on the limited amount of arable land. The farm land of the more favored valleys is fully worked under the prevailing techniques of subsistence farming, so that the growing population can survive only by diminishing the already inadequate per capita food supply or by part-time employment elsewhere. Perhaps a hundred thousand men make a seasonal trek to the mines of the Andes and the large estates of the coastal region, and earn a reputation as an unreliable labor force by abandoning whatever they may be doing when it is time to return to the mountains to harvest their own crops. Neither part-time employment in home industries, transient-labor activity on the sugar and cotton plantations, carrier work as a substitute for unavailable mechanical transport facilities, nor actual migration to the capital diminishes their faith in and affection for the land.

The region once knew an advanced civilization whose farming was characterized by development of special varieties of plants through selective breeding, domesticating of 70 or 80 different species of plants, skillful terracing of steep mountainsides, splendid irrigation works, use of fertilizer, competent preparation of the soil—"scientific agriculture" of the day. But the retrogression over the centuries has been deep and the descendants of that civilization—landless degraded peons—wait on guidance and assistance in matters quite beyond their immediate competence. The government has traditionally been concerned more with the commercial agriculture of the coastal valleys, but it has slowly come to comprehend that its major agricultural challenge may be the economic and social problem of the Indian farmers in the sierra. A North American observer has suggested that "if the standard of living of the mountain farmers is to be raised, agriculture must be commercialized and the productivity of the land increased. More machinery, modern machinery, must be introduced, improved methods followed, shifts in crop economy made, and there must be more irrigation works, reclamation, land reform and education. The cost of all that is well beyond the means of the poverty-stricken Indians. Only under

government auspices is such a program possible." [16]   But
the government notes that soil resources are shrinking steadily
while poor health and malnutrition fail to keep the population down. The ominous threat of agrarian revolt promotes
interest in correction of the difficulties, but tenure changes
alone do not necessarily assure larger productivity, resettlement is difficult and costly, the human resources available
require slow and costly educational effort, all in a country
whose overall productivity is at best low.

The Colombian Situation. With over 90% of the population
living in one-third of the area of Columbia, Colombian thinking on agricultural development is divided into two schools:
One urges that the vast areas of public lands be opened. The
other proposes policy concentration on subdivision of the large
holdings in the better-settled regions. The latter group claims
that some of the best tracts of land, such as the Cauca Valley,
the valley of the Sinu, the upper Magdalena, and the Bogotá
Savanna, are still held in large tracts; that with notable
exceptions the owners live in the cities, take little interest in
day-to-day management of the land; intensive expansion is
discouraged by the attractiveness of high-yielding non-agricultural investments, by the capacity to make profits easily
from livestock, and by the difficulty of obtaining suitable farm
labor, with the result that much of the best and most accessible
land remains in pasture. Meanwhile, the argument runs, the
land owned by owner-operators tends to be in small plots,
so small in many cases as to be uneconomic, and often so
ravaged by erosion that cultivation itself is questionable.

Two-thirds of the Colombian population depend directly
on farming for their livelihood. They operate over a million
farms, covering about 5.3 million acres of crop land and 122
million acres of pasture land. One-quarter of the entire
population depends directly on coffee growing, with the rest

---

[16] C. Langdon White, "Rumblings over the Andes," *The Pacific Spec-
tator,* Autumn, 1949, p. 418. For a discussion of the health problem in
Peruvian colonization, see Wilson Longmore and Charles P. Loomis,
"Health Needs and Potential Colonization Areas of Peru," *Inter-American Economic Affairs,* Summer, 1949, pp. 71-93.

of the people directly affected by anything concerning the coffee industry. Most of the coffee is grown on small holdings of two to twenty-five acres, and even the few large plantations are small compared with those of Brazil. Twenty years of intensive government pressure for self-sufficiency in agricultural staples has developed a price structure wholly out of line with world markets. In 1949, for instance, wheat in the highland producing area was $7.68 per bushel compared with U. S. price of under $2 in terminal markets; the minimum price fixed for domestic top-quality cotton—53 cents per pound—was far above the U. S. quotation. The extreme difficulty of moving goods from one region to another has led to development of regional self-sufficiency for staple foodstuffs, although there is some specialization for trade. In the Department of Bolívar, for instance, there are rice-growing centers without truck roads and without rice mills, so that the only way to reach the mill in the neighboring community is on mule back, with the service of the mule more costly than the value of the two sacks of rice it carries. And intercity and inter-departmental transportation is even worse. Many promising agricultural regions are handicapped by inability to move surpluses to urban centers or to ports for export. Even relatively short hauls of 60 to 120 miles may require combined use of truck and river or truck and river and rail, with serious delays at each loading and unloading point. Storage facilities are wholly inadequate, losses by insects and pests great, and absence of satisfactory warehousing and credit systems bring great loss to farmers through price fluctuations between marketing and off seasons.

When Kathryn H. Wylie analyzed the Colombian agricultural system in 1942, she reported that there were few trained workers available in agricultural economics or agronomy, that there was little local literature on correct agronomic practice for individual crops, that there were no adequate facilities for specialized training in tropical agriculture, that there was no central information service for farmers nor systematic extension work. Except for the major crops— coffee and bananas—the analysis continued, agriculture was still carried on largely in primitive fashion.[17]

In recent years the government's insistence on self-sufficiency regardless of cost has resulted in considerable progress toward self-sufficiency in sugar, rice, cacao, wheat, cotton, oilseeds, with small surpluses of some former-deficit commodities emerging. Its protectionist policy has included tariffs, exchange control regulations, multiple exchange rates, levying of special taxes on processing of certain agricultural products, fixing of minimum prices. The policy has promoted mechanization. Another movement encouraged by the government has been the co-operatives of which there were four with 1,087 members in 1933, 170 with 37,011 members in 1939, and 417 with over 120,000 members in 1948-49.

To the agricultural specialist of the U. S. Embassy in Bogotá in 1949 it appeared significant that concern with excessive fragmentation of land holdings was rising along with the debate on optimum use of the larger estates; that effective exploitation of the new public lands waited on serious attention to transportation facilities; that unless the $8 to $10 million annual tribute to insects, fungi and rodents which the cereal producers were suffering were reduced by adequate storage facilities, the priority given expansion of production seemed unbalanced; that lack of standardization and grading handicapped all commodities except coffee; that while it was true that no export commodity except coffee could be sold at prices in line with those of the mechanized exporting countries, the optimum rate at which mechanization should proceed demanded closer analysis, since development of better varieties of seed, improvement of marketing and transport facilities and similar lines of activity were no less important. And he noted quietly that in this heavily agricultural country, the government was still spending less than three per cent of its budget on the government agencies devoted to agriculture and animal industry.

The Argentine Experience. "To most non-Argentines and some Argentines," observes Carl Taylor in his authoritative

---

[17] Kathryn H. Wylie, *The Agriculture of Colombia, Foreign Agriculture Bulletin No.* 1, October, 1942 (U. S. Department of Agriculture, Washington, 1942).

study of rural life in Argentina, "the land problem of the nation inheres in the so-called land monopoly . . . but the land problem is not simple." [18] The "fifteen families which own one-tenth of the entire area of Argentina's richest province," the "300 persons who control over 13 million acres in Buenos Aires," the "two corporations which control an area larger than Switzerland and Belgium combined," have made easy targets for political revilement. And the inadequate standard of living yielded the farm population by one of the world's superlative endowments of soil resources has permitted little sympathy for the landowner. Nowhere have the advantages of a wider distribution of ownership been more generally recognized, nowhere has landownership been more highly prized, and nowhere have landowners defended their concentration of ownership more successfully.

More diversified than most Latin-American agricultural economies, the Argentine rural economy has been geared to heavy participation in world markets as a low-cost (in balance-sheet terms rather than social-cost terms) producer. It has had a relatively high degree of farm mechanization, both in the pastoral industry with its efficient fencing, windmills, "Australian tanks," motors, universal dipping vats, dehorning and branding chutes, shearing equipment, and on the farms to which more than a quarter of a billion dollars of agricultural machinery were sent from overseas in the years between the first and second world wars. It has had a large class of farm labor, but the farm-operating families, a half million of them, constitute the bulk of the farm population. By the time the mass of immigrants began arriving and crop farming began to challenge the dominance of the livestock industry, the pattern of landownership was fixed, most of the accessible public land had been turned over to private owners in large blocks, tenancy was indicated as the emerging form of operation. As grain production spread, many estates were broken up into tenant-operated family-size units, but the change to a smaller unit was in terms of operations rather than in terms of ownership. Tenancy has

---

[18] Carl C. Taylor, *Rural Life in Argentina* (Louisiana State University Press, 1948), p. 204.

been the prevailing form of operation in wheat, corn, and cattle, with lesser importance in sugar, fruit, vineyards, and cotton. The family-size farms proved that the land could produce a larger volume of marketable goods and simultaneously support a much larger rural population; the units were not small, they used considerable mechanical equipment, and they were highly self-sufficient, as well as efficient in production of commercial crops. Table 10 shows comparative yields among major producers of grains. And as a low-cost producer of fine meat Argentina never failed to demonstrate its competitive strength.

The tenant might start out using the owner's working capital and equipment, farming hundreds of acres with family help and a seasonal call on farm labor for harvesting, taking little financial risk and sharing as little in the profit. As he accumulated capital from the good harvests, he increased his share of the profits by buying his own equipment and furnishing his own working capital, with consequent rise in the risk. But as a tenant his investment, the short-term of his contract, the stipulations against diversification and limited choice left him among the commercial crops, tended to direct him into one-crop commercial farming; he found he had to get all he could out of the land while on it, and the owner, perhaps an absentee, was similarly interested in mining the land without regard for the long-range view. The agricultural ladder above the tenant status was blocked for the bulk of the farm operators; they could not find land available in small units for sale at reasonable prices. The land tended to be over-valued in terms of earning capacity in the absence of alternative outlets for investment by the landowner and because the desire to own land at best sustained a very tenuous relationship to its profitability. Taylor points out that the farm operators did not live on a relatively low level physically, i.e., they ate sufficiently, had fairly adequate shelter, suitable clothes, but that in the cultural components of the level of living they were at a low standard—educational opportunities, community life, social and recreational activities.[19] There was a common school system, literacy above the Latin American average, some rural high schools

TABLE 10

Comparison of Yields in Quintals Per Hectare

5 year average	Bread Grains				Coarse Grains			
	Argentina	Australia	Canada	U.S.	Argentina	Australia	Canada	United States
1909-13	6.6	8.0	13.3	9.7	13.0	11.4	14.7	14.3
1920-24	8.4	7.5	10.5	9.2	14.7	10.7	12.6	14.9
1930-34	9.0	8.2	9.0	9.0	17.7	8.3	10.4	12.6
1935-39	9.4	8.8	8.2	8.8	15.5	7.5	10.2	14.0
1940-44	11.2	7.6	12.5	11.3	17.4	6.8	13.7	16.4
1945-48*	10.4	8.7	10.1	11.8	16.7	8.5	11.4	18.6

* Four-year average.

Source: Food and Agriculture Organization of the United Nations, *The State of Food and Agriculture* 1949 (Washington, 1949), p. 53.

and higher institutions devoted to agricultural education, perhaps three to four per cent of the government budgets being devoted to the Ministry of Agriculture and the official agricultural services; but the North American observer continually notes that the directing personnel were rarely farm folk with a farm outlook, and the complaint is common in Argentina that the official guidance and assistance for farm operators tends to be bureaucratic and out of touch with the farmer and his problems. The farm-operating family unit had pointed the way to larger output and greater opportunity for more people for a better life, but it failed to realize the potential which was open if operating units could be converted into ownership units.

Long before the Perón Administration came in to challenge the landowners' control of the economic and political life of the nation, when the new industrial class was already establishing objectives which must clash definitively with those of the landowners, there had been some legislative activity looking to reforms in the system of tenancy, colonizing activity to provide land for the smaller farmer, adjustments in the tax burden. Tenancy reform legislation dating from 1921 sought to require contracts to be of not less than five years' duration and incapable of unilateral interpretation; to encourage tenants to build adequate housing and other improvements with certainty of indemnification by the owner; to recognize the right of the tenant to farm the properties as efficiently as he could, with freedom to buy his requirements and sell his crops as he saw fit.

The landowners did not yield easily, however. The legislation was strained as it passed through the political control of the landowners and it lost effectiveness in implementation. The landowner kept real estate taxes low, delayed the income tax until the 1930's, and then kept it among the lowest in the world. When dispersal of holdings was threatened by inheritance taxes, the landowner found the device of the company with anonymous shares to avoid death duties and income tax and maintain concentrated ownership. When laws were enacted to help small farmers buy land, he balked implementa-

---

[19] Taylor, op. cit., p. 291.

tion. The cohesion of his group's activity sharply contrasted with the lack of conscious association of the other elements in the rural community, their inarticulateness politically, the dependence of progressive programs on the interest of progressive-minded persons away from the farms. When world market crises forced the government to undertake protective action in the form of "floors" for prices and special credit assistance, the large landowner's influence in the political scene enabled him to take full advantage of it. And when in the 1940's the balance of advantage shifted from farm crops to pastoral activity, the economics of the situation stimulated concentration of ownership. Partitioning of estates among heirs, bad investments by landowners in the cities and bad management of their affairs generally, inability to wait further for the increment from rising land values, tax changes—all contributed in a small way to some breakup of some estates. But Weil, writing in 1944 with an unusual grasp of the technical devices utilized to retain control of the land, concluded that the system of large landed estates "cannot be stamped out or even retarded by merely a new kind of taxation. Only large-scale expropriation under the state's power of eminent domain would accomplish a real change." [20]

In the late 1940's President Perón set up an objective that the "land belongs to those who cultivate it." The landowners were warned that lands improperly or inadequately worked would be in danger of expropriation for subdivision; progressive taxation would be increasingly applied to the large holdings, and surcharges imposed on land not worked by owners; preferential tax rates would be offered to promote subdivision; a tenancy law would revise the scale of rents, penalize croplands carrying excessive rates, prescribe the housing, schooling facilities, and other plant required from the landowner, give the tenant freedom to buy and sell such as the owners themselves had; prompt settlement of public lands would be pushed and additional land made available by irrigation projects; a settlement law would provide long amortization periods, low interest rates, promote co-operatives,

---

[20] Felix J. Weil, *Argentine Riddle* (The John Day Company, New York, 1944), p. 104.

furnish technical guidance; termination dates of farm leases would continue to be extended in the face of the opposition of landowners who objected that this inflexibility interfered with land rotation and exercise of the managerial function. The rights of tenants were so strengthened by regulations implementing the basic tenancy law of 1948 that an officer of the U. S. Department of Agriculture noted in 1950 that "there is some indication that a situation impends where small operators would enjoy more security as tenants than as owners, impeding thereby the very transition sought by the government."

The Argentine government soon became over-extended in an over-ambitious program of industrialization, public works, military advance, foreign trade direction. It bogged down in agricultural objectives, such as acquisition and distribution of 6.5 million acres of crop land. But the inability of the landowners to challenge effectively the government's interference in marketing of their crops under which it acquired farm products at a fixed low price and marketed them abroad at an enormous profit for the government, the inability to stave off tax increases, the burdens imposed by tenant legislation, the increased availability of alternative avenues of investment, did bring about realization that the reign of the large estates might finally be breaking up. When in 1949 the government was forced to announce that after devoting three years to the non-agricultural section of its program, it was now time to consolidate the gains of that section and to devote the next period to agriculture, with a twenty-five year program for the rural areas, it was recognition that reorganization of the traditional structure of Argentine agriculture could not come á golpe de pluma, whether the legislative enactment of a constitutional government or the executive decree of a dictator. But defense of the system, it seemed clear too, would henceforth consist of a step-by-step retreat, with delaying actions at every possible point, to the inevitable dissolution of the large agricultural estates.

The Cuban Experience. In 1934 the Commission on Cuban Affairs at the request of the President of Cuba wrote a

prescription for the ills of the Cuban economy.[21] Until the
end of the first world war, an economic system based chiefly
on large-scale production of sugar had brought a high degree
of prosperity to Cuba. The boom reached its peak in 1920,
only to crash in the following year with devastating impact on
sugar mills, planters, and banks alike and a resultant increase
in control of the country's resources by foreign capital. An
era of expansion in the sugar industry again developed, with
subsequent collapse that made 1932-33 as momentously tragic
a year as 1897-98 in Cuban history.

To the Commission surveying the wreckage, there seemed
to be three reasons demanding fundamental alteration: (1)
The economic system geared to one crop in an international
market where price fluctuations were wide brought with it
instability, improvidence and social damage—in good times
as well as bad. (2) Few independent local planters and businessmen had made places for themselves under the existing
system controlled to a large extent by foreign enterprise.
Technological requirements made the sugar industry inevitably a large-scale operation. To supply the enormous mills,
the sugar companies had acquired more or less effective control over thousands of square miles of sugar land, by ownership, lease or contract. A single corporation, for example,
controlled 771,025 acres, another 520,600, another 280,760
acres. On the other hand, locally owned properties tended
to be small, and the number of small farms had declined;
there were 60,711 farms in 1899, 38,105 in the early 1930's.
(3) Finally, it was clear that the system was not providing
a decent living either for the people or the controlling class,
for although at one time the wages paid and the returns to the
planters had been relatively high, in the years since 1929
the condition of both groups was pitiful. The Commission
recognized that even if sugar revived, the absence of year-
round employment which characterized the industry, the unemployment of the dead season, demanded attention.

---

[21] The report was published as: Foreign Policy Association, *Problems
of the New Cuba: Report of the Commission on Cuban Affairs* (New
York, 1935).

Recognizing the widespread demand for agrarian reform and land colonization, the Commission nevertheless cautioned that the mere distribution of land to people who do not know how to use it was bound to prove a failure. It prescribed as a corollary of agrarian reform, education in how to farm. It found that more land had been set aside for sugar than could profitably be cultivated and recommended that the land be classified as first-class and inferior and the latter withdrawn from sugar. It recommended that each mill divert the attention of its specialists to the production of foodstuffs, that they set aside land for subsistence farming and provide guidance for such activity. And it urged an elaborate program including a detailed soil survey as the basis for land use adjustments and diversification of agriculture; reorganization of farming to be based on products that can be economically produced to provide self-sufficiency for the family unit on an adequate diet; colonization plans for independent landowning farmers; subsistence homesteads and co-operative subsistence food production for part-time workers; a program of agricultural extension, research, and education; an active effort to set up institutions for cooperative marketing and cooperative financing for small farmers and landowners; a tax on uncultivated land. The fact that most of the available suitable land was in private hands was recognized as an obstruction to ambitious plans for homesteading and colonizing.

Unfortunately the pressure for diversification is always greatest and the need most widely appreciated when an economy has been flattened by collapse of its specialized markets and is thus least able to provide the necessary outlay for the broad activity required. In the case of Cuba, the government used tariff policy to encourage diversification, passed legislation to compel small growers to devote a proportion of their acreage to subsistence crops, although many milling contracts had actually forbidden use of the land for minor crops previously, required mills with untilled land to turn over a portion to workers during the dead season free of rent for subsistence farming, encouraged small-scale planting of a hundred acres or so of cane as a cash-crop adjunct to more general subsistence farming.

Within a decade after the Commission on Cuban Affairs reported, Cuba was again in the midst of a boom. Stimulated additionally by world-wide food shortages, the government compelled producers to devote a specified proportion of their land to food crops other than sugar; distributed good seed; financed rice mills, refrigerated warehouses, and storage facilities; leased government land for small-scale farming; encouraged import of equipment; fixed prices to stimulate production, held farm wages high. From 1936-40 to 1946-48, domestic production of potatoes rose 45%, corn 30%, coffee 20%, peanuts 110%, and production of rice reached 15% of total requirements. But in the same period, the production of the export specialties—sugar and tobacco—rose by 82% and 43% respectively, to finance expanded imports of foodstuffs that provided an even larger share of the per capita increase in domestic food supply; imports of potatoes rose by 82%, wheat flour 52%, lard 54%, beans and peas 73%, meat 300%, rice 7%. It appeared that when world markets permitted Cuban land and labor to be employed in its most efficient outlet—sugar—an easier way to expand the standard of consumption was by imports in return for the export of sugar. But 1949-50 was the turning point in the post-war history of sugar, and the compulsion to expand foodstuff production other than sugar without so satisfactory an alternative seemed again to be returned. The Congreso Nacional (II) de Ingeniería Agronómica y Azucarera, attempting to outline a program for the readjustment, urged better farming through scientific instruction and guidance, formation of co-operatives, construction of roads in the rural areas where over two-thirds of the landholdings were unable to use motor vehicles during a large part of the year for transport of their goods, intensification of land use through land distribution since one-fifth of the land was still constituted by 114 holdings, 36% of the land by 894 holdings, while 85% of the holdings had only 20% of the land, increased mechanization, a system of agricultural credit for the small landowner, and a minimum price structure to stimulate production.[22]

[22] *Lineamientos Generales Para Una Política Nacional Agrícola* (Havana, 1948).

Progress in Agriculture. The prescription "better farming" presses the more urgently upon the policy-maker because production of food in Latin America has not kept up with the growth in population. In 1948-49 Latin American food production was 10 to 15% higher than the average annual output for the period 1934-38. Because exports did not rise during the period in like manner, the food supply per capita rose substantially in a number of countries, and for the area as a whole it increased slightly. But as Table 11 shows, in neither production nor per capita supply nor exports was there expansion of the type that occurred in North America.

The most significant fact is that production per capita in 1948-49 was 10% under the average for the period 1934-38. The major task of the policy-maker is to devise means of reversing that tendency, for it is unlikely that food supply per capita can be maintained indefinitely at its present level, let alone be increased, at the cost of exports. The one-fifth of food production that is currently being exported consists in considerable part of commodities that would not meet Latin American dietary requirements if retained within the area, and in any event without these exports the current balance of the economy as well as its developmental capacity would be upset by inability to finance the necessary imports.

Considerable progress has been made in the use of machinery, fertilizer, and pesticides during the last decade, thanks to the favorable level of farm commodity prices relative to the prices of these production aids and to the urgent pressure to expand production of food, as well as to changes in the labor supply in some countries. But the advances have not been adequate. The number of tractors in Latin America rose from 20,000 in 1930 to 70,000 in 1948-49, but the rate of increase was well below that of North America and western Europe. In 1948-49 Latin America still had only about 1.3% of the world's tractors on 6.3% of the world's crop land (Table 12). In 1937 Latin America had taken 22% of the world's exports of tractors and other farm machinery; in 1946-48 only 19%. It is true that data on tractors give little indication of the total amount of equipment on the farms. For instance, only about 43% of the $205 million

TABLE 11

Index of Progress in Agricultural Production

Base: 1934-38 = 100

Food

	Gross Production	Production Per Capita	Exports	Imports	Supply Per Capita
Latin America	113	90	102	111	102
Canada and U. S. A.	141	123	290	99	109

Natural Fibers

	Gross Production	Production Per Capita	Exports	Imports	Supply Per Capita
Latin America	112	89	100	183	97
Canada and U. S. A.	112	97	91	140	136

Source: Data on gross production and production per capita from *Food and Agricultural Targets and Outlook for 1950-51* (Food and Agriculture Organization of the United Nations, Washington, 1949), p. 9. Data on exports, imports and supply per capita from *The State of Food and Agriculture* 1949 (Food and Agriculture Organization of the United Nationes, Washington, 1949), p. 8, 12. Base period for food indices for Canada and U. S. A. for exports, imports, and supply per capita is 1935-39.

of farm machinery imported into Latin America in the two years 1947-48 consisted of tractors and there is a sizable local production of relatively simple implements.[23] But the

TABLE 12

Estimated Tractor Inventories

(thousands of units)

	1930	1938-39	1948-49	% of world's tractors in 1948-49	% of world's crop land
Latin America	20	35	70	1.3%	6.3%
North America	1020	1597	3700	71.0	19.9
U. S. S. R.	72	523	500	9.6	19.2
Europe	110	205	501	15.0	11.9
United Kingdom	20	60	285		

Source: *The State of Food and Agriculture* 1949, p. 134.

index of mechanical draft power provided by statistics on tractors is not too far off as a measure of the relative pace at which the region is putting machinery at the command of its farmers. As Table 13 shows, the overwhelming bulk of draft power on Latin American farms continued to be supplied by draft animals, while in North America the dependence on mechanical power was rising to produce greater speed of operation and release of about one hectare of land for each animal displaced.

Consumption of fertilizer increased by over 50% from 1936-38 to 1948-49 while North American consumption was rising about 150%. (Table 14). Latin American production of nitrogen is considerable; but even in production, while there was a four-fold increase in North America, South American production was rising only from 279,000 tons to 299,000 tons (N) and its participation in synthetic nitrogen fertilizer

---

[23] In 1949 it was estimated that "feasible investment in farm machinery" in the decade 1949-58 in Latin America was $1,145 million in imported machinery and $55 million in domestic production. This excludes simple plows and hand tools made by local carpenters and blacksmiths. *Report on International Investment and Financing Facilities* (Food and Agriculture Organization of the United Nations, Washington, 1949), p. 39.

TABLE 13

Draft Power on Farms

(Millions of Draft Power Units)*

| | 1930 | | | 1938-39 | | | 1946-47 | | |
	Tractors	Draft Animals	Total Units	Tractors	Draft Animals	Total Units	Tractors	Draft Animals	Total Units
Latin America	0.1	39.8	39.9	0.2	41.2	41.4	0.4	42.2	42.6
North America	6.1	15.8	21.9	9.6	12.3	21.9	17.3	8.5	25.8
Europe, excluding U. K.	0.7	22.3	23.0	1.2	23.0	24.2	1.9	19.3	21.2

* Draft power units as follows: Tractor = 6; horse and mule = 1; buffalo = 0.9; draft cattle = 0.5.

Source: *The State of Food and Agriculture* 1948 (Food and Agriculture Organization of the United Nations, Washington, 1948), p. 205.

TABLE 14

Consumption of Fertilizer

	1936-38	1948-49
Nitrogen (thousand metric tons N)		
South America	32	50
North and Central America	380	917
Europe, excluding U.S.S.R.	1,297	1,610
Phosphoric acid (thousand metric tons P_2O_5)		
South America	22	80
North and Central America	714	1,801
Europe, excludng U.S.S.R.	2,043	2,282
Potash (thousand metric tons K_2O)		
South America	10	18
North and Central America	417	983
Europe, excluding U.S.S.R.	1,770	2,094

Source: *The State of Food and Agriculture*, 1949, p. 130.

production was still largely in the future. Immense progress was being made in the development of pesticides (insecticides, fungicides, and weed-killers) but here too consumption tended to proceed most rapidly in countries where scientific agriculture was most advanced. Latin America was handicapped by lack of trained personnel in agricultural extension and other services to demonstrate efficiency of use and potential benefits, by lack of equipment for application; pesticides tended to be expensive, largely imported, and their use confined in great measure to specialty crops such as truck crops. Insects, the Food and Agriculture Organization estimated, continued to take one-tenth to one-fifth of most Latin-American farm crops, especially of the cereals. There were isolated instances such as the banana industry where foreign capital with its immense research facilities and enlightened effort at a more balanced tropical agriculture for Middle America had made of the whole area a veritable food and health laboratory where advances in the fight against plant and human diseases, experimental plantings and growth of new crops, development of native agrarian leadership, were creating a model of scientific agriculture. But this was the exception, not the rule.

The race between production and population was the more

ominous because of the extreme deficiencies in diet which already existed in Latin America, especially outside of Argentina and Uruguay. When the Food and Agriculture Organization studied the rather unsatisfactory data on average food supply availabilities in eight Latin-American countries,[24] it found that per capita supply had risen from 2,200 calories in the prewar period to 2,400 in 1947; but the range was extremely wide, from over 3,100 in Argentina to 1,900 in Peru. It pointed out that excluding Argentina and Uruguay, protein intake was extremely low; that in no case was there enough food like milk, eggs, and fish; that since much of the region is tropical or subtropical it would be difficult for people to reach satisfactory levels of consumption of livestock products from indigenous sources.[25] Only Argentina, Paraguay and Uruguay had an adequate meat supply. For the region as a whole, the proportion of total calories from carbohydrates was excessively high; cereals and tubers alone provided about 50% of total calories and were supplemented too heavily by starchy fruits and roots. Maize was the most important single food in Mexico, Guatemala, Venezuela, Colombia, Peru, and Ecuador, but its consumption was decreasing while that of wheat increased. Wheat was the chief cereal in Argentina, Chile, and Uruguay; manioc in Brazil was more important than all cereals; rice was the leading food in most of the Central American and Caribbean areas and the Guianas, with consumption of 23 to 122 kilograms per capita comparing with an average of 17 kilograms for Latin America. Supplies of vegetables and fruits were deficient in most countries; and

---

[24] *The State of Food and Agriculture*, 1948, p. 69. The countries studied were Argentina, Brazil, Chile, Colombia, Peru, Cuba, Uruguay, Mexico; the data are extremely unsatisfactory and inconsistencies with other statistics on volume of production and supply cannot be corrected until better statistics are available.

[25] Animal protein levels tend to be particularly low among the Indian populations, but the diet of those retaining old food habits and consuming many wild plants was found superior in vitamin A value and ascorbic acid to those who had lost such habits. In Latin America the move from rural to urban population involves a change from maize to wheat consumption and the substitution of wheat flour was seen bringing about a possibly significant decrease in calcium in the diet.

consumption of fats and oils tended to be low except in Argentina and Uruguay. Stress would have to be laid upon protective foods in the production programs if an improvement in nutritional status of the population were to be achieved. Deficiency diseases associated with low intake of vitamins and minerals were widely present, and undernutrition and malnutrition was evidenced by retarded growth of children and poor physical development of adults. Table 15 shows recent changes in production of major commodity-groups.

TABLE 15

Latin American Production by Commodities

(millions of metric tons)

	1934-38 Annual Average	1948	1948-49
Breadgrains	8.9	7.7	
Coarse grains	19.7	18.9	
Rice (paddy)	2.0		3.7
Potatoes	2.8		3.9
Sugar (raw)	7.3		11.5
Fats and oils (oil equivalent)	1.7	1.7	
Meat (carcass wgt.)	5.6	6.2	
Milk	9.1	12.2	
Hard fibres	0.12		0.20
Wool	0.28		0.35
Cotton	0.62		0.61

Source: *Food and Agricultural Targets and Outlook for* 1950-51 (Food and Agriculture Organization of the United Nations, Washington, 1949), p. 28-29. Note that the meat and milk data include only Argentina, Brazil, Chile, Colombia, Cuba, Mexico, Peru, Uruguay.

Policy. The policy-maker in Latin America starts in many cases from strong political dissatisfaction with the social inadequacies of the agricultural system and comes up against the physical realities of a crucial economic problem. He gets advice on many levels.

The rural sociologist tells him that Latin America has suffered from the failure to develop three cultural elements that enjoyed wide diffusion in North America and northern Europe—the simple iron or steel turning plow, the four-wheeled farm wagon as a substitute for the clumsy ill-balanced inefficient ox cart, and the horse collar and other elements connected with the use of horse and mule to replace the ox; that rural Latin America in the absence of widespread educational facilities had not itself been able to remedy these deficiencies by transfer of technique from abroad and had thus waited on immigration—and in areas like Argentina and southern Brazil where mass immigration occurred the transfer had been conspicuously successful as demonstrated in the quality of the farming; and that the great opportunity for Latin America lies in the introduction of such cultural traits more widely into the agricultural system.[26]

The conservationist cautions him that one-sixth to one-quarter of the Latin American population is already living and farming on inferior non-usable land, that these people must be moved off the slopes if they are not to destroy their countries' very means of existence, that resettlement is difficult and expensive. And he reminds the policy-maker that progress to date is not impressive, with Latin America spending less than $10 million a year on conservation programs, not one country in the area with an adequate forest department or suitable hydrological surveys, not more than two or three doing very much with soil research and forest research.

The labor leader warns him that he must produce a "rational exploitation of the land in order to bring about the social and economic emancipation of millions of agricultural workers," and takes comfort in the fact that farm labor is going to be made much more costly to the landowner by the efforts of organized labor.

The foreign adviser holds out to him the picture of a farm in a highly developed country—with its tractor, truck and other efficient machines, with barn and workshops, using fertilizers and insecticides and the best quality seeds, good breeds of livestock, closely in touch with the market by radio, and given a research station and extension service mentally and physically close to the farm. And he encourages him to

---

[26] See, for instance, T. Lynn Smith, "Agricultural Systems and Standards of Living," *Inter-American Economic Affairs*, Winter, 1949, pp. 15-28.

realize that some comparatively elementary improvements can work wonders—better hand tools, better bred seed, crop rotation, a little fertilizer, some insecticides and a hand duster and some means of reducing the worst of the animal-disease ravages; a simple pump for irrigation; and most of all an extension worker who can apply in practical form the modern developments to the farms of the community. He writes him a prescription: produce more nutritionally valuable foods for domestic consumption, diversify out of your few export crops, use more land for crops with higher calorie output per acre; develop extension and other farm services through government offices; conserve the soil. Then he leaves.

The economist notes that although stigma attaches popularly to the large estate or plantation, industrially advanced countries do not object to a large modern factory in an industry where labor was once sweated, and that we must similarly avoid branding all large operations in agriculture as unsatisfactory; because the great majority of large landowners in Latin America have failed to maximize the social benefits that might have accrued from the resources is hardly compensation for wiping out those areas of concentration which may be dictated by reasons of efficiencies in production, research or marketing. He reads the policy-maker the record of sweeping agrarian reforms that have tended initially at least to interfere with production and calls attention to the fact that the technological progress of Latin American agriculture relative to population has been such up to date that the pace of reform must avoid any substantial drop in national income, however temporary. He emphasizes that although there is considerable scope for redistribution—particularly in some of the richest countries—the essential problem is to raise the productivity and the income of the entire community. Social stability will still depend on a more productive system even when some equalizing of incomes has been achieved. He then endorses the prescription for better farming. And as a final note he warns that if your program results in a rise in production per capita with lower costs so that labor is released from the farm, you will need to have an outlet for the labor.

While the policy-maker is digesting all this, he is simultaneously confronted with a new "way out,"—industrialization. And he learns there are a group of factors beyond his control which may dictate the priorities he assigns to the prescription for agriculture as against that for industrialization.

SUPPLEMENTARY READING

Nathan L. Whetten, *Rural Mexico* (The University of Chicago Press, Chicago, 1948), pp. 90-151, 182-214.

George Wythe, Royce A. Wight and Harold M. Midkiff, *Brazil: An Expanding Economy* (The Twentieth Century Fund, New York, 1949), pp. 62-127.

Carl C. Taylor, *Rural Life in Argentina* (Louisiana State University Press, Baton Rouge, 1948), pp. 209-253.

Kathryn H. Wylie, *The Agriculture of Colombia, Foreign Agriculture Bulletin No. 1,* October, 1942 (U. S. Department of Agriculture, Washington, 1942), pp. 76-129.

T. Lynn Smith, "Agricultural Systems and Standards of Living," *Inter-American Economic Affairs,* Winter, 1949.

Chapter 5

Development Policy and the Land

Development policy is commonly concerned with the basic
means adopted to combat economic backwardness or to accelerate economic advance through an increase of the productivity
and the value of output of an economy. In Latin America,
however, development policy tends to be associated more
closely with the effort to reduce vulnerability to changes
in world markets. Earl Parker Hanson, discussing "the basic
philosophy of development that all the Latin Americans have
in mind in one way or another," has noted correctly that
"they want to emancipate themselves from economic colonialism; that, and none other, is their ultimate goal." [1] This
objective—however palatable to the nationalists and intelligible to everyone who is familiar with the unhappy experience of Latin America during slumps in international
markets—immediately defines the character and restricts the
potential of developmental activity in the area.

For instance, to Colin Clark, forecasting that "the world
price of farm products in 1960, relative to the price of manufactured goods and services, is expected to be about 70 per
cent higher than in the base period 1925-34" and "between
1960 and 1970 a further slight rise in the relative price of
farm products is to be expected," the implication for development policy is that the principal gainers could be the countries
with large food exports if they would "take advantage of the
situation by leaving their labour in agriculture and not attempt
an uneconomic development of industry." [2] But to the

---

[1] Earl Parker Hanson, *New Worlds Emerging* (Duell, Sloan and
Pearce, New York, 1949), p. 172.

[2] Colin Clark, "World Resources and World Population," a paper prepared for the United Nations Scientific Conference on the Conservation
and Utilization of Resources (Lake Success, 1949), pp. 12-13.

Latin American whose thinking is focused on vulnerability to world market changes, a quite different policy is indicated which deliberately ignores the possible advantages in such further international specialization. Again, in terms of priorities, North American economists frequently recommend that the productivity of agriculture be raised first in order to develop sufficient purchasing power in the rural areas to provide a domestic market for industries of economic size; and they suggest that the alternative is to have to protect indefinitely high-cost industries of uneconomic scale of production. *But for the Latin American, it is the overwhelming urgency attaching to freeing himself from contingencies in overseas markets that are beyond his control that dictates priorities.* Accordingly, agricultural policy is devised on the assumption that the volatility of international markets will continue. Given the decision that a drag on economic advance is well compensated by a reduced range of fluctuations, the problem becomes one of continually balancing this security-consciousness against the cost, much as a security-conscious individual weighs the amount of insurance he can carry without becoming hopelessly "insurance-poor."

Origin of the Philosophy of Development. The record supports and explains the reluctance of the Latin Americans to gamble on excessive specialization. (a) Visible exports comprise about one-fifth of the output of Latin America. In other regions theorists associate slumps with declines in domestic investment and prescribe measures to increase investment or consumption, but in Latin America the slump is associated with a decline in exports. It hits with devastating force, but being generated overseas it is a quite different problem to handle from the business decline which is generated at home, and it does not respond to such fiscal measures as are brought to bear upon slumps related to a falling off in domestic investment.

(b) Exports of a single agricultural commodity—coffee—are about 3% of the total national outputs of the twenty republics, and a considerably larger proportion of the national incomes of the major coffee-producing countries. Two farm

TABLE 16

Latin American Exports by Commodities

(Percentage of total exports)

	1938	1947	1949
Petroleum	17%	13%	18%
Coffee	13	13	19
Sugar	6	12	10
Cotton	4	4	3
Meat	7	4	5
Cereals and linseed	12	11	10
Hides and skins	3	3	3
Oils, nuts, etc.	2	4	3
Wool	5	3	3
Minerals	14	9	10
Other food	7	13	10
Miscellaneous	10	11	6

products—coffee and sugar—have been accounting for 25 to 30% of exports and 5 to 6% of total national incomes of the area, and again for even larger proportions of the national incomes of the countries specializing in these commodities. Table 16 shows the concentration of exports and Table 17 indicates how heavily the external purchasing power of individual countries depends on a single commodity.

(c) The volatility of international markets for its exports has been extremely great. The staggering frequency and range of price swings which characterize both agricultural products and mineral raw materials have probably been most spectacular for rubber, sugar, coffee, and wheat, the last three of which are major Latin-American exports. Coffee prices, for instance, dropped 40% when business fell off from 1929 to 1930; they dropped 26% immediately upon removal of Brazilian price-support measures late in 1937; they dropped under the impact of war to 6.75 cents for Santos 4's in August, 1940, compared with 11.37 cents in November, 1937, and by August 1941, were back to 13.38 cents; in the autumn of 1949 the price of coffee almost doubled in less than two months. It is not difficult to visualize the disturbance which such a wide range of fluctuations creates in a country like Brazil where in the late 1940's the value of coffee production was

TABLE 17

Importance of the Leading Export Commodity

(As a percentage of total exports)

	1938	1948
Brazil — Coffee	45%	42%
Colombia — Coffee	61	77
El Salvador — Coffee	92	80
Guatemala — Coffee	66	62
Haiti — Coffee	51	35
Costa Rica — Coffee	49	45
Dominican — Sugar	60	51
Cuba — Sugar	78	90
Honduras — Bananas	64	56
Panama — Bananas	77	50
Venezuela — Petroleum	92	97
Bolivia — Tin	68	65
Uruguay — Wool	44	37
Chile — Copper	52	60
Nicaragua — Coffee	47	45
Peru — Petroleum	36	26 (Cotton)
Paraguay — Cotton	27	18 (Quebracho)
Ecuador — Cacao	29	41 (Rice)
Mexico — Silver	25	17 (Lead)
Argentina — Beef	18	19 (Wheat,1947)

perhaps 6 to 9% of national income, or in a Central American country where coffee exports are 85% of total exports and perhaps 30 to 40% of the total national output. Government revenues, external purchasing power for essentials and un-essentials alike, the national credit, the pace of developmental activity, are simultaneously affected. Employment may be better maintained than in the characteristic slump of the more advanced countries, but this is chiefly in terms of the statistics of employment, for productivity and efficiency de-cline with the transfer to "disguised unemployment." The behavior of the sugar market has been another factor in making Latin Americans "insurance-conscious" in their de-velopmental philosophy. Sugar was 22.5 cents c.&f. New York in May, 1920, but plunged to 3.625 cents before the end of that year; there was a precipitous decline after 1929, reach-ing an all-time low of 1.471 cents c. & f. New York in 1930 and then continuing to decline until it reached 0.59 cents in May, 1932. The price break of more than 50% in the price of cocoa in 1949 is another illustration. Still another is the fact that from 1929 to 1930 Latin-American exports of all commodities dropped in value by 32%; from 1929 to 1932 the decline was 64%. Again, twice in less than a decade the dangerous narrowness of the base of the Latin American economies has been exposed by crises in Europe—first when the German successes early in the second world war cut off outlets for about 7% of the goods produced in Latin America, and again in the summer of 1947 when the dollar-crisis in Europe threatened markets that had been taking 40% of Latin-American exports, perhaps an equivalent of 8 to 9% of the national outputs.

The speed of the shifts in international markets has truly been bewildering for the policy-maker. During the period 1946-48 pent-up demand for agricultural commodities was so urgent that it could not be satisfied. Yet, when the Food and Agriculture Organization of the United Nations reported in September, 1949, it could write that for "sugar, cotton, certain fats and oils, and more speculatively cereals including feed grains, there is a reasonably immediate prospect of supplies in excess of demand. For some of these commodities there will be a serious problem within the next twelve months; for all of them there is a strong prospect of surplus supply within the next three years." [3] For Latin America the rapid turn meant a threat to about one-quarter of the exports.

(d) The vulnerability is aggravated by the inability to devise suitable protective measures. As Tables 18 and 19 indicate, Latin America is frequently not the decisive element in world markets, and even where its production and exportable capacity give it an extremely important position there are special difficulties in the way of exerting decisive influence. There are admittedly commodities within broad categories such as "fats and oils" for which individual Latin-American countries assume an importance beyond that for

---

[3] Food and Agriculture Organization of the United Nations, *Report on World Commodity Problems* (Washington, 1949), p. 10.

TABLE 18

Percentage of World Trade in Certain Farm Products
Accounted For by Latin America

Commodity	Period	Latin American exports as % of world exports	Latin American imports as % of world imports
Bread grains	1948-49	7%	9%
Coarse grains	1948-49	23	2
Milled rice	1948-49	5	8
Sugar	1948	70	3
Fats and oils	1948	10	4
Meat	1948	44	5
Cotton	1948	15	3
Wool	1948	22	–
Coffee	1948	88	3

Source: Food and Agriculture Organization of the United Nations, *Food and Agricultural Targets and Outlook for* 1950-51 (Washington, 1949), pp. 12-15.

the category as a whole; and for some of the bulk commodities there are special marketing positions arising out of proximity or other factors, as in the case of Argentine wheat for the Brazilian market, the Chilean-Peruvian sugar trade, etc. But the area does not function as a unit and accordingly individual producing countries often work at cross-purposes in world markets; the Cuban sugar producer's interests are for instance not always identical with those of the Peruvian, and Brazilian coffee policy has not always coincided with that of Colombia.

More significant for the basic philosophy of development is the fact that the region's capacity to compete effectively on economic grounds frequently avails nothing in the face of special objectives among the purchasing countries. Thus, Cuban sugar traditionally has entered world markets as an immensely effective low-cost producer, only to be confronted with the European drive for self-sufficiency, the North American reluctance to be wholly dependent upon foreign sources, special political demands upon the colonial powers for preferential treatment for their colonies. Argentina has entered world markets as the lowest cost producer of bulk supplies of superior-quality meat, only to be met with Empire-prefer-

TABLE 19

Latin American Production as a Percentage of World
Production Excluding U.S.S.R.

Bread grains	1948	5%
Coarse grains	1948	7
Rice	1948-49	3
Potatoes	1948-49	2
Sugar	1948-49	36
Fats and oils	1948	· 8
Meat	1948	· 23
Milk	1948	8
Wool	1948-49	22
Cotton	1948-49	11
Hard fibers	1948-49	42

Source: Food and Agriculture Organization of the United Nations, *Food and Agricultural Targets and Outlook for* 1950-51 (Washington, 1949), pp. 12-15.

ential arrangements. At the height of the surplus problem in coffee, when tens of millions of bags were being destroyed in Latin America for want of a market, the Latin Americans had to stand by ineffectively and watch preferential treatment extended to European colonies in order to stimulate production in such areas. More recently, the drive to expand production of fats and oils in African colonies has again impressed Latin America with the extreme wisdom of reducing its dependence upon foreign markets regardless of cost.

The protective measures which the Latin American considers in periods of stress are usually not impressive: adoption of an aggressive policy to seize a larger share of the market, whether by dumping, bilateral bargaining or devaluation, loses its appeal in the ability of competitors to do likewise—especially when many of the competitors have greater financial strength for a fight; the governments rarely possess the financial strength to tackle buffer stock arrangements for any length of time, or to embark too freely on a lending policy to primary producers. As far as accumulating foreign exchange in good times to tide over the slumps is concerned, the countries even in good times are too close to minimum essential requirements to permit sizable accumulations.

(e) It has been estimated that "over the two generations preceding World War II the quantum of manufactured goods obtainable for a given quantum of primary commodities declined by more than 40 per cent." [4] The Latin American finds that from the viewpoint of the advanced countries the prices of manufactured goods did not increase in real terms and in fact, rising wages and money prices of the factors of production were amply compensated by increased efficiency of production; but any improvement in efficiency in producing primary goods in Latin America during the period tended to be absorbed by the larger amount required in exchange for a given volume of manufactured goods rather than by rising standards and increased prices for the factors of production. To the argument that the relationship may be changing, the Latin American replies that this is at best an uncertain forecast. Too fresh in his memory is the thought that if the labor and resources used in producing manufactured goods had been obtained at an unchanged standard of living, the goods would have been available to under-developed Latin America at perhaps one-third of the price actually paid and the resources needed to push economic development could have come in the form of imports of capital goods without having to wait on foreign loans and investments. He is unwilling to entertain the idea of continuing to support a higher standard of living in the industrialized countries. Although there have been intervals when the terms of trade became more favorable to Latin America, the swiftness of the return to the prevailing relationship of the period has resulted in the coining of a phrase—"the tragedy of the scissors"—to cover the seemingly inevitable deterioration of trade terms and the recurring squeeze on the economy. [5]

---

[4] H. W. Singer, "Economic Progress in Underdeveloped Countries," *Social Research*, March, 1949, p. 3.

[5] When the International Monetary Fund investigated the terms of trade of 13 Latin American countries for 1946, it concluded that a number, chiefly the food producing countries, had improved their position compared with the prewar period, with substantially greater export price increases than import price increases, but that even during this period there had been deterioration for some countries, chiefly the mineral-exporting countries.

It might be noted that among students of colonial policy in recent years there has been a growing appreciation of the fact that policy must comprehend the need to avoid taking advantage of the areas producing foodstuffs and raw materials. A British report in 1948, for example, recommended that government policy avoid "recurrence of conditions in which the inhabitants of industrialized countries, with a relatively high standard of living, continued to benefit by the importation of sugar at abnormally low prices of the order of £10 per ton from tropical regions with very low standards," and suggested that policy be directed toward the "maintenance of sugar prices at a level which would enable efficient producers in tropical areas to offer steadily-improving conditions of living for their workers." [6]   The Latin-American republics functioning independently distrust their ability to persuade the consuming markets to accept such a policy line.

Wallich has suggested that the diverting of the gains from international division of labor through deterioration in the terms of trade to the consuming markets and the concentrated flow of gains largely to the owners in other cases suggest that there may be long-term economic advantage in policy which seems to be of doubtful economic benefit in the short run. "The experience in raw material countries," he writes, "shows that specialization in a few crops, involving the use of a large illiterate mass of unskilled labor, rarely redounds to the advantage of that group. In one way or another, the masses' willingness to work for a low wage stands in the way of their own progress. The gains from international division of labor therefore flow largely to the owners, or are diverted, through deterioration of the terms of trade, to the consuming population of the industrial countries. One of the best ways of raising living standards in raw material countries is to channel the laboring masses into employment where higher qualifications are required. The general human and educational improvement that comes from such work, at the same time that it increases productivity and living standards, also

---

[6] Colonial Office, *Report of the British Guiana and British Honduras Settlement Commission* (London, 1948), Cmd. 7533, pp. 291-292.

helps to justify the existence of industries that originally may have been uneconomic." [7]

Domestic Food Supply. The preference for stable conditions, if necessary at a lower standard of living, is perhaps most easily understood in the case of domestic food supplies. Although Latin America is one of the great food exporting areas of the world, a number of the individual countries depend in considerable part on imports of basic staples, and successive threats of a cut-off of supplies, whether by shipping difficulties, exchange problems, or hold-ups by exporting nations when market conditions permit, have all brought pressure for policy that would assure food for the population in quantities sufficient to ride out any such uncertainties. Curiously enough, in pressing for this objective, the efforts of the food-importing countries have clashed with the interests of other Latin-American countries that are exporters, for two-fifths of the food imports came from Latin America and one-third from the United States before the war, one-quarter from Latin America and over half from the United States in 1947, with a tendency to return to the pre-war relationship where the dominant part of the food imports was being derived from within the area. Thus, with some Latin American countries turning in their security-consciousness to less economic production because of their inability to cope with export-market problems, Brazil worked to end its dependence upon Argentine breadstuffs; Colombia pressed for self-sufficiency in sugar, wheat, potatoes; Peru sought to expand output of grain, fats and oils, and meat; Mexico pushed on the deficit in grains by adding over 4 million acres through irrigation to the cultivated area. Venezuela, for instance, in the late 1940's was importing perhaps 18% of its food consumption by calories. One-third of those imports consisted of wheat flour, oats and potatoes—the first two of which were considered very unsuitable for local production and the third

---

[7] Henry C. Wallich, "Some Aspects of Latin American Economic Relations with the United States," *Foreign Economic Policy for the United States*, edited by Seymour E. Harris (Harvard University Press, Cambridge, 1948), p. 162.

incapable of effective production during the potato-importing seasons. But the commodities making up the other-two thirds of production (12% of food consumption) appeared capable of expansion locally and the government pressed on. Cuba might be producing low-cost sugar with which Venezuela could not hope to compete and was in fact anticipating an early return of the unhappy days of sugar surplus, but the Venezuelan government offered high tariff protection, assistance in acquisition of properties, and other help to the extent that Cuban sugar interests were being attracted into the higher-cost operation.

Meanwhile, the rate of population growth added to the pressure on food importing countries. In 1934-38 the Latin-American importing countries had imported 1.8 million tons of bread grains annually; in 1948-49 they took 1.9 million tons. In 1934-38 they had imported no coarse grains; in 1948-49 they took 0.2 million tons. They imported 294,000 tons of rice in 1948 compared with 364,000 tons in 1934-38 on the average, although there had been an immense expansion of production in the exporting countries. They imported in 1948 some 90,000 tons of meat annually, 300,000 tons of sugar, 140,000 tons of fats and oils. And the drive for self-sufficiency involved for the fibers similar relationships within the hemisphere. Consumption of raw cotton rose perhaps 60% from the prewar period to 1948; but with over-supply a threat elsewhere in the hemisphere, the importing countries of Latin America continued to insist that they must find ways of supplying their expanding cotton mills with locally grown cotton regardless of the effect on the cost structure of their manufacturing industry. Still, imports of the area were 60,000 tons in 1948, five or six times the cotton imported into Latin America in 1938.

Throughout the area there is a tendency toward higher local utilization of exportable surpluses on an individual country basis. But if requirements for development—whether industrial or agricultural — in the form of foreign goods and services are to be supplied, export capacity will have to be maintained and even expanded.[8] If the requirements of the growing population are to be set at the existing standard of living, production of agricultural products must be expanded. And if higher nutritional standards are to be achieved—and development surely has that as a goal—the rate of expansion of output must exceed the rate of population growth. Latin America cannot hope to exploit the newer techniques which agricultural research has developed without a very substantial outlay of capital—for farm machinery, for fertilizers, and for the all-important development of external economies in production by investment in such fields as transportation. It is an unfortunate but inescapable dilemma that these very essential investments in lines such as transportation promise immense returns eventually, but often involve delay and lack the immediacy which the political background of development demands and which the limited available resources make desirable. Yet, to ignore the fact that a term such as "mechanization" means more than the pieces of farm equipment, means the whole application to gaining of readier access to markets, improvement of quality by storage and refrigeration and other facilities, aids to accelerated exploitation of new lands, etc.—to ignore the full scope of the new technique would be to limit the potential achievement excessively.

The productivity differential between agriculture and industry has frequently been cited to explain and even justify the priorities given to industrial development. Spiegel has found that in Brazil the value added per person in industry may be from three to six times as large as the value product per person in agriculture.[9] The Economic Commission for Latin America has reported that in Colombia the productivity per person gainfully employed in agriculture is perhaps one-sixth that of the gainfully employed person in other lines.[10] And Josué Sáenz has estimated that the gainfully employed person

---

[8] Diversification of exports is one method of reducing the vulnerability arising out of excessive dependence upon a single commodity or two commodities in world markets.

[9] Henry William Spiegel, *The Brazilian Economy* (The Blakiston Company, Philadelphia, 1949), pp. 237-238.

[10] United Nations Department of Economic Affairs, *Economy Survey of Latin America* 1948 (Lake Success, 1949), p. 86.

in Mexican agriculture produces perhaps one-eighth as much as the gainfully employed in other lines.[11] But as the attack on the low productivity of the large amounts of manpower in Latin American agriculture proceeds—by putting more capital in the form of labor-saving devices behind the farmer, by shifting the character of agriculture to permit a more continuous use and less under-employment of the labor supply, by finding new crops to level out the uneconomic labor requirements of the peak-load period—timing and priorities vis-à-vis other lines of development become all important.

A movement starting from an effort to produce enough food and raw materials to meet the domestic standard of consumption that is being sought and a surplus for export to finance external requirements of the development program creates sufficient increase in production per capita to release labor for other lines and at least enough to exclude the possibility of absorbing in agriculture the heavy annual increase in population. In agriculture's interest and in the general interest the migration from the farm has to be sufficiently large to absorb the excess rural manpower and increase the number of non-farm consumers and producers. Secretary of Agriculture Brannan has properly called attention, however, to the fact that such "migration serves all requirements best when it results on the one hand from technical progress on the farm and on the other hand from expansion in industry." [12] It is the Latin-American migratory movement to the cities for lack of opportunity in agriculture, at a time when agriculture is not meeting the food and raw material requirements despite the immense volume of manpower on the farms, that needs the most careful watching. It was such a problem that caused the Abbink Mission to note concernedly that "there are right now, from different parts of Brazil, reports of an untimely exodus of labor . . . and unless there is increased efficiency of production in agriculture, continued population shifts from the farms

---

[11] Nacional Financiera, *El Mercado de Valores*, August 26, 1946.

[12] *Report of the Secretary of Agriculture*, 1948 (Washington, 1949), p. 54.

to the cities" must not be viewed too optimistically.[13]
At this point let us examine a case in some detail.

Mechanization in Cuba: A Case Study. In 1947 it
was estimated that Cuba had about 160,000 farms, with 4.4
million acres under cultivation, excluding orchards.[14] Over
60% of the cultivated land was in sugar cane which on the
average did not have to be replanted more often than about
every eight years. Some of the other crops also did not require yearly planting, so that the acreage to be planted each
year totaled 1.6 million. New plantings of cane had to be
cultivated but only two-thirds of the old ratoon fields were
cultivated and of those only half the area (every other row),
so that the area to be cultivated annually was about two-fifths
of the total acreage in cane. Under existing conditions a
total of 2.4 million acres required cultivation each year. It
was estimated that about 5,000 cane growers had farms
exceeding 100 acres which was considered the point at which
interest in mechanizing might be stimulated.

At that time the methods of doing field work on most Cuban
farms were about the same as they had been for a century.
More than three-fourths of the plowing was being done by
oxen; planting was by hand; cultivation with oxen and much
hoeing; practically all the harvesting was by hand; 95%
of the 52 million tons of cane in the 1947 sugar crop was
hauled from the field by oxen, 5% by trucks or tractor-
drawn carts. There had been about 800 tractors in Cuba
prior to the second world war and perhaps 1,800 were imported from 1941 to 1947. More than 80% of the farm
power was still provided by the slow-moving oxen; horses
and mules were not used for field work. Oxen were eminently
suited to field work in the tropical climate, especially to the
heavy hauling of the sugar cane crop; they required little
upkeep; during the summer they subsisted on pasture and

---

[13] *Report of the Joint Brazil-United States Technical Commission,*
pp. 68-69.
[14] The data in this section are taken from a report on "Mechanization of Cuban Agriculture" prepared in 1947 by Paul G. Minneman as
Agricultural Attaché of the United States Embassy in Havana.

in the cane harvesting season they ate only the waste leaves and tops off the cane; they had been cheap up to the 1940's and when too old to work they could be sold for a relatively good price for meat; and the enormous number of oxen needed for the sugar harvest was more than enough to do the plowing and other farm work during the rest of the year. They were admittedly slow, doing 1 to 1.5 miles per hour compared with the 2.5 miles that a team of horses made in the United States, and they were extremely wasteful of man power.

To prepare the land with oxen required ten to fifteen times as much manpower as with tractors, but until farm wages increased radically during the war, no urgency to replace the oxen had been felt. Under the government-manipulated structure of minimum prices, however, agricultural wages for non-sugar work more than doubled from 1940 to 1947, and in the sugar industry where wages were tied to the price of sugar, wages came to be more than three times the rate of early 1940. Simultaneously oxen became less cheap; the large sugar crops necessitated extending the sugar harvesting season into late spring and left insufficient time to prepare land for other crops if oxen were to be used; the price of land and meat rose sharply so that available pastures were needed to produce more meat animals rather than oxen.

Mechanization seemed inevitable. Most of the land was fairly level and well adapted to mechanization, although the high content of clay in most of the soil required a heavy type of equipment. Mechanization promised a better seasonal distribution of work and a better quality of work. During the sugar season there was a heavy demand for men and oxen which consequently were not available for cultivating cane fields and for preparing land for other crops; this often resulted in failure to cultivate cane and reduced the acreage or delayed planting for other crops. The tractor promised earlier and more rapid preparation of land and larger production of other crops needed for diversification of agriculture and for producing more and better foods for local consumption. The plows drawn by oxen did not plow as deeply or evenly as the heavy tractor-drawn equipment; and by repeated cultivation with tractors weeds could be better controlled than by expensive hoeing. And mechanization offered a considerable reduction in costs and in use of labor. There are great variations in different parts of the country, and for different types of soil, and there are differences in the number of times a field has to be plowed and harrowed and in the number of oxen required per plow and in the number of men required. But Tables 20, 21 and 22 present a fair picture of the situation in time and cost. The time requirements with the use

TABLE 20

Time Requirements to Prepare Land

Operation	Power	Equipment	Rate of work time per acre of soft soil: hours
Oxen:			
Plowing	6 oxen	1 moldboard 9"	12.5
Cross plowing	4 oxen	1 moldboard 9"	11.0
Harrowing	4 oxen	Spike tooth 6"	3.5
Tractor: small track type			
Plowing	25-30 hp	3-26" disks width 27"	1.8
Cross plowing	25-30 hp	3-26" disks width 27"	1.6
Harrowing	25-30 hp	16-24" disks width 6"	0.7

of oxen are shown to be six times that of the tractor operation. Land preparation alone with tractors reduces the labor per acre to 10% of that required with oxen, and in the cultivation of sugar it can be reduced, the estimates run, to 10 to 15%. Labor costs are shown to be less than 15% those of the oxen operation for preparing an acre of land, and total costs of preparation are perhaps one-third. While there had been little experimentation with harvesting machines, it was believed that harvesting could also be mechanized; the 1947 crop was cut by hand, with some 400,000 cutters working only with machetes.

Most of the elements of the typical development problem in Latin America are present in this case. (a) From the limited viewpoint of agricultural engineering, mechanization seems clearly indicated. (b) Sugar probably represents the maximum utilization of Cuban resources. But achieving a lower cost structure offers no promise of expansion in the volume of exports, for Cuba has been a marginal supplier to world markets, dependent always on the whim of the foreign legislator and threatened always by the continuing determination

TABLE 21

Labor Saving in Preparation of Land

	Time per acre Hours	Men	Oxen	Man-hours per acre	Ox-hours per acre
Oxen:					
Plowing	12.5	2.5	6	31.3	75.0
Cross plowing	11.0	2.0	4	22.0	44.0
Harrowing	3.5	1.0	4	3.5	14.0
Tractor: small track type					
Plowing	1.8	1.5	–	2.7	–
Cross plowing	1.6	1.3	–	1.7	–
Harrowing	0.7	0.7	–	0.8	–

of the major markets to find other sources of supply. Conceivably, if the cost structure in competitive producing areas did not rise as rapidly as Cuban costs under the official wage policy, mechanization might be forced by the alternative of

TABLE 22

Estimated Cost of Preparing an Acre of Non-Sugar Land

	Labor	Equipment	Power	Total
Oxen: Heavy soil	$21.24	$0.66	$7.56	$29.46
Light soil	13.20	0.41	4.37	17.98
Small tractor: Heavy soil	2.86	1.29	6.68	10.83
Light soil	2.56	1.13	6.05	9.74
Medium tractor: Heavy soil	2.44	1.31	7.00	10.75
Light soil	2.04	1.10	5.84	8.98

Note: The use of tractors is estimated in the above table to reduce the cost of preparing land for nonsugar crops by 46% to 63%; for sugarcane land, the reduction is estimated at 61% to 75%. A larger tractor would reduce costs somewhat more.

losing even the existing outlets. But the customary reward for efficiency—greater volume, greater share of the market— is not present. (c) Under a system representing the maximum utilization of resources, when production and exports of sugar more than doubled from 1935-39 to 1948, the local food supply (as an index of general well-being) rose by "only" 7%

in calories. The reduction of this marketing position as world markets resume a more normal course would under the development thesis be accompanied by expansion into less efficient lines of resource utilization, with some advantages in the greater stability promised. It is probable that the first outlet for manpower released by the increased productivity of a mechanized sugar industry would be the food crops rather than expanded non-farm employment. Yet, it has generally been accepted that these crops offer a less efficient use of resources and that if Cuba is to have more goods for a better living the eventual absorption of manpower must be in non-farm outlets. These for the time being are not clearly indicated in the magnitudes required.

(d) If we assume a working force of 1.7 million, 0.75 million in agriculture, 0.5 million in the agricultural part of the sugar industry, there is an annual addition to the working force by population growth of some 34,000 per year.[15] A shift into non-farm activity of 1% per year would mean an additional 7,500 persons for whom outlets must be found. The capacity to absorb 41,500 persons per year in gainful employment seems so difficult that both organized labor and Cuban government officials have strenuously opposed mechanization in the agricultural part of the sugar industry. And yet these are the elements in the population pushing most impatiently for development activity that would improve the standard of living. (e) Unfortunately, as the outlook for a leading export deteriorates, the inclination to invest in costly equipment tends to be discouraged. The financing requirements are indeed substantial when there is added to the requirements for improved productivity in sugar the investment needed to move such a block of individuals annually into non-farm working force, even if the figure of only $1,000 per person be used.

---

[15] Minneman comments that the 1943 census shows 1,521,000 gainfully employed, 622,000 in agriculture, and that the latter number seems low because 500,000 are employed in the agricultural part of the sugar industry, although only part of the cane cutters employed in the sugar harvesting season find other agricultural employment during the rest of the year.

Security and Opportunity. If the philosophy of development in Latin America had no facet other than the choice of security at the sacrifice of opportunity which is involved in the search for protection against excessive reliance on foreign markets, the picture would be extremely disturbing. But the Latin American re-introduces opportunity into the developmental philosophy by research into the factors that make for differences in per capita income between countries. He finds that one such factor is the proportion of a country's working population that is engaged in the primary occupations (agriculture, forestry, and fishing), and the relative importance of secondary occupations (manufacturing, mining, and construction) and of tertiary occupations (trade and services). "With few exceptions," writes one highly competent analyst in Washington, "living standards may be expected to rise and world trade increase as the inhabitants of more and more agricultural countries go into secondary and tertiary occupations; also, with few exceptions the greater the emphasis on trade and services, as compared with manufacturing, the greater the rise in per capita income." He goes on:

> "In every region, whether highly agriculturalized southeastern Europe, China, India, Africa, Latin America, and southern United States, or the highly industrialized areas of western Europe and northeastern United States, per capita incomes are larger where the proportions of the labor force engaged in agriculture are lower; and practically everywhere, economic programs providing for readjustment out of agriculture are called for. . . . In two contiguous countries in Latin America—Argentina and Chile—the same general relations between industrialization and living standards hold. A difference of 12 points in the agricultural proportion is associated with a per capita income in Argentina nearly $200 greater than in Chile." [16]

In presenting such findings, proper note has usually been made of the importance of other factors making for differences in per capita incomes such as "capital, education, pro-

---

[16] Louis H. Bean writing in National Bureau of Economic Research, *Studies in Income and Wealth, Volume VIII*, "International Industrialization and Per Capita Income" (New York, 1946).

ductivity of resources, distribution of income, proximity to markets, living and consumption habits," and of the importance of timing and integration of efforts in both agriculture and industry. But too frequently, the creation of an elementary industrial establishment has seemed so simple, when contrasted with the action required to expand agricultural production within a highly traditional structure virtually mined with social, economic, and political obstacles, that the Latin-American policy-maker has focused on this narrower element of the problem.

Sáenz avoided this error when he adapted the findings to the Mexican situation. He found less than 700,000 persons in the industrial working force producing almost twice as much as about 4 million persons gainfully employed in agriculture, livestock, and forestry activity and speculated thoughtfully on the possibility of increasing the national income by $500 million by a transfer of 300,000 persons from the farms. "Our country," he complained, "suffers from hidden unemployment. Millions of people are working land that is almost sterile with primitive techniques; thousands of laborers work with antiquated and inefficient machines; at least 3,000 million man-hours are being wasted annually. It is thus impossible to doubt that Mexico's future lies in general improvement of productivity and in increase of industrialization and of economic activities of the secondary and tertiary type." But he noted carefully that this process of absorption into industry must avoid a decrease in agricultural production, so that the objectives become two: "The first must be the continuous application of a plan for development capable of giving employment to population removed from the soil; the second is continuous application of a plan for agricultural development tending to obtain a greater yield on the farms of optimum size from the economic point of view, located in good land and having good communications." [17] The magnitudes of the problem can be appraised in this fashion. At the period Sáenz was writing, national income of Mexico was perhaps $115 per capita, the working force may have con-

[17] *El Mercado de Valores*, August 26, 1946.

sisted of some 7 million persons, with perhaps 4.5 million in agricultural, pastoral, and forestry activities, and an annual rate of growth of the working force of 2 to 2.2%. If the increase in gainfully employed were to be absorbed in non-farm activity and if the farm working force were to be reduced by 1% per year, an effective outlet for upward of 180,000 workers needed to be provided annually. If an investment of $1,000 per person were required for effective entry into non-farm activity—and there is no intention here of estimating the actual investment per worker required for an effective rate of development—this would mean investment requirements of $180 million or more annually in an economy with a national income of perhaps $2.7 billion.[18]

The importance of proceeding with effective measures to improve the productivity of agriculture in the initial stage of the development program is emphasied also by Finer in his study of the Chilean Development Corporation when he concludes that "if the Corporation succeeded in all else but failed in improving agriculture, not only would those who live on the land continue to be miserably poor but those in urban occupations also would find little improvement in their standard of living.[19]   And the imperative necessity of balance in the development program, as between industry and agriculture, is stressed by the Abbink Mission when it finds a more productive agriculture needed to "promote industrialization by

---

[18] After reviewing investments actually made in some rapidly expanding economies and checking against rough estimates made by some countries of their postwar investment requirements, Mordecai Ezekiel used a figure of $1,000 per head as a "conservative" figure in his volume *Towards World Prosperity* (Harper & Brothers, New York), pp. 24-26. Mandelbaum in *The Industrialization of Backward Areas* (New York: Oxford University Press, 1945), p. 37, uses a range of $1,725-$2,100 capital investment per person added to the non-agricultural labor force in his study of eastern Europe.   Harvey S. Perloff in *Puerto Rico's Economic Future* (Chicago: University of Chicago Press, 1950), p. 365, suggested that an industrial development in Puerto Rico could be carried out with the provision of less than an average of $2,000 (at 1940 prices) for each new worker employed.

[19] Herman Finer, *The Chilean Development Corporation* (Montreal, International Labour Office, 1947), p. 42.

producing more economically and in larger quantity raw materials for processing in domestic industries" as well as releasing "workers for industrial employment without jeopardizing, or increasing the cost of, the food supply of the industrial and other urban population. It would provide a larger domestic market for the products of industry." And on the other hand, the "expanded and more efficient industries *would* mean larger domestic markets for agricultural raw materials and *should* mean more and better manufactured goods at prices that would bring them within the reach of larger numbers of the farm population." [20]

Toward Greater Productivity. In the United States during the past century the amount of man-labor required to produce a unit of wheat was reduced by four-fifths, corn by seven-tenths, and cotton by slightly more than one-half.[21] During the same period, no significant changes were made in the methods of producing a typical Latin-American commodity— coffee — in a typical Latin-American situation — Brazil.[22] Government experiment stations did not even begin to search for better methods for growing coffee until 1930. And although labor costs in coffee production have been estimated at 80 to 85% of operating costs and about 55% of total costs, the typical adjustment when world market prices exerted pressure on the cost structure was to implement an immigration policy that would supply an abundance of labor willing to accept wages and conditions of work stabilized at a very low level, rather than to improve yields per man-hour. This despite the fact that in Brazil coffee had contributed as much as 43% of the national income and during the period 1919-37

---

[20] *Report of the Joint Brazil-United States Technical Commission,* pp. 65-66. Italics ours. The character of the industrialization process to date has in many instances supported doubt as to the greater availability of manufactured goods at low prices.

[21] Data from an unpublished report by Frank Welch, "Adjustments in Southern Agriculture and Farm Labor Requirements," January 29, 1949.

[22] Discussion of coffee in this paragraph follows the excellent report of Henry W. Spielman, "The Coffee Future of Brazil," which was prepared in 1946 as a U. S. Embassy report.

contributed an average of 24% of the national income, dropping in the mid-1940s to about 9%; and despite the fact that as late as the 1920's coffee was providing 70% of exports, with a decreasing percentage after 1933 to reach a low of 26% in 1942, moving upward thereafter.

Typically, the large-scale landowner was interested in yield with the least outlay of money and effort, in high current earnings rather than in more moderate earnings over a period of years. He hired a poorly trained administrator to manage a $1 to $1.5 million farm at a salary of $300 to $1,800 per year plus housing. The coffee laborer, with the hoe the only widely used piece of equipment, had the responsibility for caring for the trees in the traditional fashion. The administrator made simple checks by an occasional visit to note whether the area between the trees was kept clean, and in turn suffered an occasional check-up by the owner. He was satisfied with the six or seven working days required to produce a bag of coffee, even though, as the yield of the trees decreased, time requirements rose. Throughout the line of command, there was no concern typically with living conditions and health of the employees, as befitted the technique which largely ignored the possibility of enlarging productivity per man. The abnormally prosperous period of the 1920's, when profits of 200 to 300% on investment were not uncommon, failed to stimulate a drive for improvement of production practices, and later when coffee became less attractive in world markets, the owner found that he could shift his available reserves among other places into industrialization, where thanks to the protection from foreign competition offered him by a government intent on industrializing and to the prevailing business philosophy which permitted high average profits under a low volume high-unit-profit philosophy he could hope to cash in at the initial stage. There were actually some valid arguments against mechanization: the use of mechanical equipment would mean fewer workers needed during the growing period and possibly a shortage of labor at harvest time; mechanical cultivation might encourage erosion since it loosened the soil deeper than does the hoe; and if space were inadequate between the trees the equipment might damage them. But experiments appeared to suggest that advantageous results might be obtained from cultivation with animal-drawn or tractor-drawn cultivators. And as for the possibilities of scientific research, the United States Department of Agriculture asserted in 1949 that three years of experimentation at an agricultural station in Guatemala coupled with similar data furnished from cooperating producers in five different coffee-growing areas in the 1948 crop season had demonstrated that by planting in nurseries coffee seed from known high yielding trees, coffee yields per unit of area doubled or tripled.[23] Resistance to radical changes in technique was not unique with the Brazilian coffee grower, of course, but it was clear that larger productivity per man-hour did not wait alone on transfer of resources to the urban industries.

The rise of Brazilian cotton in the 1930's to a major position in world markets demonstrated greater adaptability to new agricultural techniques, with a considerable share of the success attributed to local seed breeders. Before 1930 most of the São Paulo cotton had been of short staple type, whose grade and preparation varied widely, with the result that world markets refused to buy it except at great discounts and practically all had to be disposed of in local markets. Over a period of 12 years from 1924 to 1936 work on the selection and improvement of varieties proceeded on a highly scientific basis. By 1935 the entire state of São Paulo was planted to two varieties of cotton so nearly alike that there was no commercial difference in the fiber characteristics and length of staple, and yet the two varieties were adapted to different growing conditions within the state. Compulsory purchase of seed from the government after 1935-36, an inspection service for cotton gins to stimulate modernization and improve the quality and appearance of the cotton, supervision of conditioning, warehousing, classification, and initiation of fiber analysis, were joined with the tremendous efforts of foreign cotton firms and with European marketing conditions to bring south Brazil production from around 40,000

---

[23] Department of State, *Point Four* (Washington, 1949), p. 138.

bales per year in the five years ending 1930 to over 2.1 million bales in 1944.[24] Yet, even in this industry where man-labor economies in the United States had been less impressive than for certain other crops and where Brazilian technical progress had been faster than for certain other crops, it has been estimated that in the mid-1940's 640 man-hours were required to produce a bale of cotton, or more than double the time required in the United States. Here, too, observers stressed not only the lack of equipment but also the lack of opportunity for advancement as a factor in lower productivity. "Brazilian agricultural labor," Spielman wrote in 1946, "has little to look forward to except perhaps to escape to industrial employment in nearby towns or in the city of São Paulo." Their wages left little or nothing above bare necessities meagerly defined; there was no opportunity to save enough to buy equipment to work land of their own; there were no credit facilities for such persons, ambitious or not.

The possibilities of man-hour savings and with them the higher standard of living that is the goal of development activity are well illustrated in some recent developments in tropical animal husbandry. In tropical Latin America gen-

---

[24] Production rose rapidly following the decline in coffee prices and adoption of crop restriction program in the United States. Cotton was planted between coffee rows, and sometimes replaced coffee on plantations going out of production because of the age of the trees. Westward in São Paulo, coffee was planted on the ridges and cotton in the valleys. Soil fertility was rapidly depleted. And as price relationships in the 1940's improved in favor of coffee and food crops, cotton lost ground. This section is based on Henry W. Spielman's report, "Notes on Economics of Cotton Production in São Paulo, Brazil," written in 1946 as a report from the U. S. Embassy. Spielman notes that over two-thirds of the cotton land was farmed by hand, and the remainder largely by hand, although some operations such as cultivation were done with a one-horse walking cultivator. For the state as a whole, the only farm implement used in producing cotton was the hoe, although there were exceptions. When animal-drawn equipment was used it was primarily for plowing. In 1945-46 half the land was plowed, the other did not require plowing. On 25% of the farms, planting was done mechanically, on 15% cotton was cultivated with animal-drawn equipment. Yields per acre were about 45% below those of our Piedmont region.

erally the animals are so inefficient that the manpower required to breed and care for cattle yields little more than a meager supply of meat and dairy products for their own requirements. While the United States cattle industry slaughters at 26 months, tropical Latin America seldom slaughters before 48 months and then at weights considerably lower. Two devastating insects—the tick and the berne—have long impaired the efficiency of tropical Latin-American cattle as meat and dairy product producers and the available cattle dips have never been adequate protection against the infestations. Successful experiments with toxaphene in the late 1940's hold out a promise of greater meat production and higher-grade hides, of ability to reduce the number of animals in some areas with consequent lessening of destruction of land through overgrazing and availability of more land for production of plant proteins and plant oils, of the freeing of workers for more effective production of both food and other products.

A story that is told of the introduction of toxaphene in Brazil is illustrative of the possibilities. A Brazilian rancher owned a prize Holstein bull which was so valuable that he had refused to risk its health by using an arsenical dip strong enough to destroy the ticks. He had therefore employed a boy, full time, to keep the animal free of ticks by removing them by hand. The boy labored long hours without being able completely to free the animal from the pest. Then an entomologist of the U. S. Department of Agriculture arrived at the ranch for a demonstration of the new spray. After one treatment the prize animal was free of ticks and remained so for four weeks, with only slight reinfestation after five weeks. At the end of that time the animal registered a gain of over 100 pounds. The boy was free for more productive activity. The chemical had cost five cents.[25]

Policy Requirements. The whole structure of development activity in agriculture—the shift to tractor power, the in-

[25] Maron Simon, "More Meat for Millions," *The Lamp*, November, 1949, p. 8. Toxaphene proved its effectiveness against the tick in remarkably short order in Brazil, but the berne has proved more stubborn.

creased use of fertilizer, the development and use of better seed varieties, the increased use of cover crops and other conservation practices, improved pest and disease control, and better feeding and treatment of livestock—involves something more than agricultural policy narrowly defined. The rapid strengthening of the agricultural extension or advisory services to provide technical information and advice means not only an expenditure for such services but also educational and health expenditures to assure effective utilization of the services. And as Table 23 suggests, not only are the required technical skills scarce or non-existent in Latin America, but there are even considerable deficiencies in basic personnel needed for establishment of elementary education and public health systems. The farmer must be able to obtain local financing for expansion of production at rates sufficiently low to leave him a reasonable return on his investment — credits for improvement of his land and short or medium term low-cost credits to buy equipment; and this in turn may dictate curtailment of facilities for other lines or at least an order of priorities in financial policy. The farmer needs adequate supplies of the agricultural requisites—machinery, seeds, fertilizers—at a price which will insure their use on a sufficient scale even when the immediate price relationships of farm products and such aids are not at optimum level. This in turn may involve a decision on financing techniques and the feasibility of preferential treatment as compared with the stimulus which is sought in other areas of developmental expansion. The commonly-cited vicious circle that low agricultural output prevents financing of imported equipment and lack of equipment prevents higher agricultural output means not only a choice in local financing but also in the allocation of foreign-exchange resources if the country is to break out of the circle. And for the major schemes of improvements to yield external economies, governmental policy choices among public works are again involved.

Under optimum conditions it might be possible to proceed first with the major expenditures for transportation and similar lines with the knowledge that they would eventually permit the maximum gain from other lines of economic de-

TABLE 23

Indicators of Availability of Technical Personnel

	Year	Number of physicians per 1,000 population	Year	Number of elementary school teachers per 1,000 population
Argentina	1946	1.05	1945	5.24
Chile	1945	0.63	1945	2.54
Cuba	1944	0.63	1945-46	3.18
Venezuela	1946	0.41	1946	0.94
Costa Rica	1946	0.25	1944	4.74
Colombia	1946	0.29	1945	1.41
Peru	1946	0.19	1944	1.93
Panama	1945	0.21	1942-43	3.41
Mexico	1946	0.51	1939	2.40
Uruguay	1946	0.71	1946	2.99
Dominican	1946	0.20	1944	1.45
Haiti	1946	0.09	1943	0.63
Nicaragua	1946	0.28	1945	2.15
Guatemala	1946	0.11	1945	1.24
Bolivia	1946	0.15	1946	1.62
Honduras	1946	0.11	1942-43	1.45
El Salvador	1946	0.16	1944	1.81
Brazil	1946	0.31	1941	1.97
Ecuador	1946	0.24	1942	1.03
Paraguay	1946	0.28	1943	3.34
United States	1947	1.37	1946	4.29
Sweden	1947	0.94	1943	4.03
Canada	1947	0.95	1949	5.43

Source: U. S. Department of State, *Point Four* (Washington, 1949), p. 115.

Note: Data involve serious elements of non-comparability. Definitions of "physician" and "elementary school teacher" vary widely. There are differences in number of years of "elementary school" among the countries. It is believed that a higher proportion of total population falls in school ages in countries of lower income, so that the differential shown above is conservative, quite apart from differences in quality of instruction.

velopment. But the Latin-American country can rarely afford politically the delay in profiting in some measure from development activity and economically the delay in cashing in on some benefits when existing standards of consumption are already so low, even though postponement might mean larger gains later. Under optimum conditions it might be possible to enter simultaneously upon various lines of activity to provide what is frequently assumed to be an automatic effect of any project development, i.e., one project providing a market for the others and serving as a supplier as well; but the Latin-American country rarely if ever finds multiple activity fully within its reach and has in the past too often succumbed to the political glamor of a "show-case" operation, when it realized that only isolated projects were possible with its narrow resources. Under optimum conditions it might be possible to stress stability much less and to reach out for maximum development in those lines representing the maximum utilization of resources, but conditions of international trade hardly warrant assumption of such a risk and so the decision becomes one of setting a limit on the degree to which the pace of development should be slowed down for security reasons.

The realities of the Latin-American situation may be summarized at this point: (a) Population and capital requirements are growing very rapidly. (b) With a working force growing at the rate of 2.0 to 2.3% annually, the central problem is not one of the absorptive capacity of the land, not one of providing an outlet for immigrants, but rather how to raise the productivity of its working force so as to increase the standard of living of the growing population. (c) Since a higher standard of food consumption is basic in the development process, an increase in food production exceeding the population growth of 2% is indicated. And if the simple consumption-goods industries are to be supplied locally with fibers and hides and raw materials at sufficiently low cost to permit the increased consumption standard, greater productivity in this line of agriculture is also indicated. (d) The capital requirements for development are so great compared with the foreseeable availabilities—whether from local reductions in consumption standards and redistributions of income or from foreign sources—as to necessitate a continuing choice among lines for developmental activity. While it is clear that new difficulties would be introduced by a migration of workers to the factory before farm productivity has been increased, it is probable that an increase in agricultural productivity, with due regard for timing and priorities, can be accomplished to provide a secure basis for expanded industrial activity. Let us look next at the present organization of Latin-American industry.

SUPPLEMENTARY READING

Reynold E. Carlson, "Economic Development in Central America," *Inter-American Economic Affairs,* Autumn, 1948, pp. 5-29.

Margaret Alexander Marsh, "Monoculture and the Level of Living," *Inter-American Economic Affairs,* June, 1947, pp. 77-112.

Food and Agriculture Organization of the United Nations, *Report on International Investment and Financing Facilities* (Washington, 1949), pp. 5-31.

Food and Agriculure Organization of the United Nations, *Report on World Commodity Problems,* C 49/10 (Washington, 1949), pp. 1-73.

Food and Agriculture Organization of the United Nations, *The State of Food and Agriculture,* 1948 (Washington, 1948), pp. 64-79.

United Nations Department of Economic Affairs, *Relative Prices of Exports and Imports of Under-developed Countries* (Lake Success, 1949), pp. 66-78.

Chapter 6

Organization for Production: Manufacturing

In 1950 the Latin American in an urban community still used a very small quantity of manufactured goods by North American standards, and his rural compatriot used even less. But from the time he tossed aside the locally-manufactured covers and jumped out of a locally-manufactured bed in the morning to the time he smoked a locally-manufactured cigarette and turned out the light which burned perhaps uncertainly in a locally-made fixture at night, his simple requirements—or better put, the things he could afford—were being largely produced in the workshops and factories of his own country.

He sat down to a table whose foods had been processed locally. He drank locally-manufactured beer and soft drinks. He washed with locally-produced soap and could splurge on a variety of locally-manufactured toilet articles. His clothing —textiles, shoes, hats—was of domestic origin. His home was increasingly built with local materials — cement, paint, glass, even steel in the major countries—and outfitted by local manufacturers. He was a heavy user of patent medicines and had lived to see the change from the time that a foreign manufacturer's only concession to him was a foreign-printed label in his own language to the day that both package and contents could be of local origin. As he prospered, he acquired a few consumer durables—possibly a locally-assembled radio, even a locally-assembled automobile with locally-manufactured tires, or a locally-assembled electric refrigerator.

If he worked in an office, he still used a foreign typewriter; but the desks and filing cases could be from local workshops,

134

and pencil and paper and pen and ink were being made in a number of countries. If he worked in a factory, he saw parts for the machines being repaired and fashioned at the plant, and in the larger countries local industrialists were beginning to interest themselves in production of the simpler machinery. During the second world war he had even seen Latin American textiles going abroad to compete on such frontiers of trade as South Africa, although it was true that access to the markets was being provided largely by the inability of traditional suppliers to export goods; he had seen apparel, confectionery products and beer being manufactured for the United States; and wondrous to behold he had heard of a few machines that make machines being manufactured on the east coast of South America for export to the United States!

If he worked for one of the public utility companies, he could read in the annual reports about the increasing volume of manufactured goods, such as copper products, steel, electrical machinery, cement, office supplies, cotton goods, explosives, and rubber goods, that were being manufactured locally.[1] If he went out to the mines, he might find them using locally-manufactured explosives. If he worked for the government, the increasing emphasis on meeting requirements from local industry, pointed up especially in the promotion of great ventures like the steel mills in Brazil and Chile, furnished evidence of progress in manufacturing. The Latin American in the major countries could by 1950 be pardoned the illusion of self-sufficiency, even though the manufactured goods moved on foreign-manufactured transport facilities from foreign-equipped factories powered by foreign equipment, and even though the ingredients of his drugs, rayon,

---

[1] Brazilian Traction, Light and Power Company, for instance, in its report for 1947 noted that its local purchases had totaled $11.8 million, compared with total operating expenditures of $57.1 million which included however wages and taxes as well as materials; the estimate cited in that report was that Brazilian industrial production was supplying 60% of Brazil's needs. Many foreign corporations were finding that the policy of purchasing supplies locally when available had great public relations value; and the ability to use local currency instead of foreign exchange was another factor in the policy.

tires, and paints and even the hops for his beer might still have
to be imported.

The challenge of the import list was an old one for under-
developed countries. Late in the eighteenth century Tench
Coxe had exhorted his fellow North Americans to act on the
import list: "The very great proportion of the imports which
consists of manufactures affords constant and inviting opportunities to lessen the balance against the United States . . .
holds out a certain home market to skillful and industrious
manufacturers in America."[2] In Latin America in the
twentieth century the attack on the import list emphasized
the certainty of the market rather than the skill and indus-
triousness with which it could be won. Raul Simón, a Chilean
industrialist and engineer, put it bluntly in 1939 when he said:
"Whatever production replaces an import is and always will
represent an increase in the national wealth, independently
of its apparent cost in money values."[3]

Coupling the obvious opportunity provided by the established markets for imports with the equally obvious line of
development indicated in elaboration and processing of domestic foodstuffs and raw materials for export, Latin America
by 1950 had followed the Coxes and Simóns sufficiently to be
proceeding rapidly from light industry to metal-working and
heavy industry, although the ambitious pace of Brazil, Mexico,
Argentina, and Chile was well in advance of the other Latin
American countries, and the more backward nations were
still laboring with the problems of producing the simpler
consumer goods. The first world war had curtailed foreign
competition and stimulated local production; the depression of
the 1930's had reduced external purchasing power and given
a powerful impetus to the movement for greater self-sufficiency; the second world war had again called attention to
the vulnerability to foreign developments and freed the local
industrialists from competition; and dollar shortages in the

---

[2] Tench Coxe, *A View of the United States of America, in a Series
of Papers Written at Various Times, Between the Years 1787 and 1794*
(Philadelphia, 1794).

[3] Quoted in P. T. Ellsworth, *Chile: An Economy in Transition* (The
Macmillan Company, New York, 1945), p. 131.

late 1940's had provided automatic protection from foreign competition and even greater willingness on the part of governments to assist in the development of local industries. Rapid and intense as was the progress toward industrialization as the "way out," there was as yet little effort at critical evaluation in terms of the availability of more goods for the mass of the people. The Latin American was so intent on ceasing to be, as the Chilean cabinet officer Tinsley had once labelled him, the "last freight car of a train driven by a foreign locomotive," that he was not yet ready to investigate whether he was moving faster or even staying on the track of genuine development by moving up front.

Extent and Pace of Industrialization. By the late 1940's Latin America was producing about 90% of its consumption of cotton textiles. A decade earlier it had been importing perhaps one-third of its requirements. Domestic production had risen perhaps on an average of 6% per year, but per capita availabilities had in some cases fallen. It was producing perhaps 87% of its requirements of wool textiles, compared with about three-fourths a decade earlier. It was making tremendous progress in rayon, in plants characterized by their up-to-date installations and techniques and by their relatively higher productivity. In a decade rayon production had risen 250%; and with per capita consumption up 50% and rising rapidly, Latin America was producing 40% of its consumption compared with 18% before the war, and was moving swiftly to acquire a larger share of the market.

From the period 1935-39 to 1948 Latin America's per capita consumption of steel increased by 50%. While local production had accounted for only 8% of apparent consumption in the earlier period, the substantial expansion of facilities in Brazil and Mexico particularly enabled Latin America to produce about 27% of its requirements in 1948. And a fine new plant was rising in Chile, with the prospect of other new facilities for Colombia and Argentina, as well as further expansion in Brazil and Mexico.

Data on consumption of cement are sometimes used as an index of industrial progress and of the rate of investment activities in general. When the second world war broke out, most of the major countries of Latin America were on the road to self-sufficiency in cement, with imports running about one-fifth of total consumption. By 1948 domestic production of cement had increased by 85% and the volume of imports was larger than it had been before the war. Per capita consumption had expanded immensely, although compared with the expansion in the United States the gain was less impressive. In 1938 per capita consumption in Latin America had been about one-fifth that of the United States, in 1948 about one-sixth.

From 1937 to 1948 the consumption of wood pulp in Latin America increased by 92%, but while local production had accounted for only 10% of the requirements in 1937, by 1948 its share was 40% and rising rapidly. The failure of domestic food production to expand in such proportions explains the less impressive rise in the value added in plants devoted to the processing of meat and other food products. While comparable data have not been assembled for the metal-working and chemical industries, the increased activity in these lines in the past decade heralded an advance toward industrial maturity in the more advanced countries.

From 1937 to 1948 electric power production increased by more than 100%. During that period it is estimated that growth of industrial production may have been as much as 50% in the major countries and considerably less in the other Latin-American nations, but for the area as a whole the increase was greater than the growth in agricultural production and well ahead of the increase in population, so that per capita availabilities of domestically produced manufactured goods were larger. By the late 1940's it was estimated that manufacturing was accounting for about 15% of the national incomes of the Latin-American republics.[4] The proportion

---

[4] Wythe reported in 1949 that "in Mexico, manufacturing is estimated to account for 26 percent of the national income. In Argentina and Chile the ratio is approximately 20 percent, and in Brazil, 17 percent." George Wythe, *Industry in Latin America* (Columbia University Press, New York, Second edition, 1949), p. 13.

of the gainfully employed whose energies were devoted to manufacturing was less than that.

The Textile Industry. Latin America's consumption of textiles per capita is roughly the same as the world average, and sharply below that of Europe and North America. Command of this market has largely been won by local industrialists behind tariff walls and import restrictions of various kinds. More than a half billion dollars is invested in the industry, largely of local origin and in great part representing a steady plow-back of profits which have been high.

The principal branch is cotton textiles. Practically all the Latin-American countries have some manufacturing activity in cotton textiles; of the 5 million spindles and 160,000 looms in the area, Brazil has about two-thirds and Mexico one-fifth. The quality of the installations varies widely. The area has traditionally been a good market for equipment rejected by the more industrialized nations as technologically obsolete. Once imported the equipment has tended to stay in operation, being re-sold within the country and thereby holding productivity at a low level. Modernization has been discouraged by assurance of a market protected against efficient foreign competition, as well as by the low wage scale, lack of skilled labor, insufficient vocational training, and labor opposition to a speed-up. It has been estimated that only 5% of the looms in Brazil and Mexico are automatic. As labor costs assume greater importance in operating costs, employer interest in modernization has increased, only to be met by labor resistance stemming from fear of technological unemployment. During the second world war, the absence of competition enabled Brazil to boost exports to a high of $77 million of cotton cloth and yarn, and Mexico to reach exports of $48 million in 1946; but the position in foreign markets was quickly lost when competition returned. The installations range from a highly efficient modern industry in Colombia to the much older industry of Brazil where in the 1940's the bulk of the installations were relatively obsolete. The mills tend to be small by United States standards.

While there is some important North American participation in the industry of Colombia, Mexico, Venezuela, Cuba, and Peru among others, British participation in Argentina, and French and Spanish participation in Mexico, the textile industry is characteristically a locally-controlled industry. The major producing countries, such as Brazil, Mexico, Argentina, and Peru use locally grown cotton; others, like Colombia, are trying to expand cotton output to meet the growing requirements of their mills; a few are on an import basis; most of them import small quantities of long-staple cotton; Table 24 provides a comparison of production and consumption within the area.

Wool textiles are a less important branch of the industry. Factory activity on an important scale dates largely from the first world war, beginning with blankets and coarse woolens and proceeding slowly to the finer fabrics. The finer grades of suiting and combed yarns are still imported. The largest concentration of the industry is in Argentina which has more than half of the manufacturing activity. Home-grown fiber generally is available to the industry. Table 25 shows the current status of the industry by countries.

Since the major Latin-American countries are important producers of natural fibers, providing 15% of the world exports of fibers in 1948-49, they have felt less the stimulus of foreign-exchange considerations that have prompted fiber-importing nations to give special attention to development of synthetic fiber industries. Nevertheless, synthetic fibers are making rapid progress in Latin America. Production of rayon yarn dates from 1926 in Brazil, 1935 in Argentina, 1941 in Chile and Colombia, 1942 in Mexico, 1946 in Peru, and 1948-49 in Cuba. Latin America's share of the world's increasing exports of rayon textiles rose from 14% in 1938 to 27% in 1948, but during the same period domestic production was rising from 6,495 tons to 24,899 tons. The installations for synthetic fibers tend to be up-to-date technologically, and to compare more favorably with European and North American installations than the productivity comparisons show for the cotton and wool branches. They have been built with top-caliber foreign technical assistance and sometimes with considerable participation of foreign capital. While the

TABLE 24

Cotton Textiles: Production and Consumption, 1938-1948

(thousands of metric tons)

	Year	Raw Cotton Consumption	Cotton Yarn Imports	Cotton Yarn Exports	Cotton Manufactures Imports	Cotton Manufactures Exports	Availabilities per capita (kilograms)
Argentina	1938	33	-	0.2	38.4	0.1	5.0
	1948	81	5.0	-	10.0	-	5.8
Brazil	1938	139	0.9	-	0.6	0.8	3.5
	1948	180	0.3	0.5	0.5	6.3	3.6
Chile	1938	4	3.6	-	4.2	-	2.5
	1948	11	1.0	-	1.0	-	2.3
Colombia	1938	11	-	-	5.0	-	1.8
	1948	22	0.5	-	1.0	-	2.1
Cuba	1938	4	5.4	-	9.6	-	4.3
	1948	6.7	2.3	-	5.6	-	2.8
Ecuador	1938	1.4	-	-	1.9	-	1.1
	1948	3	-	-	1.0	-	1.2
Mexico	1938	45	-	-	1.4	-	2.4
	1948	61	0.4	0.6	1.6	9.0	2.3
Latin America	Prewar	250	20.0	-	111.0	1.0	3.0
	1948	400	17.0	1.0	30.0	15.0	2.8
United States	1938	1,330	0.5	4.5	5.8	31.6	10.0
	1948	2,040	0.6	12.7	3.3	94.0	13.3

Source: Food and Agriculture Organization of the United Nations, *World Fiber Review* 1949 (Washington, 1949), pp. 106-107.

TABLE 25

Wool Textiles: Production and Consumption, 1938-1948

(thousands of metric tons)

	Year	Clean Wool Consumption	Tops, Trade Balance	Wool Yarns Imports	Wool Yarns Exports	Manufactures Imports	Manufactures Exports	Availabilities per capita (kilograms)
Argentina	1938	15	-	0.9	0.1	3.8	0.2	1.4
	1948	28	-	1.0	-	1.0	-	1.8
Brazil	1938	7	-	1.6	-	0.8	-	0.2
	1948	7	-	2.0	-	0.5	-	0.2
Chile	1938	3	-	-	-	0.8	-	0.8
	1948	3	-	-	-	0.4	-	0.7
Mexico	1938	3.1	1.0	-	-	0.3	-	0.2
	1948	2.0	0.9	-	-	0.2	-	0.1
Uruguay	1938	2	-	-	-	0.4	-	0.7
	1948	3	-	-	-	0.2	-	1.3
Latin America	Prewar	36	1.0	5.0	-	9.0	-	0.4
	1948	49	1.0	3.0	-	5.0	-	0.4
United States	1938	130	1.4	0.2	-	1.7	0.1	1.0
	1948	314	1.7	0.6	0.8	2.1	5.0	2.2

Source: Food and Agriculture Organization of the United Nations, *World Fiber Review* 1949 (Washington, 1949, pp. 110-111.

plants still require large quantities of imported raw materials, they are serving to create a market leading to more diversified production. Table 26 shows the status of rayon production and consumption. It might be noted that the more efficient character of installations for synthetic fibers has not stopped the local industrialists from demanding and getting protection by tariffs and import restrictions of other kinds against overseas competition.

By the late 1940's all of the larger countries and some of the others had important rayon knitting and weaving industries. Requirements for clothing were being met by local industries. One field, bagging, provides an interesting example of the effort to lessen dependence on imports to the benefit of both agriculture and industry. The big crops such as grain and coffee have enormous requirements for bagging. The Brazilian and Mexican mills had early turned to producing bagging from imported jute, but in the exchange-short 1930's and the goods-short war period that followed there was a persistent effort to find local raw materials that might serve as substitutes. In 1949, for instance, the U. S. Department of State was holding out hope for kenaf, a fibrous plant, as an effective substitute for jute fiber in the manufacture of sugar bagging. It asserted that the fiber could be made fully competitive in yield, cost, and strength; its production is susceptible to mechanization and accordingly can compete with jute at the relatively high labor costs of this hemisphere; its season dovetails with the sugar season and thus promises employment opportunities for the slack period. It had already been produced commercially in El Salvador where 1,200 acres were planted, a half-dozen commercial producers in Cuba were planting 1,000 acres, and Haiti was experimenting with 250 acres.[5] Meanwhile, Brazil was encouraging local production of jute and both Argentina and Brazil were pressing for development of home-grown fibers to replace jute.

The Cement Industry. The cement industry was late in establishment in Latin America. Before the first world war,

---

[5] United States Department of State, *Point Four* (Washington, 1949), p. 138.

TABLE 26

Rayon: Production and Consumption, 1938-1948

(thousands of metric tons)

	Year	Rayon Production	Imports of staple fiber, filament, spun rayon yarn	Imports of rayon manufactures	Availabilities per capita (kilograms)
Argentina	1938	1.2	2.2	0.2	0.26
	1948	4.7	2.2	0.8	0.47
Brazil	1938	5.3	0.2	-	0.14
	1948	11.7	0.7	-	0.26
Chile	1938	-	1.2	1.0	0.46
	1948	1.6	0.5	-	0.38
Cuba	1938	-	0.5	1.0	0.34
	1948	0.3	-	5.0	1.02
Mexico	1938	-	4.4	0.5	0.25
	1948	5.2	9.0	-	0.59
Latin America	Prewar	7.0	14.3	13.2	0.27
	1948	25.0	23.7	14.8	0.41
United States	1938	130.4	11.4	0.3	1.07
	1948	510.0	22.3	0.4	3.41

Source: Food and Agriculture Organization of the United Nations, *World Fiber Report* 1949 (Washington, 1949), pp. 114-116.

144

most of the requirements were met from imports, largely from Europe which needed cargo for ships returning from Latin America with typical bulk cargoes and accordingly had a basis for low ocean freight rates. Within twenty years, however, the more important countries of Latin America were on the road to self-sufficiency. In Argentina, an American company put up the first large plant in 1919 with capacity of 400,000 tons, and by the time it built another with a capacity of 135,000 tons in 1938, Argentina's total capacity had risen to almost 2,000,000 tons. In Brazil, Canadian interests brought in the first modern plant in 1925-26 with a capacity of 200,000 tons; when another modern plant was built by U. S. interests in 1933, local capital began to take an increased interest in the industry. Chile which had one plant with a capacity of 115,000 tons before the first world war, expanded production to 313,000 tons in 1937 and increased its facilities thereafter to meet an annual consumption rise of 8%. In Venezuela the tremendous expansion of petroleum activity and public works expenditures in the 1940's occasioned a rise in consumption from 40,000 tons locally produced and 137,000 tons imported in 1938 to 215,000 tons locally produced and 421,000 tons imported in 1948. Although the shortage of fuel held back output in Argentina and other countries, the tremendous increase in construction during the 1940's paced an expansion of about 8% per year in Latin-American production.

While some of the expansion has been based on plants that would be considered marginal operations in the United States, the industry in general in Latin America is characterized by modern, well-designed, mechanized plants. Local capital has increasingly participated in the growth of the industry, although there have been substantial American operations in Argentina, Brazil, Cuba and Mexico, British participation in Mexico, and other foreign-capital activity. European technicians, particularly Danish, have participated equally with North Americans in the establishment of the industry. Table 27 contains data by countries on the recent development of the industry.

The Steel Industry. For the Latin American, the steel mill

TABLE 27

Production of Cement, 1937-1948

(thousands of metric tons)

	1937	1943	1948
Argentina	1,035	957	1,252
Brazil	571	747	1,112
Chile	313	375	540
Colombia	144	259	364
Cuba	121	170	285
Mexico	345	578	833
Peru	102	207	282
Uruguay	148	131	278
Venezuela	45	112	215
Others	176	264	339
Latin America	3,000	3,800	5,500

has become at once the symbol of his developmental aspirations and the show-case of his achievements. The values attaching to the steel mill in terms of politics and satisfaction of national ambition are such that they tend to outweigh strictly economic considerations. During World War II the United States recognized the political importance of the symbol for Brazilians, for instance, when it granted priorities for the construction of the great mill at Volta Redonda, despite the prevailing belief that the direct contribution to the war effort of the equipment involved would be greater if it were diverted to other purposes. Intergovernmental financing of projects in Chile and Mexico since that time has similarly been based in part on an understanding of the special values attaching to the steel mill.

Latin America's consumption of steel per capita is so low— less than 10% of the consumption of the United States—that national aspirations have frequently been discouraged by the inability to absorb the output of a plant of economic size. But as Table 28 shows, consumption has been rapidly increasing. Apparent consumption was estimated at 2.1 million tons in 1935-39 and 3.6 millions tons in 1948.

Mexico was the first country in the area to get a modern primary iron and steel plant. Between 1900 and 1905 a group of foreign promoters established the works at Monter-

TABLE 28

Latin American Production and Consumption of Steel, 1925-1948

(thousands of metric tons)

	Production	Net Imports	Apparent Consumption	Consumption per capita in kilograms
1925-29	100	2,237	2,337	21.0
1930-34	132	1,350	1,482	12.4
1935-39	184	1,956	2,140	16.8
1945-48	786	2,326	3,112	21.4
1948	969	2,593	3,562	24.1
1953 (estimate)	2,550	2,000	4,550	29.0

Source: United Nations Department of Economic Affairs, *European Steel Trends in the Setting of the World Market* (Geneva, 1949), p. 15.

rey; forty years later the company, now under Mexican control, was the only firm producing pig iron and mining ore in Mexico and its production had reached 150,000 tons of steel per year. A group of Americans founded a second company in 1913. And in 1944 the third major unit in the Mexican industry was inaugurated under Mexican government control and financed out of Washington. In addition there are a number of smaller plants producing ingots from electric furnaces. Although domestic production expanded from 163,000 tons in 1938 to 300,000 tons in the late 1940's, the country continued to depend on imports for 40% of its requirements as consumption rose steadily. Mexican deposits of good-grade iron ore are ample, but the development of coal mining has been so slow that it has balked expansion of the steel industry at the pace that domestic demand might have supported.

In Brazil, too, the modern iron and steel industry dates from private activity by foreign promoters, with subsequent major expansion under government control and inter-governmental financing out of Washington. Although small amounts of charcoal iron had been produced for some years, the industry really got under way when a Belgo-Luxemburg group started operations in 1921. Brazilian plants were still producing only 76,000 tons of steel in 1937, but by 1948 the 28 charcoal blast furnaces had a total annual output of 280,000 tons. Meanwhile, the mill at Volta Redonda, designed for eventual capacity of 1,000,000 tons and early capacity of 300,000 tons, had been established under government control. By 1948 Brazil was the leading Latin-American steel producer, with an output of more than 480,000 tons of steel ingots and castings. Brazil was fortunate in having perhaps 10% or more of the world's high-grade iron ore reserves, but it was less fortunate in the quality and volume of its coal, and unsatisfactory transport facilities continued to hamper development.

The Chilean record shows the same pattern of hesitant private participation in the industry and the eventual emergence of a government-controlled plant of substantial capacity. Its efforts date from a scheme projected by a French group in 1905, but only a small and costly output was available until the 1940's despite government subsidies of the works at Valdivia. Production of steel was about 30,000 tons in 1948, with consumption running about 140,000 tons a year. Finally, a government agency projected a sizable plant at Huachipato, obtained financing for external purchases of equipment in Washington, and looked forward to bringing Chilean production up and past the 100,000 tons per year mark. There were satisfactory iron ore deposits in Chile, but domestic coal was of poor quality and the size of the market was small by modern standards of steel mill operations.

Argentina has had the unhappy combination of circumstances that it is the largest consumer of steel in Latin America, but lacks commercially available supplies of ore and coal. A number of well-equipped sizable foundries have gradually expanded operations, with a dozen companies using local scrap and imported pig iron to produce a variety of steel castings and rolled products. By the late 1940's Argentina was producing up to 160,000 tons per year. Despite its deficiencies in raw materials the government succumbed to the compelling "urge" for a steel mill of substantial proportions and planned a mill with a capacity of 500,000 tons to be built under American technical direction, to use imported pig iron and local scrap and possibly some local pig iron whose supply was believed to be non-commercial, not entirely satisfactory in quality, and too far from the point of use to be economic.

Colombia, with extensive deposits of perhaps the best coal in South America, some iron ore, and a natural protection against foreign competition provided by internal transportation costs, has balanced these factors against the narrowness of the domestic market (under 100,000 tons per year) and the unsatisfactory development of transportation, and concluded that a steel mill is an urgent necessity for its economy. For many years it has agitated for a mixed private and public capital corporation to be established for the purpose, failing which it would be prepared to have the government tackle the job alone. There are some small iron works, a company with an electric furnace resmelting scrap, a rolling mill producing bars, rods and small shapes. The government has projected a plant at Paz del Río with capacity of 100,000 tons.

Peruvian agitation for a steel mill has similarly been active for many years. Here too the market is so limited as to raise questions as to ability to support a plant of economic size. In the early 1930's the government projected a mixed ownership operation which bogged down when technicians decided the iron ore contained too much sulphur. Various surveys followed, one of which came up with a project for a blast furnace at Chimbote, smelting with anthracite by special treatment, only to be discarded in favor of a scheme for an electric furnace. Peru hopes.

In Uruguay furnaces and rolling mills have been established since 1939 to produce a limited number of products from local scrap. In Venezuela the large deposits of high-grade iron ore have attracted exploitation for export to take advantage of the richness of the ore, its proximity to water transport, and special positional factors relative to American ports; local smelting has lagged; coal resources are believed to be small and of poor quality.

From the standpoint of policy, by 1950 the steel industry was characterized by government control of the larger part of the new steel-making facilities of Brazil, Chile and Mexico; inter-governmental financing out of Washington for equip-

ment that must be acquired abroad; American technical guidance; a greater degree of efficiency in installations than characterizes some of the older industries in Latin America; and continued dependence upon the government for protection from foreign competition, for financing of expansion, and for local outlets for production.

The Pulp and Paper Industry. In the decade ending in 1949, Latin-American consumption of wood pulp increased by 8 to 9% annually. The major countries had long had paper manufacturing industries, heavily protected by import duties and dependent upon imported raw materials. They had developed the production of wrapping paper and cardboard from imported pulp and chemicals, and production of paper bags and other manufactured paper products from imported kraft and other papers. War-time critical shortages of foreign materials and shipping pointed up the potentialities of local production of pulp imports which had reached 220,000 tons in 1937, the dependence of the paper industry on a continuous flow of imports, and the vital importance of the supply of newsprint for newspapers which depended largely on foreign sources. By the end of 1949 Latin-American production of pulp had caught up with the level of consumption in 1937, but meanwhile requirements had expanded immensely so that imports were also rising. Literacy was advancing, publishing was expanding, industries such as cement were developing rapidly and increasing the local requirements for bags and other paper products. In 1937 Latin America had consumed 245,000 tons of pulp and produced 25,000 tons. In 1948 it consumed 470,000 tons and produced 190,000 tons. Local production of pulp had been sought to end the dependence on imported supplies, and since efficiency is promoted by manufacture of pulp products as part of a continuous process with production of pulp, it was likely that paper production would be encouraged in the course of the development.

By 1949 Brazil was producing 90% of its paper requirements other than newsprint, of which it still imported more than half of its consumption; it still imported the higher-grade papers and certain specialized types. It had boosted production to 80,000 tons of pulp in 1947 and was counting on the expanding output of a new plant. This plant, which had been projected by local interests in 1940, was given heavy financial assistance by the government, and had a capacity of 40,000 tons mechanical pulp, 30,000 tons sulphite pulp, and 40,000 tons of newsprint. The country was rich in fast-growing trees and plants with high cellulose content, and if problems of transportation and technical difficulties could be overcome there was even the prospect that it could eventually become an exporter of pulp.

In Mexico domestic production of pulp had grown from 19,000 tons in 1937 to 51,000 tons in 1947 without a reduction in the volume of imports; the production of paper and cardboard had risen from 55,000 to 106,000 tons, but imports rose from 52,000 to 83,000 tons as consumption advanced. In Chile local factories were supplying the demand for most types of paper and paperboard and an attempt was being made to reduce dependence on foreign pulp. The Argentine paper industry as early as 1935 was producing 80% of its kraft requirements and half of its writing paper, and made rapid progress thereafter. Although a plant was set up to manufacture cellulose from grain straw in 1931, production of mechanical pulp was undertaken in 1938, and some 30,000 tons of chemical pulp and some groundwood pulp from poplar plantations were being produced in the 1940's, Argentina still suffered the deficiencies in endowment that had long made it the leading lumber importer of South America. Peru had had some success in using bagasse for pulp production, at the rate of 5,000 tons output per year.

The per capita consumption of wood for industrial purposes in Latin America in 1949 was perhaps one-eighth that of the United States, with consumption for fuelwood larger than that of the United States. The wood-working industries were expanding, there were up-to-date furniture factories, cabinet-making shops, machine manufacture of wooden articles like doors, windows, cooperage, boxes. There was a tendency in terms of world supplies to emphasize that the eventual adaptation of the tropical species of the great Latin-American forests to processing for pulp and to sawmill operation for export of high-quality lumber was of growing importance. Meanwhile, however, the area was a relatively small producer of lumber. Output was 1.5 million standards in 1948, and on balance the region was a lumber importer. Brazil, an exporter, had produced 376,000 standards of softwood lumber in 1948 but had exported half of it to the other Latin-American countries; it had expanded plywood production for the war effort, reaching 76,000 cubic meters in 1946 and then tapering off when export demand disappeared.

The immediate endowment for pulp manufacture is not a particularly good one in Latin America. The stands of those varieties of pine suitable for the most efficient production of pulp are relatively scarce. The Paraná pine forests of southern Brazil are the largest resources, with smaller stands in Mexico, southern Chile and Central America. This helps to explain the use of poplar, willow, straw, bagasse, and other vegetable materials, much of which suffer in quality of output and require mixing with imported pulp for the manufacture of paper. And the pulp from hardwoods tends to be suitable only for certain kinds of paper. But as in the related chemical field, technological advances come so continuously and rapidly that the judgment is not warranted that it may not be possible to meet local requirements for pulp efficiently in time.

The Chemical Industry. Chemical technology is so pervasive in modern industry that it is difficult to demarcate the field of the chemical industries. The extent to which the basic chemicals are produced competitively with other manufacturing areas, the alertness with which technological developments are accepted in the existing industrial apparatus, the extent to which research and training of chemical engineers are proceeding, are good indicators of the status of the whole effort at industrialization. A single heavy chemical such as sulphuric acid, for instance, is used in metallurgy, petroleum refining, leather tanning, textile dyeing and in the production of other chemicals—superphosphates, rayon, alum, copper sulphate. Thus the importance that attaches to its availability in price and continuous supply. Similarly the alkalies are basic raw materials for the manufacture of glass, soap, paper, and certain kinds of rayon, and have many uses in textile manufacture, petroleum refining, and the preparation of foods and drugs. The key position of the alkalies, in fact, has prompted several of the major Latin-American countries to regard substantial expansion of output under government direction and control as an urgent contribution to the program for industrialization.

In raw materials for the chemical industry, Latin America is handicapped by the relative unavailability of coal and sulphur, among other elements. In some cases petroleum is sufficiently abundant to offset the coal deficiency, in others the ability to bring in imported coal at low prices helps. Chile and Argentina have high-cost sources of sulphur in the Andes but most of the major countries manufacture sulphuric acid from imported sulphur, with a less important production from local pyrites or as a by-product of the smelting industry. It should be noted that many chemical raw materials are available in abundance and even exported.

In Brazil the chemical industry has been expanding steadily but the requirements of its advancing industrial structure have held imports high at the same time. Currently its requirements of acetic, nitric, hydrochloric, and tartaric acids are largely met locally. It produces sulphuric acid chiefly from imported sulphur. About one-third of its ammonia requirements are produced locally. An electrochemical plant was set up in 1936 to make chlorine, caustic soda, and chloride of lime and a second plant was set up under British-American auspices for alkalies, but the production of alkalies has been so inadequate that the government was moved to establish a company, obtain financing from the United States government, and seek to meet thereby the expanding requirements. Viscose rayon and rayon yarn by the nitrocellulose process are being produced in expanding volume. Potassium chlorate and aluminum sulphate production is developing. Substantial quantities of glycerine are produced. The Volta Redonda steel plant was yielding from its coke-oven gases some 3,000 tons of ammonium sulphate in 1949, although imports continued to be heavy. Dyes were being made although on a small scale relative to requirements. A considerable volume of copper sulphate, calcium and aluminum arsenates, carbon disulphide, and lead arsenates was being produced. Insecticide and fungicide production was a promising field. Paints, varnishes, and plastics materials were rapidly developing. Production of pharmaceuticals, cosmetics and toilet preparations had benefited particularly from foreign participation, with many branch plants and locally-licensed producers.

In Mexico, although the basic chemicals were being developed, the chief developments recently have been in the secondary industries, and imports continue to be heavy as local consumption expands. Pharmaceuticals and cosmetics are mixed and packaged locally from imported ingredients, with some manufacture from local materials. The paint, plastic, and chemical fertilizer industries are showing substantial gains. A substantial expansion in caustic soda production finally occurred in 1948 after a slow development up to that time of alkalies. The chemical industry in Mexico is among the most vocal of the groups demanding protection by tariffs and restrictions from efficient foreign competition.

In Chile the leading chemical manufacturing activities developed out of the needs of the mining and smelting industry; explosives and black-powder plants are on a large-scale and efficiently organized. As in Mexico and Argentina, pharmaceuticals and cosmetics are mixed and packaged locally from imported ingredients, with some growing manufacture out of local materials. Chilean producers meet most of the demand for sulphuric acid, hydrochloric acid, copper and iron carbonates and a considerable part of the demand for ammonia, sodium hydrosulphite, glycerin, bleaching powder, sodium silicate, and tanning extracts. Under government sponsorship and with the participation of an American firm there has been an expansion of activity in coal-tar dyes. The government has also turned its attention to the deficient production of the alkalies.

Argentina has a large production of insecticides, disinfectants, and fungicides from both local and imported materials. There were in the late 1940's eleven local producers of molding powders and plastics. Its paints, pharmaceuticals, and toilet preparations were compounded and packaged with a substantial use of local materials. Coal-tar solvents were imported. Sulphuric acid was produced from imported sulphur. The government prodding for self-sufficiency in the alkalies was helping.

In the small Uruguayan market, paints, enamels, common soap, toilet soap, perfume, pharmaceuticals are being compounded and packaged. Coal-tar chemicals are derived as by-products of a gas-generating plant; some chemical pulp is being made from wheat straw; a government agency makes and distributes ethyl and denatured alcohol. In Colombia, the government's activity in pushing for the establishment of sizable local production of the alkalies is a typical action in the drive to develop chemical industries in Latin America.

The Chemical Industry and the Cartels. One of the distinctive features of the chemical industry in Latin America has been the influence of the international cartels. For instance, in the international arrangements for alkalies and explosives, provision was usually made for control of the Latin-American markets. The emergence of local industrialists interested in producing chemicals at home, and the interest of Latin-American governments in encouraging industry, have been given special character by the presence of cartel arrangements. Sometimes local competition has been discouraged by price cuts or threats of price wars, sometimes the profit margins of the industry and the price structure of the industry have been seriously affected. A document published by the Twentieth Century Fund in 1946 throws some light on the character of the activity:

> The main factor was the apparent need for some temporary price action in the face of unusual pressure for the erection of local industries, particularly in Mexico, Brazil, and the Argentine, and with special reference to caustic soda and soda ash—and where government assistance was being sought. In Brazil the problem has been met by the formation of an exploratory company . . . to circumvent action by others, satisfy government. . . . In the Argentine ash prices were also reduced as a temporary measure because of the interest of the government in the entire alkali

picture, and owing to considerable interest by local groups in such a venture.[6]
As an illustration of the character of the activity, the Fund noted in its case studies the nature of the problems of local industrialization encountered by the Duperial companies, which had been organized jointly by the leading American and British chemical companies to serve their interests in Argentina, Brazil, Uruguay, and Paraguay:

> One of Duperial's chief business rivals from the outset was a rich, powerful, and aggressive local commercial house —Bunge & Born (B. & B.). When B. & B. learned of du Pont's and ICI's plans to pool their business in Argentina, it requested a share in the enterprise. After participation was refused it, B. & B. began drafting plans for independent manufacture of chemicals in several lines directly competitive with major interests of the Duperial partners. For this expansion program, B. & B. had ample funds and the support of local sentiment for home industries. Du Pont and ICI met this challenge by both conciliatory and warlike tactics. To discourage B. & B. from producing sulphuric acid, Duperial cut sulphuric acid prices and at the same time made a rather flattering offer to guarantee B. & B. a substantial proportion of the tartaric acid market—in which B. & B. was already an important factor and Duperial had little interest, except for bargaining purposes. To dissuade B. & B. from manufacturing carbon disulphide, Duperial offered to supply it with 25 percent of its own output for resale.[7]

The area of such arrangements extended beyond the alkalies. In 1935 Duperial organized a company to erect a local rayon factory, offered a French rayon manufacturer 15% participation in return for patents and processes, was confronted by Bunge & Born with a bid for recognition on penalty of suffering construction of a competing rayon plant, which it blocked by offering 15% participation. The manufacture of cellophane in Argentina proceeded under similar arrangements. And the safeguarding of interests proceeded in a typical pattern when in the 1930's a local Argentine

---

[6] George W. Stocking and Myron W. Watkins, *Cartels in Action* (The Twentieth Century Fund, New York, 1946), p. 437.
[7] *Cartels in Action*, pp. 460-461.

paper manufacturer ventured to build a plant to supply its caustic soda and chlorine requirements and wound up participating in arrangements to stay out of each other's primary field of manufacture, to refrain from exporting, and similar arrangements.[8] It is of some interest that when the principal American and British interests agreed to invest in local manufacturing facilities for their joint subsidiaries in South America, it was on condition that the projects promise a net return, after all taxes, of at least 17.5% in Brazil and Chile and 15% in Argentina.[9] In the pharmaceutical field, the cartels of the pre-war period, particularly under German leadership, similarly affected the character of both export and local manufacturing activity in Latin America.

It is proper to note that Latin America generally does not share the American antagonism to trusts and cartels, at least not for the same reasons. Such opposition as is to be found is likely to rise more from opposition to exploitation of industry by foreign capital than from a bias in favor of free competition. As a potentially heavy loser from the operations of cartels, the Latin American might have been expected to be more vigorous in his opposition. While it is true that Latin America went along with the United States in inserting in the Economic Charter of the Americas at the Inter-American Conference in Mexico City in 1945 a point for joint action against the cartels, the issue carries little weight in the Latin-American mind.

The Food Processing Industry. In the initial stage of industrialization in Latin America, the food-processing industries were the leading activity, and coupled with the textile industry accounted for the larger part of the investment, the value added by manufacture, and the number of workers in industry. Here were concentrated some of the most efficient manufacturing plants that Latin America has known. The meat packing plants and the sugar mills established under foreign ownership, for instance, helped Latin America

---

[8] *Cartels in Action*, pp. 462-463.

[9] George W. Stocking and Myron W. Watkins, *Cartels or Competition* (The Twentieth Century Fund, New York, 1948), p. 124.

achieve a competitive position in foreign markets wholly out of line with the many subsidized activities which were to follow in other fields of manufacturing. Here some of the great accumulations of industrial capital originated to provide funds for expansion into a variety of fields. In Brazil the great Matarazzo concentration of industrial activity which in the late 1940's included 286 separate enterprises spread from a small shop refining lard in steady succession to flour mills, bagging for the flour, cotton seed mills, soap and toilet preparations to use the raw materials in which the firm was dealing, packing cases, saw mills, box factories, tin containers, meat packing, and eventually into more advanced activity represented by rayon, chemicals, textiles, and the associated industries which keep such plants moving efficiently, and even into manufacturing in other Latin-American countries. In Argentina the Bemberg fortune, which made the family one of the richest in the world, expanded from skillful acquisition of control of the brewing industry to a wide variety of activity —tramways, dairy products, land, yerba maté, cotton, mortgage, insurance, underwriting, and banking. The great grain-trading firm of Bunge & Born in the Argentine expanded to ownership of a great chain of flour mills, jute and bag factories, edible oil factories, paint factories, textile mills, chemical plants, shoe factories, cotton gins, grain elevators, sugar refineries, tin-can factories, as well as into housing, shipping, and other fields. With the exception of the temporary activity in the export field during the wars, export from industry was largely limited to the food-processing field and is likely to continue largely to be limited to this field for some time.

As industry has expanded, the processing of meat, sugar, vegetable oils, flour, beer, and other locally-produced food products has lost ground relative to other industries. In some cases the food industries have relied on imported materials in part, such as the hops for Mexican and Brazilian beer, the flavoring concentrates and coloring compounds for soft drinks; in some cases the flour mills use imported wheat, as in Peru and Brazil. But characteristically food processing is based on domestic raw materials, and the line of development has been to do as much as possible of the processing domestically before exporting the products. As technological progress is made, the processing of domestic raw materials may be found capable of considerable expansion. For instance, in 1948 research was completed in Mexico which resulted in establishment of a pilot-plant preparatory to a large-scale production of a new high-melting industrial wax from henequen waste. The pace of such development will depend on the extent of research and training of technicians in the individual country and on the degree to which foreign techniques and foreign capital are permitted access to profitable activity in the countries.

While the variety of food-processing activities has been increasing with improvements in canning and preparation of food and with the shift to internal performance of processing formerly done abroad, there is some indication that the increasing demands of domestic consumption may result in a shift from export to domestic outlets for the industry. In Argentina, for instance, the great packing plants were built for international trade, but as plans to consume larger and larger proportions of the meat production locally proceed, the outlet for the plants will shift accordingly. *It is possible that the process may be accompanied by a lessened alertness of response to technological advances.*

Leather, Shoes, Glass, Rubber, Ceramics. Local raw materials have been the basis of several other important lines of manufacturing. In many of the countries the tobacco industry is of considerable importance, and is characterized by concentration in a small number of companies, broad protection from foreign competition, and large profits. The leather industry in many countries has developed to the point of self-sufficiency except for special leathers that continue to be imported. The related shoe industry developed rapidly after an American producer of shoe machinery expanded in Latin America in the decade before the first world war. The region has become largely self-sufficient for leather shoes, for which demand incidentally is limited to perhaps half the population. The scale of production is small, quality of the factory product poor, protection from foreign competition very great, ownership largely local with some scattered foreign participation.

In contrast the rubber manufacturing industry has profited heavily from foreign participation, either in branch factory form or in establishment with foreign technical direction and partial financing. Characteristically, the rubber product plants in Argentina, Uruguay, Brazil, Colombia, Venezuela, Cuba, Peru, and Mexico, manufacturing a variety of products from rubber-soled footwear to druggist's sundries to tires and tubes, tend to be on a more economic scale of operation, utilize more advanced techniques. The availability of local raw materials varies; Brazil, for instance, has a domestic supply of rubber, cotton fabrics and duck and is making an effort to provide more of the necessary chemicals, although it imports carbon black, chemicals, and rayon cord.

In glass manufacturing too there has been considerable technical progress, promoted in part by foreign technical and financial cooperation. Glass containers are the chief item of manufacture, but flat-glass production has also been increased. Similarly, there has been considerable progress toward self-sufficiency in ceramics in the more advanced countries.

Self-Generating Demand. As the light industries have become established, they have in turn generated a demand for manufactured goods. The consumer durables started out as strictly assembly operations based on imported parts, usually under foreign control. But gradually, the automobile, radio receiver, electric refrigerator, and other appliances have come to represent a fairly substantial local manufacturing operation. Truck and bus bodies, radio and refrigerator cabinets, batteries, gaskets, fan belts, jacks, chains, floor mats, electrical apparatus of various sorts, and a variety of other products have been found capable of local production. When the Abbink Mission reviewed the electrical goods industry in Brazil it found local production of some $20 million a year, as compared with local requirements of perhaps $100 million. The inability to make and market heavy generating equipment and large-size motors could not be allowed to conceal the substantial activity in small motors, transformers, electrical cable, circuit breakers, fuses, insulators, lighting fixtures, batteries, and welding equipment. Here too the steady drive to cut away products from the import list under the difficulties of war and the continuing difficulties of shortages in foreign exchange made itself felt. There were abundant opportunities for supplying the growing operations of the textile, paper, cement, wood-working, and other light industries. And attesting to the fashion in which such opportunities were being taken up were the signs of activity in the manufacture of the simpler textile machinery and parts, cement mixers, wood-working machinery, hardware, agricultural implements, pressing machines, cotton ginning equipment, sawmill machinery, plastic molding equipment, even transportation items like freight cars. Certainly in 1950 the metal-working industries were far from the importance which characterized them in a mature industrial nation but they were showing progress.

On December 31, 1949, for instance, the Brazilian public was treated to the first view of trucks produced by its Fabrica Nacional de Motores. When production under the franchise of Isotta-Fraschini (Italy) had been projected and work begun some six months previously, the trucks had been assembled entirely from Italian parts and materials. Meanwhile, however, local manufacturers experimented with what they might contribute to the manufacture and were able increasingly to supply parts. Thus in early 1950 Fabrica Nacional was producing locally the hood, fenders, instrument panel, steering wheel, cylinder sleeves, pistons, certain engine gears, fan, exhaust manifold, The frame was being made in Minas Gerais. The radiator, batteries, springs, fan belt, and tires were being made in São Paulo. Several types of bodies were made in Rio de Janeiro. The wheels originated in Paraná. The size of the capital investment obstructed local manufacture of some parts. The diesel motor would continue to be imported; manufacture of the crankshaft alone would have required $1.5 million of machinery, and similarly sized investments were required for production of the cylinder block and camshaft. The lack of a large forging press in Brazil made it necessary to import front and rear axles; the front and rear transmissions and the transmission shaft were being imported. There was constant activity to expand into manufacture of what was still being imported. Industry was truly on the march.

The Brazilian Situation. In 1950 Brazil was the leading industrial nation of Latin America. Its industries could draw on a wide variety of locally-produced raw materials: cotton, wool and hard fibers; iron and a group of lesser minerals although the endowment in the Big Three of the metal world (copper, lead, and zinc) was unsatisfactory; timber, vegetable oil seeds, nuts, waxes, medicinal plants, sugar, hides, elements for the construction materials, rubber; and the output of a sizable food producing plant. The government pressed constantly for use of local raw materials, whether of established supplies such as rubber or of materials that could be developed locally given a certain market. For instance, in the late 1940's, by the withholding of dollar-exchange for the import of ink one prominent American firm had been "persuaded" to invest in local manufacturing facilities which would use imported raw materials; shortly thereafter dollar cover for the raw materials was withheld in order to divert the business to the sterling area with whose currency Brazil was then more abundantly supplied; finally, the manufacturer was told to seek out local sources of raw materials since the import from any foreign source would be increasingly restricted. Brazilian industry frequently suffered from the poor quality and lack of standardization of its raw materials, but under the accompanying policy of government support against foreign competition, the contribution to inefficiency provided by unsatisfactory raw material supplies was a greater worry to the ultimate consumer than to the manufacturer concerned with short-run interests.

Its industries were weak on the fuel factor. There were extensive areas with favorable geological structures for petroleum, but no substantial quantities had yet been found and developed. Brazilian coal was low-grade, had lower calorific value than imported coal, required special processing. The water-power resources were impressive statistically, but development was very costly, particularly in view of the distances which frequently separated the potential sources of power and the prospective consumption area. Industrial growth was linked with electric power and every expansion in power facilities seemed quickly to be absorbed in the mounting pace of industrial growth. There was no proclaimed policy of a social-rate structure to encourage industrial growth, but the authorities had not granted rate increases, such as might have resulted in a heavier flow of private capital into the expansion of facilities. Industry was basing on cheap power.

Brazilian industry had the largest market in Latin America in terms of population, but the poor transportation facilities and the very size and configuration of the country had lent themselves to the creation of a number of local markets rather than to a great national market. And per capita purchasing power was still extremely low; national income estimates ran about $150 per year. It is true that there was significant concentration of purchasing power: the 30,000,000 "economic zeros," as the population lacking in any considerable buying power has been termed, contrasted sharply with purchasing power in São Paulo and the Federal District. In the latter areas per capita purchasing power was probably close to one-third to one-half that of the United States. The whole population's purchasing power per capita is frequently put at less than one-tenth that of the United States.

Investment in manufacturing facilities per worker was about one-eighth to one-tenth that of the investment in manufacturing in the United States. It was rising with the investment in the increasingly efficient plants for iron and steel, chemicals, rayon, and pulp. Investment in the worker had similarly been halting. Successive analyses of individual industries had concluded that where the employer invested in medical facilities, hot lunches, educational and training facilities, the efficiency of Brazilian labor could be made to approach more closely that of the more advanced industrial countries, but intense concern with such investment was still not characteristic of the industrial structure of Brazil, and it was customary to list in appraisals of industry the relative inefficiency of the labor supply along with such factors as the lack of skilled labor. Interest in technical training on both the professional and worker levels was growing, but slowly. It was estimated in 1949 that there were about 10,000 civil engineers in Brazil and only a small number of industrial engineers. Engineering at the college level was being taught at thirteen institutions graduating perhaps 400 to 500 engineers per year. Around the polytechnic school at São Paulo one of the most advanced centers of technological research, perhaps the most advanced on the continent, had grown up. There were over 70 industrial trade schools which suffered, however, the characteristic deficiencies of the general educational system—the shortage of trained instructors, lack of equipment, poor health of the students, slowness to adapt the program to the immediate genuine needs of the community. And industry was managing a tax-supported program of industrial training providing part-time apprentice training for boys and girls of 14 to 18 years of age.[10]

Productivity per worker in manufacturing was perhaps one-seventh to one-eighth that of the United States, but it should be noted that comparison with the most productive industrial machine in the world is hardly a fair comparison. It was significant that the new industries were raising the relative efficiency of manufacturing and notably important that productivity in manufacturing was three to six times as great as per capita productivity in agriculture. Poor factory layout, wastefulness of labor, and inadequate attention to research and technological advances were still typical, although well-organized, ably-managed factories were not wholly absent from the Brazilian scene.

Probably 85% of the capital for manufacturing had been provided locally, with the rest drawn from Europe and the United States, but the proportion of foreign capital in privately-owned manufacturing facilities was dropping steadily. To the extent that foreign participation was merely changing its form, i.e., that participation was changing from outright ownership to joint ownership of companies and to provision

---

[10] George Wythe, Royce A. Wight and Harold M. Midkiff, *Brazil: An Expanding Economy* (The Twentieth Century Fund, New York, 1949), pp. 180-183.

of technical guidance for a fee, this change need not be viewed with concern. But to the extent that it forecast greater isolation from the stream of technological advance and an additional factor in the ossification of inefficiency which protection from foreign competition was contributing, it was a serious development. There was a considerable concentration of ownership in manufacturing and there were interlocking ties among the families prominent in control of manufacturing installations, although the typical firm in the Brazilian structure was still a small one. Profits in industry had normally been high and permitted great plow-backs of capital for expansion. Compilations by decades customarily showed earnings per year of 20% to 30% on capital plus surplus, with individual firms (and, during the war, whole industries) often showing 75% to 125% per year.

In 1950 manufacturing was accounting for about one-fifth of the national income, and providing the large bulk of requirements for consumer goods and an increasing proportion of requirements of steel and other products of a more advanced stage of industry. But in terms of development policy it was important to evaluate the findings of an ace investigator who wrote in 1949:

> Retail prices of made-in-Brazil consumer goods are substantially higher than prices of similar products in the United States. Some cotton materials of good quality are made, but most of the output is very poor. Cotton cloth is narrower than in the United States, but prices calculated per square yard run from 30 to 50 per cent higher. Domestic woolen cloth of fair quality costs about $9 to $10 a meter. Kitchen utensils are 50 per cent higher. Prices of ready-made shoes are one-third higher, while trunks and suitcases of poor quality cost two or three times as much as better articles in the United States. Most of the writing paper seen in the shops is of fair quality at best and is high-priced. Subsidiaries of American firms have, for the most part, maintained the quality of their products and have attempted to follow a pricing policy that will permit the development of volume sales, but in some instances the Brazilian authorities have required them to raise their prices in order to enable higher-cost Brazilian producers to compete.[11]

[11] Wythe, Wight and Midkiff, *op. cit.*, p. 178.

Before this evaluation, let us examine the experience of some of the other countries.

The Chilean Experience. During the decade ending in 1950, the manufacturing industries of Chile expanded their output by about 4% annually. Chilean policy was directed at reducing the extreme instability arising from its heavy dependence on the export of copper and nitrates. In the years between the two world wars and since the last war, manufacturing has steadily enjoyed increasing attention from the government. It has profited from external depreciation of the peso which raised the cost of imported goods, from liberal tariff protection, from specific assistance in the issue of import licenses and in allocation of foreign exchange, from use of the lending power of the Central Bank and of the Treasury's resources both local and in terms of the ability to borrow abroad, and since 1939 from the direct intervention of a government development corporation (Corporación de Fomento de la Producción) with wide powers to plan and promote Chilean production.

There were distinct limitations in the Chilean effort to industrialize. A population of five to six million, with a per capita national income less than one-sixth that of the United States and with little prospect of a preferential position in substantial export markets by reason of proximity, was one limitation in fields where an industry's economic scale of output was defined in larger terms. Its endowment in minerals was good, including iron and copper, but commercial production of petroleum had only begun to materialize in the late 1940's; its coal was not of the best quality nor suitable for coking, although it had become the largest producer of coal in South America with government encouragement; its water-power resources were large but presented substantial problems in financing for utilization. It had local raw materials for its woolen textile industry, was near a supply of Peruvian cotton, and had a base for chemical development in the nitrate industry and a supply, though a costly one, of sulphur. It had 22% of its area in forest, 40,000,000 acres, a large part of which was characterized by trees comparatively small in size, poor in form, and suitable primarily for fuelwood. About

40% of the forest area was virgin forest with 93% hardwood. Timber production in 1948 was still in the stage where consumption of perhaps 150 million cubic feet per year compared with 682 million being lost annually by fire for lack of organized fire protection. The volume of national savings was small, estimated at 5% of national income. The labor supply was intelligent and relatively industrious, though its efficiency was reduced by widespread malnutrition and the high incidence of disease. In managerial "drive" the country compared very favorably with many of the other Latin-American nations, and this quality of enterprise was particularly notable in the competence with which support for the development activity was promoted abroad, especially in Washington.

By 1950 manufacturing was accounting for more than one-fifth of the national income.[12] The country was meeting most or all of its requirements for a wide range of consumer goods, and it was expecting the new steel mill not only to meet the bulk of its steel requirements but also to become the nucleus of a group of associated and derivative industries. Ellsworth in 1945 estimated that factory wages were one-fourth to one-fifth those of comparable labor in the United States and that labor, being relatively cheap but not proportionately inefficient, was a factor favorable to industrial growth.[13] Chilean manufacturers, on the other hand, were inclined to stress that "labor was being given social welfare standards of the middle twentieth century before Chile had enjoyed the investment of capital to create productivity to afford it" and to attribute their high costs of production partly to this labor cost. The highly developed system of social legislation was in fact a principal characteristic of the Chilean situation, as was also the increasing participation of the government in expansion of production.

There is little doubt that immediate consumer interest was

---

[12] In 1943 17% of the gainfully employed were reported in manufacturing, but this included artisans and proprietors of one- and two-man workshops who constituted perhaps one-third of this industrial working force.

[13] P. T. Ellsworth, *Chile: An Economy in Transition* (The Macmillan Company, New York, 1945), pp. 145-146.

being willingly sacrificed in the effort to boost industrial production. Periodically concern for the consumer prompted investigation. For instance, from 1937 to 1940 protest against the high cost of essential textiles for workers with low incomes occasioned an investigation which concluded that if foreign competition were permitted, prices would undoubtedly be lowered to the consumer but in the process the profits of Chilean textile manufacturers would be reduced to an "impossible" 2.5% ; the investigating authority therefore recommended a continuance of the protective measures against foreign competition. A decade later the willingness to protect industry was even stronger. There was a virtual embargo through allocation of exchange on consumer goods that could be made locally and in the unlikely event that something slipped through, the tariff structure had been reinforced. For instance, import duties and taxes on plain cotton dresses brought the landed cost in 1949 to 117.3% above the c.i.f. cost (it had been "only" 77.7% above c.i.f. cost in 1946) ; landed cost of plain woolen overcoats was 273.5% above c.i.f. cost in 1949 (86.1% in 1946) ; rayon party dresses 425.4% in 1949 (124.3% in 1946). The Chilean industrialists who had demanded that "protection by tariffs or import licenses should be established a *priori* and as an immovable economic doctrine whenever a national industry needing protection is involved" seemed to have lost sight of the possibility that the decrease of instability, if actually achieved, might be achieved only at considerable cost to the consumer.

The Argentine Situation. Since 1931 Argentina has been speeding from an agricultural economy deeply oriented in export trade to a more industrial autarchic state. An annual increase of more than 6% per year in the pace of manufacturing activity had by the late 1940's effected a drastic alteration in the character of the economy as well as a serious realignment of political power. While the physical volume of industrial activity roughly doubled from 1935 to 1948, that of agriculture and the pastoral industries increased by only one-fifth.

In this industrial development there were some distinctive

features as well as some that characterize Latin American industrial growth generally. (a) Because of the complementary character of the British and Argentine economies and the dominance of the landed interests in the making of national policy, industry up to 1931 had been less actively supported by the government than in countries where export interests were less actively concerned with promotion and maintenance of freer trade. Weil asserts that "whatever official encouragement Argentine industry has sometimes enjoyed, was, on the whole, sporadic, haphazard, irrational, half-hearted, depending on the 'pull' the interested persons could muster or the money they could spend for lobbying and other more direct ways of 'influencing the proper people'. It may be said, however, that protectionistic duties on certain products, if instituted at all, are more likely to be granted to genuine, or genuine-appearing, domestic companies than to those openly controlled by foreign capital." [14] The tariff and exchange-control policy has even been termed "protectionism in reverse" and "malevolent neutrality toward industry." After 1931 difficulties in export markets hastened adoption of a more vigorous protectionist policy for local industry.

(b) Although the population has been much smaller than that of Mexico and Brazil, per capita income has been relatively high for a Latin American country. In terms of a market for industrial goods, the fact that per capita national income has run from one-fourth to one-third that of the United States has been significant. Per capita consumption of textiles, paper, and other consumer goods as well as of steel, consumer durables, and similar products has been well above the Latin American average; before the second world war, for instance, Argentina was using two-fifths of the steel consumed in Latin America. Although it has lost ground since the 1920's, when it accounted for half of the business activity in South America, its per capita level of consumption continues to be an outstanding factor judged by Latin-American standards.

---

[14] Felix J. Weil, *Argentine Riddle* (The John Day Company, New York, 1944), p. 144.

(c) As one of the ten leading trading nations of the world, it has been a focal point for foreign enterprise—a frontier of trade at which the products of every major trading nation were to be found in active competition, a fruitful outlet for investment capital, a focus of attraction for managerial and entrepreneurial activity.

(d) It has had the most highly developed financial organization and the largest resources of industrial capital.

(e) Its labor supply, deriving heavily from southern Europe, has been more adaptable to the requirements of industrialization than populations of the cultural complex of the countries more largely influenced by Indian traditions and habits and way of life.

Yet the obstacles to organization of an efficient thoroughgoing modern industrial plant have been great. It has a great abundance of agricultural and pastoral raw materials, unusual supplies of tanning extracts, limited commercially-available timber resources, a none too broad variety of raw materials for the chemical industry and a tragic deficiency in minerals. Commercial production of minerals has been of minor importance despite efforts to plug this gap; iron ore deposits are scarce and of poor quality and not readily accessible to consuming markets; copper is not available in significant quantities; sulphur is not available on a competitive basis. The fuel deficiencies are similarly great. It has normally been able to get coal cheaply as a return cargo for the large bulk cargoes being exported, but substantial supplies of good coal are not available from local sources. In 1949 under extreme pressure from the government, the Rio Turbio deposits were being eyed hopefully, with estimates optimistically ranging from 100 million to 1 billion tons, but unfortunately full exploitation in any case had to wait on construction of a 400 kilometer railway line. In 1949 an official of the Yacimientos Petrolíferos Fiscales, the government petroleum authority, estimated that local production was supplying 40% of the requirements for coal and petroleum and that by 1951 Argentine sources would not be able to supply more than 30% of requirements. Further, Argentine water power resources compare unfavorably with those of Brazil, Chile, Colombia, Peru, and Mexico.

In the late 1940's the requirements for consumers goods of this relatively rich market were being met largely by the local industrial structure. When the Economic Research Division of the Central Bank studied the industrial situation in 1945, it could distinguish groups of industries that were fully able to meet local demand, largely able to meet demand, or only partly able to meet requirements; and it could distinguish classes of industries by their degree of ability to meet foreign competition. Typically in goods of which local production met requirements, from 1937-1939 to 1945 cigarette production had risen 34%, beer 82%, wheat flour 28%, footwear 23%. In industries moving toward self-sufficiency with considerable success the growth in production from 1939 to 1945 had been 87% for wool yarn, 39% for wool fabrics, 104% for cotton yarn, 92% for cotton fabrics, 220% for woolen carpets, 203% for incandescent lamps, 200% for brass and copper pipes. In industries only meeting requirements partly, the growth from 1939 to 1945 had been 35% for rayon yarn, 125% for paper pulp, 27% for paper and board, 64% for caustic soda, 460% for electric motors. And there were new industries, like plywood, lathes, electric clocks, calcium carbide, coming into existence. On the competitive picture, the Central Bank study found the paper industry firmly established with the exception of certain specialized types. It recognized inability to compete in higher-quality woolen fabrics and in fine cotton yarns and fabrics. It considered pharmaceutical production broadly competitive despite the dependence upon imported raw materials to a considerable degree. It deplored the slower pace of development of chemical output. It considered the infant iron and steel industry almost uniformly vulnerable to overseas competition, doubting that more than one-tenth of the expansion from 20,000 to 150,000 tons output in wartime consisted of competitive facilities. It believed that enduring gains had been made during the war in the production of small radial drills, auxiliary textile and shoe machinery, single-phase and three-phase electric motors, small portable shovels, precision types of weighing machines, certain kinds of pumps. But it found at least one-fourth of the machinery industry that had developed out of wartime shortages to be uncompetitive. It seemed that 7% at least of industrial employees found themselves in industries that would be unable to compete without unusually heavy protection.

In 1948 the official military establishment was operating steel plants with open-hearth facilities having a capacity of 50,000 tons per year, operated mainly on scrap with a proportion of home or imported pig iron, and devoted to meeting the needs of the military services. There was in addition private steelmaking capacity of perhaps 150,000 tons per year which was yielding an output of 100,000 to 120,000 tons. The only local deposits of iron ore being worked was the remote Zapla field, over 1,000 miles from Buenos Aires, where there were reserves estimated at over 100 million tons of Fe content around 40 to 55% with high silicon and phosphorus. A state-owned blast furnace had been turning out 18,000 tons of charcoal pig iron there. And high among the hopes for further industrialization stood the proposed new plant with capacity of 500,000 tons, which would still leave a wide import basis for a market consuming more than a million tons per year.

By 1949 the industrial war babies, particularly the metallurgical industries, were in retreat from competition. "Our production costs are high, very high," mourned the head of the Cámara Argentina de Industrias Metalúrgicas in June 1949, "and have driven us out of competition. Argentine industrialists who participate in tenders in competition with foreign manufacturers are astonished at the differences in prices of their offers, even for goods which before the war easily sustained the competition of the largest international factories. The producers of household appliances—cooking stoves, water heaters, refrigerators, fans—regard with anxiety the possibility of appearance of similar goods from abroad. Manufacturers of equipment for industry and for construction work—bathtubs, washbasins, piping, machine tools, motors, accumulators, door fittings, locks, iron girders, radiators, copper sheets, motor vehicle spares, bolts, screws, nails— would soon go out of existence if these goods were allowed to be imported when offered. Argentine metallurgical industry subsists as a result of an absurdity—the lack of foreign exchange while throttling us through the scarcity and high prices of raw materials is at the same time saving us from extinction through foreign competition." [15] Discounting some of the worry as incidental to a plea for additional protection from competition, the inability to compete seemed to be well established. The industry claimed that average cost per man-hour of labor in a representative metallurgical establishment had risen sevenfold since 1939, fuel was short and costly, raw materials were imported at a disadvantage, and power was so short as to discourage mechanization even if the industry had been able to put a more modern installation at the command of its workers.

The size of the typical Argentine industrial establishment was increasing. Industry had profited from a considerable degree of enterprise on the part of the local population. Although there was considerable foreign participation in meat packing, tires, rayon, chemicals, pharmaceuticals, electrical items, textiles, consumer durables, paper, and other lines, the predominant interest and investment in manufacturing was Argentine. There was a high degree of concentration of ownership in the locally controlled industries. The government was intervening increasingly in the development of industry. And politics had in the 1940's dictated a startling acceleration of welfare legislation and decrees, with an immediate effect on the cost structure of industry. But effective challenging of the industrial expansion from the viewpoint of the Argentine consumer had not yet occurred.

The Mexican Situation. In 1949 Nacional Financiera, a Mexican government entity functioning as an investment bank for the financing of industrial expansion, advertised that in the fifteen years ending December, 1948, it had been a prime factor in the establishment or development of 172 industrial enterprises, among which were 21 foundries or metallurgical plants, 18 sugar mills, 14 textile mills, 12 printing establishments, 11 cement plants, 9 packing and canning plants, 11

---

[15] *Review of the River Plate,* June 24, 1949, pp. 19-21.

public works ventures, and 10 communications and transportation firms. Manufacturing activity had been expanding at the rate of 4% per year. More than half of the value of manufacturing output was concentrated in textiles and food and beverages, but Mexico had boosted the volume of output of construction materials, including steel, cement, and glass, by 191% in the period 1939-47 and the volume of rubber, paper and alcohol by 80%, and had an expanding industrial structure devoted to the assembly and/or manufacture of automobiles, farm equipment, electrical appliances and materials, aluminum products, and containers. By the middle 1940's more than a quarter of the national income was accounted for by manufacturing activity—and expansion continued. Mexico had been a leader in Latin America in industrialization in the first decade of the twentieth century, lost ground to Argentina and Brazil in the second decade when it was going through the intense revolutionary upheaval, and then resumed its industrial advance.

For industrialization, it had at its command a wide variety of local raw materials but there were few industries which could obtain their requirements on sufficiently favorable terms to be considered as possessing special advantage in the supply of raw materials. The cotton textile industry had a local supply of cotton except for small quantities of long-staple, but it relied on imported chemicals, dyes, lubricants, and machinery. The wool clip was of poor quality and inadequate for requirements. There were native fibers in abundance but imported jute had long held a preferential position in the eyes of manufacturers. Mexico had a fine varied endowment in minerals—copper, zinc, lead, silver, mercury, antimony—but these were little used locally. It had a supply of high-grade iron ore. It had been the second largest producer in the world of petroleum in the 1920's only to see the industry dwindle relative to requirements until a net import position threatened in the late 1940's. It had good coking coal although development had been halting. Water power was the mainstay of manufacturing, but financing was difficult and there were natural handicaps in exploitation of resources in the irregular and unpredictable rainfall in the mountains, a porous soil so that rainfall seeped into subterranean channels, prevalence of earthquakes which demanded special construction for dams. Water supply might seem the easiest requirement to meet, but one of the largest American corporations had abandoned the idea of establishing a branch plant in Mexico City when its engineers discovered water supplies were inadequate. The water situation was neatly pointed up in 1947 when even during the rainy season a shortage of water forced a 40% cut in power and the closing of factories. Although the scarcity of water had been blamed partly on the rapidity of growth in population and there was optimism that the distant Lerma River could be tapped, there too the headwaters were rapidly being denuded of forests, and of an unprotected watershed probably less than 50% remained in forest.

Mexican labor had proved unusually well suited to the automatic machinery and repetitive processes of modern industry, but an imposing array of labor and social legislation had deprived industry of much of its flexibility. The effectiveness of the protests against adoption of modern machinery for such industries as textiles, out of fear of technological unemployment, promised to be a continuing obstacle to creation of efficient industries.

The market was not measured in terms of a population that had long since passed 20 million, but rather in terms of 7 million as effective purchasing power units. The President of Mexico had recognized this in his Call to the Nation speech in 1947, when he noted that some 15 million Mexicans functioning outside the marketing channels in a subsistence agriculture would have to be incorporated into the market if industry were to continue to expand effectively. And per capita national income of $120 to $150 was small by North American standards. An American firm making a market survey in Mexico in 1940 estimated that 0.7% of the population might be considered the potential market for luxuries such as electric refrigerators and automobiles, 5.5% for moderately priced items like radios and phonographs, 7% for cheap hardware and small tools, 20% for the minimum essentials, and about 65% must be considered quite out of the market picture.

Although there was a very sizable amount of foreign capital invested in Mexican manufacturing installations, it was estimated in 1949 that foreign capital represented no more than 10% of the total investment in manufacturing.[16] Industries were frequently characterized by the small number of producing units so that the generous availability of tariff protection threatened to enhance a potentially monopolistic position with disastrous pricing effects and to perpetuate inefficiency. But in the drive to expand industry, the government since 1941 has steadily broadened its area of assistance to industry. Import duties and import restrictions have been generously applied to prevent any serious test of competitive capacity, tax-exemption privileges have been freely granted to new enterprises (to about 500 firms in the period 1941-48), financing has been made available, including use of the government's credit in Washington. In fact, a feature of the industrial scene by 1950 was the growing use of intergovernmental financing for steel, ammonium-sulphate, meat packing, sugar mills, and other industrial activity. During World War II exports of textiles, footwear, and beer had brought manufactured goods up from about 1% of total exports to 34%, but the return of competition saw Mexican goods quickly lose their place in foreign markets and their competitive position exposed even in the home market.

The Colombian Experience. Colombia provides an interesting case of a small market basis for industrialization. In 1939 it was estimated that less than $175 million of manufactured goods were being consumed annually in Colombia. Per capita expenditures on manufactured goods were about $15 to $20 per year. And even in the efficiently organized coffee industry in which one-fifth of the population was directly engaged, per capita cash income on a typical coffee *finca* was estimated at only $45 per year. About $100 million of manufactured goods

---

16 House Report No. 2470, 80th Congress, 2nd session, *Fuel Investigation: Mexican Petroleum*, Progress Report of the Committee on Interstate and Foreign Commerce, p. 43.

were being produced in the country. Of the imports, about 10% consisted of quality products directed to an upper class market for which domestic manufactures were unlikely to be an acceptible substitute, 40% consisted of machinery, transportation equipment, and other heavy industry goods whose production locally seemed likely to be long deferred on any economic basis, and about half consisted of lines where manufacturing was gradually taking hold locally. Manufacturing had tended to precede the production of raw materials, creating developmental opportunities for production of raw materials. About $61 million was estimated to be invested in manufacturing facilities, financing had been largely with local capital, management was by owners. The scale of industry was small, with only 78 plants out of 1,378 having over 100 persons employed. Industry had typically developed from food processing, beer, textiles, tobacco, with the narrow purchasing power always a dominant consideration; in the manufacture of footwear, for instance, it was notable that the majority of the population did not wear manufactured leather shoes.

Industrial expansion had been accelerated in the 1930's and was popularly credited with cushioning the depression years for Colombia. With the coming of the second world war, local industry had expanded out of enormous profits, for the prevailing business philosophy was the typical Latin-American philosophy of high unit profits and low volume rather than price cuts for mass production. The typical assistance of government was present in protective tariffs, use of import and exchange restrictions to cut off the inflow of competitive consumer goods, currency depreciation, and feeling of its way into a development entity which could utilize the credit of the government abroad for expansion into steel and chemicals and the other aspirations of the new industrial states. The existing industrial plant was commonly considered superior to many of the industrial plants of the Latin American countries, but there was little inclination to test its effectiveness in the interest of the consumer.

The Tannenbaum Thesis. In 1934 Professor Frank Tannenbaum, a great American scholar, disturbed the Latin Americans greatly in a book entitled *Whither Latin America?* when he concluded that industrialism seemed destined to be confined within narrow ranges in Latin America, that it was limited by the absence of resources, skill, and capital, by the lack of opportunity for export in competition with world prices, by the low standard of living of the mass of the people. "On the side of basic resources," said Tannenbaum, "Latin America has no large-scale industrial future. . . . On the side of population Latin America's industrial development must be considered as seriously handicapped. . . . Capital saving, as a contributory element to industrial development in Latin America, is handicapped by the fact that profits from transportation, mining, industry and agriculture are to no small extent exported. . . . The discussion of industrialism in Latin America must take into consideration the fact that most of it is developed by foreign capital upon a concession basis. Now, the distinction between a concession and private borrowing by local people for industrial enterprise is that when the loan is liquidated the enterprise passes to the borrowers, while a concessionaire continued to own the property and control it as long as the concession lasts. The first species tends to develop a local capitalism and to spread the incidence of industrialism into by-ways and highways that the concessionary type of development does not. The concession rarely becomes native; the loan that is liquidated does. . . . One may ask whether under the circumstances, local capital accumulation—which in the long run must become the basis for a native industrialism—is possible." Tannenbaum found the cultural complex of Mexico, Central America, and the west coast of South America except Chile, so heavily influenced by Indian populations with their old traditions, habits, and ways of life that he did not believe there would be ready yielding of the type of response essential for industrial development, and regrettably in the Plate and southern Brazil where the cultural complex seemed more appropriate the resources were not available. In the smaller countries, in the matter of mere numbers as well as in purchasing power, the market did not suffice for any significant industrial development even if all the other factors were present.

Accordingly Tannenbaum wrote: "The absence of resources, the cultural equipment of the population, the peculiar impact of investment from abroad upon the rapid export and possible exhaustion of mineral resources, and the necessary confinement of large areas to the exportation of agricultural products in a competitive world market for what seems to have become a stationary European population, combined with the further fact that large tropical areas in Latin America may on economic grounds remain largely inaccessible, if not indifferent, to those benefits of industrialism that we set most store by, may in the long run prevent the development of those characteristics that we tend to identify with industrialism and may, in turn, lead to a very different type of civilization, less dependent upon world markets and less in need of the type of equipment that makes our civilization what it is." [17]

To the Latin Americans, bemused by industrialization, the prospect posed by Tannenbaum was devastatingly cruel. Angry efforts at rebuttal were prompt and almost passionate in their rejection of the thesis.

Villaseñor's Answer to Tannenbaum. Eduardo Villaseñor, the intelligent, well-read, fluent director-general of the Banco de México was one of those who disagreed completely with Tannenbaum's pessimistic conclusions. He argued that emphasis on the meagerness of coal resources as a deterrent to establishment of steel-making facilities ignored the possibility of technological developments that might overcome this deficiency. "Man's inventive genius may some day obtain the same results with petroleum as a reducer of iron ore," suggested Villaseñor. He argued that wide industrial expansion was possible even without the heavy industry symbolized by the steel mill. "Why," he asked, "should it not be possible to produce in Latin America all the chemicals obtainable from its vast resources, even though there be no large steel industry?" He challenged the inability to provide a solid basis for financing of the huge expenditures required for development of hydroelectric resources and suggested that

---

[17] Frank Tannenbaum, *Whither Latin America?* (Thomas Y. Crowell Company, New York, 1934), pp. 22-35.

a more thorough examination of the resources of the countries might eventually uncover a commodity position on which the financing could be based. He speculated on the possibilities of greater integration of the hemisphere's steel making resources involving greater movement of iron ore across international boundaries out of Mexico and possibly import of coal and other requirements to meet Latin American steelmaking needs.[18]

Perhaps the most significant difference between the analyses of the two experts consisted of their evaluations of the political realities under which development activity was likely to proceed. Villaseñor envisaged investment capital being attracted without the monopolistic or concessionary advantages that might act as deterrents to development. He considered industrial development to be possible without the excessive tariffs which would stifle competition and with it the increased productivity which must be forthcoming from industrial development. "With a little intelligence on the part of labor authorities, and some investment," he wrote, "the textile industries can provide both purchasing power and cloth for the inhabitants and, in some cases, like that of Mexico, can even achieve technical progress long overdue which might increase wages and cheapen the products." He assumed that local and foreign governments could now, after a long and not too satisfactory record, be depended upon to outline the basic facilities of power and transportation that promised most in the way of economic development and to assign them suitable priorities in developmental efforts, and if the selection were properly made financing must unquestionably (and unquestioningly?) be forthcoming from the United States. This concept stemmed from Villaseñor's basic premise—that the United States *must* export capital. "You may even have to give your capital away," he wrote, "lest you become a modern Midas and witness the decline and fall of the United States in the midst of a golden age of plenty. . . . I say, then: get

[18] Eduardo Villaseñor, "Inter-American Trade and Financial Problems," *Inter-American Solidarity* (The University of Chicago Press, Chicago, 1941), pp. 77-90.

rid of your treasure—lend it, give it, throw it away—if you do not want to perish in the misery of plenty." In contrast, Tannenbaum had reviewed the financial requirements for basic development facilities in terms of the normal intelligent process of investment. The conclusions obviously had to differ sharply with such varying bases. Curiously enough, in 1950 it seemed that the Mexican rather than the North American had more correctly read the Washington scene. In fact, he seemed to have forecast the Washington policy position more accurately than he had the policy potentials for economic development of his own government.

The sixteen years after Tannenbaum wrote were not a period calculated to direct developmental policy into traditionally "sound" lines. The depression years, the war period, and the rapid return to the uncertainties of export markets in the postwar period, all bolstered the position of those who insisted on greater insurance against the uncertainties of foreign markets and foreign sources. So much so, that the policymaker in Latin America was reaching the point where he must decide whether to de-emphasize industrial-expansion "insurance," or at least attempt to evaluate the point where it conflicted with the "harmony of interests" idea. *If it were true, as Alexander Hamilton had asserted in his skilfully phrased "Report on the Subject of Manufactures," that a supported manufacturing interest would strengthen rather than weaken agriculture, create further opportunities for enterprise and investment, furnish new employment possibilities, attract immigration—and the Latin American policymaker had certainly adopted the idea with enthusiasm—it was nevertheless time to determine how far the support was to go, in company with what other supporting activity elsewhere in the economy, and in what order of priority.*

SUPPLEMENTARY READING

George Wythe, Royce A. Wight and Harold M. Midkiff, *Brazil: An Expanding Economy* (The Twentieth Century Fund, New York, 1949), pp. 160-185.

Dudley Maynard Phelps, *Migration of Industry to South America* (McGraw-Hill Book Company, New York, 1936), pp. 43-90, 288-324.

Eyler N. Simpson, *The Ejido: Mexico's Way Out* (The University of North Carolina Press, Chapel Hill, 1937), pp. 529-582.

George Wythe, *Industry in Latin America* (Columbia University Press, New York, Second Edition, 1949), pp. 247-273, 325-353.

Lloyd J. Hughlett (Editor), *Industrialization of Latin America* (McGraw-Hill Book Company, New York, 1946), pp. 191-209, 264-272, 346-358.

80th Congress, 2nd Session, House Report 2470: *Fuel Investigation—Mexican Petroleum* (Progress Report of the Committee on Interstate and Foreign Commerce (Washington, 1949), pp. 40-52, 99-115.

Chapter 7

Development Policy and Industrial Growth

We cannot properly appraise the achievement, appreciate the potential, or analyze the course of Latin-American industrialization if we adopt as a standard the experience of the United States of America. It is not only that the material bases of American industrial supremacy—the natural resources and the political unity of so great an area free of internal trade barriers—are lacking. The very matrix out of which Latin American industrialization is developing differs too sharply from that out of which American industry expanded so tremendously after the Civil War to permit satisfactory comparison in terms of similar processes.

Latin American industrialism has been developing out of an undemocratic, semi-feudal conservative society, not the dynamic, pioneering, democratic base from which the American expansion proceeded. In the United States the transformation was from an agrarian society, in which the typical citizen was an independent property owner, to one in which economic inequalities were to become marked. In Latin America the original base is characterized by extreme inequalities, with the bulk of the citizens already dependent on enterprise controlled by a very small minority of the people. But while in the United States the mass of the workers accepted the shift to inequality and dependence and the discipline incident thereto, accepted the prevailing argument that everyone would eventually benefit from the freedom given the more energetic and able individuals to sweep unchecked toward power and riches, in Latin America industry has been encountering from the start an impatience with the long-

183

prevailing inequality and a demand for immediate benefits from the industrial process. That is to say, while industry in the United States could work its miracles of increased productivity and delay full sharing of the benefits, in Latin America tensions have been quickly created by the demand for privileges and benefits similar to those achieved in the older and more productive industrial economies, and slowing down of the whole process may inevitably follow from these demands.

The American was characteristically inventive and inclined to activity of practical utility, even though he lagged in pure science. The Latin American has not developed the professional training and the intellectual curiosity that make for progress in pure science, nor has he displayed the native technical inventiveness. A widely experienced engineer has commented that the "folkways and imagery are notably deficient in those elements which stimulate scientific curiosity and technical invention . . . even the keenest of Brazilian leaders seem not yet to have recognized that the condition of a dynamic and self-renewing industrial economy is that it shall be sustained and perpetually revitalized out of the alert inventive genius of the whole people." [1]   On the other hand, it should immediately be noted that the Latin Americans have at their command, provided they are willing to mobilize it by suitable action, the ready-made technological knowledge built up from generations of experience of the more advanced countries.

In Latin America industry has been developing out of uncertainty, lack of confidence in the ability to produce and market commodities in which it frequently seems to have competitive advantages far superior to its prospective industrial output, fear of being unable to sustain even the present standard of living, and constant awareness of the misfortunes of its primary producers in the 1930's and in other periods of cyclical decline. For contrast there is the American in the two generations following the Civil War, building

---

[1] Morris L. Cooke, *Brazil on the March* (Whittlesey House, New York, 1944), pp. 76-77.

his industries with supreme confidence and driving ahead in the exhilarating belief that he could and would achieve everything possible and some of the impossible. Here the individual of executive or practical technical ability regardless of his social background found encouragement to test his qualities of leadership; in Latin America the same competent individual would have to break out, to force his way through barriers created by local distinctions and lesser mobility which he found in the tightly-controlled rural economy, in closely-held banking systems, in policy-making spots in the government. He did sometimes force his way through, but there was this difference: in the United States the prevailing system encouraged him to assert himself; in Latin America he had to move up and out in spite of the system.

Capital in the United States in that stage of industrialization was active, quicker of mobilization, less attracted to luxurious spending and the contemplative life. In Latin America the familiar plaint of the inadequacy of savings for the financing of industry is coupled with the picture of incredibly luxurious living of the wealthy. Long ago Tench Coxe had taken sturdy pride in the contrast between Europe and the United States: "It is probable that all the jewels and diamonds worn by the citizens of the United States, their wives and daughters, are less in value than those which sometimes form a part of the dress of an individual in several countries of Europe. . . . (In the United States) all capital stock is kept in action. . . . All the citizens are in active habits." He would have attached importance to similar differences between Latin America and the United States more than a century later, although by 1950 he would have found the Latin American tending toward more "active habits," even toward keeping his "capital stock in action." Yet the drive did not compare with the earlier period in the United States.

All this in terms of factors determining the pace of development, rather than as a judgment on the wisdom of the character and way of life which in the United States seems to have been so ideally suited for the rapid growth of industry and which in Latin America seems to challenge the pace at which industry can be expected to develop. A great enterprise in Peru used to have emblazoned across the front of its establishment the Latin exhortation—*Tace, Ora et Labora*— which meant and meant emphatically "Keep quiet, pray and work." A return to unquestioning compliance with that exhortation is not here suggested as something indicated with labor stirring and restless in mid-twentieth century Latin America. But we could hardly evaluate the background of the drive for industry without realizing what is involved in the more articulate insistence upon immediate substantial benefits from the industrial process, without appreciating the difference between the dominant business philosophy under which American industry made such rapid strides and the recurring theme in Latin America which finds a Cuban official, extremely enthusiastic for both rapid industrialization and immediate gains to the worker, writing that "the Cuban worker knows that wage increases are obtained by joint pressure of the union on the government and not by his individual effort to increase productivity, and therefore higher protective tariffs must be given industry to compensate for the enduring inefficiency stemming from the lack of interest in increasing productivity," and a sober student of Chilean affairs suggesting that "Chile's great ill is that its workers no longer need have any ambition since they can obtain what they desire through political means."

From scattered data on the composition of income payments in Latin America, we know that income from manufacturing has increased in relative importance in recent years; that given the higher ratio of industrial capital equipment, productivity per worker tends to be larger in manufacturing than in agriculture; that productivity in manufacturing nevertheless tends to be low; and that the steady gain in productivity per worker in manufacturing from year to year which should be the source of steady improvement in the standard of living has failed to materialize in the manner in which it occurs in other industrial areas. What are the factors involved?

Labor. The productivity of Latin-American labor is low. This refers to the average amount a man produces in a given time—output per man-hour. Is this low productivity a matter of innate inability to produce effectively? At one time there was a tendency to trade in variations of the story of native labor that earned in a few days in a new enterprise more than it had earned previously in a week or two and consequently promptly took off for a vacation rather than stay on the job to boost its standard of living by producing more goods. Or the story would be told meaningfully of the native who quoted $1.00 for his basket but, when asked how much he would charge for 100 baskets exactly alike, thought for a moment and then replied "$1.25 each." Asked why the increase in price as quantity sales were offered him, he replied: "Because I would no longer enjoy making them." But we must be careful about the importance we attach to such stories in any over-all appraisal of the labor force for Latin American industry.

Admittedly industrialism imposes drastic changes in the habits and way of life, for it is an educational, organizational, and political process rather than simply a matter of installing machinery. Many of the manufacturing industries that first gained ground in Latin America did not require as high a degree of skill as some of the later industries. And the opportunities for training and the technological inheritance have been lacking. But as the demand for skilled workers has risen, the labor force with suitable training has made the adjustment successfully. Cooke, one of the few engineers who have published their findings on the subject, tells of inspecting a Latin American mining operation which was "an astonishingly antlike performance in our modern mechanized world. No fault could be found with the workers; they worked long hours at a firm steady pace and under the circumstances handled a surprising amount of coal. But they and their foremen and managers lacked our technological inheritance, the inductive analytical habit, the zest for invention." After several case studies he concluded that there was "a keen native aptitude for rapidly acquiring mechanical and related craft skills . . . a remarkable capacity for sustained labor . . . with proper health and nutritional care and competent managerial direction a work performance that compares satisfactorily with that of workmen in the industrially more mature countries."[2]   Wythe rates Mexican labor in industries using automatic machinery and repetitive processes as "superior to any except that of the United States, Germany and Japan."[3]   An officer of the International General Electric Company has suggested that "with proper training the difference in ability, skill, and resulting output under comparable conditions is slight" as compared with factory labor in the United States.[4]

The ability to produce is clearly affected by the low health and educational standards of the area. To the extent that these conditions are a function of income, they are effect *and* cause of the low income of the area. *There is reason to believe that given suitable investment in health and education, given equal training, equipment, and managerial competence, Latin American labor might be expected to perform as effectively as that of the more advanced industrial countries.* In terms of developmental policy this means that one of the primary areas for developmental activity consists of the investment in labor; to neglect health and education improvement is to doom manufacturing to low productivity and thus to inability to raise the standard of living adequately. The investment called for in labor is characterized by involving largely local currency expenditures since foreign exchange is needed at best for the "show-how" assistance, and by the fact that a considerable period of time is required for the full benefits to make themselves felt.

Availability of Capital. In addition to the investment in the productive capacity of labor, the expansion of manufacturing requires (a) capital for the manufacturing installa-

---

[2] Cooke, *op. cit.*, pp. 72, 76.

[3] George Wythe, *Industry in Latin America* (Columbia University Press, New York, 1949, Second Edition), p. 288.

[4] Quoted in Wythe, p. 370. It is noted that where the scale of operations is too small to require continuous production, workers may be employed on manufacture or assembly of widely different articles in the course of a year and that this is not conducive to the high average output per worker achieved when work is on a single operation or article.

tions themselves, and (b) capital for the broad fields of power and transportation. These are immense outlays without which the effort to achieve full productivity in the factories is likely to fail. To what extent is the supply of indigenous capital adequate for these demands?

We actually know very little about the volume and character of savings in the individual Latin American countries and about the demand for investment capital. In the absence of suitable data it has been common to assert that the lack of capital is a major, if not the most important, barrier to the development of industry. But there is reason to believe that the volume of savings available for investment relative to national income is not small in Latin America. Although the large bulk of the population have such low incomes that voluntary savings are hardly possible,[5] the extreme concentration of wealth and income creates a very large amount of savings by the relatively small group in the upper brackets. The Abbink Mission hazarded an estimate that Brazilian net savings might be 10% or more of net national income.[6] Mosk suggested that "a significant percentage of the Mexican national income is saved each year." [7] The Economic Commission for Latin America put gross investment in Chile at 8 to 11% of national income.[8] Spiegel estimated that Brazilian investment in 1944 represented from 24 to 29% of income payments to individuals, a somewhat smaller ratio to the national income proper, but "in any event, investments have certainly been very high, higher perhaps than comparable figures, for recent years, of other large countries;" and he went on to cite a capital-formation rate of 17% in Great Britain in the 1860's and 7% in the late 1930's, a rate for the

---

[5] In 1946 it was estimated that only 300,000 out of 9 million adult persons in Mexico have life insurance policies. In Brazil 400,000 to 450,000 persons are covered by life insurance, including 100,000 under group insurance, excluding insurance provided by the association of government employees and by the social security institutes.

[6] *Report*, p. 134.

[7] Sanford A. Mosk, "Financing Industrial Development in Mexico," *Inter-American Economic Affairs*, June, 1947, p. 8.

[8] *Economic Survey of Latin America* 1948, p. 38.

United States of 14% in 1900-10 and 5% in 1934-37, a Japanese ratio of investment to income of 22% in 1934-37.[9] "In the larger centers," George Wythe concluded in his comprehensive review of *Industry in Latin America*, "capital is not the major problem in connection with most types of manufacture. . . . The expansion of industry along sound lines is now conditioned more by human and socioeconomic factors than by financial limitations." [10]

The ineffective mobilization of the available domestic capital constitutes the real challenge. Historically and still characteristically, there has been a preference for investment in land in Latin America. The attraction to real estate has grown stronger, if anything, as urbanization has proceeded, and the inflationary tendency has strengthened the process. Perhaps two-thirds of the savings in Brazil in 1947 were devoted to the construction of buildings, with prominent concentration on the more costly type of construction for the well-to-do classes rather than on factory construction or on low-income residential construction. Coupled with the prevailing search for quick profits by speculation in commodities or in production that will pay off quickly, which immobilizes considerable amounts of funds for the more productive activity, Latin-American capital has typically resisted channeling into the more constructive development fields. And the fact that in most of the countries there are only rudimentary facilities for assembling and investing savings balks mobilization. The investment banking apparatus is meagerly developed, the whole institutional structure of an active capital market is lacking, the banks' role is largely confined to short-term operations. The manufacturer lacks a wide market in which to transfer part of his interests in order to obtain liquid funds and is continually furnished, therefore, with an additional incentive to aim for the highest possible profits in the shortest time in order to recover his original investment. A large proportion of the business organizations are

---

[9] Henry William Spiegel, *The Brazilian Economy* (The Blakiston Company, Philadelphia, 1949), p. 40.
[10] p. 51.

family undertakings; their stock is closely held by owners who want full personal control and who themselves share the preference for real estate especially in view of the protection afforded against a long-term rise in the general price level; issuance of new securities is typically handled by private arrangements. The large mass of the people are unfamiliar with the merits of owning securities as an alternative field for use of their savings. "In the industrial advance of Mexico," Mosk wrote in 1947, "a serious problem has arisen in the failure of domestic savings to move into industrial investment." Apart from hoarding, Mexican savers prefered to invest in urban real estate and construction or in mortgages; savings pooled by banks were directed toward industry only in small amounts because the banks were preoccupied with short-term commercial lending; and the *financieras*, theoretically the counterpart of our investment banks, failed to initiate industrial undertakings, were more important in lending than in investment, emphasized short-term rather than long-term lending, financed commercial and often speculative transactions and did little to create a market for industrial securities.[11]

In the estimate of roughly $600 million of savings in Brazil in 1947, $70 million is represented by payments to social security institutes, and $30 million by payments to insurance and capitalization companies, a total of $100 million of collective savings; business firms reinvested about 25 to 35% of total net earnings, or an amount of $200 to $300 million for the year; profit payments were sufficient to permit an estimated $150 million in savings; the large agricultural producers may have saved as much as $50 million; and the increase in savings deposits in saving banks representing the flow of middle-class savings, was perhaps $50 million. Of an estimated $375 million that went for building construction, $25 to $37 million was estimated for new factory construction, $100 million for residential housing for lower-income groups; and most of the balance represented the construction of office buildings and apartment houses for the upper-bracket

---

[11] Mosk, *op. cit.*, p. 45.

group in the main urban centers. It was unfortunate that in the speculative boom in urban real estate even the social security institutes helped feed the activity with funds that should have been more strictly confined to other uses.

In terms of development policy, the adequacy of capital refers both to requirements in local currency and to requirements of foreign exchange. The latter would be adequate to the extent that exchange from the proceeds of exports could be withheld from consumption goods for covering the cost of foreign equipment and essential supplies for industrialization—with the alternative of foreign investment. Adequacy of indigenous capital for local-currency requirements would in the first instance depend on the ability to redirect the savings into the most constructive channels and to mobilize the savings more effectively. Many policy lines have been indicated for this task: discourage excessive investment in urban real estate by discriminatory tax policy against capital gains in this line of investment; influence the investment policies of the banks to divert their resources to better uses; discourage bank financing of speculative activity; restrain inflationary forces and thereby limit opportunities for greater profits in real estate and increase the attractiveness of other investments. What is significant is that these involve action on difficulties whose roots are deep in the Latin-American economic organization. Similarly the obstacles to increasing the volume of savings are fundamental. If luxury expenditures of the upper-bracket group could be cut, if the concentration of income could be reduced, it might be helpful, although it is not certain that concentration at this time does not promote the volume of savings for the short period. Confronted with the desirability of curtailing consumption in order to provide larger investments for the requirements of this stage of industrialization, the policy-maker quickly notes that the level of consumption of the masses does not permit further reduction without great difficulties and that a counter movement is under way, stemming from the insistence of labor on immediate benefits from industrialization, which challenges his ability even to hold to the existing level of consumption without concession.

*While foreign investment in Latin-American manufactur-
ing facilities has at times been conspicuous, manufacturing
installations have to date been largely financed with local
capital.* U. S. investments in manufacturing facilities in
1948 totaled only $676 million, for instance, or less than one-
sixth the total American private direct investments in Latin
America; the increase in the 1940's was largely effected by
reinvestment of earnings.[12] It is likely that local capital is
adequate for the expansion of most of the manufacturing
industries. This has both advantages and disadvantages. It
prevents the drain which foreign ownership involves for remittance of earnings and the loss of control to outsiders and
perhaps the weighing of advantage among several countries
in which the outsiders might be operating at the same time.
On the other hand, the foreign investment is the easiest way
of tapping the accumulated technological knowledge of the
more advanced countries and of being assured the privilege
of drawing steadily on the advances made in the research and
operational facilities of the foreign country. The foreign
plants have frequently, also, paid better than the prevailing
wage scale, have adhered more strictly to the social security,
tax, and labor legislation than have locally-owned plants, and
have brought with them a pool of managerial competence
whose mobility is sufficient to raise the general level of managerial capacity in the country.

Once the mobilization of resources has improved, local
capital is likely to appear much less inadequate even for the
power and transportation requirements. But for a long
time the Latin American is likely to be reluctant to enter
fields which require a large initial investment and long years
of development before profits appear, or which require ac-

---

[12] The United States Department of Commerce estimated investments
in Latin American manufacturing activities at $192 million in 1936.
The U. S. Treasury's *Census of American-Owned Assets in Foreign
Countries* (Washington, 1947) showed $322 million in manufacturing
in 1943. In 1948 the American investment in manufacturing in Latin
America was $676 million. (Milton Abelson, "Private United States
Direct Investments Abroad," *Survey of Current Business*, November,
1949, p. 21.)

ceptance of a rate structure that will stimulate industry and agriculture and are likely therefore to produce profits out of line with the general scale. As Mr. Desiderio Garcia of the Compañía de Acero del Pacífico in Chile said in 1949: "The interest of our private investors increases as the prospects of the undertaking are more immediate and attractive and also in relation to the benefit the new concern may bring to existing or future firms in which, generally, the same investors will participate." [13]   Thus these other areas of investment are likely to be left to the foreign investor, or failing an interest on his part, to the government which in that case will choose between vigorous efforts to redirect the flow of savings into such investments and foreign borrowing by the government itself.   In many countries the requirements for power and transportation run two-thirds or more of the developmental activity required for industrial expansion, and since the process of improving the use of local resources is likely to be slow, this would seem to fix definite limitations to the pace of expansion of manufacturing.

One other problem in the more effective assembling and use of local savings might be mentioned, namely, the practice of wealthy Latin Americans of sending capital abroad. It is common for persons of wealth in Latin America, including politicians and ex-politicians but also including men not directly in politics, to hold substantial bank balances abroad and to make long-term investments overseas for reasons of security.   This is not surprising in an area of political instability and substantial personal government.   Such capital earns less overseas than it might earn at home, but since security rather than the rate of return is the primary consideration, the flow has continued — to the United States, Switzerland, and other countries considered safer than Latin America.   In the project for an Inter-American Bank and later in the establishment of the International Bank, the possibility of making more effective use of such capital in the countries of origin was a point of serious consideration.

---

[13] United Nations Economic and Social Council, *Methods of Increasing Domestic Savings and of Ensuring Their Most Advantageous Use for the Purpose of Economic Development* (Lake Success, 1949), p. 120.

Business Philosophy. The prevailing philosophy of high profits per unit of sale rather than mass markets at low unit profits has been costly for Latin America. This philosophy is characteristic not only of manufacturing but also of wholesaling and retailing. It is so generalized that there is no urgent pressure to keep costs down such as would be present in a dynamic industrial structure investing for the long pull in anticipation of moderate unit yields on a growing mass market. Inefficient competitors are safely blanketed under the umbrella; the concern with raising output per worker is less; and the rare occasion of entry into the field of a competitor, such as Sears, Roebuck with its reputation for volume sales at low unit profits, necessitates a review of competitive practices, and typically a review of the range of government assistance against such practices as the new competitor may wish to institute. "At times," said President Dutra of Brazil in 1948, "enterprises are set up without the prospect of a successful performance in the face of market resistance which aim solely to derive a high profit with the least possible effort. Present world conditions no longer support such a conception of deriving high profits on small-scale operations. Only mass production will stimulate the labor market and reduce the cost of products to meet social and economic needs, i.e., achieve a well-balanced level of wages and the cost of living." Yet, it must be noted that the "high unit profits" philosophy has been nourished by the protection against foreign competition which has been increasingly provided in practically every Latin American country. The willingness to risk capital in new factories, to keep installations up to date in line with technological advances, to press for higher productivity and the greater volume of sales that are possible in a dynamic expanding economy, is capable of yielding fine returns too, as the experience of American business reveals. But it is a far-distant record from Latin America's high-cost industrial structure created behind walls that bar any of the refreshing influence of foreign competition and comfortably adapted to yield large profits on the smallest possible volume. A disproportionate share of the sales value of industrial production for interest, depreciation, and profits is characteristic in Latin America. In 1947 a Brazilian tabulation showed 16% of the sales value for wages, commissions, and bonuses; while 36% was devoted to interest, depreciation, other overhead costs, and profits.

It is sometimes said that the high profits merely offset the deterring effect on investment of high rates of interest. Interest rates are extremely high in Latin America: higher in the more remote sections of the countries than in the metropolitan centers where modern banking facilities are likely to be concentrated; more expensive for agriculture than for capital intended for commerce or industry; more expensive for industry than for commerce. The rates reflect partly past inflationary experiences and the uncertainty of the future, partly the inadequacy of financial and credit machinery, and in large measure the pressure of demand for capital on available funds. Cognizant of the trend of prices and the repeated loss of savings by inflation, lenders demand higher rates of return than they would if prices remained stable. The interest rates are undoubtedly a deterrent to investment, especially in industries which require several years before they begin showing their earning power and in fields where profits range widely and where consequently the high interest rates add to the fixed burden excessively. The high rates are both a symptom of the risk, reflecting the general economic backwardness, and a contributing factor to the risk of investment.

Under the prevailing philosophy with respect to profits and the cooperative attitude of government with respect to restriction of competition, the pyramiding becomes unfortunate. A high-cost industrial structure is welcomed into being, and it is then agreed that prices should be set at a "reasonable" level in relation to costs so as not to further discourage the already timid investor in manufacturing. Yet it must be eventually recognized that an increase in consumption of the products must be achieved by lowering prices sufficiently and continually through improved productivity if the standard of living is to improve.

A Case Study in Impact on Business Philosophy. When

Sears, Roebuck invaded the Brazilian retail field in 1949, Brazil already had a sizable industrial plant. It had stores that featured a very wide range of goods, a chain of 19 stores of the five-and-ten type, stores with considerable familiarity with the advertising and display practices common in the United States. But the trading mechanism generally was characterized by slow turnover, haggling at the retail level, specialty shops, low-pressure selling, custom manufacture. And the production machinery had resisted the gospel of low-unit profits on mass markets.

Sears brought emphasis on turnover, volume pricing, and universal shopping appeal. It imported its technique of determining product specifications and maximum retail price points and markups in advance, and of negotiating purchases at prices scaled to known manufacturing cost plus profit. It introduced its standard practices in full-page newspaper advertising, rapid truck delivery service, delivery of parcels in exchange for cash at point of purchase, spectacular counter displays, liberal money-back policy, as well as air-conditioning, night openings, and other inducements to convenient shopping. Imported merchandise carried a prestige that locally manufactured goods could not achieve, but Sears had arrived at a time when there was a dollar shortage and import controls barred the free flow of merchandise from the United States. For this reason and for the obvious public relations advisability of trading within the country as actively as possible, Sears ranged the country to find merchandise and develop sources of supply. Its demands for accurate cost information were often impossible to meet, often regarded as an impertinence. To some manufacturers it offered partial financing to make possible tooling up to the scale of purchases that Sears could offer. To others it volunteered assistance in improving manufacturing processes so as to lower costs. To others it offered assured markets for products they had never manufactured. Mass production of items never successfully mass-produced in Brazil had been achieved by 1950 in such widely divergent lines as floor waxers, graduated cup brassières, pressure cookers, electric jig saws, hand tools, steel casting rods, graduated men's shirt sleeves, waffle irons.

It created new demands for products. It was responsible for increased consumption of paper in Brazil. It used many paper products not previously used by stores: large amounts of a good grade of wrapping paper made especially for it with its name and motto printed on it; its extensive use of paper bags was an innovation in large-scale retailing in Brazil and was followed by increased use by other stores. It put several factories to work trying to make the collapsible type of paper boxes commonly used in the United States, but not being manufactured locally. It started the manufacture of kitchen paper toweling and facial tissues. It had toilet tissue made to its own specifications for a growing market.

Its entry into the Brazilian market had been dreaded by many retail establishments because of the potential ability of a very strong competitor to drive out competition through price cutting. But in the initial period the most important impact was on the philosophy of retailing, on the development of local manufacturing to specifications, on aggressive selling which other stores found they could profitably emulate, on the development of new products and new techniques. Once the potentialities of production and sale for mass markets were established, other retailers would be able to function on the same theory, and Sears' suppliers and other manufacturers could adopt the new and potentially even more profitable way of doing business. While the parallel of the O. Henry story in which an Alabama merchant found himself stuck with a supply of shoes in a Latin American city that was not accustomed to wearing shoes and proceeded to create demand by sprinkling the streets with cockleburs should not be labored, the fact remained that the stimulus to mass marketing was as necessary for successful industrialization as the introduction of machinery in a factory or the training of workers to the requirements of tending machinery.

The Size of the Market. The limited purchasing power in most Latin American markets is clearly a handicap to successful establishment of industries in which the optimum size dictated by technological considerations exceeds the market—present and potential. But many of us tend to place excessive emphasis on the role of the giant mass-production plants even in the advanced industrial countries. Granting the advantages in continuous process industries, such as steel, chemicals, and flour, that stem from use of very specialized large-capacity apparatus to reduce costs per unit of output, the number of industries requiring very large plants is not as great as is popularly thought. As Shire has noted in his examination of *The Importance of the Small Plant in Industry* "generally, consumer goods can be economically produced in small plants." There is evidence in the experience of many of the light industries in Latin America that the protection afforded legitimately by avoidance of ocean-shipping and other charges incident to importation compensates adequately even in cases where some deficiencies do derive from the scale of operations, and thus makes economic the scale warranted by local conditions. And, of course, the system by which many of the Latin-American governments give a new industry virtual command of the local market avoids in the initial stage excessive parceling of the market.

There are admittedly inherent limitations in some industries, even where a single plant has the whole market, imposed by the smaller scale of operation—such as inability to support research and training facilities of suitable scope—and by the relative immaturity which is reflected in the time taken to develop the associated ventures such as those making essential parts or designing special equipment or providing specialized engineering and purchasing and legal services. The associated ventures that eventually build up a modern industrial center require a considerable time to establish and short cuts are few and difficult. Indeed, the disadvantages of such immaturity have been recognized in the argument for helping "infant industries" along the road to efficient operation. *It can be argued effectively that by plunging into modern industrial production the Latin American country gains an advantage in the speeding up of industrial education and in the creation of the associated network of industries and services which may compensate for the higher initial cost of the product. But the unfortunate aspect of the situation arises in the undiscriminating selection of industries and the unwise yielding to vested interests who have gained power in the political enclaves of the capital, long after they should have been prodded into greater efficiency and ability to withstand competition by their own efforts.*

Efficiency and the Infant Industry Status. After considering the improper allocation of limited savings in terms of maximizing productivity, the business philosophy of high unit profits, the consequences of inadequate investment in labor productivity, the limitations imposed by the size of the market, the high cost of money, the relative unavailability of funds to provide more and cheaper power and better transportation, the provision of excessive social security benefits before productivity can support it, and the loss of flexibility in the labor force through unwise indemnification plans for discharged workers and other devices, it may be found that the largest factor in the relatively low productivity of Latin-American industry and its failure to show suitable continuing gains in productivity is the failure of the government to provide a climate for investment in manufacturing that would encourage efficiency rather than inefficiency.

Ellsworth writes of Chile's Corporación de Fomento, the government-controlled developmental agency, that it "appears to be in danger of ignoring and even defeating its principal purpose, that of 'increasing the standard of living of the people by utilizing the natural resources of the country and lowering production costs.' This can result either from concentration upon the mere 'utilization of the natural resources of the country' without careful attention to factors determining costs of production, or from undue and ill-conceived stress upon another of its objectives, the 'improvement of the international balance of payments'." He emphasizes that the Corporación may be tending to overlook the importance of cost considerations and cites its pronouncements regarding the number of factories that are still not fully developed in Chile "because of foreign competition and the lack of sufficient protection on the part of the State." [14]

---

[14] Ellsworth, *op. cit.*, pp. 90-92.

Cooke in the early 1940's saw Brazil at the point where "from this time forward it is largely a question of consolidation of industrialization along management and technical lines, in other words the acquisition of the know-how." He warned that the size of profits under the Brazilian system was not a measure of efficiency and stressed that behind the barriers to competition generously provided by the Brazilian government, industry must stimulate itself into greater efficiency in the whole range of activity—improvement and standardization of raw materials, modernization of installations, revision of merchandising and distribution methods to achieve mass consumption. Infant industries were in danger of ossification of inefficiency through excessive protection, and he urged Brazil to remember that whatever aid prohibitive tariffs may provide infant industries, "when depended upon after the children are grown up they are an invitation to disaster." [15]

Pressed by raw material producers for tariff protection that would encourage expansion of local sources of industrial raw materials and by manufacturers to resist such demands lest the competitive cost picture of the new industries be made even less satisfactory, the Latin-American governments were tending to yield to both groups, with the result that the final cost of production compared even more unfavorably with foreign products produced from a ready supply of cheap raw materials.

And in the whole question of indiscriminate protection of industry there was an overriding matter of priority which the Economic Commission for Latin America faced bravely in 1949 when it concluded that "in a number of cases (of Latin American countries) for some time to come a further expansion of the extractive industries can contribute more to the nation's welfare than an artificial stimulation of manufacturing could achieve. This is seldom an alternative since each actually requires the support of the other. If the primary goal is more volume of goods and stability of their supply, industrialization cannot be the only means since it implies introducing labor-saving devices in all lines of production." [16]

---

[15] Cooke, *op. cit.*, p. 239.
[16] *Economic Survey of Latin America* 1948, p. 54.

In the migration of industry to Latin America from the United States and Europe, increases in tariffs and other import restrictions have provided a strong incentive to set up manufacturing facilities locally. In fact, many American industries, which in the United States have neither needed nor demanded tariff protection and have in fact advocated freer trade actively, have arrived in Latin America and become among the most vocal of protective tariff advocates in an effort to gain advantage often over their fellow-countrymen who lagged in shifting from an export to a local manufacturing basis. In some cases an agreement to lower prices locally once production was under way has been part of the original understanding with the government and implementation of the agreement has sometimes brought difficulties, but in general the governments have been lax in demanding *quid pro quos* in terms of gains from efficiency as the price of the assistance offered the manufacturer, whether he were of foreign or domestic origin.[17]

Adler has argued that some "uneconomic" industrial developments can be justified on social and political grounds so that the limits of "desirable" industrialization can be drawn even wider:

> An increase of industrial production is desirable as long as the gains in real income of those persons directly affected by the development of new industries *appear* to be greater than the losses entailed by other sectors of the economy. For instance, construction and operation of, say, a rayon factory, doubles the real income of 500 or 1,000 workers and their families, while new import duties on rayon textiles decrease the real income of rayon consumers by a fractional amount; the gain of the 500 or 1,000 workers *appears* to be large and the loss of the consumers, spread over a wide area, may pass unnoticed or at least will not raise any social and political problems.
>
> Protection through tariffs or other forms of import restrictions may, of course, result in a loss in real income of the consumers of imported goods (and their newly developed

---

[17] See, for instance, Dudley Maynard Phelps, *Migration of Industry to South America* (McGraw-Hill Book Company, New York, 1936), pp. 137-147.

domestic substitutes) which is greater than the gain of the increase in productivity of persons employed in new industries. In that case the national income in real terms declines. But at the same time a redistribution of real income in favor of industrial wage earners, and to the disadvantage of consumers of imports, is taking place. If the decline in real income is concentrated on higher income groups—as it may well be in many underdeveloped countries where the bulk of imports is consumed by the numerically small upper and middle classes—this redistribution of income may not be undesirable from the point of view of economic welfare, and it certainly appears desirable from the point of view of a government eager to broaden its bases of popular support.[18]

Unfortunately, a very substantial part of the initial industrial effort in Latin America has been directed at the requirements of the lower classes, rather than at fulfillment of the demand for better-grade textiles and other consumption goods. To that extent redistribution of income at the expense of the upper-bracket group would not occur. More important for our purposes here is that granting the fact that an unwise selection of industries to be protected has frequently been made, the error is being compounded by the failure to take steps to promote efficiency once the industry is set up.

It is especially important that in the key industries such as steel and the heavy chemicals, in which there is a tendency for the Latin-American governments to lend financial assistance for establishment as well as to continue protection from competition, and which are likely to be the nucleus for associated and derivative industries, every effort be made to prod the industries into maximum competitive capacity. In many of these cases, the very limitations to efficient industrialization that we have been examining have been eliminated. Take, for instance, the Volta Redonda steel plant in Brazil.

Initially, the Brazilians were veritably bemused by their great iron ore reserves of 65 to 69% metallic content, variously estimated at 10 to 15 billion tons; by their large deposits of

---

[18] John H. Adler, *The Underdeveloped Areas: Their Industrialization* (Yale Institute of International Studies, New Haven, Connecticut, **1949**), **p. 18.**

excellent 45 to 57% manganese ore; enough so as to shrug off the coal deficiencies with an estimate that there were 400 million tons in the Santa Catarina area which could be carbonized to coke despite the high ash content. The major existing steel producer had been financially successful behind tariff walls, with an iron ore supply immediately available at the site and domestic coal so distant that charcoal was mainly used. Local consumption of steel was small, and being divided among the various kinds of steel seemed particularly inadequate for an efficient competitive operation. And the trend line of consumption had not been impressive: Brazil had consumed about 500,000 tons of steel annually in 1928-29, of which about 25,000 tons was produced locally; ten years later, 1938-39, its apparent consumption was running about 430,000 tons per year, of which about 100,000 tons was locally produced. Bickering on the likely location of a new plant had not ended with an ideal location, final site being 500 miles from coal, 240 miles from iron ore, 210 miles from limestone. But in fostering the establishment of the enterprise the government was able to overcome some the handicaps that the ordinary industrial enterprise would encounter. It was able to obtain a considerable portion of the capital for the mill in the United States on government credit at interest rates that compare favorably with what an American steel company might pay for its money and very favorably with prevailing rates in Brazil. It could cooperate in the investment in labor to the end that the adverse productivity differential resulting from health, educational, and training inadequacies would be reduced. It could hold out the prospect that requirements of exchange for additional foreign equipment and materials would be more readily forthcoming than for other manufacturing ventures, some of which in the late 1940's were having difficulty in arranging foreign-exchange cover for machinery which they wished to install and which they were able to finance in local currency. It could hold out the prospect of again utilizing the credit of the government for cheap capital for expansion of facilities.

In addition, it gave the mill the traditional protection accorded infant industries. Government departments were instructed to fill their requirements for steel at the mill regardless of their ability to buy at lower prices elsewhere in Brazil or in foreign markets. The mill was also given tax preferences. And while it was still in the process of construction, government officials discussed with the other steel producers the desirability of raising protective tariffs which, although they were adequate for existing facilities to be run profitably, might not be adequate for the new enterprise in which the government was interested. Import restrictions through control of exchange effectively cut off competitive supplies from overseas. The enterprise produced about 245,-000 tons of crude steel equivalent in 1948, added 100,000 tons for its 1949 quota, and planned to continue expansion.

The temptation in a venture of this kind is to adopt a pricing policy that will permit the enterprise to show sufficient profits to avoid its becoming a target for political opposition, or to proclaim a social-rate policy on the theory that steel is a basic element for many industries and should therefore be made available at low cost, even though it means a sizable deficit for the government to be made up from other sources of revenue and even though such a policy encourages even greater looseness in management. Yet the plant is modern, installed under the direction of high-grade foreign technicians, financed in part by low-cost foreign capital, assured of model-enterprise treatment in efforts to make labor's productivity comparable with standards prevailing in countries where such plants are more common. And its local competitors, lacking some of these advantages, have been able to prosper and to yield very healthy-looking dividends. The experience of Latin-American industries to date does not support too much confidence in the ability to sustain a continuing drive for efficiency, but if these basic industries, under what are optimum conditions for Latin America in terms of capital, labor, and technique, cannot avoid becoming an additional high-cost element in the growth of manufacturing, great disappointments are in store for those who pin their hopes to rapid industrialization. That is the real significance of the findings of the investigators who in 1949 concluded rather gloomily that "Costs are likely to remain high, although government departments have been instructed to buy Volta Redonda products even when they are more expensive. In practice, the charcoal-iron mills are doing better than Volta Redonda." [19]

The Terms of Trade. In addition to the abuses that creep into the system of protecting local industries from foreign competition, it has been suggested that there may be a basic inconsistency in the Latin-American policy of encouraging domestic manufacturing by means of tariffs on imports of competing products. Metzler notes that the Latin-American countries have a comparative advantage in the production of foodstuffs and raw materials, that most of their leading exports are commodities for which the world demand is decidedly inelastic, and that "since the Latin American countries in many instances provide a substantial proportion of the world's supply of such goods, it seems likely that the external demand for their exports as a whole may be quite inelastic even over considerable periods of time," and that if one goes beyond the immediate effects of tariffs he may find that "tariffs may accomplish little either in protecting Latin American manufacturing or in increasing the share of the workers in national income." He continues:

This does not mean, of course, that the tariffs entail no economic benefits to the countries imposing them, but the benefits may be quite different from those originally contemplated. With the low price elasticity of demand for their products, the countries of Latin America are in a particularly good position to employ tariffs as a means of achieving more favorable terms of trade. A favorable movement in the Latin American terms of trade, however, means an increase in the prices received for exports relative to the prices paid for imports; and, to the extent that such a shift occurs, part or all of the protection intended for domestic manufacturing is wiped out. In other words, since tariffs do not alter the basic techniques of production, any benefits which they confer upon one industry or one segment of the population are likely to be at the expense of another industry or another segment of the population. The Latin American tariffs cannot, at the same time, bene-

---

[19] Wythe, Wight and Midkiff, *op. cit.*, p. 172.

fit industry at the expense of agriculture and benefit agriculture at the expense of industry; and, although these tariffs are imposed upon manufactured goods, it is possible that, in the end, world conditions of demand may be such that the tariffs actually injure the industries which they are intended to protect. . . . The favorable movement in the terms of trade may more than offset the initial effects of the tariff in raising domestic prices of manufactured goods. And, even if the conditions of demand are not so extreme, it remains true, in any event, that the degree of protection afforded by Latin American tariffs is much smaller than appears at first glance to be the case.[20]

In practice, Latin-American industrialists have not been inclined and are not likely to be inclined in their demands for protection against foreign competition to follow through to the ultimate effects on exchange rates and relative costs. And where long-established export interests, as in the River Plate countries, have had difficulty in reconciling themselves to the rise to political and economic power of the new industrial group, they have tended to protest in terms of the immediate effect on their traditional export markets of a reduction in purchases from such countries—a variation of the 'buy from those who buy from us' sloganeering—rather than in terms of the final repercussions of tariff policy. The policy-maker in the government similarly has been satisfied with the immediate purposes and effects of the protection afforded domestic industry.

It is probable that the most promising field for effective action will long continue to be initial avoidance of protection for industries which seem unlikely to achieve operations of an economic character, and continued investigation and action to minimize the stimulus to inefficiency afforded by easy access to political assistance from the capital.

Industrialization and the Policy-Maker. By 1950, industry in the major Latin American countries was moving from the status of an extension of agricultural production to that of a more balanced industrial structure, with increasing em-

---

[20] Lloyd A. Metzler, "Tariffs, the Terms of Trade, and the Distribution of National Income," *The Journal of Political Economy*, February, 1949, pp. 23-25.

phasis on heavier industry. Even in the less advanced countries, progress was being made (a) in the food-processing plants which were largely an extension of agriculture; (b) in the market-oriented industries like beer, wood products, meat products, bakeries, and flour milling, where closeness to market was a key consideration; and (c) in the labor-oriented industries such as cotton textile manufacturing, clothing, shoes, and furniture, where wages figured in relatively large ratio to total costs. It was unwise and unreasonable for the proponents of industrialization to be identifying industrialization in the public mind with a sudden improvement in material welfare of any substantial degree. In fact, the very arguments for relieving the new industrial plant from overseas competition until it had found its stride pointed to the need for time to effect serious gains. But in some of the countries the light industries had already had decades in which to consolidate their positions, and there was a growing appreciation of the need for evaluating policies affecting the growth of industry, even on the part of observers who were highly sympathetic to the motives behind the drive for industrialization.

"The Latin-American nations should . . . make sure," wrote the widely experienced Carlos Davila in 1949, "that industrialization does not become another weapon in the hands of a few for the further pauperization of the many. . . . The annual percentage of profits of most Latin-American industrial and commercial enterprises are generally two, and quite often three, four and five times larger than those obtained by similar enterprises in the United States. What this means in cost of production and in prices for the consuming masses can very easily be visualized." [21]

Leopoldo Zea had written of an earlier period in Mexican history (the Díaz regime) that nothing was accomplished except that "the privileged classes were no longer the army and clergy but a new group that called itself the Mexican bourgeoisie. . . . The government continued to be the prin-

---

[21] Carlos Davila, *We of the Americas* (Ziff-Davis Publishing Company, Chicago, 1949), p. 248.

cipal source of privileges; and the material progress that might have engendered a powerful bourgeoisie was not achieved. . . . It all boiled down to a political change: the colonial lord of the manor had given place to the Porfirian landowner. If there was progress, it worked toward greater efficiency in the methods of exploitation. . . . Instead of exploiting industry they exploited peasants or the Treasury. . . . Such industries as sprung up were due to the great European bourgeoisies, French and English in particular, to whom the progress of the country was of no concern." [22]

Now, in the midst of the widely publicized growth in Mexican industry during the 1940's, a liberal journalist, in rather disillusioned fashion, returned from Mexico in 1947 to voice the doubts that disturbed technician and publicist alike: "The problems that Mexico is facing are problems that grow . . . out of a young and newly native capitalism that has all the signs of our own 'robber baron' days of the late nineteenth century. . . . For at least 75 percent of her population Mexico's war prosperity has been all but a fraud. . . . The income tax structure of the war period left the huge profiteers almost untouched. . . . Those best able to pay, those who are profiting enormously all but escape taxation. There are thousands of Mexican businessmen who aren't interested in anything that doesn't bring them 40 percent with the sky the limit. Real estate and industrialization are their two favorite fields. The roads still need to be built, the harbors dredged and improved, the railroad lines rebuilt and newly equipped, irrigation still to be provided for." [23]

"Will the capitalists and industrialists keep faith with the people," asked Herbert Cerwin, a passionate believer in Mexico's future, "Or will prices go sky high without United States competition to keep them down?" [24]

---

[22] Leopoldo Zea, "Positivism and Porfirism in Latin America," in *Ideological Differences and World Order*, edited by F. S. C. Northrop (Yale University Press, New Haven, 1949), pp. 189-190.

[23] Alexander H. Uhl, "The 19th Century Comes to Mexico," *New Republic*, May 5, 1947.

[24] Herbert Cerwin, *These are the Mexicans* (Reynal & Hitchcock, New York, 1947), pp. 91-92.

Wallich warned that "where the market is so narrow that only small-scale plants are feasible, employing a negligible amount of labor and perhaps relying on imported raw materials, demands for heavy tariff or other protection in the name of development have scant merit; such 'development' may involve little more than the creation of a permanent monopoly for a small group of entrepreneurs; in such cases, labor fails to benefit and the consumer may be permanently worse off."[25]   And although the government's cooperation was being exacted in many cases by heavy accent on anti-foreign feelings, the prospective "new monopolists" were in fact largely local in origin, for manufacturing was dominantly of local ownership by 1950. Incontinent rejection of the warnings by unbiased observers of the direction in which manufacturing was being pushed was perhaps the most dangerous course that the policy-maker in the government could steer in 1950.

There was no easy course. The industrial plants that were being newly established tended to be more modern, more competitive with those of the advanced manufacturing nations. And the industries which had been originally developed by foreign corporations as sources of supply for export markets had tended to be well equipped. But much of the original industrial plant catering to the domestic markets had consisted of outmoded equipment, justified often as better adapted to the less-experienced labor and managerial supply of the area, and the stimulus to boost efficiency had been faulty so that a steady rise in productivity of the industrial structure had not been forthcoming. It was possible that qualitative advances in the existing industrial plant held out more hope for benefit to the consumer than did much of the expansion that was being projected locally into new fields of industrial activity.

It is true that these Latin-American economies were not so consciously planned and directed by the governments as

---

[25] Henry C. Wallich, "Some Aspects of Latin American Economic Relations with the United States," *Foreign Economic Policy for the United States*, edited by Seymour E. Harris (Harvard University Press, Cambridge, 1948), p. 163.

to enable them to dictate where capital was to flow in order to maximize the social benefits of investments, as judged by the policy-maker. Investments were proceeding in accord with the judgment of individuals as to relative profitability of different ventures, usually from a short-run point of view. Yet the potential influence of government in selection between alternatives was great in terms of stimulating and facilitating expansion in particular lines. For unlike the United States, where David A. Wells had correctly noted that the dynamic sweep of industry after the Civil War "through what we may term the strength of its elements of vitality" was largely independent of legislation, the expansion of Latin American industry in its initial stages has been heavily and characteristically associated with governmental action. Unfortunately perhaps, industrial influence was growing in the capitals, and the long tradition of government as the source of privilege yielded slowly if at all in Latin America. The isolated symbols of the era's hope—the mechanized plant with its forced increase in wages—might in the policy-maker's eyes become as unsatisfactory a beneficiary of social priorities as the great landed estate might have been. But his hands were by no means free, and even if they had been, the time table which was being thrust upon him politically failed to comprehend that development must be thought of in terms of decades and generations rather than in single years. For the policy-maker in Latin America, these were the realities of industrial development policy:

(a) An overwhelming proportion of the people could not be a significant source of savings for investment, nor a significant market for the products of industry, nor adequately productive without a substantial investment in their health and education. While one method of raising capital for industrialization was to push living standards down and thereby divert a larger proportion of production into capital equipment, this was hardly feasible in the light of existing standards of consumption. There was in fact political pressure to yield up a larger proportion of the national income to this group in advance of gains in productivity, at the expense of an investment ratio that was already inadequate, and at the same time that development activity demanded a higher ratio of investment. There was economic pressure to increase the purchasing power of this dominant group of the population because of the realization that the market must be enabled to assume economic proportions for the projected industries. And there was the insistent demand that the labor force be more productive if the cost structure of the industries was ever to become competitive with former sources of supply.

(b) The savings of the small group in the upper brackets were so large that they made the total savings of the community greater than was commonly believed to be possible. But these savings were not effectively mobilized. The demand for products of local industry of this group was too limited to compensate for the inadequate purchasing power of the larger group which was confined largely to basic necessities. In seeking to tap these savings effectively, the policymaker had to avoid too heavy pressure on local costs of production, lest a sense of insecurity be created among the investing group which would defeat the hope of more effective mobilization of resources. In fact, policy had to be directed partly to rounding up for local use funds now hoarded locally or held abroad—an objective that would not be served by contributing to the timidity of the investing class.

(c) Outlets for capital were not limited to the industrial field, for a foundation needed to be laid for agricultural advances simultaneously. Agriculture must be made to produce a supply of local raw materials that would compare favorably in quality and price with those available to industry in other countries. Demand for industrial output stemming from agriculture still comprised a very large proportion of the population and this purchasing power must be expanded by greater productivity on the farms to yield an adequate market for local industries. And since it would be necessary to call on foreign capital for assistance in development and for the equipment of a more advanced industrial and agricultural structure, agriculture must be stimulated by greater availability of capital equipment per worker to enable creation of the foreign exchange necessary for servicing foreign assistance.

(d) It was likely that the preference of local capital for the traditional money-making lines such as urban real estate, farm land, trade and speculative commercial activity, would yield only slowly. The reluctance to invest in the power and transportation improvements that were so necessary to industrial expansion might be an enduring characteristic of the private capital market. On the other hand, it was probable that the volume of local savings and its willingness to invest sufficed for the requirements of manufacturing in all except possibly those industries that require extraordinary large investments and a considerable period before they paid off.

(e) On the part of the government, the policy-maker had to mobilize sufficient funds for the investment in the productivity of labor, an investment that would yield its benefits only slowly and indirectly. He could try to impose suitable progressive income taxes and implement a broad program of social services for the benefit of the lower-income groups. All this in the face of the political resistance of the powerful industrial group and with the caution dictated by the need to avoid discouragement of investment. It was common to throw up at the policy-maker the fact that in the more advanced countries the great part of industrial growth had been accomplished before the burden of taxation reached present proportions, but the policy-maker noted as commonly that with the tax burden very low, Latin-American capital had not been flowing into the most attractive fields from the viewpoint of the national welfare. The policy-maker needed also to mobilize capital for the major investments in power and transportation and communications and the other public utilities. In other words, from 50 to 75% of the capital requirements of industrialization depended on the ability of the government either to attract foreign funds into private investment in Latin America and/or local governmental activity, or to alter the lines of investment of local savings so drastically as to impose a schedule of social priorities on the economies, through use of the tax power and borrowing capacity of the governments. Since a large share of the requirements for power and transportation involved goods which were not being produced locally, exports must be made to yield sufficient funds to cover foreign costs after everything feasible had been done to reduce imports of consumption goods, again with the alternative of calling on foreign capital to help finance the movement.

Since two of the chief sources of foreign exchange are the mining and petroleum activities, let us next examine the organization of these industries.

SUPPLEMENTARY READING

Antonio Carrillo Flores, "Practices, Methods and Problems Involved in the Domestic Financing of Economic Development in Mexico," United Nations Economic and Social Council, *Methods of Increasing Domestic Savings and of Ensuring Their Most Advantageous Use for the Purpose of Economic Development* (Lake Success, 1950), pp. 180-236.

John H. Adler, *The Underdeveloped Areas: Their Industrialization* (Yale Institute of International Studies, New Haven, 1949), Memorandum Number 31, pp. 1-30.

Morris Llewellyn Cooke, *Brazil on the March* (Whittlesey House, McGraw-Hill Book Company, New York, 1944), pp. 209-251.

A. C. Shire, *The Importance of the Small Plant in Industry* (International Technical Congress, Paris, 1946).

"Sears, Roebuck in Rio," *Fortune*, February, 1950, pp. 78-80, 151-156.

Chapter 8

Organization for Production:

Mining

The mining industry in Latin America shares certain characteristics of mining activity the world over: (a) Minerals are wasting assets that cannot be replaced. (b) The occurrence of mineral resources dictates location without regard to concentrations of population or centers of capital or outlets in industry. And sites are frequently so remote as to necessitate the organization of complete community facilities in order properly to exploit the resources. (c) Exact estimates are impossible for the volume and quality of particular deposits and potentially competitive sources elsewhere. Initial costs of prospecting and development are tremendous and there is a continuing risk that superior or more accessible resources (natural or synthetic) may be discovered. The responsiveness to price increases in the short run is limited to proven reserves and the availability of power and transport and labor facilities to utilize them. (d) The speculative character of discovery, the heavy specialized investment required, and the exhaustibility of reserves, all serve as stimulants to lessening of competition among producers by organization toward monopolistic control. (e) Metals after fabrication can reenter the market time after time as scrap; scrap supplies increase constantly and tend to affect adversely demand for primary metals when business falls off. (f) Mineral markets are erratic, frequently out of balance. (g) The importance of minerals in time of war introduces special strategic considerations in the organization of the industry, whether in a major producing nation inducing expansion of capacity beyond civil-

215

ian requirements in order to assure continuity and sufficiency of supply when war comes, or in an underdeveloped country likely to serve mostly as a supplier of raw materials, motivating inducements to expansion of capacity through stockpiling or other arrangements.[1]

In addition, Latin America's mining industry has some special features: (1) It is heavily dominated by foreign capital. Accordingly it is a primary target for nationalistic pressure, for discriminatory legislation and enforcement of legislation, for challenge by labor and politicians and even by local capitalists who shy away from the great risks and heavy long-term investments that the industry requires but become intimately interested once the industry shows promise of paying off in returns commensurate with the risks taken by foreign capital. (2) With Latin America a relatively small consumer of metals and minerals, the industry functions largely for export and is extremely sensitive to changes in international markets. (3) It provides employment for only a very small proportion of the gainfully employed, even in countries where mining has attained considerable importance, such as Peru, Bolivia, Mexico, and Chile. But in such countries it exercises disproportionate influence on the level of economic activity by reason of the large percentage of total exports created by it and the associated effects on government revenue, foreign purchasing power, etc. (4) The output of the industry has failed to keep pace with the growth of population or with the growth of manufacturing.

This last point is especially interesting to students of developmental policy, because world trends in mineral consumption are such that this might have been expected to be an optimum area for development. "The quantity of mineral products consumed between 1900 and 1949," a Canadian expert noted in 1949, "far exceeds that of the whole preceding period of man's existence on earth. . . . The increases in consumption since 1900 have covered all the more important metals and minerals. During that time production of pig

---

[1] Discussion of mineral activity in this chapter excludes petroleum. Chapter 9 is devoted to the petroleum industry.

iron, lead and tin has more than doubled; zinc and copper have quadrupled; aluminum, nickel, tungsten and others have shown even greater ratios in increase." [2] The pressure on resources occasioned by the growing importance of minerals to contemporary civilization, the continued rapid rise in population, and the universal demand for a higher standard of living, must presumably be translated into acceleration of development of new sources of supply.[3] An American specialist in 1949 calculated that world reserves in terms of years' supply at the current rate of consumption then stood as follows: copper 45 years; zinc 39 years; tin 38 years; lead 33 years, chromite 47 years; bauxite 200 years; iron ore 200 years.[4] And when an appraisal of the mineral position of the United States was undertaken in 1944 by the Bureau of Mines and the Geological Survey, it was reported that of 41 commodities studied, reserves of 15 were equivalent to more than a half century of requirements at the 1935-44 rate of consumption, reserves of 3 were equivalent to 33 to 39 years of consumption, and reserves of 23, including such highly essential minerals as bauxite, zinc, copper, lead, and tin, were equivalent to less than 25 years. (See Figure I.)

A fifth characteristic of the Latin American mining industry might be mentioned also—the ease of prescription-writing for development in this field. The scope of developmental activity in mining in Latin America depends very

[2] H. L. Keenleyside, "Critical Mineral Shortages," An Address Delivered at a Plenary Session of the United Nations Scientific Conference on the Conservation and Utilization of Resources (Lake Success, 1949).

[3] The implications of higher standards of living approaching that of the United States in terms of mineral consumption are not always understood. In 1945 utilization of pig iron, for instance, was 790 pounds per capita in the United States, 47 pounds in the rest of the world. See Edward Sampson, "Some Aspects of Mineral Adequacy," a paper presented at the Annual Meeting, Canadian Institute of Mining and Metallurgy (Montreal, 1949).

[4] Elmer Walter Pehrson, "Discussion of Estimates of Selected World Mineral Supplies by Cost Range," United Nations Scientific Conference on the Conservation and Utilization of Resources (Lake Success, 1949).

FIGURE 1

Estimated Commercial Mineral Reserves in Known Deposits in the
United States, Compared with Average Annual Rates of
Domestic Production and Consumption, 1935-44.

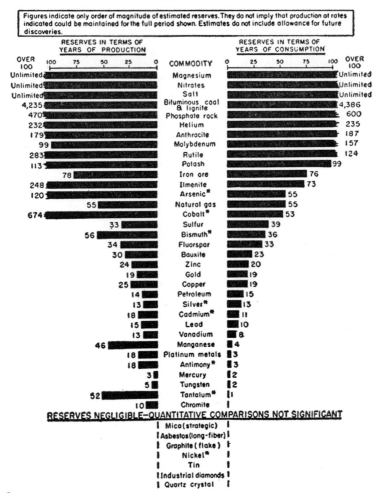

Source: *The Mineral Position of the United States,* prepared by the
Inter-Bureau Committee for Mineral Reserves Study (Geological Survey
and Bureau of Mines).

largely on the willingness of the governments to encourage for-eign capital to take the enormous risks incident to prospecting and development. In the absence of suitable encouragement, progress in mining is likely to be halting and uncertain.

Size of the Industry. The value of output of the Latin-American mining industry in 1948 (excluding petroleum) was about $800 to $850 million. The magnitude of the mining operation has been similar to that of Canada which has a population less than one-tenth that of Latin America. Of the production, Mexico accounted for about $270 million, Chile $250 million, Peru $60 million, Bolivia $70 million, Brazil $55 million. The area produced in 1948 about half of the world production of silver and antimony; one-fourth of its copper, tin, and natural graphite; one-fifth of its lead, cadmium, and white arsenic; one-third of the bismuth and vanadium; one-seventh of the zinc and tungsten; 5 to 10% of the gold, molybdenum, nitrogen, platinum, manganese, and fluorspar; about 2% of the iron ore; and less than 1% of the coal production. The proportion of the world's mineral output supplied by Latin America failed to expand signifi-cantly in the decade of the 1940's, despite the immense incen-tive and pressure for expansion of production during the war. It has been estimated that from 1937 to 1948 the output of nonferrous metals rose by 15%, output of the precious metals dropped by one-third, and the production of coal and iron ore expanded by more than 50% from an insignificant prewar level to a still insignificant level of 4.3 million tons of iron ore and 5.4 million tons of coal in 1948. Precious metals account for less than one-seventh of the total value of mineral production. Table 29 shows Latin American production of certain metals and minerals as a percentage of world pro-duction. It should be remembered that some of the commodi-ties not shown in the table, such as quartz crystals and mica, have strategic value out of proportion to the value of produc-tion.

It is estimated that less than 250,000 persons were em-ployed in the organized mining industries of the four countries accounting for more than 80% of Latin America's mining

TABLE 29
Relation of Latin American Production of Selected
Metals and Minerals to World Production

	1948	1938
Copper	24%	23%
Lead	19	11
Zinc	15	11
Antimony	48	58
Tin	25	18
Vanadium	30	38
Tungsten	13	12
Gold	5	7
Silver	48	43
Manganese	7	7
Iron Ore	2	1.3
Coal	0.3	0.3
Cadmium	19	16
Chromite	6	4
Molybdenum	4	2
Natural graphite	24	8
Mercury	7	6
Platinum	8	10
Bismuth	33	35
Nitrogen	8	8

Source: U. S. Bureau of Mines, *Minerals Yearbook*.

output in 1948 (Chile, Mexico, Peru, Bolivia). This is less than 2% of the gainfully employed. But the importance of the industry to these economies cannot be judged by employment figures. Mining accounted for more than half of the exports of these countries, ranging from 25% in the case of Peru to over 90% in Bolivia. For Latin America as a whole, mining exports were about 10% of total exports. It is estimated that the industry produced about 10% of the national incomes of the four countries. And it contributed heavily to government revenues, accounting directly for more than two-thirds of the receipts of the Bolivian government, for instance. It is not unreasonable to assume that for every person directly employed in organized mining activity another is thereby given employment in ancillary occupations—transportation, communications, services, commerce—so that the impact of international markets on the mining industry involves more than the proportion of gainfully employed would indicate. The heavy concentration on individual commodities—copper and nitrate in Chile, tin in Bolivia, for instance—increases the vulnerability. Elsewhere in Latin America, there are concentration points where mining has local importance: platinum in Colombia, precious metals in Nicaragua, chromite in Cuba, for example.

Mexico: A Declining Industry. Mexico has been one of the great mineral-producing areas of the world. Long before the Spaniards came, silver and gold were known and worked, mostly from placers or shallow pits where ore-bearing veins ran. Discoveries of mineral resources followed the conquest of New Galicia in the 1530's. A silver deposit near Compostela, discovered by an Indian in 1543, brought a wave of active prospecting throughout the region. In 1548 the San Bernade vein near Zacatecas was discovered, and by 1558 the discoveries in the neighborhood of Guanajuato had been made, including the "Veta Madre," which ranks with the Real del Monte and the Comstock Lode as the world's richest. The mines at Taxco, Sultepec and Temascaltepec were soon discovered. In 1551 the mineral region of Pachuca was discovered which, with the Real del Monte, has been called the greatest mining camp in the world. "Time after time, engineers have thought that the ore of this lode had been exhausted, but new deposits have always been found and today Real del Monte alone produces approximately one-sixth of all the silver mined in the world." In the Pachuca region too came the invention of the amalgamation process for extracting silver from the ore with the aid of mercury, the patio process, which revolutionized the mining industry, permitting profitable exploitation of ores of lower grade and not being superseded until invention of the cyanide process in the late nineteenth century. By the end of the sixteenth century most of the mineral regions of permanent significance in Mexico except in the far north had been revealed. Centuries of important mineral activity followed.[5]

---

[5] Based on Walter Howe, *The Mining Guild of New Spain and its Tribunal General*, 1770-1821 (Cambridge, Harvard University Press, 1949), pp. 4-9.

In 1948 Mexico was producing one-third of the world's production of silver, one-fifth of the cadmium, one-seventh of the lead and arsenic, one-quarter of the graphite, one-sixth of the antimony, one-tenth of the fluorspar, one-eighth of the bismuth. It was producing 3% of the copper and zinc, 6% of the mercury, and less important fractions of the world's gold, iron ore, coal, manganese, tungsten, tin, and a number of other minerals. The mining industry employed about 70,000 workers, perhaps 1% of the active labor force. The bulk of the mining and smelting activity was under foreign control, more than 90% of the foreign interest being U. S. participation. The Bank of Mexico in 1945 estimated that foreign investment in mining was $205 million, that it had apparently ceased to expand.

Important as mining continued to be, it was nevertheless suffering a downward trend, both absolutely and in relation to other activity in the economy. Metallic exports had been 67% of total exports in 1938 and dropped to 26% in 1946. While it recovered to 41% in 1947 this was partly because of higher world prices; there was no reason to believe that the trend had been reversed. The share of the national income derived from mining and metallurgy had been estimated as 13% in 1929, but it had dropped to 7% by 1946 and the industry appeared to be losing ground. The Mexican government's index of volume of metals production showed a drop of 20% from 1929 to 1947, and even at the peak response to wartime requirements was off 9% in 1942 from the 1929 level. Gold production had long been declining: a peak of 1.2 million ounces was produced in 1911, an average of 739,000 ounces annually in 1917-30, 367,000 ounces in 1948. The greater part of the gold produced was from ores in which it is found in association with other metals. Silver was being produced chiefly from base-metal ores; peak output of 106 million ounces annually had been reached in 1927-30, output sagged to 68 million ounces in 1933, improved wtih the beginning of the U. S. Treasury's silver purchase program in 1934, reached 76 million ounces in 1935 and 84 million ounces in 1937, was running 83 million ounces per year when the war broke out, and declined to 77 million ounces in 1944 and 58 million ounces in 1948. In 1929 about 96% of the silver produced in Mexico was from foreign-owned mines (three-fourths American), but agreements in 1938 and 1939 transferred control over several important properties to Mexican cooperatives or labor unions, and by 1940, 15 to 20% of current output was being produced from such mines, under leasing, royalty or profit-sharing arrangements with the former owners. In 1947 the Mexican government acquired the Real del Monte y Pachuca property from an American corporation.

In 1929 Mexico produced 80,560 tons of copper; it averaged 49,700 tons annually in the period 1925-40, managed expansion under wartime pressure to 51,400 tons in 1942, produced 63,500 tons in 1947, and assisted by good prices produced 59,000 tons in 1948. Lead production was 282,000 tons in 1938, 223,000 tons in 1947, and 187,000 tons in 1948. Zinc output reached a peak of 219,000 tons in 1944, dropped off thereafter. Production of antimony was 3,413 tons in 1929, 10,789 tons in 1937, 13,682 tons in 1943, and down to 6,790 tons in 1948. The growing demands of the steel industry have pushed iron ore production from 187,000 tons in 1944 to 229,000 tons in 1948; coal production passed the 1.2 million ton mark in 1947.

The temporary stimulus to production afforded by the high price levels of 1947-48 did not lessen the concern with the long-term tendencies in Mexican mining. The failure to attract a sustained flow of new capital for mining stemmed from a fundamental change in the climate of investment. It has been written that "perhaps never again will the mining and smelting industry find so fertile a field for development as Mexico offered in the late eighties and early nineties. . . . The Mexican product was mined with cheap labor . . . taxes were very low . . . nature had endowed her prodigally with mineral riches . . . the working in the old mines were accessible and could be easily examined . . . the many dumps containing thousands of tons of ores then considered unprofitable by the Mexicans were on the ground awaiting improved methods of treatment. . . . Furthermore, the President of Mexico looked with favor upon foreign capital and gave every official aid and encouragement to the mining companies that now began to take root." [6]

When the National Mining Congress met in 1948 to consider tendencies in the industry, the recitation of conditions was a complete reversal of the factors attracting investment in the 1880's and 1890's. "It is imperative," said Gustavo P. Serrano, "to take measures in view of the exhaustion of known reserves which will permit exploitation of low-grade ores now unprofitable." The system of taxation on production and exports was branded as contrary to rational and wasteless exploitation of the mining resources, forcing excessive depletion of high-grade reserves and impeding balanced development of the industry. The "existing labor contracts were executed under undue union pressure and contained clauses disruptive of discipline and efficiency." Transportation facilities were unsatisfactory and unreliable. And a "foreign-dominated industry sapping irreplaceable riches" (sic) had long since ceased to be able to count on aid and encouragement from the government. Tax relief was the chief issue—relief from the production tax law. The industry argued that assessment of a higher profits or net-income tax would as a replacement for the production tax have two beneficial effects: (a) It would become profitable for the industry to exploit large quantities of low-grade ore which were currently being taxed out of operation; and (b) Government revenues would eventually increase with the expansion in developmental activity, although there would admittedly be an interval between the reduction in yield from the production tax and the increase anticipated from increased mineral production when government revenue might suffer.

In terms of development policy it appeared that Mexico had had the misfortune of going from one extreme to the other. But if mining was to make its potential contribution to Mexican development, a middle ground adequate to attract foreign technology and foreign capital would have to be found.

---

[6] Isaac F. Marcosson, *Metal Magic: The Story of the American Smelting and Refining Company* (Farrar, Straus and Company, New York, 1949), pp. 189-190.

Chile: Mono-production. In 1948 Chile produced one-fifth of the world's copper, about 8% of its commercial nitrogen, 1.7 million tons of iron ore, 10,500 tons of manganese, 6,200 tons of lead, 4.9 million grams of gold, and 30,800 kilograms of silver, and minor quantities of other metals and minerals. About 2% of the gainfully employed were in the nitrate and copper industries, on which directly and indirectly perhaps one-twelfth of the population depended. Copper had produced about 8% of the national income in 1941 and nitrates about 4% ; and although manufacturing made great progress in the decade that followed, these two commodities, which accounted for three-fourths or more of Chilean exports, were still determining factors in the level of business activity. The economic history of Chile in the last century can be written around the record of the nitrate and copper industries and there are sufficient lessons in policy formulation in that record to warrant review at this point.

Chile's nitrate deposits are the sole source of natural sodium nitrate. Chilean nitrogen occurs as nitrate of soda mixed with other chemical compounds—only the nitrogen and iodine have been commercially recoverable. Commercial exploitation began early in the nineteenth century, the first exports occurred in 1830, substantial importance dates roughly from 1880. From 1880 to 1910 production multiplied tenfold. Although by-product ammonia from manufacture of coke and coal gas was another source of supply of nitrogen, in the decade 1900-10 Chile was still supplying two-thirds of the world's output of chemical nitrogen. Control of the deposits had originally been shared by Peru, Bolivia, and Chile, but as the economic value of the deposits grew, international friction was generated until finally a war gave Chile sole control of the nitrate fields.

The lack of competition in world markets stimulated the Chilean government to levy an export tax on all nitrate shipments, which represented over a fifty-year period 30 to 70% of the selling price at Chilean ports. During the half century the government drew the equivalent of one billion dollars in gold from this tax. From 1880 to 1930 revenue from the tax averaged 42.8% of the government's ordinary revenues; the peak came in 1894 when it amounted to 68% of public revenues. The apparent ease of shifting to the foreign consumer the cost of much of Chilean government activity made it possible for other potential sources of revenue to go untaxed, increased the dependence of the whole economy on nitrate, and promised eventual difficulties when nitrate markets sagged.

Neither technology nor capital requirements were barriers to new enterprises and the number of producers constantly increased. In 1901 there were 78 producers, in 1911 double that number. But as productive capacity of the refineries expanded more rapidly than world consumption, Chilean producers turned to industry agreements to restrict output. Between 1884 and 1914 there was a series of such arrangements to raise prices by restricting output, but they proved self-defeating and were regularly dissolved. Prices were raised, high-cost producers were kept in the industry, guaranty of an export quota brought an influx of new producers and encouraged old producers to expand their capacity, and as the number of units grew the difficulty of enforcing regulations became greater. The constantly increasing demand for nitrogenous fertilizers nevertheless kept the industry profitable, despite periodic market gluts and severe price declines. Meanwhile, however, serious structural weaknesses were being developed: there was little incentive to improve methods of production, inefficient techniques were perpetuated, waste was encouraged, and the industry became one characterized by obsolete and redundant facilities.

When the first world war broke out, Chile was producing 55% of the world's production of nitrogen. Demand rose and with it prices, but in the very prosperity the basis for decline was being created. Search for synthetic production processes had been under way before the war broke out, prompted partly by the Chilean price policy, by inefficiency of the technique, by the growing business appreciation of the potentialities of scientific research, and in large part by the German determination to be free of dependence on foreign sources for what was an indispensable war commodity. In 1913, progress had been made to the extent that 66,000 tons of synthetic nitrogen (7.7% of total supply) were produced, compared with 312,000 tons of by-product nitrogen, and 473,000 tons of Chilean. Cut off from Chilean sources by the Allied blockade and freely subsidized by the German government, the German industry achieved the necessary technique and scale of output and reached self-sufficiency. By 1918 synthetic nitrogen accounted for 23% of total production, Germany was self-sufficient, others of the industrialized countries were moving toward self-sufficiency, Germany was even ready to go into export markets once the war was over. By 1921-22, Chilean production of nitrogen was exceeded by production of other countries for the first time. Faced with the loss of its chief prewar market on the continent and with new competition in other markets, the Chilean industry failed to launch an aggressive competitive policy and instead clung to prewar tactics—the export tax, and controls by producers over output.

From 1920 to 1933 a veritable revolution took place in the nitrogen industry. The leading industrial countries rushed mass production of synthetic ammonia from the air; world capacity to produce nitrogen rose more than threefold from 1.6 million to nearly 5 million tons. While it is true that world consumption was also rising, more than doubling in the period, Chilean production dropped from 430,000 tons per year to 76,000 tons. Under the impact of more accessible, cheaper synthetic supplies and the widened appreciation of self-sufficiency as a necessity in case of war, the Chilean economy which had been very unbalanced was subjected to successive continuing shock. The average annual price of Chilean nitrate of soda, f.a.s. Chilean ports, had been $51.88 per ton in 1921-22, had dropped to $18.80 by 1933-34.

The Guggenheim interests since the early 1920's had been following nitrates closely and had developed at great cost a new process of ore treatment that they believed could be adapted to nitrates. This process permitted more efficiency of recovery, use of lower-grade ores, and use of more mechanical techniques to mine and handle ore, although it also involved larger investment per unit of capacity than did the old Shanks process. Two new plants were built, but it was too late to stem the advance of the industry elsewhere and their new capacity merely widened the gap between the world's capacity to produce and current consumption.

There followed successive efforts in Europe and within Chile to regulate competition. In 1931 the Chilean government effected a reorganization in which the industry formed a single gigantic corporation to control about 95% of the production facilities. The venture was one of genuinely high-finance proportions, involving the issue of securities of some $600 million. The venture collapsed, as exports, prices, and government revenues kept on declining. Production decreased 75% from 1929 to 1932; prices dropped 40%. The venture was dissolved in an atmosphere of grave charges concerning over-capitalization, acrimonious debate regarding motivation, and general uncertainty as to the future. It was succeeded by a new entity with control over production and sales, in which there was heavy government participation in organization and control and sizable participation in profits. Meanwhile with world production capacity more than double consumption in the peak year, European producers were pushing their schemes for international cartel organization, and the Chilean government encouraged the industry in the 1930's to enter into the international arrangements so as to secure a minimum position in world markets without carrying the competitive struggle to a bitter end.

At the outbreak of the second world war Chile was producing about 8.5% of world production. In 1948-49 its position was roughly the same. From 1938-39 to 1948-49 world production rose about 30%, although German facilities which had been seriously damaged by the war were slow to regain their former scale of operation and accounted for only 14% of world output in 1948-49 compared with 32% before the war. There was still great uncertainty as to the ultimate position of Chilean nitrate. It is true that there is a considerable measure of consumer preference for the natural product, that the newer modern plants in Chile had greater capacity to compete, and that world consumption of fertilizers was increasing tremendously. But with shipping charges roughly one-third of the landed costs in foreign markets, observers in the late 1940's had emphasized that the ability to compete effectively rested not only with improvement in cost structure at shipside in Chile, but also with reduction in transportation costs. On the favorable side, there was the increased alertness to take advantage of technological developments. In 1948 the industry reported that it had passed the experimental pilot plant stage with a new solar evaporation process and was proceeding to commercial-scale operations which promised ability to use residues not otherwise utilized, comparative economy in operation, and substantial extension of the life of available nitrate grounds.

The devastating experience with excessive dependence on nitrates which culminated in the disastrous episode of the 1930's has done much to develop "insurance consciousness" or "diversification regardless of economic cost" as an element in Chilean economic policy. In 1926-28 nitrates had still constituted half of Chilean exports, the value of production of nitrates was almost half that of agriculture, the industry furnished more than one-fifth of government ordinary revenue, and its contribution to the balance of payments was a major element behind the capacity to borrow abroad. The industry was concentrated in northern provinces without alternative fields of employment so that a decline in importance meant wholesale adjustments and movements of population and areas of economic activity. The decline in trade, government revenue and employment, and the intensification of political and social unrest, brought home a lesson to Chileans both in cyclical and in long-term effects of concentration on a single commodity.

While Chile's dominance of the world nitrogen markets was being lost to technological progress and European enterprise, the foundation for another concentration of activity was being laid by American enterprise and technological progress in the treatment of low-grade ores. Early in the twentieth century some 2,000 copper mines were being intermittently worked in Chile. Sensational developments came in the first decade of the century as low-grade copper ore bodies were acquired and methods of treating the ores were perfected. The Braden property was organized in 1904 and brought into large-scale production in 1912. The great Chuquicamata property was organized in 1912 and brought into production in 1915. The installations were laborious, difficult, and dangerous and required skill, experience, and capital which could not have been supplied locally. There was considerable local resentment as American control spread rapidly over the low-grade ore properties, but immense investment went on, partly out of war profits, to prove and equip ore bodies, build transportation facilities, set up whole communities.

By 1918 the Chuquicamata property was known to possess 700 million tons of 2.1% ore, the largest deposit in the world, and the Braden property was put at 250 million tons; the undeveloped Andes property had 100 million tons proven of 1.5% ore. A decade later 300 million tons of 4% ore had been added to the Chuquicamata estimate. In 1911 local activity on higher-grade ores had yielded Chilean exports of 40,000 tons. By 1916 the Chuquicamata and Braden mines were producing 42,000 tons and the other mines 37,000 tons. By 1918 total production was 127,000 tons, of which the American low-grade properties produced 90,000 tons. By 1926 U. S.-controlled properties produced 203,000 tons, the others 20,000 tons. Production grew to 353,000 tons in 1929, slumping to 180,000 tons in 1933. By the time the second world war broke out, copper was producing twice as large a share of the national income as nitrates, more than half of total Chilean exports, more than double the value of nitrate exports. There was dissatisfaction with excessive dependence on copper too, for it was an industry functioning for export markets, in a field where prices fluctuated rapidly and widely partly as a result of market manipulation by cartel members. Copper, for instance, was less than 11 cents a pound in 1914, rose to a wartime peak of 30 cents; was 18 cents in September, 1920, hit a low of five cents in the early 1930's, steadied at 10 to 12 cents in 1938-40. In 1948 the American-controlled mines produced 426,000 tons of copper, compared with less than 20,000 tons produced at the other smaller properties.

It has sometimes been argued that dominance by the American firms weakened Chile's ability to control its own position in world markets, made its economy, as the politician's phrase goes, "a pawn helpless in the hands of American manipulators at the international cartel table." On the other hand, others have pointed out that the bargaining position of the Chilean copper industry against other major areas such as European-controlled production in Africa and elsewhere had been enhanced by alliance with the powerful American interests. There was recognition in Chile, however, that the capital requirements of the industry exceeded the available resources of the country, and as late as 1948 the government entered into arrangements with the Anaconda interests for investment eventually of some $130 million for construction of a plant to treat sulphide ores at the Chuquicamata mine.[7] For purposes of comparison, it will be recalled that Ellsworth in 1945 estimated Chile's savings at not over $50 million per year. It was not at all certain, nevertheless, that Chile was prepared generally to recognize that the prescription for development in the case of mining was the relatively simple one of permitting foreign capital to risk money if domestic interests were unwilling to assume such risks, and to develop the necessary technological capacity to produce new assets for the economy.

Peru: Stagnation. A half century ago J. P. Morgan, Phoebe Hearst, D. O. Mills, and James Ben Ali Haggin, with some other enterprising Americans, risked $10 million to find out what could be done to work the deep sulphide ores in the strata around Oroya, 12,000 feet above sea level, and a place

---

[7] The ore at Chuquicamata, greatest known copper deposit in the world, occurs in three general subdivisions, namely, oxide, sulphide, and a mixture of both. From the beginning of operations to date, the recovery of copper had been exclusively from oxide ore and oxide content of mixed ore by leaching. While substantial tonnages of oxide ore remain in the mine, to provide for future operation it was necessary to build facilities to process extraction of copper from sulphide ores and sulphide content of mixed ores. Initial investment of $70 million involved a concentrator, a smelter, a converting plant, 12 miles of railroad lines, a 45 mile water-supply line capable of delivering 40,000 tons of water per day, additional employee housing, and other facilities.

called Cerro de Pasco, 82 miles from Oroya and still higher.
The decision proved a good one. In 1948 the enterprise, Cerro
de Pasco Copper Company, was employing 14,000 persons,
had annual sales of $29 million (compared with total Peru-
vian mineral production valued at $60 million).[8] Its invest-
ment, which was estimated to exceed $52 million after de-
preciation and obsolescence, was sprawled over more than a
million acres from which it fed its workers and worked its
many ventures. It is said that $25 million was risked before
a pound of copper passed through the Oroya smelter, but by
the end of the 1940's the enterprise had yielded up more than
a half billion dollars in wages, taxes, royalties and other
local expenditures. The Cerro de Pasco mine was still the
leading copper producer, but its yield of copper had gradually
become less as long intensive mining left only ores of lower
grade. But while it was producing copper ores almost exclusively, the company had been exploring and developing
lead-zinc ores and there were now said to be 10 million tons
of ore assaying 17% zinc and 6% lead, largely in the form
of marmitite. After seven years the costly Yauricocha railway and aerial tramways system had been completed and
new production was coming in at Yauricocha. The company
in 1948 produced 16.8 million pounds of copper, 29.8 million
pounds of lead, 57,932 tons of zinc concentrates, and 3.2
million ounces of silver; its purchases from custom shippers
and leased-mine output amounted to 11.4 million pounds of
copper, 46.8 million pounds of lead, 2.6 million ounces of silver,
and 1,481 tons of zinc.[9]   At Minasragra another American
group had found the largest known deposit of vanadium ore.
After thirty years Peruvian production was still about one-
third of the world output. Other foreign groups had also
been active in Peruvian development. In 1948 the country
was producing 4% of the world's production of zinc and lead,
6% of its silver, 4% of its antimony, 18% of its bismuth, and
30% of its vanadium.

---

[8] It might be noted that sales within Peru totaled $3.3 million, of
which $2.1 million consisted of silver.

[9] Data on a number of other commodities are not available.

But mining was not an advancing sector of the economy. As Table 30 shows, the peak of silver production had been reached in 1927, copper in 1929, lead in 1938. Wartime demand and good prices, despite a common shortage of labor in the mining districts, had lifted production in other minerals for a time. But despite the abundance of minerals, new investment lagged. Typically, Peruvian capitalists with few exceptions had always been unwilling to put their money into mining ventures, and in fact would have had difficulty meeting the large financial requirements of modern mineral development even had they been less timid. And North American capitalists who had financed most of the important mining ventures in the country were by the 1940's increasingly hesitant about getting in deeper, in view of the tendency of the government to tax mining enterprises directly and indirectly without due consideration for the financial risks involved, the troublesome controls over trade and exchange which militated against free use or withdrawal of capital once inside the country, and the unstable political-economic situation in which the large foreign company was an easy target for the politician. Mineral products excluding petroleum had accounted for 31% of exports in 1938, 28% in 1941, and 25% in 1948 (when prices were good). If they were to provide a foreign-exchange basis for developmental activity,

TABLE 30

Peruvian Mineral Production in 1948 Compared with Peak-Year
Production

Commodity	Unit	All-time Peak Year	All-time Peak Volume	1948 Production
Silver	kilos	1927	871,737	288,911
Gold	kilos	1941	8,870	3,458
Copper	metric tons	1929	54,366	18,069
Lead	metric tons	1938	58,044	48,538
Zinc	metric tons	1945	61,154	58,842
Bismuth	metric tons	1943	483	253
Tungsten	metric tons	1943	669	212
Vanadium	metric tons	1943	1,573	913
Antimony	metric tons	1945	2,301	1,636

it was clear that policy relating to the stimulation of investment would have to be revised.

Bolivia: Existence by Sufferance. One of the most discouraging economic situations in South America is the mineral-dominated economy of Bolivia. More than nine-tenths of total exports, the purchasing power for food and other essentials that must be imported, the stability of the currency, more than half of the government revenues, the external credit of the nation, all hang precariously on activity in the mineral industry. Within the mineral industry, tin dominates, accounting for 70% of total Bolivian exports; much of the other mineral activity depends on transport and other facilities supported by the tin industry.

Unfortunately, Bolivia is a high-cost tin producer. Its position in world markets has depended largely on the willingness of other producing areas to allow it a minimum position in cartel arrangements during the 1930's and on the ability to market regardless of price during World War II and in the immediate postwar period. Inland transportation is long and costly, with mines located at heights of 12,000 to 17,000 feet above sea level, and topography and distance unfavorable for economic transportation. Excavating in lode mines demands large capital investment. The ores are low grade, reserves are of lower grade; the rich ores were gradually exhausted during the 1930's and no new deposits of higher grade ore were discovered in large enough quantities to reverse the trend. The labor supply suffers from malnutrition and poor living conditions, tends to be unreliable and increasingly dissatisfied. Productivity per worker does not come up to that of other producing areas.

The tin industry consists of one major group, the Patiño interests, which accounts for about half of the output. It is of local origin, having been the source of one of the world's great fortunes, but the Patiño activities have long since acquired international character, for the tin industry generally is characterized by a high degree of financial integration which ignores national boundaries. A second group, the Hochschild interests, controls about one fifth of the tin activity, and the Aramayo interests about 5 to 8%. It is true that not all the mines are such high-cost operators that they could not compete in world markets. But it is generally believed that the bulk of the industry could not survive free competition in world tin markets. Bolivia's share of world production was 23.7% in 1922-24, 16.6% in 1933-36, 14.7% in 1937-40. In 1948 it was producing about one-fourth of the world's production, but as other producing areas recovered from their wartime difficulties, the prospect of surviving only by sufferance of an international cartel arrangement returned.[10]

Certain political and strategic factors exist, however, which offset to some extent the strictly economic appraisal of the industry. Bolivian tin is the only major supply in the hemisphere. Accordingly the United States has a special interest in assuring a stand-by reserve capacity in case of war. Along the same principle it has the tin smelter set up in the United States during the second world war whose maintenance is justified partly by its potential military value; and stockpiling arrangements similarly take cognizance of the limited availability of tin in the hemisphere. Furthermore, if Bolivia were left to its own resources to effect the reorganization of her economy that would be necessary if tin were left completely at the mercy of competitive conditions, the adjustment would be so serious that the United States would probably find it necessary to offer substantial economic and financial assistance as part of its good-neighbor policy. Thus the decisions on tin involve decisions on alternative policies relating to Bolivia which make the outlook somewhat less depressing although by no means happy.

In 1948 Bolivia produced, in addition to one-fourth of the world's tin, about one-fourth of its antimony, one-twelfth of its tungsten, and lesser quantities of bismuth, gold and

---

[10] On the operation of tin control in Bolivia, see Burton C. Hallowell, "Administration of Tin Control in Bolivia, 1931-39," *Inter-American Economic Affairs*, Autumn, 1949, pp. 3-24, and "Tin Control and Bolivia's Foreign Exchange Position, 1930-39," *Inter-American Economic Affairs*, Winter, 1949, pp. 61-84.

silver, lead, copper. Despite the incentives of the war period, production did not expand significantly. While the mineral resources of the country have not been fully explored, experienced mining men are not inclined to optimism regarding potential expansion. And here, as everywhere in Latin America, the inclination to blame the "excessive" portion of the national wealth that goes to owners of the mines overseas (although they are not all of foreign origin) for the nation's poverty has made the mining industry a football for the politician and as such of decreasing attractiveness to new capital investment. Despite the already unsatisfactory position of the mining industry competitively, the incredibly low standard of living of the workers evokes a continuing demand for larger returns to labor; the unavailability of alternative tax sources balks any revision of the tax structure that might temporarily reduce revenues from the industry in anticipation of eventual expansion of revenues and in fact is responsible for steady pressure for additional revenue from mining; the inability to mobilize sufficient foreign exchange for any substantial program of development prompts continued pressure for reducing the share of exchange that goes abroad for profits and external expenses and discourages further investment that might improve the technological position of the industry. The industry has been deeply involved in politics, not always to the benefit of efficiency in government or the long-range interests of the economy.

Brazil: Relative Inactivity. Brazil in 1950 presented a case of relatively unimportant mining development and continued resistance to acceptance of conditions that might make for acceleration in the exploitation of its mineral resources. In 1948-49 mineral production was estimated at $50 to $60 million. Coal accounted for more than one-fourth of that total. Quartz crystals, on which the war had focused attention as a critically needed material with Brazil a major source, had in recent years been accounting for the second highest value, with gold and diamonds next in importance. Manganese ore and mica provided about 4% each of the total value of production. Nonferrous metal production was negligible.

Although production of a number of commodities of high strategic importance had been expanded during the war, the dollar value of output was small and tended to fall off when the war ended. For instance, the peak year of exports of titanium, beryllium, zirconium, and tantalite reached less than $2 million. The peak year for exports of all mineral products was 1943 when a total of $41 million was exported. Half or more of Brazilian mineral production has been consumed locally.

From the standpoint of immediate development policy, the iron ore and manganese reserves have constituted the challenge and the problem. The strategic significance of imported supplies of manganese for the United States prompted great interest in the late 1940's in the expansion of Brazilian production, and the deteriorating position of the United States in high-grade iron ore turned attention to Brazil's resources as well as to other areas. But the reluctance of the Brazilian government to permit foreign companies to exercise dominant control over mining activity served to impede assumption of the enormous risks and investment of the great sums required for economic exploitation. There was an abundance of manganese ore, although the principal producing deposit at Morro da Mina (controlled by a subsidiary of an American firm) mined since 1904 had probably passed its peak. In most cases successful exploitation even after discovery depended on great investments in transportation and port facilities as well as in the principal mining activity. In Amapá Territory, 180 miles north of the Amazon, a large body of manganese ore was under investigation and consideration in the late 1940's but transportation to the Amazon and construction of port facilities imposed difficult and costly conditions for development. The Urucum deposit near Corumbá in Mato Grosso reportedly had reserves of 35 million tons from which there had been mined 45,000 tons. But Corumbá was on the Paraguay River, 2,000 miles above Buenos Aires; the ore was hauled 20 miles by truck to the Paraguay, dumped for loading on barges for shipment to Buenos Aires; the river was navigable to Corumbá six months of the year for vessels drawing seven feet and eight months for vessels drawing 4.5 feet; the alternative route involved a rail trip of 1,200 miles to Santos. Each discovery of manganese, and there were many known deposits already, pointed up the inadequacy of transportation facilities and the large investment that economic exploitation involved. Similar circumstances marked the iron-ore field. Probably nowhere in the world was there more high-grade iron ore. Yet, 2 million tons seemed a high target for production in 1948.

When the Rio Doce project was launched in 1942, out of a desire to expedite iron-ore movement, engineers were confronted with the task of mechanizing the mining operation at the Cauê iron mountain, including crushing, screening, and conveying to railway cars; the railway had to be improved to handle a target figure of 1.5 million tons annually; and ore-storing and loading facilities at Vitória had to be enlarged. The work was costly, difficult, and became quickly entangled in local inefficiency which impeded the financial cooperation that had been extended by the Export-Import Bank. The Rio Doce properties were not the only iron-ore deposits in Brazil, but Cauê alone was estimated to contain a half billion tons and the other two deposits of the Rio Doce enterprise—Conceição and Dois Córregos—were also sizable. Yet in 1947-48 they had had difficulty reaching the 300,000 tons per year mark out of Vitória and strained past the 500,000 tons mark in 1949. Recent investigations have suggested that an economic operation should contemplate movement of at least 5,000,000 tons per year and required construction of a deep-water port with adequate ore-loading and coal-unloading facilities as well as a new double-track standard-gauge railway from port to mines. Investment would exceed $100 million and in the developing picture of competing sources of iron ore it was not at all certain that the competitive position of the industry would be satisfactory.

The Abbink Mission pointed out that most Brazilian mineral deposits were handicapped by their distance from seaboard and by topography that dictated high-cost transportation. Reviewing the vision then current in Brazil of an export industry providing 40 million tons of high-grade ore for movement annually, it warned that even if a market could be found, the amortization and service on the huge investment required might easily raise the loaded cost of ore to a point that would cause the buyers to lose interest. It was clear that the local iron and steel industry was not going to reach proportions to tap effectively the huge reserves of the country. It was clear that local capital would not be attracted in the volume required; and the custom of granting concessions for development of mineral deposits to individuals or groups with little capital at their command was merely discouraging genuine large-scale activity. Yet the government hesitated, in the prevailing reluctance to "divorce itself from the national patrimony," to offer the degree of control and conditions of investment that alone would warrant the flow of private capital from abroad.

Capital for the Mining Industry. In 1950 more than a half billion dollars of foreign capital was invested in the Latin-American mining industry. This capital was predominantly American, and concentrated for the most part in the activity of a few very large corporations. Domestic investment was of much smaller proportions, usually limited to small-scale operations, and in many cases demanded and received special consideration from the government in the form of financing through specially created mining banks, preferential treatment in the sale of exchange created by exports from such mines, and government purchase arrangements for the disposal of their production.

Bain and Read in their authoritative review of *Ores and Industry in South America* estimated in 1934 that the commodities produced in properties under American control included "all of the asphalt and bauxite, a considerable part of the coal, about 90 per cent of the copper, one-third of the gold, practically all of the iron ore, more than one-third of the lead, one-half of the manganese, over one-half of the petroleum, approximately one-half of the platinum, 70 per cent of the silver, only one-tenth of the tin, all of the tungsten and vanadium, and two-thirds of the zinc." The most significant holdings were in petroleum and copper. They went on to say that British activity had been comparatively modest, "confined to about 8 per cent of the copper, 42 per cent of the gold, 5 per cent of the petroleum, one-half of the sulphur, and 7 per cent of the tin; obviously, from a world viewpoint, these tonnages are of little importance, but the petroleum production of a British-Dutch group, 33 per cent of the total for South America, is of considerable consequence." With respect to French activity, "French companies supplied small percentages of the copper, gold and tin." And they noted that the enormous risks, the great investments, and the importance of technological background, had served to discourage domestic investment: "the minerals produced by local capital . . . are most of the antimony, until recently all of the bismuth, most of the coal, a small share of the copper, about 15 per cent of the gold, two-thirds of the lead, one-half of the manganese, much of the nitrate, 5 per cent of the petroleum, about 30 per cent of the silver, one-half of the sulphur, two-thirds of the tin, and one-third of the zinc." [11] The significant concentrations of local enterprise consisted of the tin and nitrate interests; and it should be noted that local participation in tin was so largely involved in the financial integration of the industry generally the world over as to alter considerably its character as a locally owned field.

What is especially important is that mining in Latin America has in the past two decades failed to attract any expanding flow of capital from abroad. Rippy has estimated that paid-up capital of British enterprises in Latin-American mining in 1897 was under £5 million; in the 1880's some £20 million was pumped into the industry, partly motivated by the quest for copper, which was stimulated by the new electrical industries and more importantly by eagerness for precious metals. The volume of British investment may have been about £23 million in 1890, of which £8.5 million was in Mexico, £5.3 million in Venezuela, £2.9 million in Colombia, £1.1 million in Chile, £0.8 million in Brazil. The boom of

---

[11] H. Foster Bain and Thomas Thornton Read, *Ores and Industry in South America* (Council on Foreign Relations, Harper & Brothers, New York, 1934), pp. 346-347. Note that the data refer to *South* America, not to *Latin* America.

the 1880's was followed by a shakeout in the 1890's. With the resumption of investment on a larger scale thereafter, British mining capital may have reached £25.6 million by 1911, again dominated by the investment in Mexico which was a nominal £12 million, with £3 million in Brazil, £2.3 million in Colombia, £2.0 million in Chile. Since then there has been a steady decline in British interest, which was reversed only briefly in the 1920's. The figure for 1929 is put at £22.4 million. By 1945 Rippy estimated the nominal British mining interest to have sunk to scarcely more than £10 million, of which £2.75 million was in Mexico, £1.1 million in Chile, £1.1 million in Bolivia, £1.4 million in Venezuela.[12]

French investments in Latin-American mining probably began in Mexico and Chile around the middle of the nineteenth century. After 1870 these investments expanded rapidly. In 1902, according to Rippy, French capital in mining may have been as much as 120 million francs, including 50 million in Mexico, 20 million in Venezuela, 18 million in Chile, 8 million in Bolivia, 5 million in Colombia. French capital in mining continued to expand in the next decade and an estimate of 750 million francs for 1913 has been used. Rippy comments that "dividends paid by a few of the French mining and miscellaneous companies were enormous. . . . Such immense profits siphoned away by foreign capitalists tended to produce economic nationalists in Latin America; but for the French, big profits seem to have been very exceptional. . . . It is more than likely that the losses of many little Frenchmen far outweighed the gains of the fortunate few in Latin America." The mining investment in the 1940's has not been reliably estimated, but the suggestion has been made that French investments of all kinds in Latin America were in 1947 one-eighth the value reached in 1913, totaling perhaps $200 million and since mining was one of the less

---

[12] See J. Fred Rippy, "The British Investment 'Boom' of the 1880's in Latin America Mines," *Inter-American Economic Affairs*, March, 1948, pp. 71-78, and J. Fred Rippy, "The Peak of British Investment in Latin American Mines," *Inter-American Economic Affairs*, Summer, 1948, pp. 41-48.

important categories of investment, the total in this industry had obviously reached rather insignificant proportions.[13]

The United States Department of Commerce has estimated that in 1929 the American investment in mining and smelting in Latin America was $732 million; in 1936 the investment was $708 million, in 1940, $512 million. The heavy reduction is accounted for by capital distributions, writedowns, and exchange depreciations, which from 1936 to 1940 caused a decline in mineral investment amounting to $105 million in Chile, $45 million in Mexico and $27 million in Peru. Table 31 shows the more important concentrations of mineral investment in 1940.

TABLE 31

American Investments in Mining and Smelting in Latin America, 1940

(millions of dollars)

	Number	Value
Chile	8	$276.8
Mexico	36	168.3
Peru	4	20.2
Cuba	7	6.6
Others	27	40.5
	82	$512.4
Division by classification:		
Precious metals	28	$ 45.0
Non-metallic	9	121.1
Other metals	45	346.3
	82	$512.4

Source: U. S. Department of Commerce, *American Direct Investments in Foreign Countries*—1940 (Washington, 1942), pp. 13, 21.

As of May 31, 1943, the United States Treasury estimated the value of American controlling interests in mining and smelting enterprises in Latin America at $404.8 million.

---

[13] See J. Fred Rippy, "French Investments in Latin America," *Inter-American Economic Affairs*, Autumn, 1948, pp. 52-71, and J. Fred Rippy, "French Investments in Mexico," *Inter-American Economic Affairs*, Winter, 1948, pp. 3-16.

This included $107.7 million in Mexico, $215.3 million in Chile, $29.1 million in Peru, $10.4 million in Bolivia, $12.2 million in Argentina, $2.5 million in Brazil, $6.4 million in Cuba, $3.1 million in Ecuador. The U. S. Commerce Department reported that in 1945 direct investments in mining and smelting were $412 million. Although there was a slight increase— $22 million — from 1945 to 1948 to bring the total value to $434 million, the conspicuous characteristic of this field continued to be its inability to attract significant additions of capital under the prevailing climate of investment.[14] Meanwhile, income received from the mining and smelting investments had averaged $53 million annually from 1940 to 1943 and $36 million annually from 1944 to 1946.[15]

Iron Ore: A Case Study. At this point let us consider a specific case. In recent years it has become increasingly apparent to the steel industry of the United States that its present high-grade iron ore reserves would have to be supplemented with ores from new sources in order to maintain an adequate supply of ore for the next half century at least. Since the early 1900's over 80% of the nation's iron ore supply has come from the Lake Superior district; most of the ores are shipped in their natural state, supplemented by concentrates from simple beneficiating processes. The second world war chopped 340 million tons of the highest quality reserves out of the pits, and at its end, it seemed likely that

---

[14] Data on American investments are taken from the following sources: U. S. Department of Commerce, *American Direct Investments in Foreign Countries—1940* (Washington, 1942); U. S. Treasury Department, *Census of American-Owned Assets in Foreign Countries* (Washington, 1947); Milton Abelson, "Private United States Direct Investments Abroad," *Survey of Current Business*, November, 1949; Milton Abelson, "Movement of Private U. S. Capital to Foreign Countries in 1947," *Foreign Commerce Weekly*, August 21, 1948; Frederick Cutler, "Yield on U. S. Direct Investments Abroad Reached Peak in 1946," *Foreign Commerce Weekly*, October 18, 1947.

[15] Income in 1945 reached a low of $29 million, due primarily to a prolonged strike in the Chilean copper industry. The relative stability of the sale price of copper to U. S. government agencies during the war while production costs were rising brought an overall decline in income from the industry during the war years.

no more wars would ever be fought off Lake Superior's natural ores, and that not too many years of peacetime supply would be forthcoming from those fabulous reserves.

The industry attacked the problem on two fronts: (a) beneficiation of low-grade taconite ores which are abundantly available in the United States and for which techniques must be devised since the country cannot drift into complete dependence on foreign ore; and (b) examination of ore deposits in many foreign countries to ascertain whether or not such ores can be used economically at the present consuming plants. Iron ore is not a scarce mineral, but much of the world's ore is located so that it would be uneconomic to use it in the United States. The individual companies began costly investigations of foreign sources, using the most advanced technical methods.

Some iron ore had already been entering the country from Latin America. One company, Bethlehem Steel, especially had been interested in imports to feed its Sparrows Point (Maryland) plant. It imported more than 2.5 million tons from its Chilean proporties in 1948. In 1949 it began expanding its El Romeral iron mine to increase supplies both for the new steel mill in Chile and for foreign use; its reserves were estimated at around 20 million tons of 60% iron. It had also been operating in Cuba, bringing in small quantities of lateritic iron containing nickel and chromium. But in general Cuban laterites were not competitive with other ores; an economic method of extracting the nickel and chromium was required before the large deposits of lateritic iron could assume economic importance; and persistent surveys by a number of companies had failed to uncover any high-grade iron deposits in Cuba of sufficient size to warrant interest as a dependable source of supply.[16] Bethlehem also held the best deposit of iron ore on the west coast of Mexico at Las Truchas, but exploitation waited on use for a hot-metal operation along the west coast

---

[16] During the second world war a U. S. Government-financed corporation used the laterites to get nickel. For a few years some 3600 tons of ore carrying 30% iron was used daily. The operation was discontinued after the war.

of the United States. Eastern Venezuela had been explored in the late 1920's and certain deposits of high-grade ore had been found, then believed to approximate 50 to 75 million tons. During the 1940's Bethlehem spent more than $50 million to bring this deposit into active use, aiming at 2.5 million tons of imports annually. The magnitude of an operation of this kind may be judged from the fact that it required building a 34-mile highway, a 36-mile standard-gauge railway, all the facilities at the pit, storage bases, port installations, conveyor systems, and even design of a special fleet of ocean carriers to bring the ore into the United States.

Another company, United States Steel Corporation, had filing cases loaded with reports on known deposits, some dating to 1908, but the urgency of finding an economic source of large supplies of high-grade ore prompted the corporation to vote several millions of dollars for new surveys, and by early 1946 field forces were tracking down every reported showing of ore and every possible prospect in Brazil, Venezuela, Honduras, Guatemala, Nicaragua, Puerto Rico, Cuba, Mexico, Sweden, Canada, and a number of other countries. Ore bodies were drilled and explored in the Agalteca deposit in Honduras; at Mayagues and Jancos in Puerto Rico; on the east coast of Mexico and over 40 deposits on the west coast; the Wabana mines in Newfoundland; Little Whitefish Lake in Quebec; Texado Island, Iron Hill, and Zaballos in British Columbia; the Marampa and Tonkolili deposits in Sierra Leone, West Africa; holdings in Morocco; the Djebel Djerissa holdings in Tunisia; the Ouenza ores in Algeria; the Conakry ores in French Guiana; several possibilities in Alaska. The company had surveyed Brazilian resources periodically since 1930 but it now renewed its investigations, coming onto some excellent manganese reserves in the course of the examination. Late in 1945 air observers began to work over the Orinoco River iron ore district in Venezuela; within a year some holdings around the Bethlehem Steel concession had been subjected to magnetic survey without satisfactory results. In general, work in Venezuela had been east of the Caroni River which the Venezuelan government considered the only possible iron ore area and which it had listed as a Federal Reserve Zone on which even with the restrictions only 40-year concessions were possible. West of the Caroni was a vast unexplored land. Late in 1946 the company was persuaded to spend several hundred thousands of dollars more in a gamble west of the Caroni. Let the responsible Vice-President of United States Steel describe what happened next:

> From a study of the general topography of this part of Venezuela, our geologists knew that this area had been subjected to violent upheavals in the geological ages; they also knew that the possibilities were favorable for finding iron ore in the hills and mountains formed by these upheavals. Our company, after formal approval of the Venezuelan government, made an aerial survey and photographed 10,500 square miles of this territory. Objectives, pinpointed on these photographs, after a study of the terrain, were examined by exploration parties traveling in planes, jeeps and on foot. Magnotometer surveys showed strong magnetic indications in the areas of iron ore occurrences discovered by these parties. Diamond drills were hurried into the country to see if the magnetic indications were caused by a large deposit of high grade iron ore or by a low grade highly magnetic formation. Exploration tunnels were driven into the side of the Cerro Bolívar mountain. From information derived from drilled samples and samples obtained from the tunnels, we knew that we had found a large quantity of iron ore. Our problem . . . is one of financing the development of the property itself and determining the best methods to be used in bringing the ore from the interior to the ocean shipping points.[17]

A mountain of iron ore of almost unbelievable purity, with probable reserves greatly exceeding one billion tons, had rewarded one of the most costly and far-flung of all ore searches. Cerro Bolívar! Cerro Bolívar seemed in 1950 to have become a significant influence in the American steel industry and thus in the entire American economy. It was estimated to contain far more tonnage than the famous Hull-Rust pit in Minnesota had ever produced or would produce. And there were doubtless other deposits in the area.

---

[17] Statement by John G. Munson before the Congressional Joint Committee on the Economic Report, January 24, 1950.

Yet, from a development standpoint the expenditures were only beginning. Surveys were next undertaken to determine the best method of transporting the ore. The choices included a $114 million investment in a 274-mile railway running from Cerro Bolívar to a tidewater terminal on the north coast, including a 4.5 mile bridge (including approaches) across the Orinoco River; and a $51 million investment in 91 miles of railway from Cerro Bolívar to a river terminal at the confluence of the Orinoco and Caroni Rivers, with the Orinoco dredged to permit bringing up the ocean ore carriers to load at this terminal. Dredging the 45,254,000 cubic yards of bottom would cost $18 million, and maintenance would be $1.1 million annually. And ocean carriers possibly of battleship size would have to be designed and built, a $50 million fleet of them, to pick up the ore for transport to the United States. Meanwhile, as the industry contemplated the task of raising hundreds of millions of dollars, it had constantly to keep in mind the cost structure, for any untoward action in the producing country which upset the delicate cost structure might jeopardize not only the investment but also the extent to which this particular source of ore was to be used. For the same company was also planning to exploit a great deposit uncovered in Labrador—the famous Hollinger-Hanna concession — and work on the low-grade ores was certainly going to produce an effective supply. In 1950 it was estimated that the Venezuelan ore might show an equivalent unit cost with that of Lake Superior taconite nodules and Labrador ore and be somewhat more costly than Lake Superior natural ores.[18]

---

[18] This section on the Cerro Bolívar discovery is based on T. W. Lippert, "Cerro Bolívar; Saga of an Iron Ore Crisis Averted," *Journal of Metals and Engineering*, February, 1950. Lippert used a variety of estimates to reach a price comparison for Lake Erie ports per unit Fe as follows: 14.5 cents Labrador ores, 14.5 cents Venezuelan ore, 14.5 cents Lake Superior taconite nodules, 14.0 cents Lake Superior natural ores. He hazarded an estimate that in the late 1960's United States Steel might be drawing 15 million tons of ore from Venezuela and 10 million tons from beneficiated taconite, while the companies other than United States Steel and Bethlehem might be drawing 10 million tons from Labrador, 17 million taconite, 4 million Venezuela.

Just as the structure of the American industry was certain to be stirred by availability in the late 1950's of 10 to 15 million tons of the richest type of ore from Venezuela annually, the pace of development in Venezuela would be affected in many ways: additions of vast purchasing power overseas; large accretions to the Treasury; additional employment for local labor in an industry that paid better wages, furnished better living conditions, and usually complied more strictly with social legislation than domestically owned extractive industries; additional managerial competence which was sufficiently mobile to help grade up the local working and managerial force; new outlets for local agriculture and industry; ancillary activity in transportation and communication that would benefit the whole country.

Development Policy and the Mining Industry. It has been pointed out that "from Roman times down to the present, rulers and statesmen have struggled with the problem of trying to retain for the State as large a proportion of the yield of natural resources as possible without restricting their production." [19]   In the mid-twentieth century, the Latin-American nations were torn more than ever by the desire to avoid any draining away of their mineral resources through foreign ownership.   Every known showing of ore, every geological discovery, was hailed hopefully as a key to accelerated development of a nation; yet every suggestion of foreign exploitation of mineral resources evoked a hostile reception. Every sign of decline in established mining industries brought a demand for renewed attention to the industry; every suggestion that incentive be given to risk-taking essential to expansion in this industry seemed to meet a cold reception. There were exceptions among the twenty Latin-American republics, of course, but in general the wide gap between geological reality and economic reality was not appreciated and the myth of fabulous resources that could spring to life and bring wealth to all died as hard as that of El Dorado had for so many of the ancestors of the present population.

---

[19] Bain and Read, *op. cit.*, p. 37.

Yet the lines of policy formulation—the alternatives open to the policy-maker—were clear. If the Latin-American economies had been authoritatively administered and planned, it might conceivably have been possible for the policy-maker to focus the national savings on mining development at the expense of other lines of development. But it may properly be questioned whether any policy-maker would have been inclined to do so, having in mind the unusual risks attaching to development work in this field as compared with other areas of activity that involved greater assurance of accomplishment. Since the planning and administration of the economies had in fact not reached such a point, the directions in which the national savings were used still rested largely on the decisions of individuals and corporations. In view of the demonstrated character of investment which received preference in the use of domestic capital, it was safe to say that domestic capital would not be attracted to the enormous risks, the large capital concentrations, and the long-range character of investment involved in mining. This appeared to leave these alternatives: permit exploitation of resources by outside capital, or keep the resources unutilized until such time as domestic capital would become available for their prospecting and development. Unfortunately, this is not a full statement of the alternatives, since it assumes that the mineral resources must eventually be utilized effectively. There is actually no assurance that resources left to wait on a quarter-century or half-century of capital formation will be utilized. Technological progress constantly changes the availability of substitute, possibly lower-grade, natural resources that may currently not be competitive, and also threatens to make available synthetic materials. Whether the great nitrate resources would have been mobilized if capital had not been forthcoming in their early period of development is a case in point. Further, the existence of alternative deposits, whether in Africa or in some country in Latin America which may more astutely see the advantage of immediate development of its resources than other countries, may defer indefinitely the time when a country's conserved assets may find an overseas outlet. For example, it is possible that the Venezuelan iron ore development may point up an error on the part of Brazil in not stimulating the earlier development of its vast iron ore resources by providing suitable conditions of investment. Finally, the degree of financial and industrial integration in the major consuming areas may reduce the assurance that a country can feel in its ability to dispose of its production of minerals when it has come into the necessary domestic capital funds to develop them on its own. Thus the alternative of utilizing resources wisely now or *not ever* utilizing them effectively may be a better statement of many of the situations than the glib assumption that "we will develop our resources later rather than now, and when we do, we will get the whole benefit for ourselves without cutting in those foreign interests."

Even if eventual development were assured, the developmental policy decision involves the extent to which the present population should be sacrificed for the benefit of succeeding generations. It is commonly realized that by lowering the current standards of consumption of the population it might be possible to divert a larger share of the national production into development activity; but it has commonly been agreed in Latin America that standards of living are already so low that a further purposeful lowering of the level for the mass of the population is hardly feasible. In a sense the decision on mining involves the question of whether development should be promoted now by gaining only 90%, perhaps, of the yield from mineral development, or waiting in the hope of one day being able to retain a larger proportion of the yield within the country. We have seen that much of the development activity in power and transportation and industrialization and mechanization of agriculture requires foreign exchange for overseas purchases. Since mining is likely to be dedicated to export, for some time, the ability to support such developmental requirements of other industries is substantially affected by the degree to which mining is encouraged to expand. And since productivity is greater in mining than in many of the locally owned extractive industries, improvement in conditions of living can be achieved immediately, regardless of whether or not the full yield of the industry is being retained within the country. There is no doubt that in the past the cost of introducing foreign capital into the mining industry in some countries may have appeared exorbitant, that some countries may even have been "bled," as the politician puts it. *But if the interest in development is genuine, the policy-maker must weigh the means of attracting capital and technological competence to the mining industry in order that it may contribute effectively to development, and in so doing he is likely to find that it is possible to safeguard national interests without checking the flow of capital.*

SUPPLEMENTARY READING

U. S. Bureau of Mines, *Minerals Yearbook 1948*, "The Mineral Industry of Middle and South America."

George W. Stocking and Myron W. Watkins, *Cartels in Action* (The Twentieth Century Fund, New York, 1946), pp. 118-170.

Issac F. Marcosson, *Metal Magic* (Farrar, Straus and Company, New York, 1949), 183-228.

Burton C. Hallowell, "Administration of Tin Control in Bolivia 1931-39," *Inter-American Economic Affairs*, Autumn, 1949, pp. 3-24.

H. Foster Bain and Thomas Thornton Read, *Ores and Industry in South America* (Council on Foreign Relations, Harper & Brothers, New York, 1934), pp. 22-42, 331-370.

U. S. Tariff Commission, *Latin America as a Source of Strategic and Other Essential Materials* (Washington, 1941), pp. 53-66, 91-98, 133-142, 151-160, 169-178, 185-197.

Chapter 9

Organization for Production: Petroleum

At mid-twentieth century, an economist might have reasoned that at least in the petroleum field an orderly and precise definition of national interests and national objectives calculated to maximize the pace of healthy development seemed within reach of the Latin-American policy-maker. Petroleum everywhere held a central position as a fuel for modern industry, agriculture, and transportation, as a lubricant for the increased mechanization of the economies, as the base for a rapidly expanding chemical industry. It was especially important in a coal-short area like Latin America where the equipment of industry and transportation was proceeding on the assumption that an adequate and dependable supply of petroleum would be available, despite the tendency of petroleum to become for the oil-importing countries a more and more significant drain on their foreign-exchange availabilities. Consumption of petroleum was increasing by about 6% annually.[1]

The national interest in a Latin-American country dictated that steps be taken to assure a petroleum supply in the increasing quantities required, that this supply be assured in

---

[1] This is the rate used in the projections of an inter-governmental committee in 1949 in the report: *Statistical Summary of Individual Plans for the Development of World Oil Production, Refining and Trade (Excluding North America and Eastern Europe)*, prepared by the United Kingdom and Netherlands Governments with the assistance of Economic Cooperation Administration, September 12, 1949. In most of the Latin American countries in the late 1940's consumption was increasing at a much faster pace.

such fashion as to involve the minimum strain on the balance of payments position and thus not impede the meeting of other development requirements, that proper consideration be given the possibility of war or other emergencies which might interfere with the flow of petroleum from abroad. The national interest further demanded that, if possible, petroleum be made available in quantities which would enable it to pace development, i.e., not only assure local adequacy but also provide an export surplus with which other developmental activity might be financed. Finally, the national interest demanded that these objectives be achieved (a) with maximum efficiency in the industry; (b) with proper regard for balance in the economy so that shifts in the cyclical or long-term position of the industry should not be accompanied by drastic upheavals locally; (c) with advantage to the local economy commensurate with the removal of an irreplaceable resource which belongs to the nation; (d) without such strain on available financial resources of the community as might upset plans for development in fields deserving priority for reasons of greater assurance of yield or more immediate benefit or inability to achieve financing in any other way, for petroleum discovery and exploitation involves enormous risk and requires immense concentrations of capital and yet is sufficiently attractive to foreign interests to make foreign financing possible under suitable conditions; (e) with the largest possible ability to defend the country's export position against competitors in world markets.

There was a broad record to put up against these objectives, for by the end of 1949 almost 9 million barrels of crude oil had already been produced in Latin America. Efficiency? The major petroleum installations represented probably the maximum achievement of modern technology in Latin America. There were no barriers to the flow of technical knowledge and performance among the great petroleum centers of the United States and Venezuela, for instance, and successive installations and campaigns of exploration represented the last word in technical progress. Investment per worker in such centers as Venezuela was reported as high as $25,000, far exceeding the investment behind the worker in other

Latin-American industries. Productivity was corresponding-
ly great, supporting standards of living for the workers far
above prevailing levels elsewhere in the economy.

Commensurate gain for the local economy as a whole?
Foreign capital had long dominated Latin-American petroleum, and in 1948 foreign-owned companies were producing
almost 90% of total petroleum output. In some of the countries, particularly in Mexico, the industry had suffered a long
period of irresponsible short-sighted leadership which acted
in disregard for the long-run interests of both the companies
themselves and the local economy. The willingness to ride
roughshod over local governments and labor alike had been
matched by similar irresponsibility on the part of the governments themselves which failed to realize the imperative
need to "sow the petroleum" if the economies were to flourish
and expand enduringly under the temporary stimulus of petroleum activity. This period had perhaps culminated in the
expropriation of the industry in Mexico in 1938, but the
realization that the national interest and the interest of private capital in the industry could be more closely identified
to the benefit of both by a new policy line was already beginning to take hold before that time. In the past decade the
industry has not only assumed responsibility for making
petroleum products available to the local economy at low cost,
not only invested heavily in the health, education, sanitation,
living conditions, and well-being of its own workers. It has
also recognized through its tax and royalty arrangements
with the government a responsibility for maintaining high-
level activity in the petroleum industry, acted vigorously in
defense of the country's position in world markets, and co-
operated effectively in the government's efforts to "sow the
petroleum" so that the base of the economy might be effectively broadened. Intensive cultivation of model industrial
relations, maximum use of nationals and steady grading up
so that they might take over responsible positions as well as
the lower echelon posts, steady expansion of local sources of
supply for industry requirements, have combined with continuing increases in the proportion of the earnings of the
industry yielded up to the governments to increase the bene-

fit accruing to local economies from the petroleum industry. The legacy of the previous period—the ill will, suspicion, dissatisfaction—remained, however, as a potent vehicle for unscrupulous political exploitation and manipulation and a continuing drag on development of resources.

Financing? Well over $2 billion of foreign capital was invested in the industry in 1948. Domestic private capital was rarely seen in the petroleum industry, but for every $10 million of foreign capital risked and expended without return in Paraguay, Panama, Colombia, Ecuador, every country where exploration was permitted, even in lush and usually profitable Venezuela,[2] hundreds of millions more of foreign capital stood ready to take the gamble that might make out of a nation's ineffective buried resources a living source of better food, housing, health, security, and welfare for all the people.

If he confined himself to summary statistics, the economist might have thought that implementation had followed in a straight line from the definition of national interest. For in 1948 Latin America was producing more than one-sixth of the world's production of petroleum, which was a more respectable share than it had reached in most major lines of production. (See Table 32). It had doubled its output of petroleum from 1939 to 1948, after achieving a 25% increase from 1930 to 1939, and had lifted its share of world production from 15.5% in 1930 to 17.9% in 1948—no small accomplishment at the pace of expansion of world production and something which bespoke a development effort hardly typical of other lines of Latin-American activity. It had drawn into the petroleum industry an unprecedented flow of almost a billion dollars in the three years 1946-48. And when other exports were expanding largely because of price increases, petroleum had achieved advances in volume and was one of the two leading Latin-American exports in the late 1940's, accounting for almost one-fifth of total exports. This picture was badly distorted, however.

---

[2] Even in Venezuela, Creole Petroleum could drop $22 million between 1944 and 1948 in the Barbacoas and Tamanaco concessions and achieve only eleven dry holes and an abandoned modern camp and industrial facilities.

TABLE 32

Crude Oil Production

(barrels 42's)

	Cumulative Production Through 1948	Daily Average Production 1939	1948	% of World Production 1939	1948
Total — World	58,216,409,000	5,694,226	9,342,880	100.0%	100.0%
United States	37,099,169,000	3,465,649	5,510,000	60.9	58.9
Canada	143,200,000	20,664	32,500	0.4	0.3
Trinidad	368,986,000	53,541	55,160	0.9	0.6
Venezuela	4,536,260,000	562,829	1,338,760	9.9	14.3
Mexico	2,369,627,000	117,203	160,000	2.1	1.7
Cuba	712,000	-	300	-	-
Colombia	440,180,000	64,835	64,880	1.1	0.7
Argentina	409,027,000	50,999	64,000	0.9	0.7
Bolivia	4,371,000	589	1,270	-	-
Brazil	534,000	-	400	-	-
Ecuador	44,488,000	6,461	7,000	0.1	0.1
Peru	372,246,000	37,007	38,440	0.6	0.4

Source: L. G. Weeks, "Highlights on 1948 Developments in Foreign Petroleum Fields," *Bulletin of the American Association of Petroleum Geologists*, Volume 33, No. 6, June 1949, p. 1124.

South of Mexico there was an exporting area, consisting of Venezuela, Colombia, Peru, and Ecuador, which was producing in 1948 about 15.5% of the world's oil and largely exporting it.[3] Data for 1948 showed less than 1% of crude production used locally, with local disposition of about one-fifth of refined products. (See Table 33). One country in the group, Venezuela, had opened its doors to active exploration and exploitation of its resources by foreign capital in the belief that the national interest could be adequately safeguarded without delaying work until local capital could be mobilized to assume the risk. The performance of the industry indicated by over-all data for Latin America really involved the achievement of this one country. Venezuela alone in 1948 was producing 14.3% of the world's oil; it was responsible for 92% of the production increase in Latin America during the period 1939-48 and for practically all of the increase in export capacity; it was the destination of about nine-tenths of the capital that had been newly attracted to the industry.

Elsewhere in this exporting area, Peru was menaced with a long-range downward trend of production that threatened to convert her from an exporter into a net importer by 1952 unless some legal means could be found to open acreage to oil exploration on a satisfactory basis in the face of strong political propaganda against foreign participation. Colombia had lost ground in the petroleum field because of its reluctance to provide suitable petroleum legislation, the difficulty of conducting satisfactory operations in the prevailing atmosphere of labor activity, and the generally discouraging attitude of the government toward foreign private-owned operations. Ecuador had produced only minor quantities of oil, its receptivity to foreign developmental activity shifted frequently, and such potential fields as the country might possess seemed likely to require unusually large investments.

---

[3] The classification of an exporting area, importing area, and Mexico as used in this discussion follows the handling of statistical material in *Statistical Summary of Individual Plans for the Development of World Oil Production.*

TABLE 33

Production, Local Disposition and Sales Availability
in the Caribbean Exporting Area—1948*

(millions of metric tons)

Crude Oil:

Production	79.0
Used locally	0.6
Disposition runs to local refineries	49.6

Refined Products:

Output	47.4
Local disposition	10.0
Process oils	0.8

Available for Sale:

Crude	29.6
Products	36.6
Total	66.2

*Caribbean is defined as Colombia, Ecuador, Netherlands West Indies, Peru, Trinidad, and Venezuela.

Source: *Statistical Summary of Individual Plans for the Development of World Oil Production, Refining and Trade (Excluding North America and Eastern Europe)*, prepared by the United Kingdom and Netherlands Governments with the assistance of the Economic Cooperation Administration, September 12, 1949.

South of Mexico there was also an importing area, consisting of the remaining Latin-American countries, which in the 1940's was losing ground steadily in the effort to meet its petroleum requirements from its own resources. This area had produced 0.9% of the world's oil in 1939, 0.7% in 1948. It had increased production by less than 3% per year in the period 1939-48 while consumption was growing at a much faster pace. The area was already heavily dependent on imports, as Table 34 shows, and the intergovernmental group which projected estimates for 1950-53 on the basis of that table forecast a steady increase in imports. Throughout this area development policy was generally geared to politically articulated definitions of national interest that preferred an indefinite delay in development of petroleum resources to a more immediate development with foreign capital. Argentina

TABLE 34

Availability of Crude Oil and Refined Products
in Latin American Area—1948*

(millions of metric tons)

Local crude production	3.3
Crude supplies from exporting areas	2.9
Total crude available	6.2
Refinery throughput	5.7
Refined products—net availability:	
Movement from exporting areas	13.1
Plus, refinery output	5.3
Net availability	18.4

*Latin-American importing area is defined as all Latin America south of Mexico, and the nonproducing Caribbean Islands, but excluding the Caribbean exporting area.

Source: *Statistical Summary of Individual Plans for the Development of World Oil Production, Refining and Trade* (*Excluding North America and Eastern Europe*), prepared by the Unted Kingdom and Netherlands Governments with the assistance of the Economic Cooperation Administration, September 12, 1949.

had long ago imposed restrictions on granting of new leases for exploration by private companies and seemed intent on having all branches of the industry ultimately controlled by a government entity, despite the fact that the existing government body had lagged in its exploratory work and in developing the potentially large oil-bearing basin areas. Brazil's favorable geological structures, indicating the possibility of large reserves of petroleum, were buried under an effective propaganda line—o petróleo é nosso (the petroleum belongs to us)—which obstructed effective introduction of experienced risk-bearing foreign capital. Chile had emphatically warned that foreign participation was barred when finally in 1945 it discovered the world's most southern oil field in Tierra del Fuego. Bolivia was burdened with a government entity which had been the sole operator since the fields and leases of a foreign company were expropriated in 1937, and despite the existence of substantial reserves its production continued to be unimpressive. In Central America, Guatemala typically in 1948-1949 studied the willingness of a number of American companies to gamble on an especially costly operation in an inaccessible area where the terrain, outgrowth, and climate were especially troublesome, and where the lack of facilities would have necessitated movement of a labor supply into the area, construction of overland communication facilities, and other primary expenditures in addition to the ordinary costs. The government reasoned that the willingness of these companies to gamble might mean that petroleum development was a "sure thing," and consequently withdrew for the time being from the negotiations.

Mexico had been one of the world's great producing areas for oil, as Table 32 shows, and it still has immense petroleum reserves. Yet, in the late 1940's it found itself in the unhappy position of being threatened with becoming a net importer of petroleum as consumption advanced rapidly and the government-controlled industry failed to expand production effectively. Late in 1949 it seemed to have averted that crisis. The legacy of the experience which had ended with expropriation in 1938 was such that not even a decade of inefficiency, loose financing, inadequate personnel, and unsatisfactory labor relations of the government monopoly had turned public favor to the re-introduction of foreign participation in the ordinary forms.

It was significant that the four major industrial nations of Latin America—Brazil, Argentina, Mexico, and Chile— were vigorously pursuing mechanization of their economies in the 1940's and yet had chosen development policies for a central factor in such industrialization — petroleum — that promised either to strain the available domestic capital resources to the disadvantage of other lines of development, or to consume much of the borrowing power abroad to the detriment of other requirements, or to bear more heavily on available foreign exchange resources — in any event to delay maximum mobilization of the petroleum resources even if it involved a slowdown in the whole process of economic development.

Venezuela: Sembrar el Petróleo. In 1948 the petroleum industry in Venezuela provided 72% of the revenues of the Venezuelan government, accounted for 96% of total exports, and employed about 60,000 persons, or 4% of the gainfully employed. The petroleum resources of the country were enormous; production through 1948 had exceeded 4.5 billion barrels and proved reserves were 9.7 billion barrels, but expert opinion was that only a minor portion of ultimate potential reserves had yet been uncovered. Most of the oil found to date had been in the Tertiary formations of the Maracaibo-Falcon and Orinoco basins. The Cretaceous beds which were known to underlie much of the oil territory had scarcely been scratched as yet.[4] And a third basin, the Apure, was virtually unexplored. About 60% of the output of crude oil consisted of heavy or low-gravity crudes, serving chiefly as a source of residual fuel oil; 27% consisted of light crudes resembling the oil of east and west Texas; the intermediate crudes, 13%, were suitable for making asphalt, lubricating oils, and waxes. The high proportion of fuel oil crudes caused value of output to be related closely to world prices of competitive products for marine bunkering and industrial plants, and the volume of output to be related to the level of industrial activity and shipping activity.[5] Venezuela also had substantial reserves of natural gas. In the United States 5 trillion cubic feet of natural gas has been found for each billion barrels of oil discovered, and although the dominance of heavy crudes in Venezuela indicates a lower ratio, sizable resources are undoubtedly available. Commercial development of natural gas, however, could be expected to lag, for unlike oil it is not

---

[4] The Shell Company brought in a Cretaceous well with initial production potential of 25,000 barrels in 1944 in an old field (La Paz) northwest of Lake Maracaibo which was down to production of 8,000 barrels a day and whose facilities were headed for the scrap heap. By 1949 the field had ten Cretaceous wells producing 125,000 barrels a day; and in another field northwest of the Lake (Mara) fifteen Cretaceous wells were producing 60,000 barrels a day.

[5] Residual fuel oil is marginal among oil products, usually commands a unit price below that of crude oil, shares market with coal on competitive price basis.

exported to world markets and the economy of Venezuela does not yet afford important local outlets.[6] The structure of the industry in 1948 consisted of 12 dominant corporate units or groups, of which only three were really important: Creole (Standard Oil of New Jersey) accounting for 45% of production, Royal Dutch Shell 32%, Gulf (Mene Grande) 17%. In the six years 1943-48 the industry made capital expenditures of $1.28 billion in Venezuela. It had capital of $1.36 billion engaged in the industry at the end of 1948. Profits were large in the late 1940's when demand was expanding rapidly and prices were extremely favorable, but in 1946 about half of the operating units had not yet attained a profitable status. The industry averaged profits of 21.4% annually on capital employed in the six years 1943-48 (ranging from 6.7% in 1943 to 34.3% in 1947 and 27.7% in 1948), and paid out average dividends of only 9.8% in order to be able to finance the immense requirements for replacing and expanding crude oil reserves and plant facilities.

When the oil companies first came to Venezuela a generation ago, they found a population half sick, mostly illiterate, and wholly unskilled in the technique of finding and producing oil—a source of unsatisfactory unskilled labor and little more. Enlightened self-interest forced them to create a healthier and abler labor force by revolutionary improvements in housing, sanitation, medicine, education, recreation, and wages; and where self-interest did not adequately manifest itself, labor legislation from the late 1930's on accelerated this tendency. In 1948 about 93% of the persons employed in the industry were Venezuelans. Not only had the industry complied with the usual requirements of a fixed minimum proportion of staff to be of local origin, but with a shrewd eye to both public relations and labor relations it had engaged in a training program to increase the proportion of Venezuelans in the more skilled and managerial posts, a task which can be better appreciated when it is realized that there was

---

[6] It has been suggested that the establishment of carbon black manufacture might become practicable after a period, when the supply available for this purpose in the United States becomes inadequate and other sources are needed.

no pool of skilled specialized personnel from which to draw and the industry had largely to train its own pool of men. By 1949 one company, Creole Petroleum, could boast that it had "nationalized" its skilled oil field workers up through the top-paid rank of driller, all its foremen, many supervisors, almost all accountants and clerical personnel, that it was using scores of Venezuelan geologists and engineers and other high-grade technicians, that all of its 76 doctors, its entire legal staff, and some top management posts were successfully held by Venezuelans. At a lower level the same company had reduced the illiteracy rate in its working force from 82% to 12% in a decade. Employment in the industry was relatively stable, without seasonal layoffs. The work week was 48 hours for day workers, 42 for night labor, with 44 and 40 hours respectively for office help. Workers were paid for every day of the year which included 280 work days, 52 Sundays, 9 national holidays, 24 vacation days. In the first half of 1948 average daily take-home pay per working day was $9.84, indirect pay was $1.12, and indirect benefits were $4.17, for a total of $15.13—well above the level of other industries in the country.

The labor law of 1936, far in advance of the level of social thinking applying to most economic activity in Venezuela, had special requirements for the petroleum industry, such as modern sanitary housing, primary education for workers' children, and complete medical attention. Thereafter the contentious organizing efforts of three politically minded labor groups prodded the industry constantly into giving maximum attention to the well-being of its workers. Major strikes were absent from 1936 to 1949 but the unions backed by the government in their contract negotiations of 1946 and 1948 were able to emerge with total wage and benefit gains of 86%.

The industry depends on export markets. As late as 1948 local sales were only about 1.7% of production and there is no likelihood that local consumption will figure significantly in total production. About one-third of exports have been going to Europe, one-third to the United States, 19% to the Latin-American area, 9% to Canada, 6% for bunkering, etc. As the Middle East resources and the new Canadian resources are increasingly exploited, the pattern of marketing is expected to change with increased emphasis by Venezuela on Western Hemisphere markets. The geographical position of Venezuela is a fortunate one in terms of export markets. Transportation costs for tanker shipments to Europe are only half those from the Middle East, and the margin is even greater for Western Hemisphere outlets. But production costs have been low in the Middle East and the completion of pipe lines under construction currently are expected to reduce shipping costs. Within the Western Hemisphere Venezuela's advantage in transportation cost is likely to continue.

In 1943 the Venezuelan government received half of its income from the oil industry. In the six years 1943-48 the total government income rose from $110 million to $573 million, and the portion derived from the oil industry rose from 50% to 72%. Since a portion of the other revenues results indirectly from oil activity, these percentages understate the reliance on oil. In the 1943-48 period Venezuelan total exports rose from $204 million to $1,128 million while the proportion of petroleum to the total rose from 88% to 96%.

The legislative history of the industry may conveniently be divided into the period dominated by the dictator Gómez and the period since his death in 1935. The nation is the owner of the subsoil in Venezuela. A concession from the government is needed to engage in oil development. Prior to 1920 concessions were granted subject to the Mining Code and a number were granted to individuals who later transferred them to operating companies. By 1921 production had reached 4,000 barrels a day. In 1922 a workable petroleum law was enacted providing that concessions up to 10,000 hectares would be granted with the option to select development parcels up to one-half the total acreage. Concessions carried a life of 40 years, involved a royalty to the government of 10% of the value of the oil (7.5% for underwater and distant areas). The provisions of the law were modified successively in 1925, 1928, 1935, and 1936, but the changes were not of significant character. By 1926 the industry was producing 100,000 barrels daily; by 1937, 423,000 barrels daily. While Gómez lived the industry's problem was to deal and reach an understanding with the dictator; public relations were in large part relations with Gómez. Fortunately for the industry, Gómez' interest was in speeding the exploration and development of Venezuela's resources, so that by the time he passed from the scene, Venezuela was established as one of the great producing areas of the world. A new petroleum law in 1938 heralded the opening of a new period: the royalty on new concessions was raised to 15%; other conditions, such as requirements for continuous drilling and development, were imposed. The demand for concessions promptly fell off.

The government then began to develop the partnership theme that has come to characterize Venezuelan oil operation. It announced a policy of larger participation in the proceeds of the oil, looking to a fifty-fifty sharing with the companies in the net income. The petroleum law of 1943 resulted. It raised the royalty to 16 2/3% and provided that companies could convert all concessions obtained under prior laws into new concessions for a term of 40 years. The concessions were converted by virtually the whole industry so that the whole oil development was brought under the terms of the law. The government calculated that the law would result in a fifty-fifty participation by the government and the companies in the net profits of the industry. The government's share in every year since 1943 has actually been greater than half. The private companies did not at first welcome the principle of a fifty-fifty partnership, but within a few years were active proponents of the idea.[7]

Originally the principle had been intended to give the government equal participation with the industry *as a whole* over the life of the oil operations, i.e., to share equally in the combined results of all operators and not to penalize success-

---

[7] The 1943 law granted a period of three years for exploration after which one-half of the area of each concession reverted to the government. On the maximum of one-half retained by the concessionaire, an initial exploitation tax and an annual surface tax became payable, including usually a bonus, in addition to the one-sixth royalty. The higher royalty involved for Creole Petroleum a boost from an average of 7.9% to 16⅔%.

ful individual activity in a good year. But in 1945 the growing profits of the more successful companies prompted the government to impose an extraordinary "one-time" income tax levy on the grounds that it would otherwise fail to get the equal share in the boom profits. Negotiations followed which accepted the 50-50 partnership principle as applying to each company separately and to each year separately; this provision was included in 1948 in an amendment to the income tax law. The amendment assured the government 50% or more of the net income every year under any condition, from the industry as a whole and from each company. Table 35 shows the split of net income in recent years.

The petroleum law of 1943 had also imposed a refinery obligation linked to the granting of new areas for oil development. Except in certain cases where an alternative refining obligation was negotiated, an undertaking to refine within Venezuela the equivalent of one-tenth of the production from new concessions became a requirement in order to obtain new concessions, although the rule was not applied to converted concessions. There was some dissatisfaction with the refinery obligation and with the application of the 50-50 theory, but in general Venezuela had provided an acceptable basis for development of petroleum resources. There was not lacking in Venezuela the pressure for nationalization common to all Latin-American countries, with its useful appeal for the ambitious politician. But at the end of the 1940's the Venezuelan could compare the national policy for organization of the oil industry which his country had adopted with the alternatives elsewhere and be pleased with his findings. There were a number of countries in Latin America with favorable geological structures which might one day conceivably emerge as important petroleum producers. But while they struggled largely to meet local requirements, Venezuela had become a major world producer, a very efficient competitor in world markets, its export interests were being pushed and defended vigorously the world over. Venezuela alone had its own financial resources and a continually growing source of capital with which to launch a major developmental program; and its only problem was to determine those lines of "sowing the

TABLE 35

Net Income and Government Revenue from the Venezuelan Oil Industry 1943-1948

(millions of dollars)

	1943	1944	1945	1946	1947	1948	Total for Period
Ratio of Government's receipts to Industry's net income	63-37	52-48	62-38	53-47	51-49	52-48	54-46 (average)
Received by Government from oil industry:	$55	$94	$146	$163	$262	$411	$1,131
Of which, royalties	28	44	55	79	128	204	538
income taxes	7	14	46	53	97	151	368
other revenues	20	36	45	31	37	56	225
Net income of the oil industry	$32	$84	$ 89	$143	$246	$377	$ 971
Of which, net income reinvested	-14	22	39	74	143	263	527
dividends	46	62	50	69	103	114	444
Capital employed in the business	$477	$541	$646	$808	$717	$1,359	$ 758 (average)
Ratio of net income to capital employed	6.7%	15.5%	13.8%	17.7%	34.3%	27.7%	21.4% (average)
Ratio of dividends to capital employed	9.6%	11.5%	7.7%	8.5%	14.4%	8.4%	9.8% (average)

Source: Joseph E. Pogue, *Oil in Venezuela*, a pamphlet report published by the Chase National Bank, New York, 1949. Data in the section on Venezuela are largely drawn from the report. The compilations are based on the 12 corporate units or groups which "embrace nearly all of the oil activities."

petroleum" which would yield the largest advances in the standard of living. The level of technical and managerial ability possessed by nationals of the country was rising out of the mobility of the know-how originally imported by the industry. Great improvements in health and education had been directly effected for the group immediately concerned in the industry, and the means were being provided to spread such improvements throughout the whole population. Ancillary industries and occupations were thriving on the central industry's advances. Venezuela was on its way.

Brazil: O Petróleo é Nosso. Among the sources of inanimate energy, petroleum plays only a minor role in Brazil, accounting for about one-sixteenth of the total compared with 84% for wood and charcoal and 8 to 9% for coal. But the almost complete reliance on imports (domestic production of petroleum was only a piddling 300 to 400 barrels per day in 1948-49, or less than 1% of consumption), the estimate of an 8 to 10% increase in consumption annually if the pace of industrial development is to be maintained, and the growing burden on exchange availabilities evidenced by the fact that in 1948 petroleum already accounted for 10% of total imports all point up the desirability of vigorous action to meet this deficiency.

Interest in the supply of petroleum locally developed with the fuel shortages during the first world war. From 1918 to 1938 the geological service of the Ministry of Agriculture drilled over 70 wells and official interest expanded; finally in 1939 a well producing an unimportant quantity of oil daily was brought in in the so-called Lobato-Joanes field in Bahia. The National Petroleum Council was created in 1938 by a decree-law establishing a government petroleum-control entity, and it proceeded to take over the drilling campaign. A plan of exploration was outlined in 1944 by an American consulting engineer and work was advanced in about eight states. By the end of 1948, 147 wells had been completed in Bahia and oil reserves were estimated at 17.8 million barrels; cumulative production in Brazil, all from the Bahia basin, barely exceeded half a million barrels. Geologic explorations, started in northeast-central Brazil in 1946, had by the end of 1948 indicated that the major petroleum possibilities were defined by an area of 235,000 square miles in the central part of Maranhão. Refraction seismograph operations were begun in the Marajo area in 1946 to determine the thickness of the sediments and to outline areas which might be favorable for petroleum, with drilling getting under way as the decade ended. The large Paraná basin of southern Brazil contains a maximum thickness of 1,800 meters of very low-dipping Paleozoic sediments considered to have petroleum prospects and studies looking to the selection of exploratory drilling locations were under way. From 1938 to 1947 the appropriations of the Petroleum Council had totaled $24 million. In 1948 the President of Brazil included in his proposal for a five-year development plan (known as the Salte Plan) the suggestion that $62 million be spent during the period on petroleum exploration. It was pointed out, however, that the Brazilian area of exploration covered perhaps 300 million hectares, for which probably much more than that amount would be needed in risk capital, and given the tremendous uncertainty attending petroleum exploration work anywhere, the possibility and even likelihood of fruitless activity pointed up the policy issue of letting foreign risk capital assume the risk.

In the refining end of the industry the Salte Plan envisaged the expenditure of $73 million for a program that would bring locally controlled refining capacity up to 80,000 barrels per day, which was the government's estimate of requirements in 1952. During the war the Petroleum Council had installed two rudimentary refineries with a daily capacity of 150 barrels; one refinery was later dismantled. There were three small privately owned refineries in the south operating on imported crude. In Bahia a refinery with a capacity of 2,500 barrels daily was being constructed under government control. Private Brazilian groups had obtained concessions to construct two refineries with a capacity of 10,000 and 20,000 barrels respectively, and the government was moving forward with plans for a refining capacity of 45,000 barrels additional.

Unfortunately for Brazil national interest and national

aims were confused in the 1940's by an effective propaganda line—O petróleo é nosso—which seemed to defy any attempt to consider the problem in economic terms. Quite apart from this political maneuver, however, there was the reluctance of local financial interests to permit foreign capital to gain control of the potentially lucrative industry, although there was no inclination on their part to assume the risks. There were three positions on petroleum policy: (a) Let the government assume a complete monopoly of the industry, assume the full risks of exploration, finance exploitation and refining, or permit only Brazilian interests to share in the refining and transportation end of the business; (b) Accept the fact that local capital, governmental or private, could not shoulder the full burden of exploration and exploitation, and accordingly permit free competition regardless of nationality; (c) Open exploration and export of oil to private interests, but retain local control of the refining and transportation facilities, control of which would carry with it control of the industry in effect. While private foreign capital insisted that it could not enter Brazil without arrangements that offered the prospect of compensation ultimately for the assumption of the riskier end of the industry, while local private capital insisted that it wanted no part of the risks but would resent anything but minority foreign participation in the refining function, while the government simply lacked the means financially of developing the industry, Brazil lagged in the production of a commodity of which an adequate supply was essential to any serious attempt at industrialization, failed to develop an adequate supply, and failed to develop exports which might have carried some of the burden of external requirements for other fields of development. The Brazilian members of the Subcommission on Fuels of the Joint Brazil-United States Technical Commission warned that "petroleum exploration and the development of the petroleum industry call for abundant means and exceed our ability to carry them out, taking into account the fact that these undertakings have to be carried out speedily and on a large scale, as our growing economy requires." But petroleum was a political football in Brazil, and in 1950 an acceptable solution politically had not yet been found.

Argentina: Steps to Government Monopoly. Fuel-poor Argentina, whose ambitious plans for industrialization have always been challenged by the poverty of its mineral endowment, might have been expected to write petroleum policy around the central objective of stimulating exploration and accelerating exploitation by every possible means. Instead, Argentine policy has focused on the gradual elimination of private enterprise from the industry as an end in itself. Soon after the discovery of the petroleum field at Comodoro Rivadavia in 1907, a government entity—Yacimientos Petrolíferos Fiscales (YPF)—was set up to develop the field which had promptly been reserved from private entry. By the time that YPF celebrated its twenty-fifth anniversary in 1932 it could boast that it had 1,319 producing wells, four refineries, a fleet of tankers, a network of distributing stations, and was supplying about 25% of the fuel oil and gasoline and 14% of the kerosene used in Argentina. Other fields had been discovered since the original exploration in Comodoro Rivadavia, but Argentina had already adopted the policy of refusing to permit foreign companies to have additional field acreage for exploration and drilling, and experts were warning that reserves were not being discovered rapidly enough for the prospective requirements of Argentina. To the production restrictions stemming from the obstacles put in the way of exploration, Argentina added numerous privileges of a discriminatory nature for the government entity, such as tax exemptions, monopoly of certain local and national government business, and special franchises for street pump concessions; and it virtually compelled negotiation of marketing agreements that steadily weakened the position of private competitors. Decree 86,639 of 1936 gave YPF the right to be the sole importer of all petroleum products and granted it the privilege of distributing such imports among private firms; crude oil was to be distributed directly to such private firms as came to an agreement with YPF which retained control of the distribution and sale; participation in the market was limited to firms which reached an agreement with YPF. There was some question of the legality of the decree and YPF never fully availed itself of the powers granted to it, but the private companies preferred negotiating agreements to undertaking legal action which could only worsen their relations in an already hostile atmosphere. Thus in 1936 and 1937 marketing agreements were set up; since fixed quantitative quotas were established for a market that was expanding, the effect of the agreements was to improve the position of the government entity. In 1937 YPF had 31.6% of the gasoline market, by 1942 it had 57.7%, by 1945, 67.5%. The marketing arrangements more or less restricted YPF to marketing its own production, leaving the private companies to do the importing, although YPF had authority to import directly for its own account in case of emergency. As local production failed to expand adequately, however, YPF came to encroach on the import function as well.

In 1942 the government entity, armed with regulatory and almost lawmaking powers, was accounting for two-thirds of Argentine production. It had full rights to all petroleum reserves in federal lands and private exploration and drilling had been seriously limited, but the government effort at exploration in the large potentially oil-bearing basin areas had failed to develop the needed reserves so that one-third of the petroleum requirements had to be imported. When the Argentine five-year plan for economic development was worked out in 1946, carrying a need for vastly increased quantities of fuel, government officials found that domestic production was off 10% from the peak production of 1943, and that a 50% increase would have to be achieved by 1951 in crude oil, and major increases in capital expenditures for petroleum plant would have to be financed. But the long neglect of the foundations of any sound petroleum industry in pursuit of the objective of eliminating private competition regardless of the effect on the economy was not easily remedied and there was still no tendency to examine realistically the cause of the lack of progress. Soon after the plan was launched the country found itself overextended financially, short of the exchange required for exploration and refining programs and short even of internal financing. From 1943 to 1947 Argentine production declined from 68,000 barrels daily to 60,000 barrels, while imports of crude and petroleum products rose about 31.5%. Production was 63,000 in 1949. As for the objective of government control it could be pointed out that the government entity was producing 70% of total Argentine production. But imports were now more than 55% of total petroleum requirements. And consumption must rise steadily if development was to occur as desired in the economy. In the current organization of the industry there was no indication that petroleum would emerge as a pacemaker for the whole development program and more reason to fear that it might instead be a retarding factor.

Mexico: Expropriation and Government Monopoly. In 1917 Mexico was producing petroleum at the rate of 55 million barrels per year. In the sixteen years since commercial production had begun Mexico had moved steadily to a place among the world's great producers of oil. Exploration and exploitation were carried out by private capital in a period in which public relations and labor relations were deeply subordinated to the interests of the hard-hitting executives who were concerned with the short-run problem of getting as much oil as possible as quickly as possible at the lowest possible cost. The constitution of 1917 abandoned the principle of ownership of the subsoil by the surface owner and provided for strict separation of rights to the subsoil from surface rights. Article 27 provided that the nation has direct ownership of petroleum and all solid, liquid or gaseous hydrocarbons and that expropriation may be effected only for reasons of public utility and by means of indemnification based on the value which the property has for fiscal purposes.[8] This article was the basis of a long controversy between the Mexican government and the foreign owners of petroleum properties and foreign governments. It must be remembered

---

8 "With respect to petroleum and solid, liquid or gaseous hydrocarbons, no concession may be granted, and the respective regulatory law will determine the form in which the nation may carry into effect the exploitation of these products."

that Mexican industry at the time was largely dominated by foreign capital and there was a desire to protect Mexico against the foreigner and to increase the benefits accruing from foreign-developed industries to the Mexicans. This feeling was present also in the related constitutional and legislative activity regarding labor. The adoption of Article 27 was followed in 1917 and 1918 by decrees introducing a tax on the production of petroleum and providing that issuance of a specific permit by the Ministry of Industry is a prerequisite to exploitation of the subsoil. Article 27 raised important questions as to the status of oil rights acquired by foreigners prior to 1917, involving 80 to 90% of the total foreign holdings.

In 1921 the Supreme Court of Mexico found that the constitutional provision was not retroactive with respect to oil rights acquired prior to its adoption, provided that "positive acts" had been performed in exercising such rights. In 1923 Mexican representatives at the so-called Bucareli Conference interpreted the proviso with respect to "positive acts" to include any demonstration of intent to use acquired rights, for the purpose of exploration and exploitation. In 1925 a petroleum law granted confirmatory concessions for 50 years to foreign holders of properties, instead of recognizing in perpetuity rights acquired prior to adoption of the constitution; and it further limited the definition of "positive acts." The law and regulations pertaining to it were modified in 1928 to provide for the issue of confirmatory concessions for an unlimited period of time to holders of rights acquired prior to the adoption of the constitution. Applications were made for confirmatory concessions thereafter, and a period of relative stability in the industry's relations with the government followed.

Meanwhile, a lasting basis for controversy was being created by the constitutional provisions relating to labor and by the legislation that followed the adoption of the constitution. Article 123 fixed the basic principles to be followed in enacting labor law: strikes were declared lawful when peaceful means were employed; labor disputes were to be submitted to conciliation and arbitration boards; penalties were provided for refusal to submit disputes to arbitration or to abide by the findings. A federal labor law of 1931 followed the constitutional outline, provided for submission to an arbitration board of collective conflicts arising out of questions of an economic nature on establishment of new labor conditions. Between 1934 and 1936 strikes occurred in the oil fields as the workers made new demands. On November 3, 1936, the union of petroleum workers submitted to fifteen leading oil companies a long list of demands for wage increases and benefits to be incorporated in a comprehensive collective contract which was to be concluded with all companies in lieu of previous separate contracts.

Negotiation of a single collective contract was acceptable to the companies, but certain of the demands were not acceptable—specifically, wage increases that were considered excessive and proposals which management believed were encroachments on its prerogatives. It might be noted that the invasion of management prerogatives is an issue on which the oil companies even today are prepared to offer greatest resistance, even in countries like Venezuela, where agreements on wages and benefits have been negotiated with relative smoothness and a minimum of unfriendliness. A strike threatened and was avoided by presidential intervention in favor of a six months' cooling-off period. In May, 1937, the companies submitted a counter-proposal which was promptly rejected. A strike was called at the end of the truce period and terminated with the appointment of a panel of experts to study and make recommendations. The experts reported on August 3, 1937. The companies rejected the report. The Federal Labor Board accepted the recommendations, however, on December 18, 1937. It might be added that the experts in large measure had found in favor of the workers. The companies contended that the industry could not stand the costs that would be imposed by these findings and sought an injunction against the decision. The Supreme Court on March 1, 1938, refused to grant the injunction. With violent wild charges flying from both sides of the controversy, the Mexican government on March 18, 1938, expropriated the properties.[9]   Expropriation was a "bolt from the blue," Ambassador Daniels wrote.   "Neither the Embassy officials nor the officers of the oil companies had been given a hint that expropriation would follow the failure of the companies to accept the Supreme Court's decision.   On the contrary, the oil companies expected and had so expressed themselves to me that a receivership would follow.   I had also been told by the Secretary of Foreign Relations that if the companies did not accept the court decree he expected a receivership would follow." [10]

After expropriation, Daniels continues, "a wave of delirious enthusiasm swept over Mexico."   A barrage of propaganda followed from both sides.   The companies contended that in developing production of 1.9 billion barrels of oil from 1901 to 1938 they had spent $1.2 billion locally and contributed greatly to the national well-being, that the expropriation was a premeditated effort to deprive the rightful owners of their properties after all the risks had been taken, that Mexico lacked the ability to pay promptly and should therefore return the properties or pay up at once.[11]   The Mexican government held that they had had to expropriate in the face of a challenge to the "very sovereignty of the nation," that the companies had exaggerated the capital brought into Mexico for development of the industry, that they had failed to bring suitable benefits to labor while taking excessively good care of foreign staff, that the government would pay for the properties.   Both the British and American governments were extremely exercised over the expropriation.   The British companies were at the time producing about 75% of the oil and

---

[9] Expropriation was pursuant to the expropriation law of 1936 whose validity had been attacked by the companies earlier and been the subject of remonstrances by the government of the United States.

[10] Josephus Daniels, *Shirt-Sleeve Diplomat* (Chapel Hill, The University of North Carolina Press, 1947), p. 229.

[11] The companies also protested that the Supreme Court had not acted independently, had been merely a tool of the Executive.   Actually, separation of the Judiciary and the Executive in the Mexican Government did not exist in the form that it characterizes our own government, so that the criticism was basically correct.

had recently discovered the great Poza Rica field whose potential contrasted sharply with the semidepleted fields which the American companies were exploiting. It seemed clear that the private companies had failed to appreciate adequately the basic developments in Mexico in recent years: the growth of nationalism, the power of organized labor, the force of anti-imperialism with its enduring slogan value regardless of the presence or absence of content. The availability of another important, even superior, producing area—Venezuela —where greater cooperation in development of resources was forthcoming may have delayed the shift from company tactics which too frequently seemed to have been dictated by a textbook on "how *not* to win friends and influence people." And the readiness of the government to persist in policies similarly reminiscent of a text on "how *not* to attract foreign technology and foreign capital to a country" only helped in the deterioration of the situation. The policies of the petroleum industry the world over were to be influenced by the lessons learned from the Mexican experience, but in Mexico the damage was done.

A government entity, Petróleos Mexicanos, was set up to take over the industry and in 1939 legislation provided that foreign oil companies or Mexican subsidiaries of foreign companies could not enter into contracts with the Mexican government for exploration and exploitation of Mexican oil resources. After a long-drawn-out dispute on compensation for properties expropriated, involving the exchange of many notes between governments, heavy pressure by private interests in Washington and London, and a basically sympathetic attitude toward Mexico in Washington stemming from the good-neighbor policy of the Roosevelt regime, the governments of the United States and Mexico agreed in 1941 to appoint an expert commission to determine the amounts and terms of compensation. In 1942 the commission set a value on the American properties of $24 million to be paid one-third on July 1, 1942, and the balance in five equal annual installments, with interest at 3% payable from March 18, 1938. A few years later the British reached a settlement for compensation for their much larger properties. A few small privately owned operating properties and a large number of privately owned subsoil concessions were not expropriated and some of these private companies continued to operate on a minor scale, all being required to sell their production to the government entity or to market domestically at prescribed prices. It now remained to be proven whether government monopoly was actually in the national interest.

Mexican production in 1921 had reached a peak of 193 million barrels, with exports of 172 million. Thereafter production and exports declined sharply. Output averaged 156 million barrels annually in the period 1921-25, 58 million in 1926-30, 36 million in 1931-38. Mexico had lost much of its attractiveness to foreign capital long before the final act of expropriation occurred. To this situation the government brought a deficiency of technical and executive personnel, limited financial resources, the inability to break into established marketing channels abroad in a highly integrated private industry, a political debt to labor for its support in the showdown with foreign capital, a setting in which a tradition of successful government operation of industry was lacking and in which a considerable current of incompetence, graft, and excessive political influence would have to be accepted without challenge. Production failed to expand significantly, averaging only 43 million barrels annually from 1937 to 1947. Meanwhile domestic consumption was rising. Net exports had been 68% of production in 1921-37, 36% of production in 1938-41, 13% in 1942-47.

The financial aspect of monopoly control cannot be adequately examined since the data are not readily available and many of the reports of deficits and loose financing cannot be verified. But the situation that developed in simple terms of volume of production, volume of exports, capacity to meet domestic requirements, and capacity to create a surplus with which to assist other developmental activity is easier to judge, especially in its contrast with the situation in Venezuela. By the late 1940's the Mexican government was seeking actively to enlist either United States government financial support for the government monopoly or some method of attracting private American capital and technology to the industry without relinquishing the control which by now had become a solid political theme in Mexico that could hardly be challenged in economic terms. The government entity presented to the American government in 1948 a plan for a five-year development program for the oil industry requiring $470 million, which it was hoped might result in a lift in production from 62 million barrels in 1949 to 133 million in 1953 and 165 million in 1955. Domestic consumption was 43 million barrels in 1946, 51 million in 1948, and was believed heading for 70 million by 1955. Since American government loans were not usually available in industries where private American capital had indicated a willingness to invest under suitable conditions, the Mexican entity sought means of attracting private firms also. Originally it sought private exploration agreements in which the foreign firm would act as an agent of the government entity, and upon discovery of oil turn over operations to Petróleos Mexicanos and accept compensation in oil as produced. The legal basis of such activity was sufficiently in doubt to cause American firms to hesitate to go into Mexico without a change in the law; there was a further reluctance to accept Mexican supervision over exploratory drilling and operation; and the terms of compensation were in dispute. The Mexican entity insisted, however, that it could legally enter into long-term contracts which entitled foreign companies to a percentage of oil produced from wells drilled by them and which would give the companies a degree of managerial control sufficient to protect their investments in exploration and exploitation ventures, and upon that basis some American interest had been stimulated by the end of 1949.

Curiously enough the great wave of national indignation at the oil companies which had been stirred up before expropriation and kept alive thereafter served to retard the ability of the government entity to negotiate for private participation when the need was finally recognized. In 1949 production was increased sufficiently to eliminate for the moment the fear of becoming a net importer although Mexico was far from realizing the scale of industry which its reserves would have made possible under competitive exploitation. An American congressional subcommittee in 1948, which was so friendly as almost to be biased in favor of the Mexican government operation, reported that "Mexico presently finds itself in a peculiar and uncomfortable financial position. . . . If the industrialization process gave promise of being more stable and permanent than it actually seems to be, there would be reason to believe that the temporary financial embarrassment would be short-lived. By way of solution, the rapid and continuous expansion of Mexico's manufactures seems less feasible than a stepping up of the production and export of petroleum. This, in turn, depends largely upon the rate of expenditure on exploration and development and the making of mutually satisfactory working arrangements with foreign oil interests. . . . In the future it seems likely that the successful exploitation (of Mexico's petroleum reserves) will be the real key to her lasting prosperity." [12]

Guatemala: Some Typical Complexities. It is useful to examine the complexities of petroleum development that arise in a climate of investment where there is (a) a basic aversion to private development of the industry, (b) a recognized inability to develop the industry with government financial and technical resources, (c) an unwillingness of domestic capital to assume the risk and a simultaneous unwillingness of domestic capital to allow external capital to profit by assumption of risk, (d) a recognition of the political usefulness of repeated denunciations of the intentions of foreign capital, and (e) a regret that once this feeling is aroused orderly negotiations with foreign capital on an economic basis that protects the country adequately become virtually impossible. The case of Guatemala in 1948-49 is instructive.

The Guatemalan petroleum law was based on a draft prepared by an American expert and modified by the Congress in a nationalistic effort which made it virtually impossible for foreign firms or any other firms to operate. The law was adhered to Article 95 of the constitution which provided that

---

[12] Report of the so-called Wolverton Committee. House Report 2470, 80th Congress, 2d session, p. 4.

petroleum may be exploited only by the state and by Guatemalans and Guatemalan firms whose capital is predominantly national. Since direct participation of foreign-owned firms was prohibited and since there was no local know-how and risk capital, any activity under the law was precluded. Further, exploration concessions did not carry with them the automatic right of subsequent exploitation on a reduced area, and instead the firm making the discovery had to submit the area to public bidding. Also, after 20 years all employees, even those in executive and technical posts, had to be of Guatemalan nationality. The law itself was enacted in a form carrying previously prepared loopholes. To strengthen its plan to exploit deposits in its own name through contracting foreign firms, the state was careful to make no reference to itself in the law, which was construed to mean that even though the law makes no provision for state exploitation the omission of mention of the state cannot restrict in any way its constitutional inherent right to exploit; further, the omission of mention of the state was construed to mean that its contracts naming it an exploiting entity operating simply through an agent need not be governed by restrictions of the law.

Geological surveys more than fifty years ago had indicated the possibilities of oil in the region of El Peten. In the 1930's the Shell organization held concessions in the area, made surveys, and finally abandoned the work at the beginning of the second world war. Thereafter a number of American companies were encouraged by superficial geological surveys to indicate an interest in a sizable gamble on the area, even though it represented in their opinions third-rate possibilities as against certain other areas. The region was highly inaccessible, had only 12,000 inhabitants in an area of 35,854 square kilometers, the climate was hot and humid, movement extremely difficult, access at the moment only by air, with the terrain and overgrowth promising very difficult and costly operations if anything actually came of the gamble in drilling test wells. No test well had ever been drilled in any area of Guatemala, but this did not prevent officials and local capitalists from assuming that the willingness of the companies to invest some capital in a gamble meant that a petroleum industry was a "sure thing" for Guatemala. The rise in local consumption of more than 20% for the year served to enhance interest in the prospect of a new industry.

The companies, having made the decision to take a chance on Guatemala, were now faced with the problem of determining whether there was any legal basis for participation in the industry. One company was carrying out exploration operations in a concession area of 800,000 hectares, had no rights whatever in its own name, and had simply contracted with a local firm to exercise exploration rights which it had obtained in a concession granted in 1947. Another firm was operating under similar arrangements on an area of 600,000 hectares. A third had obtained simply a limited-period concession to explore an area of 100,000 hectares. Several other firms of local origin had applied for licenses which were later suspended when the government declared the entire area of El Peten which had not yet been licensed for exploration to be a national petroleum reserve in which the state would have preferential rights to explore in its own name. The legal talent that was mobilized to find a basis for operations convinced two of the American companies that they could function by negotiating a contract naming them as agents of the state for exploitation of deposits in the name of the state; under this arrangement instead of paying the government a certain percentage of production as a royalty they would receive from the government the larger portion of production as payment for their services. The question was raised whether this was a deliberate means of circumventing the constitution and the argument was convincingly presented that since the state has the inherent right to exploit petroleum and since it lacks the technical capacity to do so, it was proper to contract with a firm to carry out the requirements of the work. A third firm learned from its attorneys that any contract would have to be signed as an actual concession within the petroleum law and that as a prerequisite to the obtaining of such a concession both the constitutional limitations and the objectionable features of the petroleum law would have to be changed. While this firm waited on new legisla-

tion, the other two went through the laborious task of negotiating a contract which took advantage of the skilful drafting
of the law which had permitted the government to avoid the
restrictions of the law. When this whole process with its
great uncertainties had been completed, the government decided that it really did not want to risk foreign participation
and broke off the deal!

Peru and Colombia: Legislative Indecision. Peruvian production of petroleum in the years since 1937 has leveled off
and tended downward. In 1937 production was 17.5 million
barrels; in 1938, 15.8 million barrels; in 1948, 14.1 million.
In 1946 and 1947 annual production averaged 12.7 million
barrels. The failure to develop new reserves has not been
offset by the forcing of production on the old fields of the
northwestern coastal region; although some success was
achieved in the campaign of shooting oil wells with nitro-
glycerine, in 1949 the experiments in salt-water drive had
not been successful yet. Meanwhile consumption rose about
10% per year from 1941 to 1948. By 1948 consumption
locally constituted 46% of crude production and it was estimated that a continuation for five years of the pace of increasing requirements without a balancing factor in new
production might wipe out Peru's export position. This
had special significance in the Peruvian case because the local
market was supplied at a much lower profit margin than
foreign markets, at the insistence of the government which
refused to permit price increases such as were obtained abroad.
International Petroleum, an American-owned firm, which produced about 83% of the total production, supplied 94% of
the local market and refined 96% of total refinery output,
succeeded in 1947 in negotiating a concession covering a part
of the national reserves known as the "Sechura" but the
government was unable to push the measure through the
Congress. Similarly the granting of concessions in the
Montaña which was believed to be a potentially important
oil-producing region waited on the passage of new petroleum
legislation that would bring in the immense investment of
capital necessary for exploration and exploitation. Such
"wildcatting" as was being carried out, even if successful

could not be expected to alter significantly the production of oil for a number of years because the only testing area of importance was east of the Andes in inaccessible areas. The Agua Caliente property of the Ganso Azul enterprise already had a potential output of 3,000 barrels per day but was delivering less than 500 because its location east of the Andes limited marketing to portions of eastern Peru and Amazon River ports east to Manaos. A fair knowledge had been acquired of the best potential oil areas in the Montaña region by geological parties of the major oil companies, but until suitable legislation could be enacted to translate geological possibilities into economic reality this had no bearing on the immediate supply position. In 1948 a government entity was established with authority to negotiate contracts with foreign corporations to explore and exploit petroleum; it produced about 112,000 barrels in 1948 but had not yet served to resolve the legislative indecision that held back the finding of new reserves for Peru. Meanwhile, an important export was being threatened by the steady rise of consumption of the level of production. There was a great deal of land favorable for petroleum exploitation east of the Andes, but development would be unusually costly and the government was slow to act.

In Colombia, where production was much larger, there was a similar lag in the creation of suitable conditions for rapid development of the industry, a long delay in enactment of suitable legislation, a growing local market supplied normally at a low profit made up by more profitable exports, ambitious plans to have the government participate directly in the industry. In 1949 it was pointed out that Colombia was faced with a rapidly rising demand for refined products which in the absence of adequate refining capacity meant a drain on dollar-supply that could be met only by expanding crude exports. The local price structure impeded investment in the necessary additional refining capacity. Heavy expenditure was required for risky exploration. And it was regarded as not impossible that the diminishing profitability of crude production on the De Mares venture might make such production uneconomic by the late 1950's.

From 1940 to 1948 Colombian demand for refined products rose by 115%. By 1951 requirements, it was estimated, would have risen another 18%. Already in 1948 one-fifth of consumption of refined petroleum products was being imported; by 1951 it was estimated that imports would comprise 30%. Refining capacity at Barranca Bermeja had been increased 140% from 1943 to 1947 but additional expansion was being retarded by the lower profit margin on local sales and the general uncertainty of labor and legislative relations for private companies in the country. About three-fourths of crude petroleum production was exported in 1948 and production gained substantially in 1949, but the industry was characterized in Colombia by great uncertainty regarding the intentions of the government. When Law 165 was enacted in 1948, authorizing establishment of a government corporation to take over the management and operation of the De Mares concession when it reverted to the government in 1951 and to engage in refining and transport for local consumption, specific provision was made that if private capital was introduced the total capital of Colombian origin (private and government) must be at least 51%. Yet in the exposition of motives which accompanied the legislation, there was a statement of principles which should govern public policy in the petroleum field, with which compliance was entirely possible without government ownership. The objectives defined in this statement of national interest were: (a) full exploitation of resources; (b) timely development of reserves for local consumption; (c) defense of government revenue from the industry; (d) adequate refining capacity locally; (e) fair tax policy to stimulate private investment; (f) wise and equitable labor policy, including a larger use of Colombian labor; (g) fair sharing of the profits of the industry by the nation and the industry's operators.

Bolivia, Ecuador and Chile. Bolivia expropriated the properties of the Standard Oil Company in 1937 after controversy over the company's policy during the Chaco War. The company claimed to have invested some $17 million in the properties but was persuaded by the United States government to accept $1.5 million in full settlement under the agreement signed with Bolivia in 1942. The Bolivian government entity which was established to run the industry has suffered from the serious lack of capital which afflicts most enterprise in Bolivia, from the lack of technical and executive background that makes for success in such activity, and from the lack of transportation facilities which has balked efficient marketing within Bolivia as well as in external markets. The short-supply position of both Argentina and Brazil with respect to petroleum has prompted an interest on the part of both countries in securing priority to Bolivian production through construction of transportation links and has also promoted attention at times to the desirability of some cooperative scheme which would insure an orderly coordination of demand and supply in the area without deterioration to competitive and even warlike diplomacy.

Ecuador in 1949-50 seemed to have convinced the outside world of its interest in rapid development of its resources by private capital. Its production of 7,300 barrels per day in 1949 was still coming from the old oil fields of Santa Elena Peninsula. One company had carried on exploration activities for ten years over most of the basin area between the high Andes and the coast and had finally terminated its unsuccessful operation in 1947. Another corporation was conducting costly operations in eastern Ecuador in the large basin lying in the Amazon drainage east of the Andes. The costs already incurred would have been sizable items had the government needed to cover them and when and if petroleum was discovered in the new regions an immense outlay would be required to make exploitation effective, but at least for the time being Ecuador seemed willing to have the private companies incur the risks.

In Chile the government development corporation had approached the problem of petroleum by engaging American technicians to make surveys and explorations for its own account. A field was discovered in 1945 which was believed in 1948 to be capable of producing at least 3000 barrels daily, with a much higher potential, compared with a daily consumption in Chile of 16,000 to 18,000 barrels of petroleum products. By 1950 Chile had negotiated for the export of crude oil to Uruguay and was proceeding confidently with expansion of facilities. The government had made it clear that it considered petroleum a field for government activity, not private participation.

Foreign Capital in the Industry. In 1948 foreign-controlled properties were accounting for about 87% of the production of crude oil in Latin America. As Table 36 shows, the proportion of foreign-controlled production, excluding Mexico, was 96%. American capital had 62% of the production, British-Dutch capital 34%. Petroleum had become the most important field for investment of British and American capital in Latin America.

The Department of Commerce has estimated that American direct investments in Latin-American petroleum amounted to $617 million in 1929, dropped to $453 million in 1936, were $572 million in 1940. In the latter year the distribution by leading countries was Venezuela $250 million, Colombia $75 million, Mexico $42 million, Brazil $31 million, Cuba $10 million. In 1943 the Treasury Department put the value of American-controlled interest in Latin-American oil enterprises at $572 million, of which $341 million was scheduled for Venezuela, $75 million Colombia, $39 million Argentina, $11 million Peru, $5 million Mexico, $14 million Cuba, $4 million Ecuador. More than $450 million was invested in the three years 1945-47, of which $257 million went to Venezuela. In 1948 another $224 million was added, to bring the total investment up from $645 million in 1945 to $1,376 million in 1948.[13] During the same period the British-Dutch companies were attempting to maintain their relative position by similar expansion of their properties, also largely out of earnings.

The income received from direct investments in Latin-American petroleum activity has been superior to that yielded by most classes of investment. The yield in 1940 was $36.4

---

[13] Data on investments include sizable investments in ships, in sales of the U. S. Maritime Commission to foreign-flag operators controlled by American companies. Ship sales accounted for $157 million in 1946-1948.

TABLE 36

Production of Crude Oil and Refinery Throughput
Classified by Nationality of Companies—1948

(millions of metric tons)

	American Companies	British-Dutch Companies	Others	Total
Production of crude oil:				
Caribbean*	50.9	28.0	0.1	79.0
Other western hemisphere*	0.1	0.5	2.7	3.3
Total—Western Hemisphere				
excluding North America	51.0	28.5	2.8	82.3
Refinery throughput:				
Exporting Areas:				
Caribbean	25.8	23.7	0.1	49.6
Importing Areas:				
Latin America	1.3	0.6	3.8	5.7

Source: *Statistical Summary of Individual Plans for the Development of World Oil Production, Refining and Trade (Excluding North America and Eastern Europe)*, prepared by the United Kingdom and Netherlands Governments with the assistance of the Economic Cooperation Administration, September 12, 1949.

Note: *Caribbean is defined as including Colombia, Ecuador, Netherlands West Indies, Peru, Trinidad, Venezuela.

Latin America, as an importing area, is defined as all Latin America south of Mexico, and the nonproducing Caribbean Islands, but excluding the Caribbean exporting area.

Table shows data according to three groups of companies: American; British-Dutch which includes British and/or joint British-Dutch companies; and others. Operating subsidiaries are classed according to nationality of the parent company rather than according to the country in which they are incorporated.

Conversion factors: 7.3 barrels per metric ton, which is equivalent to the formula "barrels per day x 50 = metric tons per year."

million, the annual average for 1941-43 was $46 million, the annual average for 1944-46 was $104 million. In the case of Venezuela, the income received from petroleum investments was 15.6% in 1938, 8.4% in 1939 and 7.6% in 1940. The average for 1943-48 was 9.8% on capital employed.[14]

Policy-Making for the Industry. We are by now familiar with the problem of scheduling priorities in an economy which lacks the financial and technical resources to proceed full speed in all directions simultaneously. When, in the spring of 1949, the government petroleum entity in Mexico, apparently oppressed by a sense of frustration and tangled impotence, warned that it could carry forward development work "only at the rhythm which its income permits . . . but to advance with the required speed its income is simply not enough," the President of Mexico replied that agriculture and not petroleum carried top priority in Mexico's development plans. To that end, taxes, revenue from local sales of petroleum, and other factors affecting the income of the petroleum entity, were so adjusted as to reduce the resources that might otherwise have been available to it for development. The Wolverton Committee, on the other hand, had viewed petroleum as an area meriting maximum consideration if Mexico was to advance with greatest possible speed.

It was important for the policy-maker in Latin America to appreciate, however, that in the case of petroleum the choice was not limited to priority over other fields in the use of local resources. For petroleum there was a vast pool of foreign capital and technology which could be tapped under arrangements that had proved in some countries already to be capable of an immense contribution to early realization of the general development objectives. This fact was as intelligible to the policy-maker as it was unpalatable to the politician. In the potentially oil-rich countries probably no other field offered such substantial prospects of providing foreign exchange eventually in the volume required for the development needs of the economy. But there was no sense in minimizing the risks attaching to the petroleum industry investments. It was conceivable that the policy-maker could

---

[14] It should be noted that this figure refers to income actually transmitted to the owners. Net income during this period was 21.4% but the larger part of earnings was being re-invested in the enterprises.

gamble on a priority to petroleum in the use of local resources in the same spirit that the typical ill-fed, ill-clothed, and ill-housed Latin American used his own limited funds to buy a lottery ticket weekly on the theory that he could hardly be worse off than he already was and that this gamble afforded him the one chance of emerging from the pit in which he was presently lodged. Conceivably a gamble could pay off, although the Niagaras of misstatement regarding the certainty of great returns once oil was found ignored the world setting of the industry, the character of growing intertional competition, and the uncertainty of the place of any individual exporting nation in the overall picture. National policy seemed to dictate a somewhat more responsible attitude toward the use of resources. It could also be argued that delay in development to the possible benefit of succeeding generations was to be preferred to sharing of the wealth in any form today to the advantage of the present generation. But the very low standards of living that currently prevailed raised some serious questions as to such a decision.

It was clear by 1950, however, that decisive action was imperative. In the major importing countries petroleum was becoming an important drain on foreign-exchange supplies and consumption was rising more rapidly than production. In a number of producing countries for which petroleum had been a significant export commodity, the growth of consumption relative to production was reducing the foreign exchange created by the industry. And only Venezuela had succeeded in making of the petroleum industry an immense contributor to the over-all development plans of the country. Domestic private capital was unwilling to assume the risks attaching to the industry. The governments would have to mobilize their resources to the disadvantage of other fields of development if petroleum was to be made a government activity. And foreign capital was ready to come in and assume risks under suitbale conditions of investment. The alternatives were clearly indicated.

We shall examine next some major fields of development which will help us to understand the tremendous financial requirements of economic development.

SUPPLEMENTARY READING

L. G. Weeks, "Highlights on 1948 Developments in Foreign Petroleum Fields," *Bulletin of the American Association of Petroleum Geologists,* June, 1949, pp. 1029-1070.

Herbert Feis, *Petroleum and American Foreign Policy* (Food Research Institute, Stanford University, Commodity Policy Studies No. 3), pp. 1-62.

Josephus Daniels, *Shirt-Sleeve Diplomat* (Chapel Hill, The University of North Carolina Press, 1947), pp. 211-268.

Lloyd J. Hughlett, Editor, *Industrialization of Latin America* (McGraw-Hill Book Company, New York, 1946), pp. 273-299.

Eugene V. Rostow, *A National Policy for the Oil Industry* (New Haven, Yale University Press, 1948), pp. 9-15, 57-69, 108-115.

Chapter 10

Energy Requirements

Every hour of human effort in Latin America is supplemented by less than one-tenth as much non-human energy as supplements the hour of human toil in the United States. In the United States, as J. Frederic Dewhurst has aptly noted, "although many a worker still has to 'work like a horse' in the traditional meaning of the term, power-driven machinery is now doing most of our work for us; most occupations today require more horse sense than horsepower." [1] In 1937, as Table 37 shows, inanimate sources of energy (coal, wood, oil, gas, and water power) furnished 97.6% of the energy consumed for productive purposes in the United States, with 1% furnished by draft animals and 1.4% by human energy. In Latin America, however, only about two-thirds of the energy consumed for productive purposes was then being provided by inanimate sources, with draft animals furnishing 19.4% and human energy still accounting for 16.2%. Since 1937 the consumption of energy for productive purposes has been increasing at the rate of 6% per year in Latin America, compared with about 7% per year in the United States; and the increased proportion of inanimate energy consumed in Latin America has been a further encouraging sign. (See Table 38).

In coal-poor South America in 1937, wood provided about 40% of the inanimate energy, oil 30%, coal 16%, gas 3%, electricity 10%. In Middle America, oil provided two-thirds of the energy, with coal, wood and electricity providing about one-tenth each. In the United States coal accounted for almost half of the energy consumed, oil for one-fourth, gas for 14%, wood 6%, electricity 9%. (Table 39). During

---

[1] J. Frederic Dewhurst and Associates, *America's Needs and Resources* (The Twentieth Century Fund, New York, 1947), p. 681.

TABLE 37

Energy Consumption for Productive Purposes in 1937

(Millions of kilowatt-hours electricity equivalent)

	Animate Sources		Inanimate Sources	Total	Ratio of Inanimate to Total	Per capita use in kilowatt-hours electricity equivalent
	Human	Draft Animal				
South America	8,878	12,235	34,902	56,014	62.3%	631
Argentina	1,276	5,460	13,686	20,423	67.0	1,600
Brazil	4,325	4,116	11,029	19,470	56.6	450
Chile	460	343	4,537	5,340	85.0	1,162
Middle America	4,006	3,288	16,572	23,866	69.4	596
Mexico	1,915	1,795	9,017	12,726	70.9	664
Canada	1,112	1,735	56,292	59,137	95.2	5,318
United States	13,022	8,677	889,294	910,993	97.6	6,996

Source: Department of State, *Energy Resources of the World* (Washington, 1949), pp. 84, 102. This publication is referred to hereafter as "Energy Resources."

293

World War II the shortage of imported fuels in Latin America temporarily checked the movement away from fuel wood, but the long-range trend toward hydroelectric power and petroleum has continued. Consumption of electricity rose about 8% per year from 1937 to 1948 and the pace of increase seems limited only by the ability to arrange for additional capacity since the output of new installations is quickly absorbed. In 1937 industry consumed about half of the electricity, 45% of the oil and one-fifth of the coal; the railways were the principal outlet for coal. Table 40 shows the use pattern.

TABLE 38

Energy Consumption for Productive Purposes 1937-1948

(billions of kilowatt-hours, electricity equivalent)

	1937	1946	1948 (Estimate)
South America	56.0	78.0	86.2
Argentina	20.4	22.8	27.6
Brazil	19.5	24.2	25.0
Chile	5.3	5.0	5.4
Middle America	23.9	35.8	42.2
Mexico	12.7	21.5	25.7
Canada	59.1	103.7	112.3
United States	911.0	1426.8	1562.7

Source: *Energy Resources*, p. 102, Appendix G.

The Latin American policy-maker has been extremely conscious in recent years of the fact that mechanical-energy resources are the controlling factor in economic activity and that the rate at which the nation can mobilize effectively its energy potential largely determines the extent to which it can advance the welfare of its people and lessen the human toil. Harnessing more inanimate energy in order to multiply the human effort, however, implies a very large capital investment, advanced engineering and managerial skills, effective application of scientific discoveries. In 1935 Latin America was accounting for only about 3.6% of the world production of energy, compared with 3.3% for France, 13.7% for the British Isles and 37.7% for the United States. (Table 41). As we

TABLE 39

Nature of Fuel and Power Consumed in 1937

(Percentage of the total)

	Coal	Wood	Oil	Gas	Electricity
South America	16.1%	39.7%	30.6%	3.2%	10.4%
Argentina	18.7	9.7	50.0	7.0	14.6
Brazil	16.4	62.7	11.6	0.4	8.9
Chile	18.3	56.5	13.8	0.6	10.8
Middle America	9.1	10.5	65.4	3.4	11.6
Mexico	9.8	9.0	51.3	8.3	21.6
Canada	44.2	10.0	13.8	3.8	28.2
United States	46.2	6.1	24.4	14.1	9.2

Source: *Energy Resources*, p. 92.

have seen, the endowment in coal is poor. While petroleum may eventually prove more abundant than it has yet been proven to be in some of the more advanced countries, we saw in the previous chapter that the process of mobilizing these resources has been retarded by introduction of policy considerations other than that of accelerating development. The area's resources are most promising in water power, on which the countries have been placing their greatest hopes. The potential water-power output of South America is more than six times its *total* current energy consumption, that of Middle America is at least three times the total current energy consumption of the area, while that of North America is only about one-quarter of its total energy consumption. In 1937 about half of Chile's electricity, three-fourths of Peru's and Colombia's, 85% of Brazil's, and 60% of Mexico's electricity was produced in hydroelectric plants, and the remaining portion in thermoelectric plants operating on domestic fuel. By contrast, about 4% of Argentina's electricity came from hydroelectric plants and the remaining part from thermoelectric plants that imported nine-tenths of their fuel. Since that time hydroelectric activity has gained in importance in Latin America.

Character of the Power Industry. The policy considerations affecting the production of electricity in Latin America have

TABLE 40

Uses of Energy in 1937

(Percentage of the Total Used)

	Military	Overseas Bunkers	Local Bunkers	Rail-ways	Auto-mobiles	Domestic, Commer-cial, etc.	Industry	Stored or Lost
South America	3.4	1.1	2.5	19.5	4.7	39.2	22.9	6.7
Argentina	1.6	2.5	3.8	27.7	8.7	17.5	36.0	2.2
Brazil	0.7	1.8	4.3	24.6	3.5	49.1	14.7	1.3
Chile	2.1	4.4	-	7.0	1.4	62.7	20.8	1.6
Middle America	5.0	15.9	1.0	11.6	4.0	17.0	32.2	13.3
Mexico	-	2.1	0.3	15.0	4.3	17.1	57.9	3.3
Canada	-	0.9	2.3	13.5	6.7	35.9	37.6	3.1
United States	0.3	1.2	1.9	11.9	11.4	28.6	40.9	3.8

Source: *Energy Resources*, p. 88.

included prominently:
(1) The desire to make electricity a low-cost source of energy as a stimulus to expansion of economic activity generally.
(2) The fact that the industry has been dominated by foreign capital which was concentrated in a few companies whose earnings have been closely controlled by regulatory bodies and which were vulnerable to popular prejudice against foreign activity and the easy mobilization of that prejudice for cause or without cause, as it happened to suit the pur-

TABLE 41

Ratios between Energy Production and Resources: 1935

(Percentage of World Total)

	Area	Energy Produced	Resources
World	100.00%	100.00%	100.00%
Latin America	15.796%	3.626%	2.312%
Mexico	1.488	0.622	0.209
Central America	0.422	0.011	0.169
West Indies	0.180	0.153	0.010
Argentina	2.110	0.186	0.174
Bolivia	1.007	0.003	0.084
Brazil	6.430	0.122	0.845
Chile	0.561	0.128	0.109
Colombia	0.878	0.227	0.141
Ecuador	0.232	0.023	0.034
Paraguay	0.346	0.033	0.068
Peru	0.944	0.228	0.167
Uruguay	0.141	....	0.010
Venezuela	0.689	1.890	0.151
United States (continental)	5.922	37.695	28.992
Canada	7.209	1.488	6.048
France	0.416	3.300	0.386
British Isles and Eire	0.236	13.743	2.042
U. S. S. R.	16.900	8.584	15.152
Africa	22.613	0.916	8.823

Source: Abbott Payson Usher, "The Resource Requirements of an Industrial Economy," *The Journal of Economic History*, Supplement VII, 1947, pp. 44-45. Latin America is defined to include the foreign-owned possessions (Guiana, etc.).

poses of government officials and would-be officials. In Brazil, for instance, one foreign-owned corporation supplied about 65% of the power and 80% of the telephone service while another company supplied 15% of the power generated. In Argentina a single foreign corporation supplied about 65% of all the light and power, two others accounted for 25%. In Chile, one company provided 80% of the light and power service. In Mexico, one foreign company accounted for about half of the power generated, another for almost one-third.

(3) The immense capital requirements of the industry.

(4) The clash of interest between the capital requirements for installations in the growing industrializing areas which under existing conditions in themselves tended to exceed capital availabilities (foreign and domestic) and the requirements for laying down the basic power, communications, and transportation facilities in newer areas, without which the nations could not hope to develop beyond existing population concentrations.

(5) The continuing pressure to nationalize the industry, stemming partly from the hope that it might thus be possible to use the earnings of the more profitable regions to subsidize the development of newer areas, partly from simple hostility to foreign enterprise, partly from impatience with the pace of foreign expansion, and in some cases from a reasoned calculation that under government ownership a social-rate structure could be established which would accept deficits on operation of these basic facilities as a proper cost of achieving more rapid expansion of industrial production.

(6) The lack of interest on the part of domestic private capital in an industry whose earnings tended to be low compared with alternative investments, partly because of the unwillingness of the government to permit remunerative rates which would yield profits more in line with the prevailing returns on Latin American industrial and real estate investments.

(7) The general inability to finance the capital requirements of the industry from the resources which the governments could mobilize at home.

(8) The fact that power installations generally do not

directly increase the foreign-exchange earnings of the economies. Consequently, foreign financing imposes a drain on exchange resources until such time (if ever) as the increased industrial and agricultural production made possible by expanded power capacity creates additional foreign-exchange earnings through increases in exports or decreases in essential import requirements.

The Electric Power Industry in Mexico. When the second world war ended, 95% of Mexico's rural population was without electricity. Consumption in the urban centers had been increasing by about 7% per year and investment had not been made sufficiently attractive to draw financing for expansion of facilities to meet demand. Shortages of power were threatening to be a brake on the process of industrialization.[2] Installed power-plant capacity was about 700,000 kilowatts. The bulk of installations were foreign-owned. Mexican Light and Power Company, which supplied about half of the power, had originally been organized in Canada with Canadian, British, and Continental capital and entered Mexico in 1902, taking over the original concession granted in 1896 out of which had come the first commercial development of electric power in Mexico. American & Foreign Power Company was supplying about 30% of the power. Developed hydroelectric power was little more than one-twentieth of the potential. Electric power was being primarily applied to productive uses. Even in the Mexico City area, which had a relatively large well-to-do residential population, half or more of the power generated was being used in industry and mining.

In 1937 the government had established a Federal Electricity Commission to organize and direct on a nonprofit basis a national system for generation, transmission, and distribution of electrical energy. The government appreciated that rural electrification for the sparsely populated rural areas with their extremely low purchasing power was not practicable on a commercial basis, but it set an objective of

---

[2] This refers to continuing shortages, rather than the familiar periodic restriction of consumption made necessary by droughts.

furnishing electricity at least to the large villages and smaller towns. In the urban communities, as the pressure on existing capacity grew, the companies increasingly curtailed the promotional effort to develop new business even in areas adjacent to the cities which they had once cultivated. The government decided to accelerate the flow of capital into the electric power industry, even if it had to use government credit. It adopted the role of supplementing where necessary the activities of private enterprise in the provision of electric power, partly by constructing generating and transmission facilities which it operated itself and partly by assisting private companies in financing expansion of their capacity. The Commission is financed by (a) a 10% tax on electricity consumption which went into effect in 1939, yielded $0.9 million in 1939, $3.5 million in 1948, and continued to produce increasing sums; (b) the sale of power which yielded $0.05 million in 1943, the first year, and by 1948 was yielding over $2.5 million with expectation that sales would yield over $22 million annually when the projected construction program was completed. It also has the authority to negotiate loans and float bonds, although in 1947 the authority to borrow abroad was delegated to an official specialized financing agency, the Nacional Financiera. The Commission prepared a program of power expansion for 1947-52 which contemplated expansion of Mexico's installed power-plant capacity to 1.5 million kilowatts (compared with capacity of 1 million kilowatts at the end of 1948).[3]

In the course of implementing this program a new formula for the structure of the power industry slowly evolved. A Rate Commission was reorganized and raised to independent status in 1948, with the task of verifying and approving the property valuations which the companies wished used as the basis for the rates, under the legal provision that rates were to be geared to earning a reasonable return on investment. The credit of the Mexican government has been offered as a guarantee of loans that can be effected by the industry in

---

[3] In addition to the Commission's work, the Ministry of Hydraulic Resources which was charged with irrigation programs had some $25 million of hydroelectric plants in its $391 million program.

Washington. In 1949, for instance, the government borrowed $10 million from the International Bank for Reconstruction and Development which was made available to the Mexican Light and Power Company, with the additional arrangement that when the company completed reorganization of its capital structure, the government would guarantee a long-term loan to the Company by the Bank. And the government has undertaken to borrow directly abroad for its direct participation in the industry, as in the case of its loan of $24.1 million in 1949 from the International Bank for Reconstruction and Development. Nine-tenths of the capacity projected by the Electricity Commission involves marketing in areas already wholly or partly served by existing private companies or in areas that are considered natural areas of expansion for them. With this fact in mind, the Commission has asserted that it intends to wholesale its energy to private companies wherever possible in such areas. In the Mexico City area, for instance, where until recently the Mexican Light and Power Company had produced and distributed all electric power, the Commission has been constructing an hydroelectric system whose output is being sold to the private company. By 1948 public-plant capacity under the program was estimated already to have been installed to the extent of 100,000 kilowatts and it was expected that when the Commission had completed its ambitious plans the capacity of the public plants would exceed that of the privately owned installations.

It remained to be seen whether the government would be content to extend the use of its credit for the financing of private companies and to provide additional investments for generating capacity without following through with parallel or competitive distributing facilities. There was some quiet satisfaction with the thought that participation by the government might help the companies get a more favorable rate structure, on the theory that the yardstick provided by the Mexican government's operations was likely to consist of a less efficient operation; and the possibility was recognized that the need to service obligations which involved the government's credit as well as that of the companies might serve as an inducement to provide a rate basis that would yield a more "reasonable" rate of return. Whether these advantages would balance the injection of the political element into the business operation remained to be tested. In the meantime, consumption of electricity was mounting more rapidly than ever, with an increase of 10% annually from 1946 to 1949.

Electricity for Brazil. In 1948 President Dutra estimated that Brazil needed an annual increase of 200,000 kilowatts in its installed power plant, an investment of $75 million per year in electrical service, of which $25 million would require foreign exchange to cover expenditures abroad. Brazil's production of electricity had been increasing by 10% annually, existing capacity was overloaded, and every addition to capacity was quickly absorbed in what seemed to be an insatiable demand for power. The installed power plant had been expanded by 11% annually from 1920 to 1930, 4.8% annually from 1930 to 1940, 3.5% annually from 1940 to 1947. An annual increase of 14% in capacity for at least six years was now sought in order to allow the supply of power to lead Brazilian development rather than to be the retarding factor as it had become in the 1940's. Capacity of 39,000 kilowatts per year had been added in the period 1920-1930, 36,000 annually 1930-40, 56,000 annually from 1940 to 1947; there had been individual years when more than 100,000 kilowatts of capacity were added. Now a pace of 200,000 kilowatts annually was set as a target. The 1.5 million kilowatts installed by the end of 1947 gave Brazil the very low per capita capacity of 0.03 kilowatts; the target of 0.05 per capita by the end of 1954 would still be low, if plans for railway electrification and continuing industrial development were to be effectively carried out. The resources were available. Brazil was still mobilizing less than 10% of its enormous hydroelectric resources.[4]

The electric power industry was dominated by foreign enterprises. Brazilian Traction, Light and Power Company, a Canadian corporation with predominant Canadian ownership and important American and British participation, was producing and distributing about two-thirds of all the power produced in Brazil, controlled over 80% of the telephones in service, had 53% of installed power plant. American & Foreign Power Company was producing 15% of the power, controlled about 14% of the installed capacity. More than half of the power sales of Brazilian Traction were to industrial users; in 1948 railway electrification accounted for one-seventh of the energy it distributed. It should be noted that Brazilian Traction's activities were concentrated in the most highly industrialized areas of Brazil — the São Paulo and Rio de Janeiro areas.

In the Brazilian power problem were practically all of the policy alternatives which can confront the policy-maker. First, there was the problem of more intensive cultivation of existing centers against development of primary facilities in new areas. There had, for instance, been recurring interest in the middle São Francisco valley as a problem area whose development might be stimulated by construction of sizable power installations. It was argued that a large hydroelectric installation at the Paulo Afonso falls about 200 miles from the mouth of the São Francisco River might supply power not only to adjacent areas in Bahia and Alagoas but also eventually to the coastal cities from João Pessoa to Salvador. The river's minimum flow, it was estimated, sufficed for an eventual installation of 440,000 kilowatts, an immediate installation of perhaps 110,000 kilowatts. A transmission line to Belém, extended eventually to Boa Vista, was outlined. The valley land on the left bank of the river was capable of irrigation, with the suitable crops including long-staple cotton, bananas, fruit, local food crops. On the other hand,

---

[4] Resources had been mobilized unevenly. In 1948 hydraulic potential of about 14 million kilowatts compared with installed hydroelectric capacity of 1.2 million; in São Paulo, potential of 1.9 million compared with actual installed capacity of 0.6 million. While hydroelectric installations dominated the electricity industry, it should be remembered that they were not alone the answer to the energy problem; some of the hydroelectric potential was too far from likely markets; some could furnish the rated capacity only when there was normal rainfall and therefore required stand-by thermal plant capacity with the accompanying problem of fuel for such plants; some communities were too far from hydroelectric potential and needed thermal energy.

opponents of regional development at this time argued that it was too early to construct transmission lines and receiver systems to serve coastal cities, with the distances making costs excessive; the prospective industries were not large users of electric power, and increased supplies of oil and natural gas seemed in prospect; the light traffic and inadequate character of the railroads in the northeast did not make electrification feasible in the near future. Since the capital requirements to reach the objective of 200,000 kilowatts per year might prove beyond the reach of the economy, the challenge of a multiple-purpose river development in the São Francisco valley with its associated developmental costs had to be weighed against further investment in the older industrialized areas which were crying for more power and where expansion of activity was sure to follow immediately upon addition of power capacity.

Second, there was the relationship of power to other developmental requirements. Domestic private capital had little interest in the low earnings of an industry dependent on government-controlled rates, even though there was great security in such investments; it had demonstrated a similar lack of interest in petroleum where the risk was enormous and returns high *if* the venture were successful. The investment in power would not create foreign exchange directly; it would add a burden on existing foreign exchange availabilities for the servicing of the investment; and it was not likely to be attractive to foreign capital unless an expansion of the nation's foreign-exchange supply by simultaneous development in other fields (possibly petroleum or mining) seemed to be adding assurance of eventual availability of funds for remittance of profits and interest when the companies wished to remit. There were limits on the government's borrowing power abroad and it might be feasible to use that power for those lines in which private capital was less interested in flowing into the country.[5]

Third, cheap power had been a recurring theme of development in the São Paulo and Rio de Janeiro areas. If the rate structure that yielded cheap power had been partly responsible for the reluctance of equity capital to come forward in the amounts required by the industry, there was at least a suggestion that the country might have to decide whether it wanted to subsidize, in effect, the industries whose profit ratios were notoriously high and not likely to be seriously affected by more costly power, or to suffer continuing difficulties in the matter of adequacy of power supply. The constitution recognized that "control and revision of rates shall be determined so that the profits of the concessionaires, not to exceed a fair return on their capital, may permit them to meet the need for improvement and expansion of these services." All too frequently in Latin America rate regulation for the utilities has meant merely a demand that rates be lowered rather than an attempt to determine the value of properties on a fair basis and the fixing of rates to yield adequate returns.

Fourth, there was the question of the degree to which the government itself should participate in the industry. In the government's plan for 1948-53 it was assumed that private capital (in this case foreign capital) would continue to be the dominating element in the structure of the industry; about three-fourths of the expansion was to be accomplished by private capital. Yet, such were the difficulties of raising equity capital for the industry at home and abroad that in 1947-49 the utility companies began to use the facilities of U. S. government and inter-governmental banks in Washington. In 1948 American & Foreign Power Company borrowed $8.3 million from the Export-Import Bank for certain dollar requirements of its expansion program, and in 1949 Brazilian Traction, Light and Power Company borrowed $75 million from the International Bank for Reconstruction and Development. The latter loan was guaranteed by the Brazilian

---

5 It might be noted that when the International Bank for Reconstruction and Development announced a loan of $75 million to the Brazilian Traction, Light and Power Company in 1949, it pointed out that the expansion of hydroelectric capacity promised to be economical in the matter of foreign exchange since it would take imports of at least $10 million of coal to provide energy equivalent to what the projected hydroelectric expansion would yield, and that this exceeded what would be needed to service the loan.

government. For the many smaller companies in Brazil—many with outdated installations and inadequate engineering staff—it might be necessary to establish some sort of central agency to assist in financing and planning. And there would probably be foreign financing too for that portion of the power plant which was to be undertaken by national and local governments. It was clear that the credit of the Brazilian government, even for private activity, was increasingly to be involved in the expansion of the industry, and rate policy was likely to become a more important element in intergovernmental financial relations.

Argentine Power Policy. In Argentina the familiar pattern of foreign ownership and demand rising so fast that the increase in capacity of installations has recently tended to lag behind demand has been complicated by the policy of nationalizing the public utilities. The constitution adopted in 1949 declared that the public services shall belong to the State and that utilities currently under private control shall be transferred to the State by means of purchase or expropriation with prior indemnification, supported in each instance by national law. The development of this policy, however, has been in process for a long time, and has had the effect of discouraging investment. "Because of the unfavorable conditions under which the subsidiaries are operating," reported one of the largest factors in the industry in 1949, "the Company has made no new dollar investments in Argentina for many years." [6]

At the outbreak of the second world war, about two-thirds of the light and power had been supplied by a European-controlled enterprise, Compañía Hispano Americana de Electricidad ("Chade"). An American firm, American & Foreign Power Company, supplied about 13% although it did not operate in heavy-consuming Buenos Aires. A Swiss-German-Italian controlled firm, Compañía Italo-Argentina de Electricidad, supplied about 12% of the light and power.

---

[6] Annual Report, 1948, American & Foreign Power Company, Inc., p. 7. The Company had already suffered expropriation of some of its properties and had had difficulty in negotiating reasonable settlements.

Consumption had been increasing by about 7% annually in the past decade. Per capita power-plant installed far exceeded that of Brazil. Soon after the war ended, the government announced a five-year "plan" of economic development which recognized the importance of power by assigning to it some 25 to 30% of the expenditures involved in the program. It was proposed to erect 45 hydroelectric stations and 11 thermal power stations with aggregate capacity of 1.6 million kilowatts, more than the existing power-plant installed; included in the plans was a 400,000 to 500,000 kilowatt plant, the most powerful in South America, to be erected on the Uruguay River jointly by Argentina and Uruguay.

Unfortunately for Argentina, although it could mobilize impressive statistics of hydroelectric potential, most of the sites were far from the consuming area which, as is the case with most economic activity in Argentina, was heavily concentrated. Not only were some of the contemplated power stations so distant from consumption centers as to be of questionable economic merit, but also the flow of the rivers on which they must rely for water supply was exceedingly irregular. There was the added misfortune that fuel-poor Argentina had to use imported fuel for its thermal installations. Production of electric energy rose by only 5% annually from 1937 to 1948, but demand pressed constantly on capacity and it was clear that installed plant would have to be sizably expanded or the development process retarded.

From the standpoint of policy, the decision to nationalize was especially important because the capital requirements to meet normally expanding demand for electric energy and to make abundant power a stimulus to economic expansion already appeared to strain foreseeable availabilities of capital. If the country were to acquire existing plant, it must inevitably slow down the expansion, for the capital requirements for indemnification of private owners would preclude availability of capital for large new investment. And it must be remembered that in its associated fuel problem (oil) Argentina was also adopting the policy of doing without foreign participation. Without going into the merits of private vs.

public exploitation of power resources, the decision seemed certainly to threaten a slowdown in the process of development.

Chilean Power Policy. "The capacity of a nation's industry for production," asserted a policy statement of the Chilean government somewhat recklessly in 1942, "is practically independent of the population and, if we disregard the capital invested in its equipment, depends solely upon the available supplies of mechanical energy. From this we arrive at the indispensable need for actively developing the generation of hydroelectric power."

The potential yield of Chile's waterpower reserves is about 4% of the total Latin American waterpower potential. In the years immediately preceding the second world war Chile was already utilizing a higher proportion of its potential than any of the other major Latin American countries. Since its petroleum resources were then very uncertain and its coal resources satisfactory only in relation to the even poorer endowment of neighboring countries, the Chileans appreciated the importance of hydroelectric development. In 1938, of total installed capacity of 470,000 kilowatts, about 188,000 was accounted for by public utilities, 227,000 by nitrate and copper companies, 55,000 kilowatts by industrial and smaller mining concerns. More than three-fourths of the light and power service was being provided by the American-owned American & Foreign Power Company. There had been no major hydroelectric installations accomplished from 1932 on, and perhaps two-fifths of the existing capacity was hydroelectric.

When the government set up the Corporación de Fomento de la Producción in 1939, it immediately set out to increase power plant capacity by 50% in three years and set a target of double the capacity by 1950. The times were not immediately favorable to such an accomplishment. In 1942 the plan for electrification was produced on which Chilean economic development was to be based. The government proposed a fourfold expansion of installed power plant exclusive of facilities of the nitrate and copper companies. It enunciated boldly a policy of making power a positive force behind development by relegating profit-making to a distinctly secondary role, if indeed it was to be considered at all. It anticipated that capital requirements would be far beyond the capacity and interest of domestic private capital, that the pace of expansion would prove beyond the capacity of foreign companies to raise capital abroad especially in view of the plan to gear the rate structure to a cheaper power policy, and accordingly it planned to rely on the credit of the government to finance the program. The initial estimate of $100 million, even spread over a decade and a half, was not negligible in an economy whose savings had been estimated at $50 million or less per year.

The electrification plan called for the government to build and retain ownership of central generators and main transmission lines and substations which would produce and integrate energy in large quantities to distributive enterprises, industries and other important consumers, rural electrification cooperatives and associations for mechanical irrigation works. In retaining ownership the government hoped to be able to influence the price and availability in lines in which it was particularly interested in rapid development. For the north, where hydroelectric resources were limited, new steam generating plants and distributing systems were laid out. To serve the Santiago area the Sauzal plant was scheduled to provide 75,000 kilowatts, and estimates made that 80,000 tons of coal might be saved in the process of displacing steam plants with similar savings by making possible further electrification of the railways. The first 25,000 kilowatt unit of this development began to furnish power to American & Foreign Power Company in 1948, with the second and third units going into use in the following year. This area also benefited from substantial additions to private capacity. For the Concepción region, the Abanico plant was designed to stimulate coal and steel activity. And on the Pilmaiquén River a plant would furnish power to the Osorno region and also provide power for transmission to other urban areas.

By 1948 the Corporación de Fomento had installed 128,000 kilowatts, assisted largely by loans from the Export-Import Bank, and was hoping to add another 200,000 kilowatts by

1955. Production of electrical energy was growing by 14% per year, and yet demand continued to run ahead of available supplies. In 1948 the Corporación obtained a loan of $13.5 million from the International Bank for Reconstruction and Development, with which it proposed to finance an 81,000 kilowatt expansion of installed power plant, all connected with mechanical irrigation projects and the secondary distribution of electricity. The Bank pointed out that existing installed capacity for public service was then 450,000 kilowatts, of which one-third was water-generated. Meanwhile the American & Foreign Power Company in 1947 had outlined a six-year $35 million expansion program which it proposed to finance also through the financial agencies in Washington, once the Chilean government had given assurance of a rate structure to permit a minimum net revenue. The proposed arrangements sought to maintain net revenues at a point where full interest and dividends would be assured on securities presently outstanding and to be outstanding, with adequate provision for assured remittance of profits and interest.

Power Policy Elsewhere in Latin America. The other Latin-American countries account for less than one-fifth of the electrical energy produced in Latin America. But the prevailing characteristics of the industry are present here too; demand pressing eagerly on any capacity made available, domestic capital uninterested in such investment, foreign capital heavily involved but showing increasing signs of being unable to secure adequate support from private equity financing channels, growing government participation in direct exploitation and in financing, increased reliance on the financing agencies in Washington.

The Uruguayan government had long participated directly in the production of energy. Lacking fuel, the curtailments of activity necessitated successively by wars and foreign-exchange stringencies compelled a bold solution. In 1937 a German group was engaged to construct the hydroelectric development at Rincón del Bonete on the Río Negro, and when war made it impossible for the Germans to complete

with respect to developing new exports or expanding exports by encouraging exploitation of its natural resources, each country would have to bear in mind its need for simultaneous expansion of its exchange-earning capacity if it was to attract the investment in power and transportation which was basic to its economic development.

SUPPLEMENTARY READING

U. S. Department of State, *Energy Resources of the World* (Washington, 1949), pp. 3-34.

Morris Llewellyn Cooke, *Brazil on the March* (McGraw-Hill Book Company, New York, 1944), pp. 193-208.

J. Frederic Dewhurst and Associates, *America's Needs and Resources* (The Twentieth Century Fund, New York, 1947), pp. 680-687.

Lloyd J. Hughlett, Editor, *Industrialization of Latin America* (McGraw-Hill Book Company, New York, 1946), pp. 319-345.

Annual Report of American & Foreign Power Company; Brazilian Traction, Light and Power Company; Société Financière de Transports et d'Enterprises Industrielles.

Guida Berrigan Hall, "Power: Hub of South America's Industrial Development," *Foreign Commerce Weekly*, April 10, 1950, pp. 10-13, 42-43.

Chapter 11

Transportation and Communication

On the subject of transportation the Latin American policy-maker in 1950 still struggled in a megatherian rut as elusive of egress as those which so frequently made motoring in Latin America a test of endurance and a tribute to patience. Although some three and one-half billion dollars of foreign capital had been invested in railway facilities, Latin America had only about 85,000 miles of railways, slightly more than one-third the mileage of the United States in an area more than two and one-half times as large.[1] Financially, the railways were unremunerative, had fallen largely into the hands of the governments to serve as a further drag on the limited budgetary resources of the nations. Physically, the railway plant was run down; the right of way, rolling stock and other facilities were badly in need of improvement and modernization. Technically, the railways suffered the unfortunate inheritance from the period of construction—the diversity of gauge, frequently poor construction, dependence upon imported fuel, sometimes the long winding trackage that reflected original conditions of construction contracts, the steep grades and sharp curves reflecting topographical obstacles and capital shortages in construction. The highway mileage was less than one-fifth that of the United States, and more than 70% of it was unsurfaced. Perhaps 25,000 miles were paved in cement or high or low type bituminous.

The coming of air transportation had been hailed hopefully in Latin America. The new form seemed especially

[1] Feis estimates that more than $3 billion of European capital was devoted to railway construction in Latin America, either directly by foreign companies or through the borrowing of governments. Herbert Feis, *Europe, the World's Banker* (The Council on Foreign Relations, Yale University Press, 1930), p. 193.

suited to Latin American requirements since it could avoid the forbidding geographical obstacles that balked surface facilities and since it imposed smaller capital requirements better suited to the limited financial resources of the area. In the absence of a fully matured rail and road system, the delay and conditioning of the new form of transport which would be necessitated in the more advanced countries by the desire to protect the huge investment in older forms might be avoided. So promising did air transport appear to be that even private local capital trickled into the industry at the start, some $3 million being added to $4.6 million of local government investment in air transport by 1941. Great as was the contribution of air traffic to the movement of passengers, however, by 1950 it had not yet demonstrated significant capacity to solve the problem of bulk freight and of the opening up of areas involving heavy cargo movement.

"Transportation," Wilfred Owen has written, "reflects the success with which the economy as a whole is functioning. Achievements in providing transportation service furnish a measure of the general state of the nation's development and the standard of living." [2] Latin America's failure to achieve a significant approximation of maximum mobility with economy, speed and safety was in 1950 more than an index of the current failure of the economies to function at relatively high levels of efficiency. It seemed to fix definite limits to the developmental potential, and in this role the failure generated considerable pessimism. For instance, Tannenbaum in a brilliant work on Mexico in 1950 reviewed the requirements estimates of some $2 billion for primary capital goods for the Mexican economy if development was to proceed effectively (included in which was a minimum of over $600 million for transportation), and having in mind the fact that such investments would not in themselves directly contribute materially to expansion of exports with which to service the investments, asked whether Mexico should not be devising "an alternative program, one more consonant with Mexican realities . . . a way out on a local parochial basis in thousands

---

[2] Dewhurst, *op. cit.*, p. 226.

of little communities . . . a philosophy of little things."[3]
Again, when the American Technical Mission was in Brazil
in 1942, the Brazilian associates of the group joined in pointing out that "the savings and borrowings of a century would
scarcely be enough to throw railways across the vast distances of Brazil." It was easy to be pessimistic. If these
countries had capital they could build railway facilities if
they had foreign exchange with which to pay for fuel and
equipment. If they had gasoline and motor vehicles they
could have satisfactory highway facilities if they could raise
the capital to build and maintain the roads and the foreign
exchange required for basic facilities and user requirements
alike. If air transport were not still inherently an expensive
method of transportation they could have an efficient transport system if they had the financial and technical resources
with which to pay for an air network or if they could service
foreign investments for the purpose. All other developmental problems were dwarfed by the magnitudes involved
in creation of a satisfactory transport system, without which
an effective industrial structure geared to a national market
could not be created. Yet, it needed to be noted and stressed
that however distant maximum mobility might be, it was
the day-to-day policy decision that was preventing the countries from reaching a more satisfactory position than they
currently achieved.

The Railroads. The Latin American railroads were largely
constructed as local extensions of the commercial interest in
foreign trade rather than as instruments of national unification, were designed to expedite the movement of the staples
of foreign trade to the ports rather than to develop a larger
internal market for local production, were destined largely
to lag behind economic development rather than to be trail-
blazers into new territory for the farmer and the miner and
the industrialist. The main lines, more than two-thirds of
the existing mileage, were built before the first world war.
In Argentina the rail network radiated out of the port of

---

[3] Frank Tannenbaum, *Mexico: The Struggle for Peace and Bread*
(Alfred A. Knopf, New York, 1950), pp. 242-243.

FIGURE 2

The Railroads of Latin America

RAILROADS OF LATIN AMERICA

This map of railways in the other Americas illustrates the comparative lack of railway development in the interior of Central and South America—especially of trans-continental latitudinal rail lines. Note the tendency of rail networks to extend fan-wise into the interior from principal seaports, with few or no connections between major coastal cities.

Source: *Foreign Commerce Weekly*, January 27, 1945, p. 11.

Buenos Aires, was concentrated in the rich agricultural provinces of the east and north central parts of the country, one-third of the mileage in the province of Buenos Aires, about three-fourths serving six provinces. In Brazil nine-tenths of the railway mileage is in a narrow coastal belt of about 300 miles in width, heavily concentrated out of Rio de Janeiro for effective service of São Paulo, Santos and Rio, leaving three states and the territories carved out of them with 35 miles of railway and 70 miles of highway in an area half the size of the United States. Systems converge on Montevideo in Uruguay, on Santiago in Chile. The basic outlines of the Mexican surface system consist of the three lines to the United States from Mexico City and the two to the Gulf from Mexico City; the railroads to the Gulf primarily facilitate the movement of foreign-trade traffic into and out of Vera Cruz; most of the rural communities are without railway service. With the great period of railway construction long past, Latin America finds itself with about 10 route miles of railways per 1000 square miles of area, perhaps one-eighth the ratio of the United States system. Less than a fifth of the area lies within twenty miles of a railway. Fairly adequate facilities have been provided for the great staples—coffee, nitrate, cereals, etc., but the concept of a national railway system is remote from realization in the major countries. Figure 2 and Table 42 indicate the extent of the railway network.

During the period when the railways were largely owned and operated by private capital, the Latin American countries with rare exceptions were not able to develop and enforce a consistent philosophy of user-protection through regulation. It is true that some of the railroads were profitable, some extremely so, but in general the Latin American governments were confronted with a continuing challenge in the precarious finances of the railway networks as a whole. Costs of construction and maintenance were high, partly so from necessity in overcoming the unfavorable topographical and climatic conditions, partly less justifiedly from the financial control out of London and Paris with its manipulation of stocks and its interlocking relationships with the construc-

TABLE 42

Route Miles of Railways Per 1,000 Square Miles

	Route Miles (000)	Route Miles Per 1,000 square miles of area
Argentina	25.8	23.9
Brazil	22.0	7.1
Chile	5.5	18.5
Colombia	2.2	4.8
Peru	1.9	3.9
Uruguay	1.8	24.8
Venezuela	0.6	1.6
Other S. America	2.9	3.1
Central America	2.9	13.1
Mexico	14.2	17.3
Cuba	3.8	85.6
Dominican and Haiti	0.3	11.3
Latin America	83.9	10.5
United States	237.5	78.5

tion companies and the companies that sold the equipment. Politically the governments found themselves driven to provide facilities themselves, when private capital was not forthcoming, for thinly populated areas which could not hope to develop within a reasonable time the necessary traffic to support such investment. They found themselves forced to take over lines that had been floated by private capital under government guarantees only to succumb to the unremunerative traffic potential or unforeseen costs of construction.

If there was an underlying stimulus to policy direction, it was not the regulation of rates or service to meet the needs of the user, not the regulation of rates so that the industry's financial health might be systematically preserved, but rather the fact that the lines were largely foreign-owned. When motor traffic offered itself as a competitive form of transportation, the first thought was not its integration into the transportation system so as to achieve more economical and efficient service but rather its encouragement as a protest against and as a lively competitor to the foreign-owned railways. While the railways cried for feeder roads, the governments encouraged duplicating facilities, further burdening the already unsatisfactory state of the industry.

As a field for enterprise and investment, the Latin American railways matured too early. Instead of a continuing flow of capital to expand and improve facilities constantly, they had to cope with the fact that capital could not be attracted in competition with alternative fields of investment. They ceased to attract the aggressive driving management that naturally gravitated to other fields. As the profits of stock manipulation and stock issue tapered off, the railways settled down to a holding operation counted upon to produce a fairly constant flow of dividends for the immense number of foreign investors who had been induced to add an Argentine rail or a Brazilian rail to their portfolios. Railway labor, given an investment per man far exceeding that of other local industries and become accordingly more productive, early reached a status superior to that of other fields, early became articulate as a factor with which management had to contend. Remote control dictated maintenance of dividends. If this necessitated that the railways assert themselves in local politics, they were not averse to doing so. (Had not Alberdi written: "Shower them [private enterprises for construction of the railways] with advantages, with privileges. Let treasure as well as men come from abroad to live among us. Surround it with immunities and privileges so that it will take out citizenship and stay!") There were devices—local boards, local attorneys, even local politicians—to help create an air of identification with the community. If it necessitated that the properties be allowed to run down and service deteriorate, they were not unwilling to permit this.

What was important in 1950, however, was that the railways were now largely in government hands. Sterling balances acquired in the Plate and Brazil during the second world war had been used to acquire the British and French properties. The State owned the railways in Argentina and Uruguay; in Brazil the government had owned one-third of the railways as early as 1889, two-thirds in the early twentieth century, and continued to acquire properties. The Mexican network was dominated by the government lines, the State lines were the heart of the Chilean system. Three-fourths or more of the railways were government owned and operated. It was extremely unlikely that foreign private capital would ever again in the foreseeable future flow in substantial quantities into Latin American railway investments. And the governor of São Paulo in proposing the acquisition of the Mogiana lines had spoken for most of Latin America when he said that "in the present condition of the *local* financial market and probably for a long time in the future there is no possibility of counting on the favor of the public in the investment of its savings in railways."

Henceforth the maximum utilization of what were at best limited resources had to become the underlying requirement of Latin American transportation policy. Yet the very fact of government ownership and operation challenged the ability to write policy in such terms. Integration of facilities and avoidance of duplication of road and rail, which could once be ignored in order to slap at foreign capital, was certain to be challenged by users unwilling to submit to the protection of the State's investment in rundown railway properties, although a conscientious Brazilian Congressional committee had properly posed the question when it asked: "Can it be desirable, while we seek to increase the flow of traffic on certain railway trunk lines, to impose on them the competition of wide and attractive parallel highways?" The tradition of over-staffing, of corrupt administration, was deeply rooted in Latin American government practice. Would unstable governments be able to mobilize the determination to overcome it? Almost every acquisition of a private railway line, frequently promoted by trouble with labor and the inability to get relief from the government, had been followed by demands on the government for rewards for labor. Would characteristically unstable governments be able to resist such demands when their properties were already losing money heavily? The United States Railway Mission in Mexico in its concluding report in 1947 had noted that the crux of the railway problem in Mexico was the existing labor employment contracts which were the source of most of the problems confronting management in Mexico.[4] And when the Argentine government took over the foreign-owned railways after the second world war, with profession of gratitude for labor's support and unlimited promises of things to come, it was soon driven to seeking a formula for profit-sharing and participation in management as a substitute for yielding to the demands of labor which must otherwise inevitably doom the railways. Finally, in practically every country there had been unceasing pressure to extend the railways into thinly populated and unproductive areas. Would governments be allowed to choose the alternative of developing greater density of traffic in areas already served by railways?

Almost universally the Latin American government railways were losing money, were failing to earn enough even to maintain existing standards of service, let alone create funds with which to rehabilitate the plant. The railroads were generally in poor physical condition. The capital requirements for achievement of an adequately improved railway service were so great as to strain the total availabilities of foreign credit—and it must be remembered that the countries depended largely on foreign sources for the equipment used in railroading, which meant that foreign-exchange had to be created. And such credits were unlikely to contribute adequately to maximum mobility with speed, economy and safety (the objective of transportation policy) unless the governments themselves could subordinate the pressure of labor, political management, army interference, and ward off at least the less deserving demands for uneconomic extension of service and for duplication by other forms of transportation.

The Highways. In 1948 Latin America had fewer motor vehicles on the roads than Canada with a population less than one-tenth that of Latin America was using. Argentina had one motor vehicle in use for every 44 persons, Mexico one per 94, Brazil one per 149 persons, while there was one

---

4 The Institute of Inter-American Transportation, *The United States Railway Mission in Mexico*, 1942-1946 (Washington, 1947), pp. 79-80. The Mission noted that practices in use and standards of operation and maintenance were low by modern criteria, attributable in great part to inexperienced and untrained management, that rolling stock, roadbed, rails, were unsatisfactory, and emphasized that the single most serious obstacle was labor's vigilant adherence to the principle of seniority in all promotions without regard to skill and efficiency.

TABLE 43

Motor Vehicles in Use in 1948

(thousands)

	Motor Vehicles	Cars	Trucks	Buses
Argentina	363.5	223.6	139.9	*
Bolivia	12.6	3.7	8.4	0.5
Brazil	318.4	162.8	145.0	10.5
Chile	65.9	35.6	25.2	5.1
Colombia	59.1	31.9	20.4	6.7
Cuba	73.3	44.9	24.5	3.9
Guatemala	9.7	5.2	4.0	0.5
Mexico	249.5	142.1	92.2	15.2
Paraguay	2.7	1.4	1.0	0.3
Peru	40.5	22.3	16.0	2.2
Uruguay	45.8	30.2	15.6	*
Venezuela	97.1	46.0	47.8	3.3
Latin America	1,398.8	782.4	555.4	49.9
Canada	1,948.7	1,473.6	468.5	6.6
United States	41,151.3	33,398.4	7,555.3	197.6
France	1,715.0	985.0	730.0	*
Australia	1,060.0	669.0	386.0	5.0

* Included with trucks.

Source: Automobile Manufacturers Association, *Automobile Facts and Figures* (Detroit, 1949), pp. 26-27.

per 3.5 persons in the United States, one for every six persons in Canada, one for every 24 persons in France. (See Table 43). The possibilities of road transportation as a means of overcoming the stagnation that had set in when railway investment stabilized had been early appreciated. But the financial requirements for subsidizing road traffic by construction of the basic facilities, the burdensome dependence on foreign sources for vehicles and parts and in many countries for petroleum, the physical barriers to cheap construction, as well as the resistance of the railways to competition, all helped to slow the development. Activity was stimulated by adoption of special taxes earmarked for road-building and by use of such revenues as guarantees behind bond issues, although in practically no case were user-revenues scaled high enough to cover the cost of highway programs.

Argentina had only about 1,200 miles of paved roads in 1932 when the decision was made to embark on a highway program supported by a special gasoline tax which resulted in a 90% increase in highway mileage in the decade ending in 1940. The twenty-year program which gradually evolved required expenditures of more than $600 million dollars, and when the Five-Year Plan was hastily assembled in 1946 it also measured requirements at about $30 million per year. In Brazil a thumbnail sketch showing less than 2,000 miles of paved highways and about 40,000 miles of all-weather surfaced roads in an area larger than the United States almost suffices to describe the position in 1950. (In 1941 the United States had had 3.3 million miles of highways of which 1.7 million were surfaced, 0.3 million paved).[5] Highway construction had gotten off to a healthy start in the 1920's, slowed down during the Vargas regime (1930-1945) when the basic transportation plan was emphasizing strategic railway development rather than road development, revived with the legislation of 1945 which reorganized the National Highway Department and created a Highway Fund which was to receive certain revenues from petroleum taxes and special appropriations for road construction. In 1946 road traffic was accounting for one-tenth as much freight as was carried by the railways. In 1947 the Highway Department had revenue of $42 million, of which $23 million was diverted to state and territorial highway authorities; its revenues were expected to exceed $65 million in 1949-50. By the end of the decade officials were setting a minimum construction target of $30 million per year, of which two-fifths, significantly, involved essential imported commodities.

Chile spent $20 million on its roads in the decade 1929-1938, $30 million in the period 1938-1944, and officials in presenting the six-year public works program in 1945 estimated that another $150 million would need to be invested in the basic highway facilities. With continuous north-south rail service,

---

[5] Definitions of "paved," "improved," "surfaced," "unimproved" vary so much in Latin America that any overall discussion of the Latin American problem gains in its capacity to confuse as such statistical breakdowns are introduced.

the trucks had been slow to break into the long-distance field competitively, but they had not lagged in becoming an important factor in short-haul light cargo traffic, especially foods. As early as 1932 the State Railways introduced door-to-door transportation service to meet road competition; by 1938 it was forced to cut short-haul rates to meet the growing competition (offsetting the loss by boosting rates on the long-distance traffic where competition was not being felt). With traffic still concentrated on a very small portion of the highways, the trucks in 1943 were carrying 24% of the revenue freight of agricultural products, compared with 15% in 1937. An official study in 1943 revealed that only one-sixth of the road mileage was used by as many as 100 vehicles daily; on more than half of the road mileage less than 20 vehicles per day were in use.

Colombia had set up a commission in 1930 to survey its transportation requirements when it became obvious that the irregular chaotic fashion in which improvements were being effected was wasteful. An organization for road construction was established, a basic plan for systematic construction outlined, and a beginning made on a civil service system to develop and conserve trained technical personnel. A vigorous effort was made thereafter, hampered by the limited amount of funds and by the inability to get assurances of funds for a sufficiently long period to make programming and coordination of activity effective. In 1940 the national government was devoting $12.8 million to roads ($8.7 million for construction and $4.1 million for maintenance) which was an extraordinary effort in a federal budget of $50 million and in total national, state and local government expenditures of perhaps $85 million. It was estimated then that about half of the highway system planned remained to be built and that $80 million more would be needed.[6] When the Ministry charged with the highway program reported in 1948 it noted that costs of construction had doubled from 1942 to 1948,

---

[6] Unpublished report prepared by an inter-agency group functioning under the direction of the Office of the Coordinator of Inter-American Affairs.

that mileage on the national highway system added in fiscal 1947-48 amounted to one-seventh of previous mileage, but that the government was appropriating funds for maintenance in amounts only one-fourth what was needed.

The Peruvian highway construction had been promoted by a road-minded President in the late 1920's who proclaimed that "the future and the prosperity of Peru rest in its roads and the rapidity with which they can be built." Despite topographical difficulties, Peru had achieved a relatively respectable mileage of surfaced and improved roads by the late 1940's.

When an American advisory group studied Mexican transportation in the late 1940's, it concluded that the existing first-class paved highways represented less than 15% of the mileage of this type that was needed. The highway program launched in 1925 had produced 5,500 miles of roads by 1940, another 6,850 miles from 1941 to 1946. By 1949-50 Mexico was adding more than 2,000 miles of roads per year to her national system. More than $40 million annually was being devoted to the road program. Highway policy had been defined in terms of (a) hastening completion of federal highways linking Mexico City with the borders of the republic; (b) preferential attention to certain important state roads; (c) slowly growing attention to a vast network of country roads. Four-fifths of the highway appropriation was being used for the national highway system, one-fifth for federal aid to the states on a fifty-fifty matched-contribution plan; and aid for rural roads was evolving on a basis of not over one-third federal contribution. While revenue from user-taxes was reaching sizable dimensions, road construction and maintenance still required more than the prevailing scale of the gasoline tax and other revenues could yield.

In Mexico as elsewhere in Latin America the roads were making an enormous contribution to flexibility in transportation, to national unification and the creation of a national market, to faster less-expensive and more certain movement over short distances, but they did not appear yet to be an answer to the problem of moving the heavy freight of industry, the heavy bulk movements of mining and agricultural

FIGURE 3

The Highways of Latin America

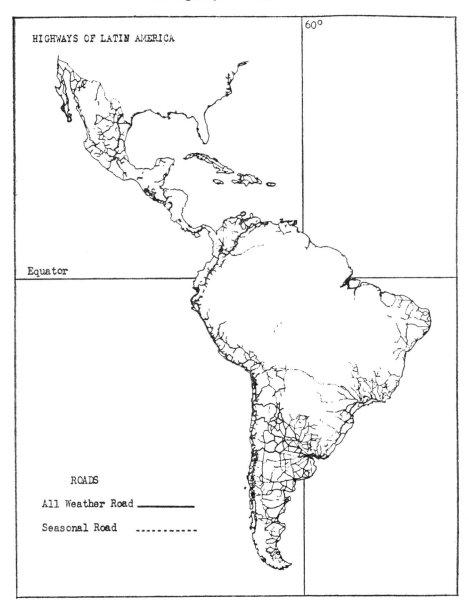

Source: *Foreign Commerce Weekly*, January 27, 1945, p. 9.

communities whether for foreign or domestic use. There was a great temptation all over Latin America to over-emphasize main or super highways competing with railways and to aspire in a few cases at least to a standard beyond what the traffic might support, rather than to build the feeder and supplementary roads. Perhaps from similar motives there was a tendency also to neglect maintenance. The region was definitely not maintenance-minded. The desire to leave a distinguishing and distinguished mark of one's Administra-tion was more easily satisfied by new construction than by maintenance, by main line construction than by a multitude of small feeder lines. But the highway capital requirements were so great of themselves, and in competition with other transport-media requirements and in competition with de-velopmental needs in other fields, that decisions were being forced on officials regarding the service and rate regulation of commercial road traffic, the means of assuring maximum integration of rail and road as well as air and water facili-ties, the means of achieving more effective movement of heavy freight for which alternative media were still lacking. And always running through the problem was the foreign-exchange question, for it was not only the surfacing of the roads that required imported machines and materials; if effective use was to be made of a highway network, a constantly increasing flow of trucks and automobiles and a steadily mounting volume of petroleum must be provided. Figure 3 shows the high-ways of Latin America. Table 44 is a rather inadequate tabulation of highway mileage data.

Air Transportation. The first successful airline in South America and one of the first in the world was established in Colombia in 1920 by an Austro-German group. The venture had an extremely favorable route connecting the isolated capital, Bogotá, with the seaport of Barranquilla; the connec-tion was made by air in seven hours, while the only surface connection by rail and steamer down the Magdalena River took a week in the wet season and as much as a month in the dry season. The tremendous saving of time, which was to be the key factor in air expansion, produced heavy traffic

TABLE 44

Latin American Highways: By Country and Classification

(thousands of miles)

Mileage Surfaced

	Cement, Bituminous, etc.	Other All-Weather Surfaced	Total Paved	Graded and Drained	Total Improved	Total Unimproved	Grand Total
Cuba	2.2	-	2.2	-	2.2	-	2.2
Argentina*	3.3	1.9	5.2	16.8	22.0	13.1	35.1
Brazil	1.8	38.1	39.9	120.3	160.2	-	160.2
Chile	1.4	8.8	10.2	10.1	20.3	11.1	31.3
Peru	1.5	6.2	7.6	11.6	19.3	1.9	21.2
Uruguay	0.6	5.0	5.6	-	5.6	0.2	5.8
Colombia	0.8	2.3	3.0	0.7	3.7	8.0	11.7
Mexico*			9.6	0.3	9.9	35.6	45.5
Others			9.3	7.5	17.4	20.2	37.6

Source: Data taken from a survey made by Esso (Standard Oil Company, New Jersey), which was released in 1949.
*Data for Mexico are for 1942. Argentina data appear to be for the "national" network. The total mileage of highways shown in this study runs close to that shown in the compilation made by the Secretariat of the Economic Commission for Latin America (*Economic Survey of Latin America*, 1948) but the breakdown by countries differs considerably. Both studies are unsatisfactory.

despite extremely high fares and the enterprise prospered without government assistance.

In 1927, after seven years of airline development, Latin American lines had 5,100 route miles, compared with 8,900 for the domestic lines of the United States; passenger-miles totaled 1,270,000 compared with 1,900,000 carried in the United States. There were still no trunk lines joining any two countries and no air connections with other continents.

From 1928 to 1934 trunk line service was established under the sponsorship of various foreign governments and several important local transport companies were organized, some under private control, others sponsored by the governments, utilizing military personnel which was the only available pool of men on which to draw. By 1934 the route mileage of the Latin American lines totaled 52,700 miles, compared with 28,100 for the domestic United States system; passenger-miles flown were only about one-quarter that achieved in the United States; Latin American fares per mile had dropped from 30 to 40 cents in 1927 to 8 to 14 cents in 1934, compared with 6 cents in the United States. The airline structure was largely under foreign ownership and required subsidization by foreign governments.

From 1934 to 1938 the local governments began to make effective the reservation of cabotage privileges for national companies except where the service could not be provided by local sources. Stipulations that companies be nationally incorporated if they were to engage in local traffic gained ground, legislative requirements specifying a higher proportion of national employees went into effect, and progress was made toward requiring all air transport companies to be controlled by nationals, although enforcement was lax in the common absence of sufficient capital or technical competence locally. Passenger traffic grew very rapidly since great savings of time could be accomplished at an extra cost that was not excessive; frequently the saving in travel time was 80 to 90%. And it must be remembered that the alternative transport medium was usually not the safe comfortable facilities available in the United States but rather an uncomfortable and often dangerous method of travel. The subsidies given the local lines were less generous than those which were used to stimulate the industry in the United States, and profits of the lines were small; satisfactory profits were the exception rather than the rule. At the same time that nationalism made its influence felt increasingly in Latin American air transportation, an external factor in the shape of German expansion was gaining importance.

At the outbreak of the second world war, there were 10,500 route miles of completely Axis-controlled lines in operation and an additional 7,600 miles in which German influence was substantial. The American republics in collaboration with the United States joined in an effort to eliminate Axis influence and in a relatively short period succeeded in grounding all Axis airlines and replacing them with *bona fide* Latin American operators or United States companies. The change was accompanied by provision of better planes, financing of improvements in airport and radio facilities, and in some cases by increased mileage. From 1937 to 1947 there was a sevenfold expansion in the mileage flown by scheduled services in Latin America. In the latter year the mileage flown was about one-fifth that of the United States domestic lines. Review of the experience of individual countries commonly revealed: peculiar adaptability to air transport by reason of terrain or population distribution; tendency for operating costs to be higher than in the United States and for rates to be higher; tendency for investment to be discouraged by rather precarious earnings records; the failure to find in the air the solution to the problem of bulk traffic.

In Mexico the major northwest-southwest mountain systems impeding surface transportation, the lack of populated support points for a lengthy highway system, the unavailability of competitive water transport for the principal population centers, all promoted interest in air transport. From 1927 to 1937 miles flown increased from 146,000 to 3,500,000, passengers carried from 1,500 to 70,000. From 1937 to 1947 miles flown increased six-fold, passengers carried showed a ten-fold increase. The 55 million pounds of mail and cargo flown in 1947 represented an 800% increase over 1937, but although air transport was being resorted to for high-cost cargo such as coffee and chicle from inaccessible interior points and for urgently needed tools and machines, the bulk freight field had not been seriously affected. The leading Mexican airline companies were utilizing American technical cooperation and partial financing. In the late 1940's operations tended to become unprofitable and several carriers were forced to abandon the field. The air carriers had co-operatively established facilities for traffic control, meteorological information and other services essential to safety of operations, and had provided much of the airport facilities.

In 1950 Brazil was one of the leading nations in the world in volume of air traffic. The great distances, meager development of surface transportation, physical barriers to construction of surface facilities, high cost and poor service of existing transportation forms, had all helped to promote air-mindedness. The cargo carried on Brazilian lines in 1947 was about one-seventh the tonnage of the domestic United States lines, mileage flown was about one-fourteenth, passenger-kilometers flown about 5%. Mileage flown was more than one-third that of all Latin America. The traffic was predominantly passenger—82% passenger, 16% freight, 2% mail. In 1940 the four airlines, foreign-controlled or influenced, had flown 3.3 million miles and 25.9 million passenger-miles. With one exception all new lines since 1940 had been organized and financed locally, stimulated by the availability after the war of war-surplus planes. In 1947 the lines flew 26 million miles and 326 million passenger-miles. The traffic was expanding rapidly. Yet in the face of expansion the industry seemed a sick industry, especially in its relation with prevailing levels of industrial earnings in Brazil. The profit-making airline operation had been an exception. Local investors were losing their enthusiasm for investment in the industry. Airline rates had been relatively low, for passenger traffic about the same as rates in the United States, whereas Latin American rates generally tended to be 50 to 100% higher than those of the United States. Airline costs were higher; the lines maintained their own navigation and communications facilities; aircraft utilization was far below that of the United States with lower route density and slow maintenance, etc.;

the air fleet was operating on a pay-load less than one-third of its capacity which led in turn to considerable rate cutting; labor costs were high despite the lower wage rates. A solution to the question of financing airports had not been found in the form of private capital, which meant a sizable problem for the government. As the decade of the 1950's opened, the need for systematic regulation of routes, rates and standards of operation seemed indicated if the industry was to continue in private hands on a sound basis. In civil aviation Brazil's problem was less one of attracting facilities than it was of intelligent regulation to assure sound development.

Air transportation in Latin America had broken the traditional pattern of regional isolation. Acceptance of the new form had come rapidly. It had quickly carved out a place in the passenger field, was viewed hopefully for high-value freight. But this was inherently an expensive method of transportation, at least at the stage of technological progress that had been reached in 1950. Power had to be expended to sustain as well as to move the load. As Robert Ramspeck put it, "The airplane has to lift physically everything which produces revenue while its competitor has to pull. Personnelwise it is estimated that it takes 2,626 employees to produce 100 million ton-miles of air transport while the railroads can produce that amount of transportation with only 72 employees." [7] The Latin American was continually being exposed to bright dazzling pictures. In Bolivia, for instance, 1,160 tons of meat were flown in from the Beni in 1949 and it was loudly proclaimed that some day the whole 15,000 tons of requirements might be flown in, with savings in foreign exchange and improvement in the diet. But the railways in Latin America were moving some 25 *billion* ton-miles in their freight traffic. The air cargo of 25 *million* ton-miles to which the Latin American lines were ascending in the late 1940's assumed less importance in the light of such a comparison.[8]

---

[7] *Law and Contemporary Problems*, Volume 15, No. 1, Winter, 1950, "Air Cargo."

[8] At the peak of its operations, our Air Transport Command, flying 3,000 aircraft and using a quarter of a million men, carried tonnage at the rate of 2 billion ton-miles per year.

The policy-maker had still to think in terms of the immense cost of improving freight movement under the older forms of transportation.

Waterways and Ports. Internal waterways, coastwise shipping and port improvement all figure in developmental requirements although in most cases they are relatively less important. With over 25,000 miles of navigable rivers, of which 15,000 miles are in the Amazon basin, Brazil in 1946 was moving only about 700,000 tons of freight on its rivers and lakes, less than 2% of the national freight movement. The larger part of the river traffic was handled by private non-subsidized companies and while minor improvements were constantly under review, major projects waited on integrated plans for regional development rather than on integration with other transportation schemes. With a long coastline and population concentrated near the coast, coastwise shipping has normally been important. In 1946 about 7% of the freight movement was by coastwise shipping in Brazil; it was not an efficient operation, required a subsidy; the field was reserved for Brazilian companies and in practice divided among government and private entities; one government organization had about one-fourth of the business, two other government entitles divided another quarter of the business. The airlines have drawn off some of the passenger traffic and completion of through north-south surface facilities may be expected to offer additional competition, involving subsidies to both competitors.

In Colombia the Magdalena system has traditionally been an important avenue of transportation, but the service is costly. In recent years the condition of the river necessitating trans-shipments, delays in delivery of merchandise to inland points, diversion of ships from Barranquilla to Cartagena has been a continuing source of irritation to shippers, combining with the feather-bedding practices of the labor unions to stimulate developmental interest in alternative means of transportation. In Argentina the river fleets are now in the hands of the government, meaning that to its responsibility for improving waterways has been added the financing of river craft of adequate type. In Venezuela the Orinoco has waited for improvement on population and an interest in the resources of the area it served. Mexico's waterways have been appraised in an engineering report in 1949: ". . . . generally undeveloped and in unsatisfactory condition . . . where traffic exists vessels are usually inadequate in space, antiquated as to machinery, inefficient in handling methods . . . operations on waterways where dangers to navigation are far too numerous involving snags, submerged obstructions, etc. . . . vessels are not operated economically, many not adapted to the type of traffic in which they are engaged."

The port congestion of the post-war years stimulated great interest in port improvement. With few natural harbors, limited facilities in artificial ports, limited mechanization of loading and unloading, attention has been focused on physical facilities. In terms of the improvement of the port of Santos which involved some $24 million in the late 1940's, requirements for Latin American port improvement ran in the hundreds of millions of dollars. But it needed to be noted that the efficiency of the ports waited also on correction of employment practices, excessive paper work, inadequate security measures, and similar characteristics of utilization of existing or improved facilities.

Telephone and Telegraph Facilities. In 1949 Latin America had about 2 million telephones in use, about 70% as many as were installed in New York City. Until the Argentine government had made its momentous decision to take over the telephone system in 1946, ownership had been overwhelmingly private. In 1949, 60% of Latin America's telephones were still under private ownership: Brazilian Traction, Light and Power Company had 380,000 installed in Brazil, International Telephone and Telegraph Company after the sale of its Argentine operation still had 121,000 telephones in service in Chile, 93,000 in Cuba, 91,000 in Mexico, 40,000 in Brazil, and 33,000 in Peru; and there were a number of European companies operating in the region. In most of the countries there were substantial lists of prospective subscribers awaiting service, but the investment in the necessary equipment to meet expansion was in some instances, as for example Chile in 1949, being discouraged by the reluctance of the governments to permit upward adjustments of rates. The telegraph system were already in most cases operated by the governments, and the inevitable antagonism toward foreign-owned utilities was at work in the case of the telephone systems as well. But domestic capital was not interested in the low yields of the industry, and the magnitudes of the investments were such that nationalization could not be accomplished without seriously reducing the already limited resources for development. Table 45 shows the telephones in service in 1949.

TABLE 45

Telephones under Government and Private Ownership, January 1, 1949

(thousands of telephones)

	Total	Ownership Government	Private
Argentina	679	599	80
Bolivia	8	–	8
Brazil	484	1	483
Chile	126	–	126
Colombia	70	62	8
Ecuador	19	14	5
Paraguay	5	5	–
Peru	44	–	44
Uruguay	78	76	2
Venezuela	55	1	54
Mexico	248	1	247
Cuba	101	1	100
Others	48	17	31
Latin America	1,965	777	1,188
New York City	2,769	–	2,769
Chicago	1,460	–	1,460
France	2,232	2,232	–

Source: American Telephone and Telegraph Company, *Telephone Statistics of the World*, January 1, 1949 (New York, 1949).

Central America: Special Financing Devices. In Central America resort to unusual financing devices has only served to point up the difficulty of providing basic transportation facilities. In the late 1940's a report drawn up by a group of government engineers in Washington concluded that $290 million was required to provide Central America with a reasonably efficient highway system and that at least $4.9 million annually would be needed for maintenance by machine methods.[9] At that time the budgets of the governments for all purposes were running about $125 million per year, with revenues frequently insufficient to cover expenditures. Gross highway-user revenue had totalled only $7.5 million in 1945 and was expected to reach $16 million by 1965 on prevailing standards.

The region then had less than 900 miles of paved highways and a total of about 5,000 miles of paved and all-weather roads. (See Table 46). There were about 2,900 miles of railways of various gauges, three-fourths of which consisted of main lines and the remaining mileage of sidings, industrial trackage, etc. It was estimated that 7.2 million tons of freight had been moving annually, of which 2.6 million had been moved by rail and about 4.5 million by road. On a unit-haul basis the railways had been developing 243 million ton-miles and the highways 110 million ton-miles annually. The railways had been accounting for 182 million passenger-miles, the highways for 321 million passenger-miles. The engineers concluded that expectation of any substantial construction of additional railways was unwarranted, that while air transport had been significantly successful in this area its potential for freight traffic was definitely limited, and that reliance must therefore be upon the highways, for which a reasonably efficient network required some 8,600 miles of suitably surfaced roads.

They emphasized that rates by all modes of transportation were then excessive: the rate for general commodities per ton-mile was $0.845 for interior air transport, $0.065 for inland water, $0.086 for domestic rail traffic, $0.116 for motor transport on the Inter-American Highway and $0.175 on other

---

[9] Unpublished report of a government agency. Much of the data in this section are taken from the report.

TABLE 46

Rural Highways in Central America 1946

(kilometers)

	Paved	All-Weather	Dry Weather	Trail	Total
Guatemala	16	3,000	3,600	1,352	7,968
El Salvador	352	1,758	106	4,000	6,216
Honduras	–	550	80	510	1,140
Nicaragua	190	160	320	4,000	4,670
Costa Rica	640	480	320	370	1,810
Panama	199	889	667	–	1,755
	1,397	6,837	5,093	10,232	23,559

Source: Unpublished report of a United States government agency.

roads, $0.680 by oxcart, $0.200 by pack animal, and $0.880 by human portage. Operating costs for motor vehicles were double those in the United States partly because of the poor roads and partly because of the high cost of imported fuel and vehicles and parts. It was suggested that improvement of the highways would result in a 30% to 50% reduction in operating costs of motor vehicles, involving a possible saving of $8.3 million per year on the basis of 1945 traffic and $19.8 million per year on the basis of 1965 traffic. Unfortunately, however, achievement of these savings by a ten-year highway construction program would have required an addition of about 25% annually to the budgets of the governments and even a twenty-year program would require additional expenditures of at least 13% annually, to say nothing of the unexpected complications that usually arise to increase the costs of such a program. And already the countries were finding it difficult to meet their existing international commitments for highway construction and the day-to-day maintenance requirements, without which they were continually threatened with rapid deterioration of the existing network of roads. It was necessary also to remember that the burden of construction and maintenance was not uniformly distributed among the countries. Costa Rica, for instance, required far larger expenditures, far larger additions to its expenditures, than did some of the more prosperous countries, if the standard of highway efficiency was to be achieved; yet, its ability to assume such a burden was among the lowest in the area.

It was in Central America that the government of the United States had introduced special financing techniques in connection with the Inter-American Highway project. The hope of continuous transportation through the other American republics had passed from an unrealized dream of a Pan American Railway to a somewhat more feasible project to join up the existing roads and trails to form a continuous modern highway. The section from Laredo, Texas to Panama, known as the Inter-American Highway, consisted of about 1,750 miles in Mexico and 1,510 miles in Central America. The promoters of the Highway have envisioned great advantages in promoting more efficient trade among the countries, citing freely the possible correction of such situations as that in which "Costa Rica when it suffered a shortage of rice had found it cheaper to import from Saigon via Hamburg and the Panama Canal than to get it from Nicaragua, a stone's throw away." [10] The enlargement of internal markets, decreased dependence on the two or three commercial export crops, the possibility of extensive tourist traffic, have all been held out as desirable objectives.

The interest of the United States, from which grew sizable financial assistance, has been less clearly defined. It is generally believed that the Department of State regarded the Highway as a means by which it could demonstrate the sincerity of the good-neighbor policy by an act in the economic field, where implementation of the policy had been conspicuously less successful than in the purely political aspects of the policy. The importance of the Highway for national and hemisphere defense has frequently been cited, but the War Department refused to support financial assistance "purely on the basis of its military importance" and conceded only that the Highway might contribute to national defense by its influence on the development and maintenance of more

---

[10] Maurice E. Gilmore, "Pan American Highway," *Foreign Commerce Weekly*, October 20, 1945, p. 42.

friendly relations with the countries concerned.[11]   A Senate committee investigating the national defense program has asserted that "the Congress approved construction on the Inter-American Highway partially for defense and partially as an artery of international commerce, not to provide a scenic mountainous route for American or other tourists, nor to serve local internal traffic."[12]   Wary of the financial and political complications that were likely to arise out of the effort to support the construction of the Highway, both the State and War Departments seem, in the opinion of the Senate committee, to have been unwilling to face squarely the question of motivation for American participation in the financing.   For instance, in 1942 the War Department seems to have invaded the province of the State Department in asserting that the Highway's contribution to *continental solidarity* made its construction an urgent *military* necessity while the State Department's earlier emphasis on its military usefulness seems to have been an improper invasion of the War Department's sphere of policy determination.

Whatever the motivation, agreement was more easily reached on the fact that the Central American countries were financially unable to build the Highway out of their own resources.   In 1930 the Congress of the United States had appropriated $50,000 to conduct a survey of possible routes and to prepare estimates of the cost of constructing such a highway.   A report was filed in 1934 indicating that up to this time all road building along the route had been local construction designed principally to serve the larger cities and that existing all-weather roads accounted for only 510 miles out of the 1,510 miles required for the highway.[13]   In 1934 an appropriation of $1 million was voted to be spent on bridges and roads forming part of the Highway.   In 1941 the Central American governments estimated that they had spent up to this time $24.7 million on roads that might ulti-

---

[11] U. S. Senate, Special Committee to Investigate the National Defense Program, 80th Congress, 1st Session, *Inter-American Highway* (1947), p. 13.   This report is referred to hereafter as *"Senate Report."*

[12] *Senate Report*, p. 11.

mately form part of the Highway. The United States Public Roads Administration estimated that it would cost $58 million to close the gaps and improve the existing inferior roads. To make the project more palatable to the Congress, the State Department had the estimate revised to fix $30 million as the sum needed to complete the project, although it was known that this would not finance a highway capable of supporting any substantial volume of through traffic. It is probable that the approach to the Congress involved the familiar strategy of "getting a foot in the door" rather than risking a complete turndown of the project by presenting a fully competent estimate of the cost of the project. In addition, the Department introduced the principle of matching contributions, under which the United States would make available $20 million on condition that the Central American countries put up $10 million of their own, construction to proceed on a plan acceptable to the countries concerned.

The recommendation of the State Department was accepted by the Congress and $20 million was voted. Part of the funds to be contributed by the local governments was borrowed from the Export-Import Bank ($8 million), so that the venture had a distinct all-American flavor. At this time (1941) there were 376 miles of paved roads, 587 miles of gravel roads used throughout the year, 260 miles of dirt roads impassable in the rainy season; the completed sections of the Highway were separated by long sections of trails through mountain jungles and swamps; and United States engineers estimated that there were 650 miles of unimproved gaps in

---

[13] An estimate for 1932 put the Central American highway system at 2,780 miles of gravel and paved road, much of it narrow and with steep grades but passable in rainy weather, and 6,280 miles of trails and very poor dirt roads passable only in dry season. The better roads were nearly all in the vicinity of the larger cities or connecting links between ports and inland cities. Guatemala alone had some type of roadway-connection with bordering republics. No republic had a coast to coast road. The railway mileage, of six different gauges, was mostly designed to connect banana, coffee and other plantations with ports or to connect inland cities and ports. Only one country had rail connections with neighboring countries. Only in one were the Atlantic and Pacific coasts connected by rail.

the route to be followed.[14]   Mexico had completed about 1,000 miles of the 1,750 miles of the Highway that was its responsibility, and it now elected not to participate in the matching-contribution device, utilizing instead the facilities of the Export-Import Bank from which it borrowed $40 million for highway construction.

The funds appropriated, not at all surprisingly, were inadequate. By 1943 the State Department was back seeking another $12 million from the Congress. This amount was to be spent on a specifically defined section in Costa Rica, this time without matching contribution from Costa Rica in consideration of its poor financial condition. The Congress yielded to the request. Unfortunately, an attempt was made by the engineers to economize on the basic survey, unforeseen difficulties developed on the route selected, and it was learned too late that although the whole job might have been completed with the $12 million on an alternative route, the unfortunate drafting of the bill in the Executive Branch of the government committed the funds to the specified section.[15] By 1945 the State Department was back for more money; this time it sought $25 million for the Highway, of which $17 million was to go into the troublesome Costa Rican stretch, again without a matching contribution by the local government. By this time, however, charges of waste and inefficiency in a related project in Central America had reached the Congress and a Senate Committee undertook an investigation.

Before and after approval of the original financing, the

---

[14] It should be remembered that the Inter-American Highway is only part of the Central American highway network.

[15] The particular Costa Rican section involved literally carving a roadway out of a steep mountain side. It was one of the most difficult engineering feats attempted in Latin American road-building since it passed over extremely rough terrain and mountains reaching 11,000 feet requiring tremendous cuts and fills. After work was started, it was discovered that suitable local material for rock and gravel surfacing was not available, that expected rock formations did not exist, that thousands of tons of dirt had to be moved in the rainy season, that a swampy area 8,000 feet up had to be traversed.

official position of the War Department had been that an overland route to the Panama Canal was not required for the
logistical support of our forces in Panama. By mid-1942 the
War Department, disturbed by war developments, while still
not rating the project a high-priority expenditure of men and
materials, found it sufficiently meritorious to warrant acceleration of the effort.[16] Army engineers proceeded to Latin
America and managed to spend in excess of $36 million net in
an effort that partly duplicated work already under way on
the Public Roads Administration's program. It had been
originally estimated by the War Department that 905 miles
could be made ready for military traffic at a cost of $14
million. A wide variety of inefficiencies (documented by the
Senate investigating committee) developed and when the
War Department abandoned the project in 1943 it had completed only 347 miles at a cost of $36 million. Much of the
activity was on roads not acceptable to the Public Roads
program, the estimate being that one-third of the work done
by the Army engineers at best was useful for the future
Inter-American Highway. Disputes between the two agencies
of the United States, the Army and the Public Roads Administration, resulted in work occasionally being done on
parallel roads while other sections of the Highway with no
road at all were being neglected.[17] It was estimated by the
Senate committee that after an expenditure of about $30
million by the Public Roads Administration and $36 million
by the War Department, the Highway was at best half completed. In 1946 it was believed that another $75 million would
be required from the United States. The original appropriation of $20 million had turned out to be only a costly open-

---

[16] General Somervell did write on May 23, 1942 that "an all-weather
pioneer road from the United States to Panama City as a military
road is urgently needed as a means of supply and communications,"
but the Senate committee asserted that no factual basis for such a conclusion was found in War Department files. General Eisenhower termed
the utility of the road "problematic" and therefore rated it low-priority.
The effort to justify it as an urgent military necessity in terms of the
need for continental solidarity (a State Department determination
properly) continued. *Senate Report*, pp. 17-18.

ing commitment. In 1950 the State Department secured an additional appropriation of $8 million to inch the project along.

Nor was financing of construction the only problem. The Congress had immediately recognized that whatever the merits of a policy of paying for roads in foreign countries, such a policy could not be justified unless safeguards were laid down regarding maintenance of the Highway and freedom from onerous tolls and restrictions that might impair its effectiveness. It proposed that the appropriation of funds be conditioned upon compliance with specific stipulations regarding maintenance and operation. The State Department, however, somewhat more familiar with the process of lending or giving money than with the task of negotiating *quid pro quos,* protested that insertion of such stipulations in the legislation would be excessively binding on the delicate relations with Central America, that it fully understood the commitments which the Congress desired. It requested freedom to work out the details. The Congress yielded. The Department promptly defaulted on its obligation to obtain such safeguards.

---

[17] Various non-economic considerations entered into selection of routes. In Nicaragua, for instance, the Inter-American Highway was routed to pass by and benefit property owned by a former President despite the fact that it meant a detour adding 42 miles to the length and routing through more rugged country where construction would be more difficult and costly. Probably the most violent disagreement between the Army and Public Roads engineers came on the merits of the high road vs. the low road. Public Roads favored the high road, asserting that it was more scenic for tourists, the climate more healthful and cooler, that it connected the more populated areas taking advantage of existing roads to the maximum, that the low road was in coastal areas that were hot, humid, insect-infested, that the low route would involve higher construction costs for bridge and culvert work that would offset the terrain-imposed costs in the mountains. Army engineers claimed the mountain routes would be winding and steep and dangerous, that vehicles would have to operate through dense fog or clouds at the 10,000 to 11,000 feet altitudes, that efficiency of gasoline motors would drop 10% at higher altitudes, that the highway would have less capacity for through traffic because of the slower speeds and more difficult operation on the winding mountain road, that cost of earth-moving would be higher in the mountains.

As the Senate committee reported: "The matter of maintenance of the highway after completion and the matter of protection against exorbitant tolls or onerous restrictions and
regulations was wholly neglected." [18]   As it happened, the
Central American countries were not maintenance-minded.
Honduras definitely needed to be convinced of the necessity
for adequate maintenance work. Nicaragua would only slowly adapt itself to the need. Guatemala knew maintenance on
the basis of poll-tax labor but that type of service was being
abolished.   Further, maintenance costs in the case of Costa
Rica were estimated to be so large that competent engineers
suggested that even if the officials could be convinced of the
need, the cost would run 5 to 10% of total government expenditures and suggested that Washington might have to be
asked either to provide for maintenance out of the United
States Treasury or to lend continually for local-currency expenditures with little prospect of repayment.   In securing the
appropriation of 1950 for the Highway, the State Department
assured the Congress that it had now arranged the necessary
safeguards regarding use of the Highway.

It should be noted, as indicated in Table 47, that despite
the wide publicity attending the Inter-American Highway
project, it represents only about one-fourth of the estimated
cost of creating a reasonably efficient highway system for
Central America. By 1950, however, the experience with
the Inter-American Highway suggested that construction of
the basic transportation facilities at the expense of the United
States was not a principle likely to be given wide application
in Latin America. No "easy way" out of the great problem
of the area had been discovered.

Brazil: Policy Requirements for Greater Mobility. "Brazil

---

[18] The committee went on to point out: "It is perfectly obvious that
with a highway passing through seven separate sovereignties, gasoline
taxes alone might be imposed by any one of these sovereignties in the
absence of an agreement regulating the same, which would be so high
as to be extortionate. . . . We may find ourselves in the position of
having built a great international public work and see it lie idle and
unused simply because we failed to provide for sensible and workable
border controls." *Senate Report,* pp. 47-48.

TABLE 47

Estimated Cost of a Reasonably Efficient Highway System

(millions of dollars)

	Construction	Annual Maintenance	Needed to Complete Inter-American Highway as of December 1946
Guatemala	$85	$1.5	$18.0
El Salvador	25	0.5	0.5
Honduras	54	0.5	4.0
Nicaragua	36	0.6	7.5
Costa Rica	40	1.0	26.1
Panama	50	0.7	18.5
	$290	$4.9	$74.6

Source: Unpublished report of a U. S. government agency. It is believed that the estimates of maintenance cost are altogether too low.

has not got around to building any sort of integrated system of transportation at all," wrote a great friend of Brazil impatiently in 1944. He went on:

Most of her hundreds of rivers are laced with rapids and shoals so that freight carried along them has to be frequently portaged. Only on the Amazon, which is in effect an estuary, can ocean ships make their way far into the interior. Brazil has not yet made her water highways navigable. Her roads are still the paths of men on foot, of horses, mules and oxen, of wheeled vehicles drawn by animals; they are not yet adjusted to automobile traffic. Her railroads are still largely made up of short lines radiating from the coast towns like sticks of a fan. Only one line crosses the country from east to west; only one inland road of about 125 miles cuts down the windings and twists of the river it parallels along the western border. Rails have not been laid to some of the most important sources of raw materials; still fewer connect the places where they are produced with the places where they are fabricated; fewer still carry them to the consumer. Traffic between the coast towns is mostly by cargo boats that ply the ocean.

"None of this traffic," he cried, "is rapid in the modern sense or adequate in an age that wants things *now!*"[19]

[19] Cooke, *op. cit.*, pp. 145-146.

But this was an old refrain in the economic literature of Brazil. The newer forms of transportation had not provided a substitute for the railways for the five billion ton-miles of freight moved by rail. Freight rates were at least double those of the United States, yet the government which owned the larger part of the 22,000 miles of railroads was already being drained of $50 million or more annually for support of the railways, and most lines were run at a deficit even without considering depreciation or return on invested capital. The railway system had entered the second world war with antiquated plant, emerged after a fairly good record with even more serious need for improvement of right of way and rolling stock. But the financial requirements were immense in terms of the capacity to support. When the Minister of Transportation estimated requirements in 1947, he found that more than $90 million per year for five years was needed, half of it in the always-scarce foreign currency. Half of the sum involved track and rolling stock of existing lines; half for connecting links to west and south, north-south connections, electrification of narrow-gauge lines, new construction.

There was considerable agreement among foreign advisory groups and local students of the problem as to the policy indicated. The five-year plan submitted in 1948 emphasized "the necessity for increasing density of traffic in opposition to the immoderate extension of the railway network into poorly populated and unproductive zones." The Abbink Mission urged that expansion into new areas be postponed except where an integrated development of mining or other productive capacity was contemplated. And there was recognition of the fact that maximum returns from existing resources were not going to be achieved as long as excessive numbers of employees were used, modern accounting methods were avoided, political and military management was permitted regardless of its competence. But policy still yielded to local pressure from outlying areas for service which they could never support, to the memory of wartime interference with coastwise shipping which had stimulated demand for construction of competing north-south rail facilities, to the political requirements that confront any government enterprise and especially enterprises with such a background as that of Brazil. These drags on development needed to be understood, since they involved policy decisions that must be made by the country itself.

In the late 1940's, for instance, when certain Russian-controlled minerals which figured largely in the defense requirements of the United States threatened to become unavailable, a vigorous interest was displayed by the United States in increasing Brazilian production. But military administration of the railways involved was such as to force investigators to conclude that external interest alone could not suffice to support the development effort and serious expansion of production would wait on Brazilian action on its railway management. In other cases there were political relationships with other countries that dictated lines of decision out of accord with the findings of the economist. For instance, Brazil was racing Argentina into the important city of Santa Cruz, Bolivia. By the end of 1949 in her effort to establish a rail connection with Santa Cruz, trains were already running a distance of 403 kilometers out of Corumbá, rails were laid to the 435 kilometers mark, out of a total distance of 650 kilometers. Meanwhile the Argentine effort on the Yacuiba-Santa Cruz connection showed rails laid only to kilometer 101 on a 550 kilometer route, with the Argentines falling behind because of their diversion of funds to other projects, once funds became scarce. Both routes might one day justify themselves in terms of development of theretofore isolated areas considered potentially rich in resources. But for the moment the engineering and financing expenditure involved a selection among outlets for limited resources largely on a political basis.

In the case of the highways, the government was called upon not only to decide on the rapidity and direction in which it would improve basic road facilities, but also to determine the extent to which it wished to make foreign-exchange available for purchase of motor vehicles and petroleum products, bearing in mind that demands upon resources far exceeded foreseeable availability of exchange. There was at least growing appreciation of the problem. When a Congressional committee reviewed the highway section of the five-year plan, it posed the question: "Let us assume that all the proposed highway projects were clearly desirable and some highly essential. Before we have discovered petroleum fields and built refineries, would it be wise to open up all highways which we desire and to pave the principal highways at a high cost? Even if (*and this was a very broad assumption*) we had ample financial resources and the necessary mechanical equipment, would there be enough workers for simultaneous construction of the majority of our railroads, for meeting the needs of intensified rural programs, and for also opening up and reconstructing so many highways? While we seek to increase the flow of traffic on certain railway trunk lines, can it be desirable to impose on them the competition of wide and attractive parallel highways?"

The impact of the day-to-day policy decision could be seen in the decision to expand the merchant marine. Along with many other Latin American countries which were heavily dependent on foreign trade, Brazil had long sought to carry a larger part of the traffic in Brazilian ships, to put the Brazilian flag on all the seas. In 1938 Brazil had a merchant fleet of almost half a million tons (gross tonnage) of vessels over 100 tons each. By June 1949 it had achieved an almost 50% increase. The increase had involved heavy use of the foreign credit of the government for expansion of the government-owned shipping entity, which also required subsidies. It is not difficult to understand the reluctance to be at the mercy of foreign governments for shipping in times of emergency, and at the mercy of foreign shippers as to rates and service in peacetime. Yet, it must be noted that the decision to divert resources to merchant shipping meant diversion from fields where alternative financing was not available or not as easily available to a field where foreign capital and management was readily available. It could not fail to affect the pace of development. And it was a decision questioned by some competent observers. For instance, Wythe, Wight and Midkiff argued that "the possibility of developing a big international merchant fleet, on a sound and economical basis, is limited in a country with large undeveloped internal resources, a shortage of manpower and capital, and limited metallurgical industries and skills. Certainly improvement of the transportation problem at home should come first." [20]

Decisions on the optimum use of limited resources were of course not the only determinations involved. To the extent that acceleration of development was genuinely sought, the policy decisions that promised a more rapid enlargement of total available resources, as in the cases cited in the discussion of petroleum and mining, were also pertinent.

Transportation for Colombian Coffee: A Case Study. A fine American scholar in a highly competent investigation of the history of the Colombian coffee industry has shown the interrelationship of transportation developments and expansion of export industries.[21] The high cost of transporting coffee relative to market price early confronted the Colombian farmer with the necessity of reducing the cost if he was to compete successfully in world markets. In the period 1865-1875 the cost of moving coffee from local market to Colombian port ranged from a minimum of 15% of the wholesale price in New York by the Cúcuta-Maracaibo route to 24% by the Bucaramanga-Barranquilla route. Adding transport cost from farm to local market and ocean freight to New York brought transportation to about one-third of market price. This ratio did not stem from any peculiar characteristics of coffee. With adequate bagging materials available, care assured undamaged delivery; there was an advantage over other products in the fact that coffee did not spoil provided it were kept dry and uncontaminated by odors; and the ratio of weight to price gave coffee a competitive advantage for production for export over most other products that were important in the economy of Colombia.

The early development of the industry stemmed from (a) production for local markets which minimized the importance of the transportation factor; (b) realization by producers that the quality of coffee grown on the volcanic soils of the

---

[20] *Op. cit.*, p. 215.

[21] Robert Carlyle Beyer, "Transportation and the Coffee Industry in Colombia," *Inter-American Economic Affairs*, Winter, 1948, pp. 17-30.

mountainsides was such as to promise returns in export markets sufficient to compensate for the transport factor in large part; (c) ability to exploit a certain limited area more accessible to the sea. In 1874 nine-tenths of the coffee was grown in this area, Santander. Such coffee was collected in Cúcuta, carried by mule in three or five days to the river port of Los Cachos on the Zulia, taken by barge to Encontrados on the Catatumbo in five days, thence to Maracaibo in a day. The 310 miles of journey from plantation to port could be accomplished in 12 to 14 days; the return trip usually took three to four weeks.

The steamboat had appeared early on the Magdalena but not until the temporary boom in tobacco and indigo in the 1850's and 1860's was service regularized. More regular service at lower rates by steamboat enabled coffee to penetrate a narrow band of the central interior. The steamboat was a vast improvement over poled barges and dugouts and saved months in transit, but the route was still extremely hazardous. Sandbars, rocks, logs and bursting boilers, prolonged winters making impassable the mule trails to the river, prolonged summers preventing boats from passing the shallows, the vagaries of the Magdalena, were familiar plaints in Colombian transportation. While the steamboat in regular service was an improvement, the industry waited on improved land transportation to expand from narrow margins along the Magdalena. Coffee seemed in the early 1890's, having become in the 1880's the chief export of Colombia, to be reaching the limit of growth in Norte del Santander and along the Magdalena.

Surface transportation consisted principally of the heavily-laden mule which could bring its 250 pound load safely along the treacherous mountain trails. There was some use of horses. And on the trip to Medellín and in Caldas where their strength enabled them to plow through deep mud with heavy loads, oxen were frequently used. Wagons never assumed general importance in the mountain terrain although there were some exceptions in a few localities. But mule transportation was slow, permitted no reduction in costs, and in other producing areas of the world the producers enjoyed

more direct and easier transportation to port. World consumption of coffee was increasing rapidly. Examining the
cost pattern, the Colombian found that there were no mechanical processes that could cut into the differential significantly;
labor costs could not provide a further source of savings;
and although for a long time there was hope that a different
species of coffee adapted to the coastal regions might enable
Colombian producers to overcome the disadvantageous transportation differential, it turned out that the inferior quality
of the coffee and the special production problems it introduced offset the gains in transportation.

The railway altered the picture. By 1898 there were 367
miles of railroads, of which 262 miles were used to move coffee;
by 1914, 709 miles of which 570 miles were used for coffee;
by 1922, 974 miles, of which 857 miles were used for coffee;
by 1940, 2,066 miles, with 1,537 used for coffee. As the
mileage multiplied, coffee provided more than half of the
outbound cargo; promoters successively measured the coffee-
freight potential in determining the feasibility of construction. The railways replaced both water transportation and
mule traffic, often paralleling old routes and bringing advantages of speed and economy. The rivers characteristically
tended to shorten in navigability as a result of erosion so
that the motivation of economy frequently joined with the
lack of alternative means of transportation as old river routes
became impassable or passable for only a shorter season. New
producing areas were brought into play. Production more
than doubled from 1899 to 1914, doubled again from 1914
to 1923, again from 1923 to 1938. Meanwhile the ratio of
transportation costs to New York wholesale price was falling
to 2% on the Bogotá-Puerto Salgar route, 3% on the Cúcuta
to Maracaibo route, 4% on the Bucaramanga-Barranquilla
run. Meanwhile the highways were building, with influence
at first primarily in shortening and cheapening transport
into individual coffee areas served even until the 1930's only
by mule, and influence also as trunk roads sharing the burden on water and rail facilities. In the valley of the Cunday,
for instance, coffee was originally carried by mule all the way
to Girardot. Later it was trucked to Girardot from the town

of Melgar where the mule trains were met. The highways were gradually extended—in 1935 a highway was completed as far as Cunday, in 1942 it was opened above Cunday as far as Las Margaritas, in 1943 as far as Andalucia; each extension shortened the mule trails, cut costs. When the whole trip to Girardot had been by mule, the cost had been 2.5 pesos per sack. By 1946 the cost by truck was 0.75 pesos.

Mexico: Magnitude of the Problem. In Mexico it remained for the railway to reduce transportation costs sufficiently to permit a wider variety of commodities other than minerals to enter the market. When corn was 20 pesos a ton, wheat 30, and it cost 110 pesos to send a ton of freight from Mexico City to Vera Cruz or from Guanajuato to Tampico, a national market could be defined only in terms of commodities that could absorb very high costs. Thus, writes one student of the Mexican problem, "the historically preponderant role of the mining industry in the economy of Mexico is to be explained, in part, by the high cost of transportation." [22]

From 1837, when the initial railroad-construction contract was signed, to the end of the century the Mexican government encouraged private capital to undertake construction of railroads, assuming responsibility for subsidies that weighed heavily on the public finances.[23] Several hundred million dollars of American and British capital poured into the railroads in the course of an economic penetration which was in a sense an extension of the Far Western frontier movement of the United States. By 1885, about 3,700 miles of track had been laid down. In the following quarter century this expanded to about 12,000 miles. In the subsequent two decades of civil war, revolution and reconstruction, less

---

[22] Tannenbaum, *op. cit.*, p. 203.

[23] Pletcher asserts that "by the end of the century railroad subsidies weighed so heavily upon the Federal Government that highway construction and repair were left more and more to the states—at first by informal agreement and after June 12, 1895, by law. In general, the states shirked their duties, apparently preferring to spend their funds on urban improvements in an effort to keep up with Mexico City." David M. Pletcher, "The Development of Railroads in Sonora," *Inter-American Economic Affairs*, March, 1948, p. 9.

than 500 miles were added. The hit-or-miss policies followed in granting of concessions made for creation of a sprawling network rather than a systematic utilization of capital and energy, although American railway experts have termed the Mexican railways "well-engineered and well-constructed." [24] Construction was costly by reason of physical factors, and made more costly by the characteristic financial manipulation of the period. Traffic load was not high by American standards, freight per mile being estimated in 1910 at one-sixth that of the American railways. Freight rates were high by American standards, although the comparison was less unfavorable when it was more properly made with facilities replaced or in consideration of the virtual non-existence of facilities in some areas previously.

In the first decade of the twentieth century the Mexican government adopted a policy of participating directly in ownership and operation. With the organization of the National Railways majority control was assumed by the government under conditions intended to safeguard the interest of foreign investors. During the revolution and civil war period that followed, rolling stock was destroyed, roadbed wrecked, properties deteriorated; in 1916 the Director General of the Railroads, for instance, reported that 35% of the bridges had been destroyed, over 3,800 freight cars wrecked, 49 million pesos of damage done to the lines. The government assumed administrative control of all the railroads from 1914 to 1926. Before 1910 all positions above those of brakemen and firemen had been held by foreigners but these officials and skilled technicians now largely left the lines, so that the government was deprived of its experienced personnel. Bonded indebtedness of the lines rose as their physical properties deteriorated, interest payments were suspended by the ever hard-pressed government. Attempts were made successively in the 1920's to reorganize and to consolidate the debt, but the frequent political upheavals, the disorganization of the economy, and the influence of railway labor balked the efforts.

In 1937 the government expropriated the National Rail-

---

[24] *The United States Railway Mission in Mexico, op. cit.,* p. 3.

ways, tried to run the system for a year.[25]   In 1938 it turned
the system over to the Railroad Workers Union.   One of the
most serious problems was the disproportionate expenditure
on wages and salaries.   For instance, Jesús Silva Herzog,
writing in 1937, stressed that labor costs were excessive, cited
data that machinists, conductors, train dispatchers were earning more in Mexico than in the United States; labor costs were
running two-thirds of expenditures, compared with less than
half in the United States and Britain.   The union, serving
simultaneously as employer and employee, strengthened provisions of the labor contract which were destined to harass
management for many years, and jeopardized discipline and
operating efficiency as well as discouraging ambitious workers.
In 1940 the workers' administration was replaced by a
separate entity functioning directly under the President of
the Republic.   At that time the National Railways constituted
a system of some 8,400 miles, almost entirely of standard
gauge; additions were made, notably the transfer of the Inter-
oceanic Railway which added 1,019 miles of meter-gauge
line, to give it a mileage of 9,600 miles on December 31, 1946.
The total mileage of federally-owned railways then constituted
about 86% of the total operating mileage of the country.

When the United States entered the second world war, the
need to expedite movement of tremendous quantities of critically needed materials out of Mexico prompted a survey of
transport facilities.   The investigation revealed that although
rail transportation was the very foundation of the whole
economic structure, the National Railways were in incredibly
bad physical condition, and management and operating personnel, enmeshed in political fortunes and misfortunes, was
inadequate.   Rails, ballast, ties, bridges, structures, cars,
locomotives, were in poor and often unsafe condition; the inspection of locomotives in railway shops was lax and little
discipline was possible in the shops because of labor union

---

[25] One of the many difficulties was that the government had built
some showy highways paralleling the railway lines rather than providing
transport service to areas wholly without transport facilities; and this
road competition hurt. This was, of course, only one of many difficulties.

interference; trains were permitted to run with defects so glaring that they would have been barred from any track in the United States; accidents and derailments happened at the rate of one per hour around the clock; safety appliances and practices were largely absent or ignored; efficient use of locomotives was unknown; repair facilities were obsolete; 30% of locomotives were regularly out of service; although most of the lines were of standard gauge and equipment was interchangeable with U. S. equipment, National Railways locomotives and cars were not permitted to enter the United States lest they be legally attached in satisfaction of the railway debt; the labor union could have any employee discharged for criticism of union leaders, and all vacancies had to be filled on the basis of seniority. Under these conditions it was clear that the Mexican contribution to the war effort would be sharply reduced.

The governments of the United States and Mexico decided therefore to establish a United States Railway Mission in Mexico to work with Mexican authorities in the rehabilitation of 1,900 miles of key lines of the National Railways. From 1942 to 1946 Mexico expended some $40 million and the United States $6.8 million in a joint effort ranging from instruction in modern railway practices to detailed repair and modernization activity. When the program terminated in June 1946, the freight traffic on all Mexican railways had risen to a rate of 5.3 billion ton-miles per year, compared with 3.3 billion in 1937, and the Mexican government was anxious to proceed with rehabilitation and reconstruction of its whole system, envisaging an early doubling of the traffic. Financing was difficult, however. The government had borrowed $19 million from the Export-Import Bank for railway equipment in 1945. It borrowed $7 million more in 1947, $19.9 million in 1949. But this was only one of many fields for which external assistance was being sought. There had been some $210 million of dollar bonds of the expropriated railways outstanding with annual contractual interest of $9.4 million, and in 1946 an agreement was negotiated with the International Committee of Bankers (amended in 1949) providing for resumption of

payment on a modified basis.[26]   But it was not likely that
private capital would ever again interest itself in the Mexican government's railway financing problem.   The railways
were losing money, failing to cover interest charges and provision for repair of roadbed and replacement of worn-out
equipment.   Even if modernization of equipment and structure had not been beyond the financial capacity of the government, it was not at all certain that traffic could be developed
adequately to amortize the investment before bankrupting
the government, for the lines were still hauling only about
one-sixth the traffic load per mile handled by United States
railways.   Meanwhile there was new construction to be
financed also, for the development plans of the government
contemplated an expansion of 25% in the railway mileage,
much of it in areas where construction would be costly by
reason of topography and where service would be furnished
well in advance of traffic that could support it.

During the six years 1940-45, an active period of investment in Mexican industry, the aggregate investment in industry has been estimated by the Bank of Mexico to have
reached a quarter of a billion dollars.   The investment in
private construction for the period has been put at something
less than that.   By comparison, the requirements of the transportation network in the late 1940's were being estimated at
a minimum of $600 million (much of it for imported goods),
with steady investment required to follow the initial planned
outlay, and with the likelihood that continuing deficits would
have to be carried by the government where it participated
directly in ownership and management of facilities.

The Investment in Merchant Fleets. From 1939 to 1949 the
tonnage of the Latin American merchant fleets almost
doubled.[27]   By June 30, 1949, Argentine tonnage was 630,000
tons, Brazilian 641,000, Chilean 160,000, Mexican 103,000,
Venezuelan 130,000, Uruguayan 70,000, Peruvian 77,000,

---

[26] In 1942 the Mexican government had reached an agreement on the
external debt of the government which reduced obligations to about 10%
of nominal value.   A similar scaling down of the railway debt was
negotiated in 1946.   Rippy has estimated that in 1939 British investments in Mexican railways were £90 million.

Colombian 36,000, Cuban 25,000 gross tons. The fleets had been expanded by acquisition of Axis-shipping during the war, by purchase of surplus ships after the war, and by placing of orders for fine new craft in yards the world over. More shipping for the Latin American fleets was building. Brazil had borrowed in Washington for the expansion of her merchant fleet. Argentina had eagerly sought ships in her bilateral trade negotiations. In the minds of policy-makers the expansion of merchant shipping had achieved top priority. It had been widely argued before the war that a country should have its own fleet to protect itself against discrimination and excessive foreign carriers' charges, that its ability to negotiate in the event of war was improved by having some service under its own flag, that in view of the growing volume of traffic generated by the government itself it was a field where preferential assistance could easily be given such a young industry. The wartime shipping shortages and the dependence upon the United States added to the determination to enlarge the merchant fleets which had hardly exceeded one million gross tons in 1938. This was again a decision fully within the competence of the local governments, again an instance where mobilization of the maximum resources for current developmental activity was not being achieved, since the activity in merchant shipping served to replace foreign service which had in many instances achieved an efficiency that the new lines might lag in reaching and served to take funds and energy away from projects which could not find substitute financing and support overseas.

The case of the Flota Mercante Grancolombiana warrants examination.[28] Pressure for locally-controlled merchant fleets in Venezuela, Colombia and Ecuador was not new. In 1933 the Conference of Colombian Coffee-Growers had demanded

---

[27] Since the majority of the ships registered in Panama and Honduras are foreign-owned, they are excluded from this discussion. The data refer to seagoing steam and motor merchant vessels of 1,000 gross tons and over.

[28] Data in this section are based largely on Robert S. Willis and Clifton R. Wharton, Jr., "Flota Mercante Grancolombiana," *Inter-American Economic Affairs*, Summer, 1948, pp. 25-40.

immediate establishment of a national merchant marine "to remedy the high and ruinous freight rates which are being paid to foreign companies," to meet defense requirements, and to save the 15,000,000 pesos "which is the tribute that our industries and commerce now pay to foreign companies." With nationalism growing, by 1939 an official of the Ministry of Foreign Affairs proposed initiation of a merchant marine possibly in connection with neighboring countries which "similarly needed one." By 1940 Colombia had put legislation on the books for a Colombian merchant fleet, but implementation was unavoidably delayed until 1944. In Ecuador and Venezuela there was also a background of persistent dissatisfaction with shipping conference practices, readiness to attribute the high cost of living partly to excessive ocean freight rates, effort to blame the unsatisfactory market position of some of the export staples on the transport charges, and easy arousing of nationalistic feeling for a merchant marine. In Ecuador the Executive in 1944 decreed establishment of a merchant fleet and suffered an unsuccessful experience with one ship for a year. At the Chapultepec Conference the Latin American republics supported enthusiastically a resolution that "the creation and development of their merchant marines" was "essential to their economies," although the qualifying clause calling for provision of service "without discrimination, at the lowest possible cost, consistent with safe and adequate service" might later introduce difficulties. In 1945 and 1946 officials of Venezuela, Colombia and Ecuador discussed the possibility of a jointly-owned merchant fleet and finally set up the Flota Mercante Grancolombiana, on the basis of 45% participation each for Venezuela and Colombia, and 10% for Ecuador. The non-petroleum traffic was estimated at 2.2 million tons, a target of 20% to be won by the Flota was set, and in its first six months of operations the Flota carried about 200,000 tons, or a pace close to the objective. Steady additions to the fleet were made in 1948 and 1949.

From the standpoint of developmental policy, what considerations warranted investment of $9 million each by Venezuela and Colombia, warranted borrowing by Ecuador of $2 million for its participation, with the reasonable expectation that additional calls on their capital would be required? (a) None of the countries had a shipping tradition or experience making it a field particularly suited for their participation. (b) None had a successful record in public administration of business activity, and there were notable failures in all three which could have been used to document the comment of the Comptroller-General of Colombia in his report for 1946 that "there is general economic disorder in Colombia but the greatest disorder is to be found in the public budgets." (c) The American Advisory Economic Mission to Venezuela in 1939 had answered the charge that high shipping costs were responsible for the fantastically high level of prices by demonstrating that the original landed cost of imports was a relatively small factor in the final price to consumers, and shipping costs within the original landed price were a minor matter.[29] (d) Coffee represented two-fifths of the export traffic and some of this could not become available competitively to the Flota since shipping lines were themselves engaged in the trade; and special marketing arrangements for such commodities as bananas where critical timing and arrival-at-market in certain condition was part of an integrated operation made

---

[29] "For most articles," the Mission reported, "ocean freight and insurance, while appreciable, do not constitute a large fraction of the costs defrayed by retail prices. The table below is taken from the report:

MAJOR COSTS OF IMPORTING AND DISTRIBUTING IMPORTS

(Retail price = 100)

	Original c.i.f. Cost	Duty	Other Cost of Landing	Total Cost at Warehouse	Whole-saler Margin	Retailer Margin	Total
Wheat flour	17	44	4	65	5	30	100
Rice	25	44	5	74	4	22	100
Lard	22	48	3	73	5	22	100
Sardines	36	18	4	58	8	34	100
Oats, unmfg.	29	22	3	54	6	40	100

Source: *Report of the American Advisory Economic Mission to Venezuela* (Washington, 1939), p. 33.

it unlikely that the companies would relinquish control of the traffic. (e) On the other hand, a semi-official entity in Colombia was increasingly branching out into all phases of the coffee trade and was in a position to throw an increasing volume of business to the Flota unless international treaty obligations were allowed to interfere. And in Venezuela the government was embarking on an immense developmental program which would generate very large traffic that could be diverted to the Flota. (f) The financial requirements of the operation were small in terms of the lush revenues that Venezuela was deriving from petroleum, but they appeared large in terms of the resources at the command of the impecunious Ecuadorean government. And when it is remembered that the $10 million of external requirements occasioned by the damage done during the political unpleasantness of April 1948 had been considered beyond the financial capacity of the Colombian government and an urgent subject for external borrowing, the drain on Colombian resources by $9 million initial participation in the fleet could not properly be brushed aside as unimportant.[30]

(g) Of the major cost items, the only area of substantial saving compared with foreign-owned shipping appeared to be in the lower wage factor. Capital was more costly locally. The experience, size and private ownership of existing carriers were presumed to give them an advantage in day-to-day operations in purchase of supplies, connections with established sources, savings arising out of the breadth of operations. A rate war based on lower wage scales would be the type most

---

[30] It may help in an appreciation of the magnitudes involved to note that in 1939 the appropriation for the school lunch program was $1.1 million. There was a serious problem of child malnutrition. About 60% of the potential school population attended primary school, i.e., about 600,000. Of these, about 150,000 were seriously under-nourished and about 250,000 inadequately fed. One-fifth of the children came to school without breakfast. It was estimated that another $5 million per year would be required for an adequate program. But the Ministry of Education was forced to announce that assumption of responsibility for such a program would involve a costly administrative establishment and a financial burden beyond the capacity of the Treasury.

likely to provoke compensating subsidies for the American lines, and in a subsidy race the balance of advantage would not lie with the Latin American countries. (h) Profits of the private carriers were running far below the prevailing level of earnings in alternative fields of local investment.

It was argued at the time that if the Flota were intended as a yardstick for measurement of the performance of the private lines, it would properly be limited to the smallest scale consistent with establishing the standard, would not be the subject of continuing expansion, would not be given extraordinary preferentials depriving it of the character of a fair yardstick. But the participating countries soon indicated that the Flota was to be given the fullest possible support and its expansion promoted at every opportunity. The Venezuelan government, for instance, exerted pressure on government agencies and on importers bringing in goods for government account to use the Flota, it gave exemptions from port charges and other burdens, and it even considered use of the fleet on a loss-basis as a disciplinary threat to competing lines. In Colombia the argument that the line might result in a saving in foreign exchange even if it operated at a loss in terms of local currency was supported by the powerful agricultural group and by industrialists pressing for higher tariff protection. For the coffee producers, a government-subsidized shipping operation provided one more element in the integration of the coffee-marketing machinery, and it was conceivable that when and if coffee prices sagged, the shipping service might provide a means of shifting part of the burden on the government. Colombia was not slow in using pressure to support the Flota. It exempted the Flota from payment of income and inheritance taxes and from payment of port dues; it granted preferential treatment to Flota ships by discretionary discriminatory tactics in the ports. And it attempted to force use of Flota facilities for movement of coffee bought from the Colombian Coffee Federation, with the argument that the Federation had invested capital in the fleet and must therefore protect its investment. Since the Federation had great power in its ability to withhold supplies of coffee from exporters who refused to accept dictation as to shipping arrangements, the United States protested ineffectively on the basis of discrimination in conflict with the Treaty of 1946. Whether the preferentials should be considered part of the protection given an "infant industry" and as such not open to the criticism made of assistance given on a continuing basis to inefficient industries was a question that could not yet be answered. But it was significant that the history of tariff legislation in Colombia and the other countries supporting the Flota had shown that industries refused to relinquish protection once it had been obtained and that the tendency had been for protection to be so extensive as to discourage efficiency. But in 1950 there was no inclination in Colombia, Venezuela and Ecuador to admit that entry into merchant shipping at the expense of alternative uses of limited resources had been an error. Ecuador, for example, was losing $0.9 to $1.0 million per year in consular fees as a result of preferential treatment given Flota cargo, and its share of the profits (with dividends slow to come) promised to be far less than this loss even if operations were exceptionally successful. Yet, its enthusiasm for the operation continued. The extent of the Flota's progress may be seen in the fact that by January 1950 its participation in the U. S. Atlantic to east coast Colombia run had increased to 86% of the traffic, from 8.9% in 1947; on the west coast run from 6.9% to 80%.

Argentina too in 1950 refused to admit that steady expansion of its merchant fleet represented any but the optimum use of its resources. In 1949 it acquired the last remaining privately-owned railway, resigned itself to an enormous operating loss on the railways, learned that rehabilitation of the lines would require immense subsidy from the national treasury. In 1949 the commercial airlines which had been organized as joint private-government entities became fully state owned, giving the government undisputed responsibility for the financing of deficits which had averaged more than $25 million annually in 1948 and 1949. In the same year it absorbed the remaining river-shipping enterprise to gain complete monopoly on the rivers. The transportation operation maintaining services in the city of Buenos Aires had by

1949 run up a deficit of 450 million pesos, with continued increases in the burden. The requirements for modernization of the railway network alone had been put at more than $200 million, and perhaps twice that was needed for the broad internal transport improvements being planned. With transportation facilities so largely in government hands, the policy-maker in Argentina was faced with the imperative necessity of allocating limited funds with maximum wisdom. It might be development of its largest coal potential in the Rio Turbio fields, which waited on a large outlay for rail transport. It might be hastening of the connection with Santa Cruz, for reason of the political rivalry with Brazil or for the economic potential that might conceivably exist in such a connection. It might be expansion of airport facilities and improvement of air service, or it might be accent on the international air services which though expensive carried an air of prestige very stimulating to the national pride. It might be the more pedestrian task of providing adequate equipment for the old network of railways, or outlays for extensive port improvement, or rapid expansion of the highway network on which $75 million of work was already under way and delayed by lack of equipment at the end of 1949. Whatever the specific policy determination, it appeared certain that the country would not be able to finance the whole operation contemplated in its developmental vision, and that it would have to count on a heavy continuing drain on the national budget for the many transport functions which had been put under government control.

Transport Policy. "When there were but eighty-four pleasure carriages in Philadelphia," laments a Latin American writer probing into the failure of Latin America to keep pace with development in the United States, "Lima had about 5,000 and Mexico City even more. Paced streets and sidewalks were unknown in the cities of Anglo-Saxon America until the nineteenth century, by which time Latin America had had them for 200 years." [31] But when the North Ameri-

---

[31] Davila, *op cit.*, p. 211.

can neighbor had become a nation on wheels, it was still being written that "at least half of the efforts of the producing caste of tropic Latin America is spent, not in growing more corn or lard or yucca, wool, cotton or rice, but in carrying what someone else had produced to someone (probably a non-producer) who will eat or use the product," and in 1949 none of the Latin American countries were using as many motor vehicles as Cuyahoga county in Ohio with a population of only 1.4 million. Before "The Rocket" had been dreamed of, young Robert Stephenson,, sent out by British interests as engineer in charge of their mines, had already in 1825 surveyed a line to Caracas from the coast. But despite the billions of dollars of foreign capital that flowed into Latin American railways in the century that followed,[32] transportation continued to be a factor delaying expansion of national markets and development of the hinterland, and the freight traffic on the railways failed to reach one-twentieth the ton-miles activity on Class I railways in the United States. Extravagant hopes of becoming nations on the wing and thereby hurdling the obstacles imposed by the financial requirements of surface transportation had settled in the realization that surface facilities might long be irreplaceable for heavy freight.

As the railway and inland waterway facilities came increasingly into government hands, the enunciation of policy that would achieve maximum coordination of transport was in a sense being facilitated. There were signs by 1950 that the magnitude of requirements for a satisfactory transport system was making more comprehensible to the Latin American policy-maker the imperative urgency of a coordinated program for transportation. But it would have been unrealistic to under-estimate the pressures upon him that must inevitably militate against achievement of adequate integration. The necessity for outside assistance by reason of the relation of

---

[32] Rippy has estimated that in 1939 British investments in Latin America railways amounted to £478 million. J. Fred Rippy, "British Investments in Latin America, 1939," *Journal of Political Economy*, February, 1948. At that time there were British investments in railways in every Latin-American country except Haiti, Panama, Honduras and Nicaragua.

these requirements to total national resources and by reason also of the important share of the expenditures which must be financed in foreign exchange was also appreciated, although here too there were obstacles to policy determinations that would maximize the flow of foreign capital. No cataracts of disaster threatened to descend upon the Latin Americans if they were unable to resist local political pressure for uneconomic action or if they failed to act so as to attract the largest possible amount of assistance from abroad. But the pace of development throughout the economy inevitably depended upon these decisions. And they were decisions that could only be made by the individual countries.

SUPPLEMENTARY READING

David M. Pletcher, "The Development of Railroads in Sonora," *Inter-American Economic Affairs,*" March, 1948, pp. 3-45.

Robert S. Willis and Clifton R. Wharton, Jr., "Flota Mercante Grancolombiana," *Inter-American Economic Affairs,* Summer, 1948, pp. 25-40.

Julian S. Duncan, "British Railways in Argentina," *Political Science Quarterly,* December, 1937, pp. 559-582.

The Institute of Inter-American Transportation, *The United States Railway Mission in Mexico 1942-1946* (Washington, 1947), pp. 23-80.

William A. M. Burden, *The Struggle for Airways in Latin America* (Council on Foreign Relations, New York, 1943), pp. 10-79.

Robert Carlyle Beyer, "Transportation and the Coffee Industry in Colombia," *Inter-American Economic Affairs,* Winter, 1948, pp. 17-30.

Royal Institute of International Affairs, *The Republics of South America* (Oxford University Press, 1937), pp. 34-58.

Special Senate Committee to Investigate the National Defense Program, 80th Congress, 1st Session, *Inter-American Highway,* pp. 1-49.

Chapter 12

Development Policy and the Foreign Investor

In the summer of 1913 William Jennings Bryan brooded over the problems created by the foreign debts of the Latin American governments. These debts then amounted to more than two and one-quarter billion dollars. The history of the Latin American public debt had been marked by four characteristics: (a) The extremely great importance of the loan promoter and loan contractor in marketing debt overseas. On the lending side, the aggressive bankers who were interested in marketing as many securities as possible, the intermediaries who knew the "right" people in the governments, the men who charged a finder's fee for "finding" a government willing to borrow, were in large part responsible for the continued marketing of bonds despite successive defaults and embarrassments. On the borrowing side, there were the officials eager to match the zeal of the lender, ranging from officials who profited directly from flotation of securities to those who considered the benefits from public works expenditures to be worth any price that might be paid for the money. (b) It was indeed costly borrowing. Interest rates, commissions, incidental charges, associated contracts for purchase of merchandise, imposed a high burden of financial service. But the promoter could point out with considerable justice that the risk was also immense. (c) While the United States and the western European countries were burdened with debt accumulated in large part from war expenditures, the Latin American debt to a greater degree originated in public works expenditures. The most common purpose of borrowing was the construction of public works, and although funds were

369

frequently diverted to cover of budgetary deficits and to careless and irresponsible expenditures, the proportion of the debt that originated in public works was nevertheless very large. (d) In the absence of an internal market for government bonds, the long-term debt bought voluntarily by investors was largely a foreign-held debt. Borrowing internally was largely limited to government paper money, loans forced upon the banks, securities issued to fund unpaid claims.

The whole rather unhealthy process—contracting of debt at high interest and commission charges, irresponsibility and instability of governments leading to default and neglect of claims, renewed efforts to borrow in response to promotional activities of aggressive bankers coupled with the eager cooperation of officials cognizant of the potential gains (personal or public) from the loans, irresponsible expenditure of new funds obtained in the course of funding old obligations, repetition of the process—had continued without extension of political control by the lending countries in Latin America. Occasionally the patience of the lending countries was exhausted and there were brusque threats or interventions by the governments but in general they displayed equanimity beyond what might have been expected in the face of the successive exasperations. Latin America was outside the main sphere of European rivalries, any act of interference or pressure against a single country brought quick resentment from all of Latin America, and there was increasingly the assurance of United States support in the event of European pressure or interference. But as American funds flowed in increasing amounts into Latin America, Bryan was concerned with the government support that American investors had come to expect and with the unsatisfactory alternative that the Latin Americans might find funds in Europe and in the course of difficulties in meeting the terms might create problems of foreign interference and foreign pressure for the United States. A number of episodes showed the concern to be warranted. Up to this time, practically all Latin American government debt, except that of Cuba and Mexico, had been contracted in Europe, largely in Great Britain. But the period of European lending was coming to an end.

Bryan as secretary of state therefore addressed a memorandum to President Wilson in which he proposed a new formula to meet Latin America's requirements for development financing:

"They (the Latin American republics) are now compelled to pay a high rate of interest and to sell their bonds at a discount. . . . If the United States offers to loan them its credit to the extent that such a loan is safe, the bonds could be made to draw four and a half per cent, which would be an immediate saving to them in the way of interest and the difference of a per cent and a half between their bonds and ours could go into a sinking fund which would, in a reasonable time, at compound interest, pay off the debt and leave them free. We could, in this way, relieve them of the debts which embarrass them, and enable them to construct such railroads as are imperatively necessary for the development of their countries. The second advantage would be that the plan would give our country such an increased influence . . . that we could prevent revolutions, promote education, and advance stable and just government. . . . We would in the end profit, negatively, by not having to incur expense in guarding our own and other foreign interests there, and positively, by the increase of trade that would come from development and from the friendship which would follow the conferring of the benefits named." [1]

President Wilson was deeply moved by the belief that "they (the Latin Americans) have had harder bargains driven with them in the matter of loans than any other peoples in the world. Interest has been exacted of them that was not exacted of anybody else because the risk was said to be greater. And then securities were taken that destroyed the risk." [2] Bryan's proposal that the United States by his formula furnish "the modern example of the Good Samaritan" was to suffer a twenty-year wait before it could be implemented in somewhat different form as part of the "good-neighbor" policy. And later experience would demonstrate the difficulty of finding a satisfactory formula.

---

[1] Ray Stannard Baker, *Woodrow Wilson: Life and Letters* (Doubleday, Doran & Company, New York, 1931), Volume IV, p. 433.
[2] *Ibid*, p. 284.

Development of the Public Debt. In 1820 a vice-president of Colombia reached London, with quite dignity consolidated all the claims against his government, avoiding any quibbling over the exact amount due and settling for a 10% interest rate. With further negotiation these claims were pyramided into a £2 million loan, and after paying commissions and interest for two years Colombia netted £640,000 with which it acquired a miniature navy and some military supplies. British merchants and officers had helped in the independence movement in Latin America, and as the new nations found that they could consolidate claims and acquire new assets in the London money market, their representatives flocked to the scene. By the end of 1825 a group of loan promoters had brought together a speculation-mad investing public and the Latin American officials who felt apparently that no price was too high to pay, and £17.5 million of securities had been unloaded. Simultaneously there was a flurry of excited interest in Latin American mining and other ventures which proceeded to drain off several millions from the market. Before the decade ended, the mining boomlet had subsided and most of the public debt was in default. For a quarter of a century British investors showed less interest in Latin America; returns from investments were negligible and the continuing effort to evolve conversion schemes that might yield also a little new money only seemed to make ultimate soundness more distant. British investments of all kinds in Latin America by the mid-1850's may have been about £35 to £40 million.[3]

In the 1860's, the memory of the early episode had faded somewhat, more stability in the Latin American regimes seemed indicated, and the promoters joined with would-be borrowers to create renewed interest in Latin American securities. The new investing period reached a peak in 1870-1873 and by 1875 a Parliamentary Committee was investigat-

---

[3] Leland Hamilton Jenks has provided an excellent account of the flow of British capital in *The Migration of British Capital to* 1875 (Alfred A. Knopf, New York, 1927). The book has the quality unusual in American scholarly works of being very readable.

ing the disastrous loans that had been floated! The same story of promoters persuading not-too-unwilling governments that they needed loans and persuading not-too-hard-to-convince people with money that they wanted Latin American securities was brought out. The characteristic irresponsibility mixed with outright dishonesty in the dealings of borrowers and lenders and the terms that were little more than arrangements in gambling, had continued. The burden of some of the loans may be illustrated by the Colombian venture which netted the government $560,000 per year for the period 1866-1873 on condition that it pay $800,000 per year in interest and amortization for twenty years. By 1876 British investment in the public debt of the Latin American governments was about £120 million; in addition, some £50 million of British capital was invested in other Latin American ventures. The holdings of government bonds in 1876 included the debt of every independent country except Nicaragua and Haiti, and the bonds of all but four (Argentina, Brazil, Colombia and Chile) were in partial or total default and almost worthless.

But neither the financial depression of the 1870's nor the disastrous series of defaults could cause British investors wholly to lose interest. Either in patient disregard for successive disappointments or in extraordinary gullibility at the hands of promoters—and more likely in a combination of these factors and the interest in the commercial activity that accompanied the loans—Latin American debt was soon absorbing more capital than ever before. From the 1880's to the first world war, investments particularly in public works and in the more stable countries expanded. Banking houses with a greater sense of responsibility strengthened their connections as bankers to individual countries. And after 1900 the larger better-established countries gained in economic effectiveness and in standing in world money markets, with a steadily improved public credit position compared with other borrowers in European markets. In 1913-14 the British portfolio contained the bonds of sixteen governments and only Honduras and Mexico were in default. British investment in government obligations was put at £316 million for 1913. See Table 48.

Meanwhile the Continent was showing increased interest in Latin American securities. There had been a dribble of French investment in government securities as far back as 1825 when an issue of 30 million francs was floated for Haiti; in the 1850's some Peruvian bonds were floated in Paris, some Mexican and Honduran securities in the 1860's, and an increasing volume of Argentine and Brazilian offerings in the last two decades of the century. By 1900 it was estimated that about a billion francs of Latin American government issues were being quoted on the Paris Bourse, of which about one-third were Argentine obligations and one-half Brazilian debt. After 1900 activity increased so that by 1913 it was estimated that 2.6 billion francs (nominal value) were invested in Latin American government securities, of which one-third Brazilian, one-fourth Argentine, almost one-third Mexican.[4] (It should be noted that these figures include some railway securities carrying government guarantees). At the some time that French banking syndicates were making their influence felt, German participation began to become effective also. Both the German and French governments showed a direct interest in the participation of their banking syndicates, an interest in expenditure of the proceeds within their countries, and a hope that the strong position that had been built up by British banks might be challenged. The German investment may have been half that of the French by 1913. In addition, participation on a somewhat less regular basis by Belgian, Swiss, Dutch and other European capital was also occurring.

In the United States the rather optimistic hope of supplementing the efforts of British capital in Latin American government financing dated to the 1820's when unsuccessful efforts were made to market loans for the government of Chile, Mexico and other countries at about the time that the short-lived boom was on in Great Britain. In the 1860's a

---

[4] J. Fred Rippy, "French Investments in Latin America," *Inter-American Economic Affairs*, Autumn, 1948, p. 62.

TABLE 48

British Investments in Latin America, 1913 and 1939

(millions of £)

	1913				1939			
			Economic Enterprises				Economic Enterprises	
	Total	Government Obligations	Railways	Others	Total	Government Obligations	Railways	Others
Argentina	£358	£82	£215	£61	£429	£65	£264	£100
Brazil	224	117	52	54	261	159	37	55
Mexico	160	29	104	26	173	39	90	44
Chile	64	35	20	9	86	26	20	41
Uruguay	46	26	15	5	39	19	15	6
Cuba	44	10	26	9	34	3	29	3
Peru	26	2	—	24	29	6	—	23
Colombia	7	4	3	—	6	3	2	1
Others	70	11	22	38	71	4	21	51
Total	£999	£316	£457	£226	£1128	£324	£478	£325

Source: J. Fred Rippy, "British Investments in Latin America, End of 1913," *The Journal of Modern History*, September 1947; J. Fred Rippy, "British Investments in Latin America 1939," *Journal of Political Economy*, February, 1948.

rather sticky operation was carried out for Mexico, and a Peruvian loan was floated. By the late 1890's a number of loans for Mexico were being floated successfuly by American bankers and some Cuban obligations were successfully absorbed. In the period 1901-1905 loans exceeding $30 million were floated for Mexico, Cuba, Nicaragua and Costa Rica, and with an additional $430 million in other foreign securities floated during the same period, John Hay, secretary of state, was moved to exclaim that "the financial center of the world which required thousands of years to journey from the Euphrates to the Thames and the Seine, seems to be passing to the Hudson between daybreak and dark." The South American financing was largely monopolized at this time by European bankers although issues for Bolivia and São Paulo were floated in New York in 1906. Primary official interest was in replacing European lenders in the Caribbean and Central America to avoid possible intervention problems and to open up new markets. From 1906 to 1914 about $77 million was raised for Mexico and $90 million for other Latin American countries. It was estimated that in December 1914 U. S. participation in Latin American securities publicly issued in the United States and still outstanding consisted of $35 million Cuban obligations, $70 million Mexican, $26 million Argentine and $25 million for other countries, for a grand total of $156 million; Mexican railway securities acquired in exchange for direct investments in the railways were estimated at $197 million; and the remainder of the portfolio acquired prior to 1897 plus securities privately acquired in foreign markets may have totalled an additional $15 million.

By the end of the first world war the financing picture for Latin American governments had taken on a new form. European investors were no longer available to absorb large quantities of Latin American government securities. The political disturbances and wholesale defaults in Mexico had eliminated Mexico largely from the international money market. But a "taste" for Latin American securities was developing in the United States. Net dollar loans to Latin America exceeded $50 million in the period January 1, 1915 to April 5, 1917, with another $400 million added by December 31, 1924.

There now followed a fantastic episode in international finance during which American investors repeated most of the mistakes that had been made by European investors in the previous century and added some new variations on the old theme. Another $1.5 billion in Latin American bonds was absorbed! In the decade of the 1920's the Latin American governments had thus borrowed about $2 billion in the New York market; 14 of the governments participated in the flood of securities, with the bulk of the capital destined for South America rather than for Mexico, Central America and the Caribbean which had been the focus of American investing interest theretofore. Once again there had been the familiar experience with promoters coaxing governments into borrowing, with officials interested in borrowing for the ancillary advantages that might attach on a personal basis, with assumption of servicing burdens out of line with foreseeable capacity to repay, with squandering of loan proceeds despite a common use of "public works" as the stated purpose of loans, with replacement of internal debt by foreign debt and disregard for the serious matter of assuming foreign-exchange requirements for local-currency expenditures not calculated to create additional exchange.

At one time, witnesses told a Senate investigating committee, there were 29 representatives of American financial houses in Colombia alone seeking to negotiate loans. In Peru the process of "persuasion" included financial "cooperation" with individuals high up in the official family. In the United States little more than the relatively high interest rates was noted by investors whose memory of seventh-grade geography constituted frequently the only knowledge of Latin America. After 1930 new investment in Latin American bonds came to an end and the period of default began its unhappy course. Many of the countries had taken on obligations exceeding their capacity. Most of them, heavily dependent upon a single export crop or upon two, were hard hit by the collapse of world markets. The terms had in many instances been extremely onerous. And the loose methods of lending had precluded systematic use of funds on projects calculated to create proportionate increases in productivity and in capacity to service investments. By the end of 1933, except for Argentina, Haiti, and some local governments in Argentina, the Latin American governments had defaulted on their obligations. During the next six years a non-governmental organization known as the Foreign Bondholders Protective Council succeeded in negotiating permanent adjustments covering about one-sixth of the dollar bonds in default. But in 1939 an American investor who wished to liquidate his Latin American holdings would have had the prospect of receiving 14 cents on the dollar for his defaulted South American bonds, 36 cents for the Central American, and 46 cents on the dollar for the West Indian bonds in default. Only 18% of the Central American bonds, 32% of the South American bonds, and 86% of the West Indian issues were still paying interest; and these bonds were selling at an average of about 70 cents on the dollar.[5] An interesting compilation of the experience with the Latin American bonds is shown in Table 49.

In 1939 the Latin American governments had outstanding obligations in foreign currencies of $3 billion, of which $1.6 billion consisted of dollar loans,[6] $1.2 billion in pounds sterling, and $0.2 billion in other currencies (French francs, Swiss francs, etc.). The private investor in the United States was no longer interested in further commitments to governments in Latin America. The European markets had long been closed to any significant contribution to the financing of the Latin American governments. Were the Latin American governments to be thrown back upon their own resources for development financing? The Roosevelt Administration thought not, for it had begun to implement a new policy instrument. Before we examine its use and potentialities, however, let us look first at the experience with direct investment during the period when the private market for Latin American government securities was expanding.

---

[5] Willy Feuerlein and Elizabeth Hannan, *Dollars in Latin America* (Council on Foreign Relations, New York, 1941), p. 14.

[6] It should be remembered that not all dollar bonds were held in the United States. The United States Treasury has estimated, for instance, that in 1943 only 35 to 40 percent of all outstanding foreign dollar bonds were owned in the United States.

TABLE 49

An Accounting for the Latin American Loans Issued 1921-31
(millions of dollars)

	Amounts Actually Invested	Repayments, Interest and Principal	Market Values December 31, 1935
Argentina	$694.9	$615.6	$285.0
Uruguay	51.8	31.4	20.0
Brazil	373.3	240.3	72.9
Chile	335.5	163.5	37.9
Peru	89.6	45.0	8.9
Bolivia	58.4	34.3	4.5
Colombia	143.4	97.3	18.7
El Salvador	7.4	7.6	1.8
Guatemala	0.6	0.3	0.1
Panama	22.8	14.4	11.4
Cuba	109.7	96.4	37.2
Dominican Republic	23.5	18.5	9.9
Haiti	15.4	16.8	7.8
	$1,935.6	$1,386.0	$491.1

Source: Compiled by Feuerlein and Hannan from John T. Madden and Others, *America's Experience as a Creditor Nation*, Table 25. Willy Feuerlein and Elizabeth Hannan, *Dollars in Latin America* (Council on Foreign Relations, New York, 1941), p. 16.

Experience with Direct Investments: British Capital. Foreign capital had not limited itself to financing governments. It moved vigorously into land and construction companies, built the railways, operated mines, set up industries, exploited the forests, provided the public utilities, promoted concessions at the ports, expanded banking facilities, provided shipping and insurance services. Decade by decade the investment grew. Production of raw materials was expanded, costs of production were reduced, competitive access to world markets was achieved, exports grew. By 1913 European direct investments exceeded $4 billion, perhaps more than twice the amount that had been invested in government obligations.[7] The larger part of the investment was British, con-

---

[7] Tables showing nominal value of investment tend to over-state the actual investment (Tables 48 and 50) and are more helpful in showing areas of greater and lesser interest than in showing actual volume of investment.

TABLE 50
French Investments in Latin America, 1902, 1913, 1938
(millions of francs)

	1902			1913			1938		
	Total	Government Obligations	Economic Enterprises	Total	Government Obligations	Economic Enterprises	Total	Government Obligations	Economic Enterprises
Argentina	923	310	613	2000	640	1360	4000	125	3875
Brazil	696	490	206	3500	880	2620	3357	2357	1000
Mexico	300	–	300	2000	750	1250	2275	2125	150
Chile	226	8	218	212	70	142	430	190	240
Colombia	246	–	246	15	7	8	90	73	17
Uruguay	297	48	249	200	65	135	310	138	172
Others	3253	961	2292	8375	2590	5785	11340	5084	5906

Source: J. Fred Rippy, "French Investments in Latin America," *Inter-American Economic Affairs*, Autumn 1948, pp. 52-71.

Note: Rippy points out correctly that global figures even if merely nominal are generally welcomed and "*if not taken too seriously* may prove useful." He notes that "the franc of 1913 was equivalent to 32.8 cents in the United States currency of 1938 while the franc of 1938 was worth about 4 cents." "Converted into United States currency the value of French capital in Latin America steadily declined after the first World War, shrinking from some $1,600 million in 1913 to approximately $450 million in 1938 and around $306 million in 1943." Feis estimates French investment as about $1 billion in 1914.

centrated heavily in railways, with Argentina the prime field for British enterprise and capital, as Table 48 shows. In Argentina, British merchants early beat off the challenge of the Americans in the trade rivalry. They established the foundations for a modern pastoral industry, introduced new breeds and practices such as fencing, promoted the export of wool, live animals, hides and tallow and eventually of frozen and chilled meat. British capital financed the railways, installed port facilities, built packing houses, gave Buenos Aires waterworks and street transportation, established department stores, improved the banking and insurance and shipping machinery of commerce while participating directly in export and import trade. It became customary to call Argentina a British dependency economically, with ties as close as those which bound the countries politically affiliated. British enterprise and capital were not merely a factor to be measured in terms of the expansion of production, however. The relationships that accompanied the development under British stimulus were far-reaching. The heavy foreign indebtedness and the dependence on a continuing flow of capital from overseas helped make Argentina's international economic position extremely vulnerable. British capital tended to identify its interests with those of the great landowning and governing families, showed the same lack of concern with broadening of the internal market and with hastening of a general rise in the standard of living. Railways owning land defined their interest in terms of holding for eventual price rises and sale in large blocks rather than in rapid disposal of land looking to intensification of agricultural activity and early settlement and colonization. The railway routes and rates focused on problems of foreign trade, rather than on the internal market. The tariff structure could be set up to protect British export interests and simultaneously protect the landowning group which was not enthusiastic about the growth of local industry. Local entrepreneurial ability found very limited opportunities in the locally-controlled sector of the economy and found equally limited opportunities in the British ventures that kept key posts in British hands.

The nature of the flow of capital—and this was true of other European and of American capital as well as of the British activity—was such as frequently to reduce the net gain from the development process:

(a) Inevitably, where a large portion of the economic activity of a country developed under foreign enterprise and continued under its direction, problems arose in terms of the "plural economy," the imperfect connection of the foreign-controlled sector with the rest of the economy, which was heightened by over-conspicuous differences between the "Anglo-American spot of civilization in the wilderness" and the low standard outside it. It was true, of course, that the dualism was even more conspicuous and important in the contrast between the ruling local interests and the bulk of the population, but foreign enterprise was an easier target politically and in fact in many countries served to divert attention from the local dualism which was the real heart of the problem. Holding down local entrepeneurial ability could not fail to create instability, the full potential gains to the mass of the population were not realized, and social problems were created.

(b) The flow of capital was erratic. Fads, speculative crazes, boomlets not always grounded in economic factors, saw an outpouring of capital into particular fields or particular countries for short periods and an abrupt reversal of the flow. A boom like that of the 1880's in mining enterprises, for instance, saw quick formation of 130 companies in London—42 in a single year—and an investment of £20 million ranging from non-existent resources of the Plate and Dominican Republic to the more abundant mineral resources of Mexico, Chile and Colombia and from disorderly Central American countries to the more stable countries, and then a quick halt and suspension of interest for a decade.[8] The wide fluctuation in the pace of investment added instability to the

---

[8] See J. Fred Rippy, "The British Investment Boom of the 1880's in Latin American Mines," *Inter-American Economic Affairs*, March, 1948, pp. 71-78, and J. Fred Rippy, "The Peak of British Investment in Latin American Mines," *Inter-American Economic Affairs*, Summer, 1948, p. 41-48.

international economic position of the Latin American countries and intensified the distress occasioned by cyclical changes in business activity. All this served to retard the accumulation of local capital.

(c) Capital flowed in response to appraisals of profit potentials, often of quick profit potentials, rather than to meet the priorities that might be established by requirements for long-range development of the country. Frequently there were associated factors in the decision such as the relative volume of business in capital equipment that alternative investments might generate, which did not necessarily bring investment in the field calculated to contribute most to sound development of the country. And if profit-making possibilities seemed best in a field like Cuban sugar or Chilean copper, the foreign investor was unlikely to accept responsibility for avoiding further concentration and the associated consequences of monoproduction.

(d) Finally, foreign investment established a tendency toward large enterprise. If the investing entity were floating securities to the public, sizable offerings and sizable corporations behind the offerings were likely to be more attractive. And if it were a corporation planning to expand from capital generated in its domestic activities, foreign investment was a field which frequently introduced too many complications for the small company to handle.

Experience with Direct Investments: Continental Capital. The French experience with Latin American investments was not a happy one. Serious expansion in the volume of investment occurred in the quarter century before the first world war. There had been some probing into Latin American mining possibilities at mid-century and some investment in land by immigrants and promoters of emigration, but activity lagged until the 1880's when French banks were established in Mexico, Argentina, Brazil and other countries, mining investment in Mexico, Chile, Venezuela and Colombia began to expand, and participation in railway construction in Argentina, Brazil and Mexico assumed more important proportions. By the end of the century French-controlled enterprises had raised twice as much capital as had found its way into government obligations. From 1900 to 1914 the investment more than doubled. On the eve of the first world war, perhaps three-quarters of a billion dollars of French capital was invested in various economic enterprises. The returns were meager. A few isolated ventures paid handsomely—the concession in the port of Rosario, Argentina; the Dos Estrellas Mining Company in Mexico and the El Callao Mining Company in Venezuela, for instance. But the disastrous venture to build a canal across Panama in which was sunk ultimately one-sixth of all the French capital ever invested in Latin America was more characteristic of the French experience. There were French promoters and construction companies that profited from railway building and there were investment bankers who could thrive on the volume of securities put on the market. But Rippy, reviewing the record of "interferences, defaults, expropriations, reclamations, protests, diplomatic disputes, disappointments and calamities" concludes that the "Frenchmen of moderate means who placed their savings in this region, and in the end nearly all French investors, encountered an unhappy fate." Some statistics on French investment are presented in Table 50.

With a relatively late start, German investments in Latin American industry, agriculture, banking and commercial enterprises may have reached a third to a half billion dollars by 1913. German capital did not move significantly into the railways which had absorbed so much of the energy and capital of the British and French investors, but otherwise there was a pressing interest in competing for concessions, government issues, and extension of the domestic industrial and banking power to industry and commerce in Latin America. The Italian contribution to development consisted more largely of manpower than of capital, with almost 5 million Italians entering Latin America between 1825 and 1940. In this case too the active period of capital flow was the quarter century before the first world war when Italian interest in banks, mercantile houses and manufacturing expanded. By 1913 Italian direct investments were perhaps $100 to $125 million, with substantially larger holdings by Italians now resident in Latin America. Estimates of the investments of the other European countries are even more unreliable than those for the major powers, but it may be safe to put the total at less than a quarter of a billion dollars in 1913.

Experience with Direct Investment:U. S. Capital. American capital early began to feel its way into Latin America, but by 1897 only about $300 million had gone into direct investments, about two-thirds of it in Mexican mining and Mexican railroads. Although a cargo of American goods had been shipped to Argentina in 1801 while the area was under Spanish rule and an American firm had been organized to engage in trade with Argentina in 1833, American interest in South America was slow to expand and at the turn of the century was well under $100 million. By 1914 U. S. direct investments in Latin America were $1.3 billion, less than one-third the European investment. Mexico was still the focus of American interest; Mexican petroleum had drawn $85 million, the investment in mining and smelting had risen from $68 million in 1897 to $302 million in 1914. In Chilean mining, $140 million had been invested in less than a decade. The Cuban sugar industry had been in the process of reorganization and by 1905 there were about 29 American-owned mills handling 21% of the crop; the investment in Cuban sugar grew from $20 million in 1897 to $50 million in 1908 to $95 million in 1914. American utility interests simultaneously expanded in Cuba and Mexico.

During the first world war the Cuban sugar crop rose 50% from 1914 to 1919, prices were favorable, and American investments expanded to $315 million. Investment in Mexican petroleum more than doubled, while sizable expansion of Peruvian petroleum investments also occurred. Tremendous profits in Chilean mining helped expand the investment to $306 million. Meanwhile American branch plant activity in South America began to acquire significant proportions. In the decade ending in 1929, the total direct investments of the United States in Latin America rose from $2 billion to $3.7 billion. The utility interests, particularly International Telephone and Telegraph Company and the American & For-

TABLE 51

United States Investments in Latin America, 1897-1935

(millions of dollars)

	1897	1908	1914	1919	1924	1929	1935
Direct Investments:							
Cuba and other West Indies	49	195	281	567	993	1025	731
Mexico	200	416	587	643	735	709	652
Central America	21	38	90	112	143	251	160
South America	38	105	323	665	947	1719	1718
	$308	754	1281	1987	2818	3704	3261
Direct and Portfolio Investments:							
Cuba and other West Indies	49	225	336	606	1101	1154	872
Mexico	200	672	853	909	1005	975	912
Central America	21	41	93	115	155	286	192
South America	38	130	366	776	1411	3014	2574
	$308	1068	1648	2406	3672	5429	4550

Source: Cleona Lewis, *America's Stake in International Investments* (The Brookings Institution, Washington, 1938), p. 606.

eign Power Company, gathered up almost half a billion dollars worth of properties. The first great period of Venezuelan petroleum expansion saw a quarter billion dollars added to the investment. The sugar industry in Cuba, Dominican Republic and Haiti came to command more than $600 million of American capital. American manufacturers had established only one branch plant in South America prior to 1900, but they established 15 in the decade 1910-1919, 29 in the decade 1920-1929, and another 21 in the four years 1930-33; their investment had reached $170 million by 1929. As import restrictions multiplied, American companies were hurrying to get behind tariff walls and to take on the protective coloring of local industries. Tables 51, 52, 53 show the distribution of capital by areas and by industries.[9]

[9] It will be noted that the data used by different authors reach different totals. Data on foreign investments are at best very uncertain. The statistics presented are valuable, however, in providing an understanding of relative magnitudes by categories and by areas.

TABLE 52

United States Direct Investments by Classes of Investments 1897-1935

(millions of dollars)

	1897	1908	1914	1919	1924	1929	1935
Selling Organizations	16	24	34	71	95	119	
Cuba & other West Indies	4	5	9	10	12	15	
South America	10	16	20	55	75	94	
Oil Distribution	4	13	23	40	60	78	86
Cuba & other West Indies	1	3	3	10	10	10	9
South America	3	10	20	30	50	68	77
Mining and Smelting:							
Precious metals	58	142	173	144	151	164	155
Mexico	50	119	140	100	112	116	105
South America	6	14	23	31	32	41	43
Mining and Smelting:							
Industrial Minerals	21	161	376	516	562	638	618
Cuba & other West Indies	3	6	15	21	21	18	21
Mexico	18	115	162	122	124	133	133
South America	–	39	198	372	416	486	463
Chile	–	30	170	306	330	382	363
Oil Production	3	55	107	286	473	653	632
Mexico	1	50	85	200	250	206	206
South America	2	5	22	83	220	444	426
Venezuela	1	2	5	18	100	240	240
Colombia	–	–	2	20	55	136	126
Peru	1	3	15	45	65	68	60
Agriculture: Sugar	24	57	118	360	678	659	384
Cuba	20	50	95	315	575	544	300
Dominican Republic	–	–	10	20	56	60	37
Agriculture: Fruit	10	31	62	72	95	161	63
Agriculture: Other	23	73	66	79	77	74	54
Manufacturing	3	30	37	84	127	230	258
Cuba & other West Indies	3	18	20	26	30	47	45
South America	..	2	7	50	90	170	200
Railroads	131	110	176	211	261	229	187
Cuba & other West Indies	2	43	24	41	72	84	69
Mexico	111	57	110	123	139	81	61
Central America	16	9	38	43	46	64	57
Public Utilities	10	52	99	102	163	576	592
Cuba & other West Indies	..	24	58	59	113	105	103
Mexico	6	22	33	32	32	90	90
Central America	..	1	4	6	13	33	34
South America	4	5	4	5	4	348	365
Argentina	1	1	1	2	2	148	165
Brazil	..	..	..	..	..	97	97
Chile	1	1	1	1	1	67	67

Source: Cleona Lewis, *America's Stake in International Investments* (The Brookings Institution, Washington, 1938), pp. 578-603.

The Position in 1939. On the eve of the second world war, foreign direct investments in Latin America exceeded $7.5 billion. The British and American investments were of roughly the same proportions, about $3 billion each. One country, Argentina, had attracted more than one-third of the total, with 10% each for Brazil, Cuba, Mexico and Chile. One industry, the railroads, had attracted about one-third of the investment, with one-fifth in the other utilities, and another fifth in mining and petroleum. Foreign-controlled enterprises were originating more than one-third of all the exports of Latin America. British investment on a selective basis had resumed after the first world war but new investment continued to be a smaller and smaller proportion of the earnings of previous direct investments. France had ceased to be a significant source of investment and Continental investment generally was on a highly selective basis and lacking significant volume. American investments were earning about 9% per year, a higher earnings ratio on equity than was afforded by the investments of most of the other countries, and more than one-third of the earnings on American investments were being reinvested.

From the standpoint of developmental policy, a dangerous hiatus in the process of foreign investment which had brought industrial civilization to Latin America seemed threatened. On the one hand, the great capital markets of the world were virtually closed to the Latin American governments whose defaults in response to the fantastic gyrations in export prices had pointed up the vulnerability of the international economic positions of countries so heavily dependent upon foreign trade narrowly based. On the other hand, an exaggerated nationalism, an anti-foreign capital movement which had long been building, threatened to interrupt the flow of private capital into direct investments. The expropriations of petroleum properties in Bolivia and Mexico, the mounting burden of social legislation obviously directed against the foreigner first and the local vested interests secondly, the maneuvers against the private oil companies and meat packing companies even in Argentina which had willingly accepted sacrifices in order to maintain its credit standing and had been regarded as least

TABLE 53

American Direct Investments in Latin America, 1929-1948

(millions of dollars)

	1929	1936	1940	1945	1948
Manufacturing	$231	$192	$210	$388	$586
Agriculture	817	400	359	360	459
Distribution	119	100	82	139	207
Mining and smelting	732	702	512	414	418
Petroleum	617	453	572	553	1064
Public utility and transportation	887	937	962	887	847
Miscellaneous	116	57	74	42	100
	$3,519	$2,847	$2,771	$2,784	$3,680

Source: U. S. Department of Commerce, *American Direct Investments in Foreign Countries*—1940 (Washington, 1942), p. 23; U. S. Department of Commerce, *The Balance of International Payments of the United States*, 1946-1948 (Washington, 1950), p. 94.

likely to interfere with the foreign investment process from which it had benefited so heavily, the increasing restrictions on the use of foreign personnel, the refusal to recognize the importance in exchange-control operations of permitting adequate remittance of earnings if investment was to continue to be attractive, the disadvantageous consequences of currency instability, the general air of hostility, the legislative definition of certain fields in which foreign investment would be discouraged, and the shrewd shift to "silent" expropriation with its greater ease of implementation without political involvement,[10] all constituted a challenge to the continued flow of capital which had heretofore been considered an essential to acceleration of economic development.

---

[10] "Silent" expropriation is a term used to cover the creation of conditions making it virtually impossible for an investor to continue operations in a country, as for instance multiplication of unreasonably restrictive social and labor laws, confiscatory tax laws, establishment purposefully of directly competitive government enterprises to function without regard for normal earnings objectives. The advantage over outright expropriation which exposes a country to difficulties with the Foreign Office or the Department of State and to demands for payment immediately for a profit-making enterprise are obvious.

It was to be expected that in Latin America as elsewhere industries affected with a public interest such as railroads, utilities, banks, would be subjected increasingly to government regulations and controls. But while in the United States such industries were locally controlled, often with wide holding of their securities, and protected by the tradition and practices of a mature capitalist system, the industries in Latin America were controlled by foreign investors living abroad and exposed to a tradition of personal government. Furthermore, the tremendous dependence of the economies on exports caused the Latin American, understandably, to view the great export industries also as "affected with a public interest" and therefore reasonably the subject of special government attention. Unfortunately, perhaps 90% of the foreign investments fell into the category of industries "affected with a public interest" when thus broadly defined. While the foreign investor commonly felt that the final blow of social revolution was unlikely to fall upon him as long as the *domestic* property-holding class continued in its powerful position, nationalistic measures nevertheless found him a more vulnerable target.

"The machine process and all it entails—transportation and communication facilities and the entire scheme of financial and business organization," wrote Max Handman in 1940, "was either introduced or its progress greatly accelerated by foreign investments."

Technicians and technical equipment, the possibilities of teaching machine and financial techniques to the national population, are due in large measure to foreign investments. Much of the medical progress which has lowered the mortality rate and increased population has come through portfolio investments. Natural resources which would have lain dormant for many decades have been made available through both portfolio and direct investments. Areas which would have been uninhabited now have been settled by the facilities furnished by foreign investments. New sources of wealth have been discovered and the sum total of goods and services available to the community are directly traceable to the fact that foreigners have sent their capital—which means tools, skills, goods, craftsmen, trained advisers and supervisors—into foreign countries, have shortened the process of waiting, and have speeded up production by at least half a century.[11]

But now, Handman continued, there was a tendency in Latin American thinking to seek a substitute in the form of a planned economy. He outlined the reasoning of the Latin American as follows:

Until now our modern instruments of production have been created capitalistically, that is, we have borrowed them from foreign countries through the instrument of foreign investments. But what have we actually borrowed? We have borrowed machines and people skilled to run them. We have also borrowed money which we have paid out to our own nationals for land on which to build railroads and for food produced at home to feed the workers who were building these railroads. Now assuming that the Government were to step in in place of the banker or foreign or native entrepreneur, could we not accomplish the same result or almost the same result? The food with which we feed the workers is raised in Brazil or Argentina. Why would not the native producer of food part with it for money or tokens issued by our Government instead of the foreign investor? The same may be said to be true of the owner of land. There is unused productive capacity which can be tapped, provided there is a good governmental organization and confidence in that organization. Not only that, but there is also a considerable amount of capital available which now seeks investment in foreign countries or in secure real estate in urban centers. Why not make the terms sufficiently attractive for this capital to flow into investments industrially productive? The answer runs in terms of lack of confidence in our governmental structure and political organization. What we need is a strong central government in which the community can have confidence or which can impose such confidence if it does not come willingly.[12]

This theoretical explanation, Handman pointed out, led to an authoritarian or totalitarian state. The Latin American had reduced the problem to "one necessary element in the desired substitution of native initiative for foreign invest-

---

[11] *Economic Relations with Latin America* (Michigan Business Papers, Number 6, University of Michigan, Ann Arbor, 1940), p. 33.

[12] *Op. cit., p.* 35.

ments and that is the machine, the instrument itself which is to be installed and operated by native skill and labor. Obviously we are dealing here with a question of technological skill primarily. The technological skill is again a matter which can be acquired by the native population if the educational system and the national organization are properly directed. . . . Looked at from the angle of large social policy, the question of being able to continue the process of civilization started or accelerated by foreign investment turns out to be, in the eyes of proponents of *economiá dirigida* nothing but a question of social and political reorganization. And that, they claim, is a matter of will, enthusiasm and devotion—and perhaps the color of the shirt." [13]

While the Latin American was fumbling for a substitute for foreign investment and examining the cost of the alternatives, variations of the old process of investment were also being devised in the creditor countries.

Government Lending. Bryan and Wilson had been driven to search for a formula for financing Latin American development out of worry over the problems of intervention, reluctance to accept the thesis that refusal to allow European intervention implied that the United States must on its own account take action to enforce payments to European creditors, rejection of the complacency with which Taft and Knox had allowed American investors to assume that government support would be forthcoming to them. By the time that the orgy of lending of the 1920's had ended in collapse and default, it was already recognized that the government would not intervene in behalf of holders of foreign bonds.[14]   The

---

[13] *Op. cit.,* p. 36.

[14] The formal position of the United States government, write Feuerlein and Hannan, "requires that other states shall respect their obligations vis-à-vis American creditors, and that in case payments are scaled down or delayed American creditors shall receive treatment as good as that accorded to other foreign creditors. Our government will protest against repudiation by a foreign government of its indebtedness to American citizens; it will protest discrimination against them. But it will not undertake to determine how fully, at what date, and in what currency the obligations of a debtor country shall be fulfilled." *Op. cit.,* p. 30.

government did not intervene. The period of the 1930's was not in any event characterized by sympathy for "international bankers" or for that matter for bankers of any stripe. Official Washington began to turn its attention to a formula for development financing now out of realization that assistance for Latin American governments from the old channels was unlikely soon if ever to be resumed. The Export-Import Bank had been established by the government in 1934 to "aid in financing and to facilitate" the foreign trade of the United States. Before the United States entered the second world war, the Bank made loans to finance coinage operations for Cuba, extended credits to meet seasonal or emergency shortages of exchange, assisted in unblocking the balances of American exporters which were unpaid because of the unavailability of exchange. It assisted increasingly in developmental activity through the financing of exports of capital equipment, loans for highway construction and similar activity. The influence of the Department of State on the Bank was great during this period, and charges that the Bank was used as an instrument of political policy are not without justification. By 1939 the Administration was convinced that the Bank should participate more actively in developmental credits not only to further the interests of capital-equipment exporters in competition with European manufacturers but also to provide the basis for expansion of the economies that had normally been supplied by the private capital markets. There was increasing dissatisfaction with the slowness of the Foreign Bondholders Protective Council to reach settlements on the defaulted dollar bond issues. In the summer of 1939 President Roosevelt sought a half billion dollar expansion of the lending authority of the Bank for development activity, and although temporarily balked by the Congress, he won support for the proposal in the autum of 1940 when the European war situation had altered the world picture considerably.

Up to July 1, 1940 the Export-Import Bank had disbursed only $73 million on the credits extended to Latin America. In proposing to strengthen the economies of Latin America to reduce their vulnerability to rapidly changing currents of world trade and to expand their productivity particularly of commodities that might be imported by the United States, President Roosevelt brushed aside the practices of the "ancient frauds" as he termed the dollar-bond issues and offered an "approach to sound lending practices." The Administration believed that there had been inadequate supervision of the proceeds of the dollar bond issues, that expenditure had not been restricted to specific projects but instead had been freely dissipated on general balance of payments deficits and on budgetary deficits in local currencies, that proceeds of the loans had been used to cover disbursements for local materials and labor which might better have been financed within the country itself and thereby made to entail no burden on the country's foreign-exchange resources, that there had been little guidance in the selection of projects or pressure to compel establishment of suitable priorities with a view to the relative contribution to an increase in productivity of the economy.

The Export-Import Bank accordingly developed a policy-statement providing: (a) That the Bank generally would make loans only for specific purposes, would not make lump-sum advances, would extend credit only for purposes which it had previously approved, would make disbursements under a commitment only upon receipt of satisfactory evidence that the purposes of the loan have been carried out; (b) That the Bank would make only loans which offered reasonable assurance of repayment, which meant that applications for loans would have to present convincing proof of the engineering, financial and economic soundness of the proposals in terms of anticipated increases in productivity and/or contribution to the balance of payments position whether by reduction in imports or by expansion in exports; (c) That the Bank generally would not finance outlays in the borrower's own currency.

From 1940 to 1943 the Bank disbursed $140 million on its Latin American credits, from 1943 to 1945 $73 million, from 1946 through 1949 $310 million. At the end of 1949 it showed net authorizations (authorized credits minus those cancelled and expired) of $755 million, against which there had up to that time been disbursed $595 million. (See Table 54). The Bank had extended credits of more than $100 million for the steel mills of Brazil, Chile and Mexico, more than $100 million each for highway transportation and for railway equipment; its portfolio ranged from financing of $38 million for Lloyd Brasileiro to help realization of Brazil's long-range planning for a merchant fleet to quickly granted assistance for reconstruction work after the Ecuadorean earthquake of 1949.

Significantly, however, as the decade of the 1950's opened, the Bank was under sharp criticism for the slowness with which financing had been forthcoming for developmental activity. It had not been handicapped by a lack of funds, for it customarily had enjoyed half a billion to a billion dollars in unused lending authority. The experience of the Bank by 1950 seemed to indicate that financing coud not be accelerated unless sound principles were abandoned in favor of a compromise toward the practices which had brought such harsh denunciation of the New York bankers who had floated the dollar bond issues in the 1920's. First, the Latin American governments had been slow to adapt themselves to the requirement of serious economic and engineering analysis of projects as a prelude to consideration of loan applications. A notable exception was Chile, and Table 54 furnishes significant demonstration of the fruits of its adaptability. Second, it had proved almost impossible to work out satisfactory developmental mechanisms or corporate structures under which joint planning and expenditure could proceed in the less developed countries like Bolivia, Ecuador and Paraguay. In fact, even in Brazil, the successive loans to Companhia Vale do Rio Doce had bogged down in local politics, and participation of the Bank's engineers in the decisions of the directing board long proved inadequate for effective expenditure of funds. Third, the large requirements for financing not directly related to the creation of additional foreign exchange had emphasized the ease of becoming "loaned up" in terms of capacity to service loans. Fourth, the tendency for developmental ambitions to step up the pace of activity excessively generated a demand for foreign goods beyond the ability to create exchange and

TABLE 54

Export-Import Bank: Statement of Loans and Authorized Credits
As of December 31, 1949
(millions of dollars)

	Authorized Credits	Cancelled and Expired	Not Yet Disbursed	Disbursed	Principal Repaid	Principal Outstanding
Argentina	$93.7	$93.1	—	$0.6	$0.4	$0.2
Bolivia	37.0	—	16.1	20.9	2.2	18.7
Brazil	287.5	114.1	9.1	164.3	64.0	100.3
Chile	141.6	8.6	43.7	89.4	32.9	56.5
Colombia	65.3	2.5	17.4	45.3	23.0	22.3
Costa Rica	8.7	1.5	—	7.3	0.7	6.6
Cuba	90.4	34.2	—	56.2	45.6	10.6
Dominican Republic	3.3	—	—	3.3	3.0	0.3
Ecuador	27.6	1.1	13.2	13.3	2.5	10.8
Haiti	17.3	2.7	4.0	10.7	5.7	4.9
Honduras	2.7	1.7	—	1.0	0.7	0.3
Mexico	155.7	7.5	28.4	119.8	42.1	77.7
Nicaragua	5.2	0.6	—	4.7	3.1	1.5
Panama	6.5	2.0	0.9	3.6	2.5	1.1
Paraguay	7.8	1.6	—	6.2	2.2	4.0
Peru	37.4	37.0	—	0.4	0.1	0.3
El Salvador	1.7	0.2	—	1.5	0.5	1.0
Uruguay	43.7	29.2	0.2	14.3	0.7	13.6
Venezuela	52.5	37.0	7.5	8.0	4.3	3.7
Miscellaneous	119.0	74.8	19.6	24.6	24.6	—
	$1,204.8	$449.3	$160.1	$595.4	$260.9	$334.5

Source: Export-Import Bank, *Ninth Semi-Annual Report* (Washington, 1950).

by 1949 the Bank was yielding reluctantly to deviations from the basic policy of project-financing. Fifth, the reluctance to take suitable measures internally was reflected in the increasing desire of the Latin American countries for external financing to cover local-currency expenditures.

The International Bank for Reconstruction and Development, an inter-governmental institution in which the Latin American governments participated directly although the dominant influence on policy was here also exercised by the United States, had made available $142.6 million in developmental financing for Latin America in 1948 and 1949. Of this amount, financing for power development totalled $135.1 million (Chile $13.5 million, Brazil $75 million, Mexico $34.1 million, El Salvador $12.5 million) and loans for acquisition of agricultural machinery $7.5 million (Colombia $5 million, Chile $2.5 million). Its findings, which coincided with the experience of the older Export-Import Bank, were that "perhaps the most striking single lesson which the Bank has learned in the course of its operation is how limited is the capacity of the under-developed countries to absorb capital quickly for really productive purposes." The impatience of the Latin American countries with the pace of financing was evidenced in the renewal of demands for an Inter-American Bank. Such a bank had been projected by the American republics in 1939-1940 but had not been brought into existence. From the viewpoint of the United States, which appeared to be the only significant potential source of development financing whatever the structure under which the funds were made available, the issue by 1950 had reduced to this: if the pace of lending were to be stepped up to the degree desired by the Latin Americans, it would be necessary to alter the policy-directive which called for "reasonable assurance of repayment" and/or to move into fields which had been barred to the lending agencies up to this time because of the policy of the United States not to provide government financing for risks which are within the scope of private capital or which private capital is prepared to assume without government assistance, i.e., the policy that institutions in which the United States government participated would "not compete with private capital but rather supplement and encourage it."

There were undoubtedly wide areas of investment in Latin America which could not hope to attract capital from the United States—the activity popularly defined as "public works," fields of basic facilities commonly provided by government, fields where a social-rate structure was strongly indicated. These fields represented immense financial requirements. But unless the capacity to create exchange to service such loans could be simultaneously expanded by investment in other fields, the lending agencies found it difficult to certify that there was "reasonable assurance of repayment." The Latin American countries generally did not share the views of the United States on the role of private capital in development and pressed for inter-governmental financing of projects in competition with private capital or to make possible the exclusion of private capital. The issue was clearly joined by 1950.

It was probable that the volume of domestic savings and the concentration of such savings in many of the Latin American countries by 1950 was such that local capital could largely meet the requirements for the less complex manufacturing enterprises and even some of the more complex activity which characterizes the initial and intermediary stages of industrialization. The major area of investment for foreign private capital was therefore the mineral, petroleum and extractive industries generally whose large risks and immense technological and financial requirements made them unattractive to private local capital. It was precisely those lines which held out the maximum hope for expanding Latin America's capacity to export and providing thereby the basis for servicing investments in public works, for importing the goods needed to speed industrialization. Unfortunately it was precisely those fields too where resistance to entry of private capital was most often encountered in Latin America. In the Latin American mind, these exports of raw materials were associated with a "colonial status," with dependence upon world markets. The Latin American was thinking of "decolonization" regardless of cost. He preferred to reserve further development of the raw-material export potential to

locally-controlled enterprise and was not particularly disturbed by the thought that the local enterprise might have to
be government activity in the absence of risk takers among
the local population. It is true that some countries displayed
less of this fear of "colonial status" but even where private
capital was being permitted access, the underlying preference
could be detected. In the United States it was widely believed that deviation from the basic inter-governmental lending policy that barred loans for fields in which private capital
was willing to flow would jeopardize the climate of investment
for all private investment. The Latin American did not share
this viewpoint.

The Position in 1950. In the decade ending in 1948 substantial changes occurred in the foreign direct-investment
situation in Latin America. British sales of properties on the
east coast of South America alone brought in more than $1
billion; included were the great railway investments in Argentina and utility and railway properties in Uruguay and
Brazil; the properties disposed of had previously been valued
in estimates of investment at more than $1.5 billion.[15] The
disposition of Axis-controlled assets was clouded in the
maneuvers of their owners, but the assets in large measure
had been converted into locally-controlled properties — at
least temporarily. There was a tremendous expansion in
American investments, largely in the period 1945-1948, and
consisting largely of additions to the investment in Venezuelan
petroleum. As Table 55 shows, the net movement of American capital in the period 1945-1948 exceeded $900 million,
of which 70% was accounted for by petroleum investments.
American-owned telephone properties in Argentina were sold
for almost $100 million; and there was notable disinvestment
in the Cuban sugar industry where from 1942 to 1946 alone

---

[15] Cleona Lewis lists repatriation of British long-term investments in
Argentina as £247 million for the period 1939-47, investment in Uruguay
£14 million, investments elsewhere in South America £57 million. She
notes that the Argentine railways had previously been estimated at
£250 million, but were sold at £150 million (90% of the investment
was held in Britain).

TABLE 55

Movement of U. S. Direct-Investment Capital into Latin America, 1945-1948

(millions of dollars)

	1945	1946	1947	1948
Total	$140	$ 56	$408	$318
Manufacturing	21	16	51	16
Distribution	4	8	31	34
Agriculture	47	6	−11	12
Mining and smelting	−7	−12	18	22
Petroleum	71	104	261	223
Utilities	2	−80	18	7
Miscellaneous	3	13	40	3

Source: United States Department of Commerce, *The Balance of International Payments of the United States*, 1946-1948 (Washington, 1950), p. 136.

28 American-controlled mills were transferred for a sales price of $56 million.

In 1948 foreign direct investments in Latin America were probably on the order of $6.5 to $7 billion, of which American investments were $4.2 billion. British investments constituted perhaps half of the total of about $2.2 to $2.5 billion controlled by European investors. Earnings on the equity of U. S. direct investments had been reasonably attractive, averaging 9.5% in the four years 1941-44 and 14.5% in the four years 1945-48 when the high level of business activity in Latin America and the especially favorable conditions affecting the petroleum industry generally contributed greatly to the effectiveness of the investments. Earning power among various classes of investment was uneven, as Tables 56 and 57 indicate.

Back in 1892 *The Economist* had marvelled that "South American investments have for a half a century been a thorn in the flesh of British investors, and it is, perhaps, because we have become so accustomed to the infliction that the country has, time after time, shown its readiness to increase the sore." [16] In the case of securities sold to the public, the chain

---

[16] August 20, 1892.

TABLE 56

Ratio of Earnings to Equity of U. S. Direct Investments in Latin
America, 1945-48

(Value and earnings in millions of dollars; ratios in percent)

	1945	1946	1947	1948
Value of investments	$2784	$2999	$3145	$3680
Earnings	312	395	504	639
Ratio to equity	11.2%	13.2%	16.0%	17.4%
Manufacturing: investment	388	433	487	586
Earnings	50	70	94	115
Ratio	12.9%	16.3%	19.4%	19.8%
Distribution: investment	139	146	166	207
Earnings	17	33	34	48
Ratio	12.5%	22.5%	20.4%	23.0%
Agriculture: investment	360	421	446	459
Earnings	55	74	86	66
Ratio	15.2%	17.5%	19.2%	14.4%
Mining and Smelting: investment	414	412	398	418
Earnings	36	40	53	77
Ratio	8.7%	9.8%	13.4%	18.4%
Petroleum: investment	553	645	769	1064
Earnings	113	134	194	302
Ratio	20.4%	20.8%	25.2%	28.4%
Public Utilities: investment	887	898	822	847
Earnings	33	32	31	14
Ratio	3.8%	3.6%	3.8%	1.6%
Miscellaneous: investment	42	46	59	100
Earnings	8	11	12	17
Ratio	18.9%	23.3%	20.3%	16.6%

Source: United States Department of Commerce, The Balance of International Payments of the United States, 1946-1948 (Washington,
1950), p. 94.

Note: Foreign earnings include total income receipts from foreign
operations as reported in the balance of payments plus reinvested earnings of foreign-incorporated enterprises. Equity is defined as book
value of investments at the beginning of the year.

of history repeating itself—investors' hopes, promoters' profits, borrowers' wastes and defaults, investors' inability to
learn anything from history, investors' hopes, and so on—
now seemed finally to have been broken for some time to
come. Certainly an inspection in the 1940's of the returns
to bondholders after most of the countries had reached settle-

ments scaling down their obligations was not calculated to stimulate further interest.[17]

TABLE 57

Income Received from American Direct Investments in Latin America, 1940-1948

(millions of dollars)

	1945	1946	1947	1948	Annual Average 1940-44
Total	$235	$306	$376	$469	$186
Manufacturing	27	33	46	51	21
Distribution	14	21	24	27	11
Agriculture	35	55	61	48	19
Mining and smelting	32	43	51	75	50
Petroleum	96	115	160	239	56
Public utilities	24	29	24	15	23
Miscellaneous	7	11	10	13	5

Source: United States Department of Commerce, *The Balance of International Payments of the United States*, 1946-1948 (Washington, 1950), p. 91; United States Department of Commerce, *International Transactions of the United States During the War*, 1940-1945 (Washington, 1948), p. 74.

But the corporations in industry and commerce had in the first half of the twentieth century fared sufficiently well to be interested in refinements of the process of investment. By mid-century they had perfected an intelligent approach to the problem of successful investment overseas that remedied many of the recognized deficiencies. Part of it was pure public-relations technique, part of it stemmed from abandonment of a hit-and-run attitude toward foreign investment in favor of an attempt to identify the interests of the foreign investor indefinitely with the long-range interests of the coun-

---

[17] In 1943 the U. S. Treasury estimated the market value of American-owned Latin American dollar-bonds as 38 cents on the dollar, on the average. In 1950 the U. S. Commerce Department reported the average rate of return on par and market values of Latin American dollar bonds as follows: South American issues, 1.8% on par value during period 1945-1948, 4.4% on market value; Central American and Mexican issues, 1.5% on par and 4.6% on market value; West Indian issues, 4.1% on par and 4.2% on market value.

try in which capital was to be placed. It was an entirely valid criticism that at one time many foreign investing entities had neglected to furnish an outlet for local entrepreneurial ability, had preferred to differentiate sharply between posts that could be filled locally and those that must continue to be occupied by foreigners, had failed to develop local sources of supply for the goods they used, had been satisfied to provide conditions of work more or less in line with prevailing standards established by local interests whose business philosophy was frequently as unsympathetic to community requirements as was imaginable. It was a valid criticism that many foreign investors had yielded to the temptation to "throw their weight around" in the arena of local politics.

But the direct investment for some time had been based on a new conception of integration with the community's interests. Nationals of the country were being trained as rapidly as possible to assume top-level posts in many of the leading foreign enterprises in Latin America. Sizable expenditures were being made for training intended to grade up the labor force. While it had become customary for the Latin American countries to fix a minimum proportion of the labor force that must be of national origin, foreign companies as rapidly as possible built local staff beyond legislative requirements. Although social legislation and tax legislation had frequently been shaped specifically to hit the foreign investor, sometimes with preferential treatment for fields where domestic interests were dominant, managers of the foreign companies were instructed to adhere strictly to the requirements of the law. Local productivity was expanded in the course of developing local sources of supply. In the many small things that go to make up public relations—foreign-staff that speaks the language of the country, assiduous coaching of staff to conduct themselves diplomatically in their dealings with nationals, participation in local non-political activities (charities, sports, "do-gooding") on a scale proportioned to the importance of the enterprise—the foreign investor had learned his lesson. He had learned to stay out of politics, especially as it became clear to him that his government would not support him if he got into trouble while engaged in such activity.

The motivation did not need to be questioned. It was good business. And fortunately, what was good business was good for the community.

Not only were the practices of foreign investors being subjected to constant improvement but also the structure of foreign investment was undergoing experimentation. For instance, by 1950 considerable support had developed for the joint-capital device in which foreign companies joined with local interests in joint ownership of a venture. Advocates of the device argued that whether the foreign company merely contributed "know-how" and patents to complement capital furnished by the local investor, whether it matched the financial investment on a 50-50 basis or whether it joined in a more uneven investment, the foreign investor took on the protective coloration of a local company by this device. They argued that it was good public relations, that "sharing" in the development of local resources made good sense.

It was still by no means certain, however, that the "partnership" in foreign investment was as happy a device as claimed. The foreign investor was buying "insurance," in the form of the local origin of his partner's investment, in the form of the influence which the local member of the firm might exercise in his own country, possibly in the form of an ability to gain access to certain industries which were barred to the foreign investor by legislation. To the extent that the foreign investor was fully able and willing to make the full investment, the country was mobilizing that much less foreign capital when it encouraged foreign companies to "cut in" local interests for a part of the ownership. Too frequently the legislative encouragement given to the device was simply a form of blackmail to compel foreign firms to share with ambitious local vested interests. And as "insurance," it was by no means certain that the "policy" would pay off in time of need, for in many cases the foreign investor was linking himself with reactionary elements in the community whose business philosophy and attitude toward labor and social and tax policy resembled that of mid-nineteenth century American businessmen rather than that of mid-twentieth century business leadership. The full force of the growing progressive movements in the Latin American countries was likely to be thrown against such elements in the community, and yet it was largely with them that the foreign investor linked himself when he accepted the joint-capital device. In some countries where the larger relationship with the United States made governments extremely sensitive to Washington's policy positions and opinions, it was likely that American businessmen by the joint-capital device might be underwriting the reactionary element in the community, and it is not at all unlikely that the local interests were aware of the strength gained from such a partnership. In domestic business practice in this country the partnership is an extremely delicate form of business organization in which selection of partners is an extremely important problem. It is likely that proponents of the joint-capital device who glibly recite the advantages of assuming a greater degree of "local" coloration have ignored some of the difficulties that joint ownership might add.[18]

In addition to the operating policies and structural changes that the business community was adopting in 1950, support had developed in the United States for assumption by the government of a portion of the risk of investment overseas. The Truman Administration in 1949-50 argued that the United States Government might well guarantee, for a fee, United States investors against the risk of expropriation and transfer of profits and capital, so that if a corporation made profits abroad it would not have to worry about its ability to convert them into dollars and get the profits home to its stock-

---

[18] It might be noted that a number of corporations have already found ways of getting around legislative requirements that make local participation in certain proportions a condition of doing business. In Mexico foreign participation in most types of enterprises requires that the permission of the Ministry of Foreign Relations be obtained. Such permission may be, but need not be, conditioned on the requirement that over one-half of the capital stock of the enterprise be owned by nationals and that the majority of directors or partners be Mexican. A number of foreign corporations have accepted the condition of certain local participation and been able to retain control in the degree desired by special arrangements with their "local partners."

holders, and if a property were expropriated it would be assured of prompt and adequate compensation in dollars. There had been some criticism of the claims of the Export-Import Bank that it had suffered no substantial defaults on its loans on the ground that foreign countries gave preferential attention to their obligations to the Bank as against their obligations to private investors, and there was some fear that as the countries assumed a larger and larger burden of debt at the Bank the interests of private investors might be jeopardized.[19] A guarantee system, it was argued, would still leave to the management of the private company the challenge of operating at a profit in the foreign country, but once it had earned a profit it would no longer have to worry over the ability to obtain dollars for its local currency for remittance to its owners. Whether the guarantee of the United States would serve as a deterrent to expropriation, whether it would stimulate prompt effective and adequate payment in the currency of the investor, or whether it would simply involve the United States Government in controversy with foreign governments from which it could emerge eventually only as a harsh collector or as a helpless "fat boy," formed part of the debate over the proposal for guarantees in 1949 and 1950. Further stimulus to the flow of capital was also sought in tax relief measures. It was proposed in 1950 "to postpone the tax on corporate income earned abroad until it is brought home, to extend and generalize the present credit for taxes paid abroad, and to liberalize the foreign residence requirement for exemption of income earned abroad."

In addition to reviewing its tax policy and to studying the feasibility of certain guarantees for foreign investments, the United States Government was also engaged in attempting to establish a code of rules under which foreign investment might proceed with greater orderliness. At the Ninth International Conference of American States in Bogotá in 1948 an attempt was made to spell out specifically some of the

---

[19] In its Ninth Semi-Annual Report the Bank noted that payments were delinquent as of December 31, 1949 on loans totalling only $1.7 million compared with principal outstanding of $334.5 million; loans in default were only $0.25 million.

principles that had been discussed and established at previous conferences and to establish more definite commitments for their implementation. In the particular interest of countries seeking investment, the Economic Agreement provided:

(a) That the States reaffirm their right to establish measures to prevent foreign investments from being utilized directly or indirectly as an instrument for intervening in national politics or for prejudicing the security or fundamental interests of the receiving countries, and standards with respect to the extent, conditions and terms upon which they will permit future foreign investment.

b) That foreign investments shall be made with due regard not only for the legitimate profit of the investors but also with a view to both increasing the national income and accelerating the sound economic development of the country in which the investment is made and to promoting the economic and social welfare of the persons directly dependent upon the enterprise in question.

c) That each State shall within the framework of its own institutions seek to liberalize its tax laws so as progressively to reduce or eliminate double taxation and to avoid unduly burdensome and discriminatory taxation.

d) That no State may apply or encourage coercive measures of an economic and political character in order to force the sovereign will of another State and to obtain from the latter advantages of any nature.

In the interest of stimulating investment, the Economic Agreement of Bogotá provided:

a) That the States agree not to take unjustified, unreasonable or discriminatory measures that would impair the legally acquired rights or interests of nationals of other countries in the enterprises, capital, skills, arts or technology they have established or supplied. That foreign capital shall receive equitable treatment.

b) That the States shall reciprocally grant appropriate facilities and incentives for the investment and reinvestment of foreign capital, and shall impose no unjustifiable restrictions upon the transfer of such capital and the earnings thereon.

c) That just and equitable treatment shall be accorded to all personnel, national and foreign, and that the development of the technical and administrative training of national personnel shall be encouraged.[20]

d) That the States shall take no discriminatory action against investments by virtue of which foreign enterprises or capital may be deprived of legally acquired property rights for reasons or under conditions different from those that the Constitution or laws of each country provide for the expropriation of national property. Any expropriation shall be accompanied by payment of a fair price in a prompt, adequate and effective manner.[21]

In addition to the multilateral efforts typified by the Economic Agreement of Bogotá, during 1949 and 1950 the Department of State conducted negotiations on a bilateral basis looking to signing of commercial and economic agreements that would stimulate the flow of capital. On November 23, 1949 a Treaty of Friendship, Commerce and Economic Development between the United States and Uruguay was signed — the first comprehensive commercial treaty which the United States had entered into with any of the other American republics since 1927. Officials of the Department of State at the time considered the provisions of the treaty relating to investment to represent the maximum achievement possible in bilateral negotiations with the other American republics. The provisions included:

a) "National treatment" for firms engaging in commercial, manufacturing, processing, financial, construction, publish-

---

[20] It was also provided that "it is desirable to permit enterprises, without prejudice to the laws of each country, to employ and utilize the services of a reasonable number of technical experts and executive personnel whatever their nationality may be." But the qualifying clause "without prejudice to the laws of each country" was considered as materially weakening the value of this provision.

[21] The United States has always taken the basic position that any expropriation shall be accompanied by prompt, adequate and effective compensation. Some of the Latin American delegations found it difficult to accept this unqualified undertaking lest it appear that more favorable conditions were guaranteed foreign than national property holders. Eight countries filed formal reservations or interpretative declarations on this subject which weakened the value of this formulation substantially.

ing, scientific, educational, religious, philanthropic and professional activities, for obtaining and maintaining patents of invention and rights in trade marks, trade names, trade labels and industrial property of all kinds, and for having access to the courts of justice and to administrative tribunals in pursuit and in defense of their rights. (National treatment was defined as treatment upon terms no less favorable than that accorded in like situations to nationals of the country.)

b) In cases where national treatment cannot be granted, there shall be accorded most-favored-nation treatment with respect to exploring for and exploiting mineral deposits (including petroleum) and for organizing and participating in companies of the other country.

c) Permission to engage technical experts, executive personnel, attorneys and other specialized personnel of their choice, regardless of nationality.

d) Tax treatment not more burdensome than that borne by nationals.

e) Permission to introduce capital funds freely and to withdraw capital and earnings freely, at just and reasonable exchange rate, with the qualification that the right is retained in periods of exchange stringency to restrict exchange to assure availability for payments for minimum essential requirements for the health and welfare of the people, with the further qualification that such restrictions shall be followed within three months by provision for the transfer and for opportunity for consultation.

f) National treatment shall be accorded the investor in the event of taking of property. Any expropriation shall be made in accordance with the applicable laws which shall at least assure the payment of just compensation in a prompt, adequate and effective manner.

g) Repetition of certain provisions of the Economic Agreement of Bogotá: equitable treatment for foreign capital; no unreasonable or discriminatory measures that would impair the legally acquired rights or interests in enterprises established or in the capital, skills, arts and technology supplied; no denying without appropriate reason of opportunities and facilities for investment of capital.

Policies Affecting Foreign Investment in Individual Countries. The climate for private foreign investment is indicated partly by the provisions of the constitution and pertinent legislation in the individual countries. In Argentina, the sphere of investment was limited by a structure of State operation of so-called basic industries and by widespread government intervention throughout the economy. The Argentine constitution of 1949 provided that concessions for the operation of public utilities may not be granted to private entities and that utilities in private hands were to be transferred to the State by means of purchase or expropriation with prior indemnification. Beyond the utilities the State was intervening "to safeguard the general interest." A trading organization had been entrusted with monopoly of export of many leading products and permitted to engage in imports of a variety of goods. There was a government petroleum organization that dominated production and marketing of petroleum. The government monopolized reinsurance activities. It was promoting a "mixed" capital device under which the government might participate with private capital in certain industries, the private capital being domestic or foreign as the government determined the feasibility. No new charters for foreign banks were being granted although existing banks were being allowed to function in a system dominated by the Central Bank. Insurance, excluding reinsurance, was carried on by foreign companies but they were subject to higher tax rates than domestic companies and the government was trying to reserve for local companies insurance cover of goods entering or leaving the country at the risk of Argentine enterprises. There was control of international capital movements and regulations governed the transfer of earnings and capital of investing entities strictly; the government in principle had agreed to treat capital entering the country since the beginning of 1948 more liberally than previously established capital.

The basic income tax rates applied to income derived from Argentine sources without discrimination as to nationality of ownership, but certain additional burdens were imposed on remittance of income abroad and on agricultural enterprises under absentee ownership. Special taxes were levied on foreign transportation companies engaged in international traffic between Argentina and other countries, on foreign press services, foreign insurance companies, foreign motion-picture companies. There was no general law requiring that a certain percentage of the working force must be of national origin, but in the "mixed" capital enterprises the charter of each enterprise could be used to stipulate such a ratio.

The official "line" in the executive branch of the Argentine government in 1950 consisted of pious statements that the government wanted to cooperate with private foreign capital that took a genuine interest in Argentina's development, of severe and continued criticism of the high profits and inadequate service of foreign enterprises in the past, of discouraging policy decisions with respect to individual industries in which foreign capital was already committed, of declarations that until nationalization of the utilities including transportation and communications had been completed, the terms of concessions would be revised to facilitate Argentine participation on an equal or dominant basis, to assure greater benefits to the Argentine people and to avoid excess profits by private owners.

In Uruguay the government had long been active in industry, assuming monopoly positions in some fields, competing directly with private enterprise in others. There was a government insurance entity with authorization to monopolize all insurance risks although it was not yet invoking the power in all lines. There was a government entity with power to monopolize the import, manufacture and sale of fuels, alcoholic beverages and cement; it monopolized the refining but not the import of crude oil, import and sale of coal, import and sale of cement for public works. A government meat packing plant had been given a monopoly of slaughter for the supplying of the city of Montevideo, and it had been given a share of export markets in competition with the private packers. A government organization had a monopoly of power and telephone service, the railways were State-owned, a government port authority was in control of port services, the government also dominated telegraph service, commercial radio, fishing-trawler fleet, manufacture and sale of fertilizers. There was a central bank, and a State mortgage bank with monopoly of issue of securities against the security of real property.

In fields not specifically reserved to the government, the foreigner could compete. With minor exceptions taxation was not discriminatory. There was no fixed ratio of national employees to total force for the ordinary industrial and commercial firm, but organizations of sizable proportions could be required to use 60% to 90% nationals. There was no restriction on the entry of technicians, managerial staff, etc. The bilateral treaty signed with the United States had not involved any significant change in the laws, regulations and policies of Uruguay.

Cuba, on the other hand, had as yet seen little government participation directly in industrial and commercial enterprises, although there was continuing policy guidance for the basic industry—sugar. The Constitution had given foreigners the same right as nationals to engage in agriculture, industry, commercial banking and other enterprises. National treatment applied. Taxation generally was non-discriminatory although foreign companies could be required to pay a special tax on their gross receipts if it could be established that profits of local branches were understated as a result of inter-company transactions. There was also a tax on all remittances abroad, including earnings and capital of foreign investments. Half of the payroll had to go to nationals, half of the wage-earning and salaried personnel had to be Cuban. This ratio applied not only to total staff of an enterprise but also to individual categories of work within each enterprise. Vacancies were to be filled by nationals when personnel was available, and in case of release of personnel, aliens had to be discharged first. It was provided that foreign technicians could be used only when it could be proved that no Cuban of adequate qualifications was available. Technicians were permitted to enter Cuba but they could stay for only one year and were required to train nationals to replace them; this permission could be renewed for two additional years provided that no replacements were available. The Cuban provisions restricting the use of technicians and executive personnel had by 1950 proved very confining to foreign enterprises and had given rise to considerable controversy.

Peru in 1950 had monopolies in distribution of salt, tobacco, guano, industrial alcohol and participated in their manufacture; it was in the petroleum business on a small scale; and it participated also in coal mining, construction, power, food distribution. Except where fields were exclusively reserved to the government, foreign capital was permitted to enter on the same basis as nationals, except for insurance where the majority of shares were to be owned by Peruvians who must also have a majority of directors, and shipping where it was provided that 75% of the shares must be owned locally; in the case of oil, one-fourth of the shares of oil companies were required to be offered to local investors or the government. Foreign enterprises were subject to a "complementary" tax on income. It was specified that not less than 80% of all persons employed in an enterprise had to be nationals who were to receive at least 80% of the payroll. There were no restrictions on the use of foreign technical and managerial personnel.

The Venezuelan constitution offered foreign capital the same rights as national capital in participation in industry, agriculture, commercial mining; banking and petroleum enterprises had to be organized under the laws of Venezuela. The government participated directly in air transportation, ocean shipping, distribution of essential foodstuffs. It had evolved an operating basis for the petroleum industry under which taxes were adjusted to yield at least half of the net profits for the State and industrialization was encouraged by requiring a minimum proportion of the product to be refined locally. Funds were transferred freely to foreign owners. On the matter of labor force: no wage differentials were permitted because of nationality; foremen and other employees, except specially qualified technical experts, who came in direct contact with workers must be Venezuelans; at least 75% of the salaried employees and of wage-earners must be nationals.

Colombia had reserved the airlines and coastal shipping fields under special provisions: 51% of airline shares must belong to nationals, coastal shipping was reserved to nationals or corporations of which 60% of the shares were owned by nationals. But in other fields the foreigner was not legally restricted from ownership of industrial or commercial enterprises. The constitution gave foreigners the same civil rights as nationals, but provided that these rights might be curtailed by law for reasons of public interest. The constitution provided due process of law and prior compensation in event of expropriation but it authorized legislation in special circumstances to determine that there shall be no compensation. The government had already moved dominantly into transportation, communications and power. Through a State development entity it was participating in steel, minerals, glass, tires, and other industrial ventures. It was in the ocean-shipping business. Tax legislation did not formally discriminate against foreign investment. The labor laws provided that not more than 10% of wage-earners and not more than 20% of salaried personnel can be foreigners; managerial staff was exempt from these provisions; 60% of the wages had to go to workers of local origin; no discrimination in rate of compensation was permitted as between local and foreign workers.

The Chilean government had monopolized the export of nitrate and iodine through a public corporation with private participation. It had reserved the petroleum production and refining field for the government. It dominated the railway system through ownership of the larger part of the facilities. It had established special restrictions on nationality of ownership for such fields as coastal shipping, air transport, insurance, fishing. All investment was subject to governmental scrutiny as to its desirability in terms of preventing overproduction or excess competition. The government's development entity was participating widely in industry, ranging from steel manufacture to distribution of farm equipment, from simple loans to local industry to direct establishment of facilities, with a stated policy of selling its equity holdings in enterprises to private investors as soon as the enterprise reached a position where it no longer needed official support of this kind. Social legislation was extensive. Employment of Chileans to the extent of 85% of staff and payment of 85% of payrolls was mandatory, except for technicians who were not available locally. An "additional" tax on income of foreign-owned companies applied over and above the normal tax on business incomes. The official "policy-line" of the executive branch of the government was that the government welcomed foreign private capital in fields not reserved to the State and assured it treatment "which is just, free from discrimination with respect to nationality, and in an atmosphere of democratic life which is a guaranty of stability and security."

Brazil in the 1930's had introduced a number of restrictions on the participation of foreign capital, but the constitution of 1946 modified these to some extent, establishing the basic principle that there was to be equality of foreigner and national in matters affecting investments. There were specific restrictions on outside participation in coastal shipping, insurance, radio broadcasting, aviation. Delay in drawing up a new mining code had left the position of foreign investments uncertain despite the new constitutional authorization for exploitation of minerals by concerns incorporated in Brazil and by Brazilian nationals. In specific cases that came up in the mining field in 1949-50 the government was pressing to assure majority participation by local interests in mining companies in which there was foreign participation. In the case of petroleum the constitutional relaxation permitting concessions to be granted to corporations organized in Brazil as well as to Brazilian nationals was likewise stalled in the debate over policy to govern the field generally. While the constitution of 1937 had limited operations in power to nationals except for existing investments, the constitution of 1946 permitted them to be conducted by companies locally organized regardless of the nationality of the owners; legislation in the period between the constitutions had liberalized the restriction to permit foreign investment at government discretion. In the banking field, legislation of 1941 had provided for liquidation of all foreign banks within five years, the period was subsequently extended, and the constitution of 1946 contained no provisions relating to foreign banking. In the case of insurance, legislation prohibits the licensing of new foreign insurance companies. The place of foreign capital was being influenced not only by reservations with respect to fields but also by increasing government participation directly in the steel industry, chemicals, and other fields where it was impatient with the pace of development.

Brazil, too, enforced provisions relating to the minimum proportion of the labor force that must be of national origin or aliens with ten years residence and married to Brazilians; the proportion here was two-thirds, and the same ratio had to be enforced as a minimum for the distribution of wages. There was no discrimination in pay for equal work permitted. While technical personnel not available locally was permitted access to the country, increasing attention was being paid in individual company concessions to the establishment of training facilities looking to eventual replacement of foreign personnel. Controls had been imposed on the transfer of capital and earnings to help overcome the balance of payments difficulties. In general, foreign enterprises were subject to the same taxes as domestic concerns.

In Mexico, foreign investment required the specific permission of the Ministry of Foreign Relations. Majority participation on the board of directors and 51% control of stock by Mexicans could be required, but in practice the Ministry had limited application of this 51% procedure to a few fields such as radio broadcasting, motion pictures, domestic air transportation, urban transportation, publishing. There was also authority under the law governing monopolies to control investment and production so as to avoid excessive competition and over-production. In insurance and commercial banking, the investment requirements for reserves of banks and the capital requirements for foreign insurance companies which were higher than for domestic insurance companies had discouraged foreign activity. The government controlled the larger part of the railroads, maintained tight control over petroleum production and the petroleum market, and steadily expanded its participation in industry through the financing facilities of the government development entity (Nacional Financiera) and the investment in power generation by the Electricity Commission.

Taxation was considered non-discriminatory. Mining, controlled largely by foreign capital, was subject to higher income tax rates than other business income. Enterprises with more than five employees were required to employ at least 90% Mexican help, but the provision did not apply to managerial staff; technicians were admitted to the country when it could be proved that qualified local technicians were not available to the enterprise. In a country which had invoked the power of expropriation frequently, it was important to note that Mexico had entered a reservation to the clause on expropriation in the Economic Agreement of Bogotá to the effect that the principle established shall be subordinated to constitutional procedures of the expropriating countries.

Public Policy and the "Bearded White Man." But the climate of investment is not defined alone in terms of formal legislation. The immense area of discretionary decision on the part of the executive branch of the government, especially in a region with a long tradition of personal government, figures equally in the appraisal of the feasibility of making investments. Tax systems and social legislation seemingly may avoid discrimination against foreign capital in favor of domestic investments; yet, the type of taxation and regulation adopted for lines in which foreign capital is dominant can demonstrate the willingness to burden the foreign investment more heavily. Exchange-control systems and import-control systems may have the perfectly valid objective of assuring adequate exchange for essential imports; yet, they can be used to impose grossly inequitable burdens upon the transfer of earnings and capital of foreign investment and to impede efficient operations by obstructing the flow of necessary materials and equipment. Equitable procedures can be established by labor laws for management-labor relations; yet, they can be easily disrupted by prejudice in the executive branch. Adequate safeguards against expropriation without suitable compensation may seem to have been set up by law or by the constitution; yet, they can be avoided by a government shrewdly proceeding with a program to make investment unprofitable and the investor eventually anxious to abandon his investment. Legislative pressure to use qualified local technicians may appear both sensible and fair; yet, it can develop into an instrument whereby unqualified personnel can be forced upon the foreign enterprise to the extent that even the ability to employ top personnel of a confidential personally-responsible basis is obstructed. The definition of industries "affected with a public interest" and reserved accordingly for government participation or special government regulation may not be unusual; yet, the steady broadening of the definition and the continued threat that the definition will be further expanded, the persistent political bombast to the effect that the foreigner's contribution in these fields had been inadequate and his reward excessive, the tendency to reserve to government precisely those fields in which the major inflows of foreign capital might be expected, cannot help influence the decision to invest or abstain from investment.

What was important by 1950 was that many Latin American countries had succeeded in destroying confidence in their willingness to assign a suitable developmental role to private foreign capital and to permit it to undertake that responsibility with a prospect of reward commensurate with the risks assumed and the function performed. Finance Minister Beteta of Mexico had put the problem aptly when he accused many Latin Americans of suffering a Quetzalcoatl complex. 'They want the bearded white man to come," he said, "but when he has come they are afraid of him." Even more unfortunately this attitude had been promoted in a number of countries by groups whose own interests were served by obstructing the inflow of foreign capital, who had themselves lagged behind foreign capital in revising their business philosophy to embrace full recognition of responsibility to the community, who flogged with great political effect the outdated business practices long abandoned by foreign companies as if they were the characteristics of modern business philosophy.

Public policy in this field in 1950 revolved around these factors:

(a) Service on the external debts had largely been resumed. The fixed charges on these public debts were now small in terms of the financial capacity of the debtor countries. The debt totalled well under $2 billion, nominal value.

(b) Domestic markets for public issues of government securities were gradually evolving. Although in many countries there was still no substantial market outside of the more or less compulsory purchases by banks and individuals, there was a prospect eventually of larger domestic public-debt operations.

(c) While it was unlikely that foreign markets would at any early date if ever renew their interest in public issues of the Latin American governments, the new financial institutions in Washington offered a source of funds at low cost. (The Export-Import Bank loans, for instance, had been made at interest rates of 3.5% to 4.5%.) But this source of funds was not unlimited in volume, there was competition for available funds with other areas of the world, and the weight of United States policy influence was still being thrown against the use of such funds in fields to which private capital was prepared to flow under suitable conditions.

(d) Private capital could be mobilized in large volume if its position were deemed reasonable by the Latin American policy-maker. The elements in this position included: acceptance of the principle that investments are entitled to a fair return, as protection against the risk of operations being made unprofitable through unreasonable encroachment by social and tax legislation; guarantee of adequate effective and prior payment in currency of the investing country in the event of expropriation; maintenance of a stipulated (or tacitly understood) minimum flow of exchange for earnings-remittances even in cases of stringencies on the theory that financial requirements are not usually very large in terms of availabilities even in cases of stringency and that a time of balance of payments difficulties is precisely the moment when an inflow of capital is desired and accordingly should not be made unattractive by suddenly cutting off earnings remittances; freedom to employ attorneys-in-fact, managers, auditors, confidential and key employees without regard to nationality, and the right of such persons to enter and remain in the country for specified periods; freedom from obligatory participation of a specified proportion of local capital or local directors.

(e) The ability to draw on the existing sources of foreign capital for government expenditures for public works depended in part on the ability to expand sources of foreign exchange. The tendency to exclude foreign capital from precisely those fields where its willingness and ability to bear risks and its technological competence were particularly needed militated against the necessary expansion of exports to create foreign exchange.

(f) The philosophy under which private capital moved abroad had changed drastically in recent years. To cite continually the case of the British railways which had refused to allow Argentine nationals to rise above the grade of foreman or the practices of American petroleum interests in the early days of the Mexican industry in vilification of the foreign investor currently was as ridiculous as to use the case of the loan to the mythical "Kingdom of Poyais" in the 1820's as characteristic of government-to-government lending in 1950.[22]

(g) It could not be denied that the pace of economic development could be greatly accelerated by wise use of private foreign capital. But the decision to use it was one which only the individual countries could make for themselves.

----

[22] Jenks tells the story that in the 1820's when Latin American securities were being accepted so eagerly in the British market "the comedy turned burlesque when a loan was eagerly taken up for the "Kingdom of Poyais," a fictitious political entity on the Mosquito Coast of which a Scotch officer had assumed the title of "Cazique." Jenks, *op. cit.*, p. 47.

SUPPLEMENTARY READING

Alexis Coudert and Asher Lane, "Direct Foreign Investment In Underdeveloped Countries: Some Practical Problems," *Law and Contemporary Problems,* Summer-Autumn, 1946, pp. 740-759.

Dudley B. Bonsal and Milo A. Borges, "Limitations Abroad on Enterprise and Property Acquisition," *Law and Contemporary Problems,* Summer-Autumn, 1946, pp. 720-740.

United Nations Economic and Social Council, *Survey of Policies Affecting Private Foreign Investment* (Lake Success, 1950), pp. 72-92.

Cleona Lewis, *The United States and Foreign Investment Problems* (The Brookings Institution, Washington, 1948), pp. 141-169, 321-333.

Cleona Lewis, *America's Stake in International Investments* (The Brookings Institution, Washington, 1938), pp. 173-206, 218-245, 264-288, 292-306.

Samuel Flagg Bemis, *The Latin American Policy of the United States* (Harcourt, Brace and Company, New York, 1943), pp. 142-168, 226-242, 276-294.

J. Fred Rippy, "The British Investment Boom of the 1880's in Latin American Mines," *Inter-American Economic Affairs,* March, 1948, pp. 71-78.

Eduardo Villaseñor, "The Inter-American Bank: Prospects and Dangers," *Foreign Affairs,* October, 1941, pp. 165-174.

Chapter 13

Foreign Trade and An
Expanding Economy

While the pace of private foreign investment in potential export capacity is in large measure determined by Latin America's readiness to provide a satisfactory climate of investment, the Latin American policy-maker does not exercise by his decisions a similar command over the availability of foreign markets. This fact has been demonstrated repeatedly in recent years with great effect: by the discouraging deterioration in trade and trade practices in the 1930's, by the effect of the war on normal trade channels, by European post-war balance of payments difficulties, by the efforts of particular commodity interests in the United States to discourage the competition of foreign petroleum and foreign copper and foreign sugar and other foreign commodities. The uncertainty of access to foreign markets regardless of capacity to compete effectively has compelled the Latin American policy-maker to compromise on the primary objective of acceleration of economic development in the direction of "insurance" against exigencies arising out of decisions of foreign policy-makers over which he can have no control. The task becomes one, therefore, of seeking the optimum balance between the objective of development to a higher economic plane as rapidly as possible and the objective of security for the current economic position.

The European Market. Europe has normally taken about one-half of Latin America's exports, the United States about one-third. The dependence upon the European market has varied considerably among the individual countries, however. The River Plate area (Argentina, Uruguay, Paraguay) has been heavily dependent upon Europe which took two-thirds to three-fourths of its exports. Its production is competitive with that of the United States, and the great cereal and pastoral industries have been oriented toward the European market, although the United States has taken some hides, wool and canned meat, was long heavily interested in linseed, and has turned to the Plate in poor crop years for coarse grains. On the other hand, Cuba, Mexico and Central America marketed less than one-fourth of their exports in Europe. Here, export capacity was complementary to American production; coffee, bananas, sugar, for instance, contrasted

TABLE 58

Relative Importance of Trade of Various Areas 1938-1948

(Percentage Participation)

Exports	1938	1946	1948*
Latin America	100.0%	100.0%	100.0%
South America	75.7	76.6	77.1
Argentina	23.8	25.8	24.9
Brazil	17.2	21.3	18.0
Chile	8.2	5.0	5.0
Colombia	4.7	4.4	3.9
Venezuela	10.6	10.4	17.4
Central America	3.3	2.5	2.6
Mexico	11.4	8.6	7.3
Caribbean	9.6	12.3	12.6
Cuba	8.3	10.4	10.8

Imports			
Latin America	100.0	100.0	100.0
South America	78.8	68.6	74.9
Argentina	28.7	16.7	22.9
Brazil	19.8	19.7	19.7
Chile	6.9	5.8	4.7
Colombia	6.0	6.8	6.7
Venezuela	6.5	8.6	12.0
Central America	5.1	5.3	4.8
Mexico	7.7	16.0	9.2
Caribbean	8.4	10.1	10.9
Cuba	7.1	8.8	9.2

*Some of the data for 1948 are estimates.

sharply with the traditional lines of agricultural production best adapted to the climate and soil in the United States. For the west coast countries in South America, the European markets were somewhat more important than the average for the whole region—50 to 60 per cent. The distribution of Brazilian trade tended to follow the average pattern—about half to Europe, about one-third to the United States. Colombia's coffee has moved largely to the United States. Venezuela's oil has depended in large measure on European markets. *Of Europe's total imports from Latin America, from 80% to 90% has normally come from South America.* Table 58 shows the relative importance of the South American countries in the total foreign trade of Latin America and Table 59 shows the geographical distribution of Latin American exports.

TABLE 59
Markets for Exports and Sources of Imports 1938-1948
(Percentage Participation)

	1938	1946	1948*
Exports to:			
United States	32.3%	40.2%	38.0%
Continental Europe	30.6	21.0	24.9
United Kingdom	17.5	12.2	11.9
Canada	1.1	1.5	2.0
Latin America	6.3	13.0	8.3
Africa	0.5	2.2	1.1
Asia	1.6	2.8	2.4
Oceania	0.1	0.1	0.1
Other**	10.0	7.0	11.4
Imports from:			
United States	33.8	59.2	59.1
Continental Europe	35.9	9.6	12.6
United Kingdom	12.1	6.2	8.9
Canada	1.0	2.2	2.0
Latin America	9.2	18.1	10.9
Africa	0.3	0.7	0.3
Asia	5.4	1.1	1.3
Oceania	0.1	0.1	0.1
Other	2.2	2.8	4.7

* Some of the data for 1948 are estimates.

** This includes petroleum shipped to Dutch West Indies for reshipment.

During the first world war, the loss of the German market which had been taking one-eighth of Latin American exports was offset by greater dependence upon the American market. By 1929, however, the trade had resumed its normal pattern, with one-half going to Europe. The devastating collapse of foreign trade thereafter—exports falling off in value by two-thirds from 1929 to 1932—ushered in a period of sober study of the relative importance in policy-making that must hereafter be attached to the "security" factor. Exports recovered partly. They were at 60% of 1929 by 1935, at 83% by 1937, down again to 63% in 1938. But the future of the European market seemed uncertain.

In the great period of expansion of Latin American exports of farm products, the European population had been advancing rapidly, British industry had created a growing market for imported food and raw materials, German industry had expanded rapidly to create an industrial population that needed to be fed and factories that must be supplied with raw materials while there was an accompanying willingness to rely on foreign sources in larger measure, the American market was growing to divert exportable surpluses of such products as meat to domestic needs, and colonial competition had been slow to develop. By the 1930's the Latin American policy-maker was confronted with a different situation: the European population increase had been slowing down; British industry was losing ground and there was more interest in meeting the requirements of a stabilizing population from politically affiliated countries whose export capacity was growing; American farm production had created embarrassing surpluses; Germany was moving toward greater balance between industry and agriculture; and Europe was blanketed with a spirit of economic nationalism focused on reducing dependence upon foreign sources.

This change affected the basis of developmental policy decisions in two ways. First, the policy-maker reasoned that he could no longer count on a steadily increasing market for his foodstuffs and raw materials and might even have to cope with a diminishing rather than expanding outlet. Second, his ability to control imports so as to increase the supply of capital equipment and reduce the flow of non-essentials was directly affected. In the 1930's the Latin Americans were experimenting with the rationing of inadequate supplies of foreign exchange to the end that after meeting urgent food and medical requirements (if the country were on an import basis for food), priorities might be given to the industrial plant and other producers' goods. Previously they might have created a surplus on their trade with Europe and spent their net earnings in the United States on goods which could be more satisfactorily supplied from that source. Now their freedom was challenged by European demands for bilateral balancing, and in setting up more closely balanced trade relationships with individual countries—for instance, Germany —they were not always free to choose imports in keeping with their plans to give developmental requirements high priority. Their bargaining power in a period when raw materials and foodstuffs were frequently in excessive supply was such that they might be compelled to take harmonicas from Germany at a time when they would have preferred to spend the proceeds of their exports on railway equipment instead of contributing to the pleasure of local music-lovers. Control of imports was conceived as a way to shift purchasing power to developmental essentials and simultaneously to stimulate local manufacturing by shutting off the supply of competitive imports of less-essential items. Such control was difficult to implement when the bargaining power in bilateral negotiations was inadequate.

The second world war quickly demonstrated the vulnerability of the economies, particularly those whose foreign trade was more largely directed toward Europe. Continental Europe alone had taken about 30% of Latin American exports. The loss of this trade and the uncertainty over Britain's ability to maintain imports occasioned great concern. Fortunately, the expansion of United States requirements of Latin American goods during the war, the special assistance given by the United States in maintaining the price of coffee at remunerative levels, the broad financial cooperation that permitted the allies to maintain imports at higher levels than would otherwise have been possible, averted more serious damage, although there were many "soft" spots in the export picture. The lesson of the vulnerability to changes in foreign markets was not lost on the Latin Americans, however, They determined not to permit their economies to be so exposed to breakdowns as a result of curtailment of supplies of imports from abroad or as a result of modifications in markets for exports.

In the immediate post-war years the demand for Latin American export commodities was heavy. It took time to bring European production back to its prewar levels and prosperity in the United States held American demand at very high levels. Exports to all destinations had been $1.7 billion in 1938. They were $4.6 billion in 1946, $5.9 billion in 1947, $6.5 billion in 1948. A very large proportion of this increase derived from the rise in prices. The United States Department of Commerce, analyzing United States imports from Latin America, has for instance estimated that "import prices were 70% above the prewar average in 1946 and two and one-third times prewar in 1948." But volume rose also. By 1947 the volume of exports to the Marshall Plan countries from South America was 97% that of 1938.[1] By 1946 Continental Europe was taking 21% of Latin American exports compared with 30.6% in 1938. By 1948 it was taking 24.9%.[2] The proportion taken by the United Kingdom fell from 17.5% in 1938 to 12.2% in 1946 and 11.9% in 1948 as the British made strenuous efforts to adjust their imports to their capacity to pay. The Marshall Plan helped greatly to sustain the flow of exports to Europe, after many of the European countries had drained down their investments and reserves to a point where these could provide little additional help in covering an import balance.[3]

---

[1] The dollar-value of these exports was about 160% higher than in 1938. The estimate of relative volume of exports was made by Organization for European Economic Cooperation, *Interim Report on the European Recovery Programme*, Volume 1 (Paris, 1948), p. 54.

[2] These figures understate the proportion taken by Europe since Venezuelan oil is not fully distributed in Table 59 by ultimate destinations.

[3] ECA-financed paid shipments from Latin America to Europe were $467.3 million from April 3, 1948 to December 31, 1949.

But by 1950 the Latin American policy-maker perceived that the war had merely interrupted the trends which had caused so much concern in the 1930's. There was the same concentration of exports that depended upon European markets, the same commodities for which no alternative market could be found in the United States. Although advancing domestic consumption promised to reduce the burden of some export surpluses, this also reduced the capacity to pay for the immense developmental requirements that must be met from overseas sources. A typical breakdown of European requirements is furnished by the import programs of the countries participating in the ECA (Economic Cooperation Administration) financing for 1948-49. Out of scheduled imports from Latin America of $1.9 to $2.0 billion excluding petroleum, grains constituted $330 million, fats and oils $250 million, meat $170 million, sugar $200 million, other human and animal food $340 million, cotton $160 million, wool $75 million, hides $140 million, metals and minerals $150 million.[4] Europe before the second world war had still enjoyed very sizable revenues from its investments in Latin America, from shipping and insurance, from emigrant remittances and other "invisibles" in the balance of payments. But when the Organization for European Economic Cooperation analyzed the prospective "invisible" items in the balance of payments with South America in 1952-53, it forecast net earnings of less than $100 million, so that Europe could no longer anticipate financing so substantial a share of its imports from South America with its earnings on "invisible" account.[5] Europe was engaged in a feverish effort to become more self-sufficient. While the even greater urgency that attached to reduction of

---

[4] It should be noted that ECA or Marshall Plan countries do not include all of Europe. One-tenth of Latin American exports to Europe (including United Kingdom) in 1948 went to countries not covered by the ECA program.

[5] It estimated that in 1952-53 investment income would be $62 million, net debt service a minus $5 million, tourist income $23 million, transportation revenue $69 million, other invisible items minus $67 million, for total net earnings of $82 million. Op. cit., p. 69. Italian receipts from emigrant remittances in South America were put at $80 million.

its import requirements from the United States caused the European countries to suggest that they would be willing to divert enough demand to South America to bring the *volume* of imports by 1952-53 to 22% above that of 1938, the means of paying for such a volume were hardly clear and the Latin Americans foresaw that they might be on the way to the same sort of pressure in trade practices as had existed in the 1930's.

For, Europe could not support this volume of imports from South America unless its exports in 1952-53 reached a volume double that of 1938. The volume was about 75% of 1938 in 1947, exceeded 90% in 1948, fell off in 1949. The relationship to developmental policy became clear when the European countries indicated the urgent need for balancing trade with individual countries and presented suggestions as to what exports to Latin America could be increased. The export program of the Marshall Plan countries for 1948-49 contemplated shipments to Latin America of $1.0 to $1.1 billion, comprised of $250 million of machinery, $110 million of transportation equipment of all kinds including passenger cars, $100 million of iron and steel products, $130 million of textile manufactures, $70 million of pulp and paper, $40 million of chemicals, $40 million of glass, $75 million of metal manufactures, the remaining items in large measure consumers goods. To increase exports and consequently maintain their purchasing power in Latin America, the European countries wished to export high-priced passenger cars, the Latin Americans wanted petroleum refineries. They wished to ship perfume and liquor, the Latin Americans sought farm machinery. They wished to ship textiles and other consumers goods which had normally been leading exports from Europe, but the Latin Americans were engaged in building their own industries, especially in the more simple consumers goods, and were unwilling to accept such competition. The clash in policy over "unessential" imports was extremely important, for the heart of the Latin American policy of mobilizing export capacity for the developmental effort was the ability to shut off the flow of luxuries and to broaden continually the definition of "unessentials" so as to make possible the largest possible import of capital equipment. Concessions would be made, preferential treatment might be accorded the more essential imports which Europe offered in competition with other sources even though they were not priced competitively, but the Latin American saw what was at best an unsatisfactory and uncertain market for his exports in Europe, did not dare anticipate any such steady growth in the outlet for his raw materials and foodstuffs as had promoted the expansion of trade decades before, feared a narrowing of the market even in peacetime and its loss in case of another war

The United States Market. In the American market Latin America did not have to cope with balance of payments difficulties nor with the tying of export volume and export proceeds to particular importations. The basic outlook was good: the American population was growing; the standard of living was rising; American production of raw materials, particularly the minerals, seemed likely to have difficulty keeping pace with the enormous demands of its industries so that greater dependence upon foreign sources was in prospect.[6] The continuing underlying hazard was the instability of the American economy which subjected the exporting country to the threat of sudden reversals in the volume that the market would absorb and of the serious impact on prices that any shift in American demand exercised. And there were the day-to-day policy uncertainties stemming from the pressure of individual commodity groups within the country.

In 1938 Latin American exports to the United States were $0.5 billion, in 1941 $1.1 billion, in 1945 $1.8 billion, in 1946

---

[6] It should be kept in mind that in the case of both exports and imports progress is continually being made in substitution for goods that formerly entered into foreign trade. For instance, in 1950 the U. S. Department of Agriculture had hopes that canaigre, a plant fairly common from Texas and Colorado to the Pacific Coast might provide the substitute for quebracho formerly imported from the Argentine. The desire to avoid dependence upon foreign sources for tanning materials in the event of war had long prompted research for domestic replacements. On the other hand, throughout Latin America in 1949 and 1950 there was great interest in the use of sugar cane bagasse for the paper industry, with prospect of decreasing Latin American imports thereby. The process of substitution works both ways.

$1.9 billion, in 1947 $2.3 billion, in 1948 and 1949 about $2.5 billion.[7] The United States Department of Commerce has estimated that the physical volume in 1946-48 was about double the volume absorbed by the American market during the period 1936-38. While some of the trade represented shifts in currents of trade occasioned by being shut off from certain areas or by slowness of some areas to resume production and while some of the increase represented special requirements occasioned by the war, there was no doubt that a considerable portion of the increase in physical volume represented enduring gains in the capacity to market Latin American exports in the United States. In 1949 coffee comprised one-third of the value of Latin American exports to the United States, cane sugar 14%, cacao and bananas 5%, petroleum 13%, copper, lead and tin 11%, wool and hides about 5%. The consumption of coffee, cacao and bananas was growing steadily, sugar was a special problem in American commercial policy (discussed below), the outlook was good for continued rise in the consumption of petroleum although importation from Latin America was challenged by the political importance of domestic producers and by competing Middle East production, and the prospect was good for greater consumption and larger dependence upon foreign sources of copper, lead, tin, hides and certain grades of wool. On the other hand, there was the sobering fact that for a bloc of commodities constituting some 30% of Latin America's total exports (other foods, animal feedstuffs, oils, cotton) there was little prospect of early significant expansion of the American market to relieve the uncertainty of the relationship with Europe. Table 60 shows leading U. S. imports from Latin America from 1947 to 1949.

The United States Market: Sugar. A quota system for sugar has been in effect almost continuously since 1934. The Sugar Acts of 1934, 1937 and 1948 took into consideration the relationship that had previously existed between imports and

---

[7] Latin American data differ somewhat from U. S. statistics of trade with Latin America. This accounts for a figure for 1949 that differs by $0.2 billion from that used in Table 60.

TABLE 60

United States Imports from Latin America 1947-1949

(millions of dollars)

	1947	1948	1949
Total imports	$2,150	$2,330	$2,300
Coffee	591	685	781
Cane sugar	410	290	322
Bananas	48	49	51
Cacao	71	86	54
Petroleum	171	254	295
Copper, crude and semi-mfg.	149	171	155
Tin	31	37	38
Lead	25	47	65
Hides and skins	32	40	16
Unmanufactured wool	70	136	94
Nitrate	15	23	26
Oilseeds	30	35	23
Vegetable oils	58	22	28
Tobacco	35	23	24
Sisal and henequen	24	29	20
Tomatoes	21	23	15

domestic production. Application of the quotas was suspended from April 1942 to the end of 1947. Under the quota system the total quantity of sugar to be marketed in the United States is allocated, in a manner specified by law, among the domestic supplying areas (including insular areas), the Philippines, Cuba (which enjoys a preferential duty) and countries paying full duty (of which Peru has usually been a leading country).

During the decade in which the Sugar Act of 1937 was in force, major changes occurred as a result of the war in the relative importance of different sources of supply. Imports from the Philippines were entirely shut off during American participation in the war and could not be resumed until 1948; and the war affected the movement of sugar from other areas to the United States as well as the production within the United States. The change in political status of the Philippines has an important bearing on the quotas. During the period of "commonwealth" status (1936-1946) the quantity of Philippine sugar that could enter this market free of duty was specifically limited by the Independence Act. This quantity in the years before the quotas were suspended was sometimes less than the Philippine quota (free and dutiable) under the Sugar Act of 1937, but since imports in excess of the free quota would have been subject to the full duty which was much higher than the rate on Cuban sugar, the Philippines actually filled only their duty-free quota. Thus in some years there was an excess of the total quota under the Sugar Act over the duty-free quota and this excess was available for reallocation to the full-duty countries, Cuba being excluded from such allocation. The Sugar Act of 1948 provided a fixed quota for the Philippines—the same as the duty-free quota provided by the Philippine Trade Act of 1946 (equivalent of 982,000 short tons of raw suger).

The Act of 1937 provided for the domestic areas (mainland beet, mainland cane, Hawaii, Puerto Rico and the Virgin Islands) specified percentages of the total quantity of sugar permitted to be marketed and guaranteed them a minimum in the aggregate of 3,715,000 tons annually. Usually the percentages specified resulted in an aggregate for the domestic areas slightly larger than the minimum. The Act of 1948 fixed no percentages for the domestic areas but allotted each an annual absolute quota, fixed in the Act. These absolute quotas are maximum quotas and aggregate 4,268,000 tons for all domestic areas.[8] There is a provision assuring to Cuba under certain conditions a minimum share of the United States market and providing for pro rata reduction in the fixed quotas of the domestic areas if necessary to accomplish that purpose.

Since the quotas for domestic areas and the Philippines are fixed, the ratio of permissible imports from Cuba and the full-duty countries to the quantity of domestic sugar permitted to be marketed varies with the magnitude of the total quota for sugar marketings, apart from the effect of reallocation of deficits. Thus in some years the shares of Cuba and

---

[8] Sum of absolute quotas for the domestic areas under the Act of 1948 exceeds the guaranteed minimum under the Act of 1937 by 15%. Population of continental United States increased 14% between July 1, 1937 and July 1, 1948.

the full-duty countries (Peru and others) could be larger under the Act of 1948 than under the Act of 1937; in other years these shares could be smaller. While the quotas for the domestic areas and the Philippines remain at figures specified by law, the normal growth of population would tend to raise gradually the share of Cuba and the full-duty countries in the American market. The basic quotas allotted to Cuba and to the full-duty countries under the Act of 1948 and under earlier Acts are revealed upon examination not to have changed the relative shares of the market appreciably. With respect to possible deficits of the Philippines in supplying their quota, the Act of 1948 provided that the deficit should be allocated to Cuba and the full-duty countries according to ratios specified in the Act; the ratios give Cuba 95% of the deficit in any case and more than 98% under certain conditions.

Since U. S. sugar legislation is highly political and always subject to change by the Congress, since the United States has been the major market for Latin American sugar, since sugar comprises about one-tenth of Latin America's total exports, and since the European countries are simultaneously pressing for self-sufficiency, it is not difficult to understand the relationship to development policy of the great uncertainty over policy-decisions in this area which are being made by foreign policy-makers.

The United States Market: Latin American Aspirations. Periodically the Latin Americans have put forth proposals looking to support by the United States of parity price systems for the major Latin American farm crops similar to the arrangements which have been adopted to protect the American farmer. The Inter-American Conference on Problems of War and Peace in 1945, for instance, watered down such demands to a resolution urging that a "fair and equitable relationship be sought between the prices of agricultural and mineral products and those of manufactured articles." [9] Other

---

[9] Following adoption of this resolution, the United States was charged by the coffee-producing countries with unwillingness to act in accord with it.

proposals have been made for a system of hemisphere preferentials which would give easier access to the American market for Latin American goods as against the competition of other foreign-produced supplies. But in 1950 the hope for expansion of trade with the United States was linked with the liberal trade philosophy which the United States was championing, the official commercial policy looking to reduction of trade barriers, freer competition in the world market, non-discriminatory trade practices, multilateralism. This did not mean that the Latin Americans could proceed with expansion of export capacity on the assumption that ability to compete would assure them free access to this market, however.

Indeed, many of the long-standing grievances still remained. The virtual prohibition of imports of Argentine beef allegedly as a protection against introduction or dissemination of hoof-and-mouth disease had long poisoned Argentine-American relations. It demanded a scientific study and report by an impartial investigatory body whose findings would be accepted and implemented, but the pressure of American livestock interests against alteration in the embargo continued to be strong.[10] The tax on imported copper had been lowered dur-

---

[10] Previous to 1930 the U. S. Department of Agriculture had authority to impose sanitary measures against imports from foreign countries or regions within a country in order to prevent the introduction or dissemination of the contagion of any contagious, infectious or communicable disease of animals. In 1926 the Department exercised this authroity by ordering that "on and after January 1, 1927 no fresh or frozen beef, veal, mutton, lamb or pork shall be permitted entry into the United States from any *region* in which either of the said diseases exists." The regulation was incorporated into the Tariff Act of 1930 with the substitution of the words "foreign country" for "region." The Argentines cried out that this "neat little change embargoed a whole region, Patagonia, where the disease is not known, just because the cattle-growing region one thousand miles north was infected." Previously meat from the disease-free regions could have been admitted; now it was prohibited. An investigating group found that Patagonia was free from hoof-and-mouth disease and in 1935 the Roosevelt Administration in an effort to improve relations with Argentina reached a sanitary convention which would have placed the region in a separate category and legalized shipment of non-cooked meat from the area to the U. S.

ing the war, but the deterioration of the American copper reserves, the fact of American ownership of foreign reserves, and the high level of the market for domestic production, did not suffice to stop agitation for restoration of higher rates on copper in 1950. And the tremendous prosperity of the oil industry, the great interest of American investors in foreign petroleum production, and the basic philosophy of liberal commercial policy, could not suffice in 1950 to quiet opposition to a dribble of foreign petroleum into the American market and to fears that the flow might increase. Nevertheless, the good faith of United States government officials charged with implementing a program of liberal commercial policies could not be doubted. It merited support from the other American republics unless they were prepared to resign themselves to the idea of steadily narrowing volume of foreign trade, with all that implied in retarding the creation of resources with which to finance developmental expenditures overseas.

For, not all pertinent policy decisions could be made by the United States. When the United States Tariff Commission reported on the operation of the Trade Agreements Program early in 1950 it noted that agreements negotiated before the Geneva agreements were in effect with fourteen Latin American countries and that three Latin American countries were associated with the United States under the General Agreement on Tariffs and Trade negotiated at Geneva in 1947.[11] Yet, at the end of 1949 one out of every three Latin American countries was already involved in questions as to conformity

---

But the Senate refused to ratify. Since the Argentine and American farm production is largely competitive, Argentina was intensely interested in any means of broadening its trade relations with the United States, especially in the case of meat where the quality was very high, cost of production relatively low, and competitive capacity great. Also, leverage was desired for dealings with the United Kingdom which was the principal and indeed the only large market for the meat industry. The Argentines argued that even a small proportion of their production (10 to 20%) diverted to the American market would help greatly; and they pointed out that such an amount of meat would be a negligible amount in the total U. S. consumption of meat. They labelled the sanitary restrictions a fraud and a disguise for unwarranted protection of the American livestock interests.

with their trade agreement obligations largely because of their intense interest in protecting domestic industries.[12]   In balancing "security" considerations against the objective of accelerated development Latin America was showing reluctance to embrace the liberal commercial policy advanced as the key to an expanding world market and in so doing was feeding opposition to the program in the United States and discouraging concessions from which it might profit in the American market.[13]   Also from the viewpoint of the Latin American policy decision, access to market alone does not suffice. The country must have something to sell. We have already seen, for instance, that in a period when United States dependence upon foreign minerals promised to increase to the potential advantage of Latin American and other mining areas, progress in mining was being stalled in many countries by policies adopted toward investments. Even in the case of the perennial disturber of good relations—Argentine beef—the restrictions on market had to be considered in relationship with the growing internal consumption in

---

[11] The agreements dating from adoption by the United States of a policy of trade agreements in 1934 authorized the President to negotiate for reductions in duties and amelioration of other trade restrictions by foreign countries and to make reciprocal concessions as to United States imports.   The General Agreement on Tariffs and Trade was a multilateral agreement in which the United States and 22 other countries participated; the tariff negotiations were conducted bilaterally on a product-by-product basis, each country usually negotiating as to each particular import commodity with the country that had been its principal source of imports.   The understandings reached in the bilateral negotiations were combined to form the schedules of concessions of the several countries set forth in the agreement.

[12] See United States Tariff Commission, *Operation of the Trade Agreements Program*, Second Report, April, 1948-March, 1949 (Washington, 1950), pp. 35-42, 64-70.

[13] It should be remembered that legislative restrictions on the American market affect different countries and different commodities in markedly different fashion.   In the 1930's about two-thirds of U. S. imports from Latin America were free of duty.   In 1929 the proportion of dutiable merchandise to total U. S. imports from Argentina was 62.6%, from Brazil 2.2%, from Cuba 95.4%.   In 1938 the proportion of duitable merchandise was 73.8%, 10.2% and 92.2% respectively.

Argentina and the failure to expand production significantly which now combined to challenge export capacity perhaps as much as did the foreign policy-maker by his decision on permitting the product access to market.

TABLE 61

United States Exports to Latin America 1949

(millions of dollars)

	To South America	To Others
Total exports	$1,552	$1,149
Machinery and vehicles	722	404
Industrial machinery	292	117
Motor vehicles and parts	178	88
Metals and manufactures except machinery and vehicles	236	112
Iron and steel	51	30
Chemicals and related items	127	96
Non-metallic minerals	89	83
Food	120	186
Inedible animal and vegetable products except fibers and wood	43	44
Textile manufactures and fibers	103	110
Wood and paper	26	34
Miscellaneous	85	80

Paying for Imports. Expansion of export capacity admittedly is not the only way to finance developmental requirements overseas. Latin America has sought a partial solution to the problem of paying for necessary imports from the United States by curtailing the import of so-called unessentials. Table 61 shows Latin American imports from the United States in 1949. Skillful use of import restrictions and exchange controls have made possible an increasing concentration of dollar availabilities on the industrial, transportation and power plant of the nations. Yet, continuing development at a rising pace demands a growth in imports beyond the savings that are possible through slowing down the inflow of "unessentials."

Examine Table 62 carefully. In 1940 Latin American trade with the United States was roughly in balance. Primarily because of heavy income on its investments, the United States had a surplus on invisible or service items of $114 million. American travellers in Latin America spent $84 million compared with the $39 million yielded to the United States by the expenditures of Latin American travellers; this travel activity was largely limited to Mexico, for which the comparable figures are $57 million and $31 million. Long-term capital transactions were small, netting Latin America only about $8 million. In the period 1941-44 United States imports expanded steadily in value. Exports rose too, but the war had necessitated a shift from the promotion of American exports to a policy of licensing exports so as to involve the least possible drain on American supplies. While the interest of the United States dictated exports consistent with maintenance of the economies at a stable level without disturbance to political relationships, this reduced itself to holding down exports to "minimum essential requirements" largely as defined in Washington. The earnings of American direct investments increased with the expanded demand for minerals and farm products and with the higher price levels. Government service payments—military expenditures, war programs such as the Inter-American Highway—expanded considerably. And transfers under such programs as that of the Coordinator of Inter-American Affairs increased the flow of dollars. Disbursements on loans from the United States government were not large and the net private long-term capital movement produced an adverse balance for Latin America. *It is estimated that in the four years 1941-44 the balance of payments of Latin America with the United States may have been favorable to Latin America by $1.5 billion.*

In 1945 the trade balance continued to be favorable to Latin America. The remittances of Mexican workers in the United States which had become a major source of foreign exchange for Mexico during the war continued to be sizable. Investment income fell off slightly, largely as a result of higher taxes on the oil companies in Venezuela. The net flow on government lending account was small and the total long-term capital movement was $65 million net. *The United States deficit*

TABLE 62

Transactions of the United States with Latin America, 1940-1949

(millions of dollars)

	1940	1941	1942	1943	1944	1945	1946	1947	1948	1949
Exports of goods and services:										
Merchandise adjusted	682	902	711	830	1112	1284	2150	3858	3158	2704
Transportation							232	294	283	276
Travel	165	221	209	298	346	398	78	86	101	104
Miscellaneous services							87	96	93	110
Income on investments	170	198	196	200	260	239	332	406	501	380
Total	1017	1321	1116	1328	1718	1921	2879	4740	4136	3574
Imports of goods and services:										
Merchandise adjusted	670	1076	1166	1445	1726	1772	1898	2284	2573	2440
Transportation							114	191	276	251
Travel	211	271	269	310	331	328	164	167	169	183
Miscellaneous services							66	83	59	66
Income on investments	10	9	8	8	8	8	10	11	13	12
Total	971	1409	1602	2073	2415	2428	2252	2736	3090	2952

Unilateral transportation (net):										
Private							−31	−24	−27	−16
Government							−19	− 9	−10	− 9
Total	−1	−7	−47	−182	−271	−75	−50	−33	−37	−25
Long-term capital (net):										
United States private							+74	−346	−272	−379
United States government	−4	+46	−21	−3	+92	−91	−55	− 60	− 42	− 42
Foreign capital	−4	2	7	4	14	26	6	− 4	+11	+ 3
Total	−8	48	−14	1	106	65	25	−410	−303	−418
Gold and short-term capital:										
Net purchases (−) or sales of gold	−122	19	109	579	406	473	−167	−809	−179	+136
Net movements U. S. short-term capital abroad	−6	−26	−16	−5	−36	−27	− 53	−344	33	+100
Net movements foreign short-term capital in U. S.	106	−7	252	158	278	160	119	193	94	+225
Total	−22	−14	345	732	648	606	−101	−960	− 52	+461
Errors, omissions, third-country transactions	−95	8	43	−116	−136	−279	−501	−601	−654	−640

Source: U. S. Department of Commerce, *International Transactions of the United States During the War* 1940-1945, p. 132; U. S. Department of Commerce, *The Balance of International Payments of the United States* 1946-1948, p. 202. Data for 1949 provided by Department of Commerce.

on all transactions with the other American republics was about $330 million.

The period 1946-48 witnessed immense changes. With American exports more freely available, Latin America's pent-up demand made its influence felt strongly. The unavailability of alternative sources of supply in Europe made the demand for American goods all the greater. In three years, United States exports to Latin America exceeded $9 billion. In the peak year of 1947, when U. S. exports were $3.9 billion, they were four times as large in terms of constant prices as in the period 1936-38; in value, U. S. exports were three times as high in 1947 as in 1945, almost six times as high as the value of exports in 1940. American investments during the period were immensely profitable, thanks largely to the prosperity of the petroleum industry; income from investments exceeded $1.2 billion in three years. U. S. travel outlay was heavy, about $167 million per year in Latin America, but Latin Americans had money to spend too and their travel expenditures figure in the balance of payments at $88 million per year. The movement of U. S. government capital on loans was $52 million net per year, and despite repatriation of certain sizable investments the new outflow of private capital exceeded $148 million per year during the period; in the two years 1947-1948 the total net flow of private long-term capital was $618 million.

Latin America's deficits on its transactions with the United States during the three years exceeded $3.5 billion. It drew on three sources chiefly to cover these deficits: (a) Dollar earnings from third countries. During 1943-45 Latin America had enjoyed net dollar earnings from transactions with countries other than the United States of about $500 million. In the period 1946-1948 such earnings rose to nearly $1.8 billion. (b) United States capital investments including short-term credits. The net outflow of long-term and short-term capital exceeded $1 billion during the period. (c) Drawing down of gold and dollar reserves. About $750 million in gold and dollar reserves were liquidated during the period.[14] In 1946 the deficit on transactions was largely covered by the half billion dollars in earnings from third countries. In 1947 such earnings mounted to $600 million, the net flow of U. S. capital was about $750 million, and gold and dollar liquidations were $600 million. In 1948 the drain on gold and dollar reserves was largely stopped ($75 to $100 million), foreign earnings totalled about $650 million, the net flow of capital investment about $280 million.[15] A comparison of Latin America's balance of payments with the United States and with other countries is shown in Table 63.

In 1949 Latin America made further adjustments in the task of living within its foreign-exchange means. Imports from the United States were reduced by almost a half billion dollars while exports to the United States dropped less significantly. Paid shipments to Europe under ECA financing amounted to $320 million, helping to reduce the pressure on gold and exchange resources, as well as to maintain the flow of goods to Europe that might otherwise have backed up in the absence of alternative markets. Earnings remitted to the United States for account of American investments fell off sharply from $501 million in 1948 to $380 million, while net long-term private investment increased by $107 million. By the fourth quarter of 1949 Latin America had developed a surplus on its transactions with the United States, and it ended the year with a substantial gain in gold and dollar assets, reversing the trend of the period 1946-1948. There

---

[14] The totals for Latin America conceal widely differing experiences of the individual countries. The third-country earnings in 1946 were shared largely among Venezuela ($190 million), Cuba ($100 million), Argentina ($100 million), Mexico ($70 million). In 1947 the bulk of the liquidations was accounted for by Argentina ($534 million); while the loss of gold and dollar reserves was characteristic of the area in 1947, Cuba whose holdings rose sharply and Venezuela whose reserves climbed slightly were important exceptions. While the loss of reserves was largely stopped in 1948, Argentina continued to liquidate about $200 million.

[15] Data in this section are largely drawn from U. S. Department of Commerce, *International Transactions of the United States during the War*, pp. 131-144, and *The Balance of International Payments of the United States*, pp. 182-188. The student is urged to read these sections of the publications carefully.

TABLE 63
Current and Capital Transactions of Latin America with Rest of
World, 1947
(millions of dollars)

	U. S.	Other Non-Latin American Countries	Total
Current Account:			
Exports, f.o.b.	$2,284	$3,726	$6,010
Imports, f.o.b.	−3,741	−1,797	−5,538
Trade Balance	−1,457	1,929	472
Non-monetary gold, net	−	50	50
Investment income, net	−385	−195	−580
Transportation and insurance, net	−103	−413	−516
Travel, net	81	− 54	27
Other services, net	− 44	− 21	− 65
Donations, net			
Private	30	− 37	− 7
Official	34	− 10	24
Total	−1,844	1,249	−595
Errors and Omissions, and			
Multilateral Settlements	564	−778	−214
Capital Account and Monetary Gold			
Private long-term			
Direct Investments (liabilities)	287	− 7	280
Other	− 33	15	− 18
Private short-term, total	− 48	200	152
Official long-term			
Credits received & extended (−)	103	−202	− 99
Amortization payments, net	− 56	− 24	− 80
IMF and IBRD gold			
and dollar subscriptions	− 67	−	− 67
Other	− 12	−165	−177
Official short-term			
IMF advances	31	−	31
Other liabilities	169	− 3	166
Foreign exchange holdings	30	−287	−257
Monetary gold, net	876	2	878
Total capital and monetary gold	1,280	−471	809

Source: International Monetary Fund, *Balance of Payments Yearbook*
1938-46-47 (Washington, 1949), p. 59.

Note: Column headed "United States" includes International Monetary Fund (IMF) and International Bank for Reconstruction and Development (IBRD).

was food for thought, however, in the observations of a wise official of the United States Treasury who noted: "In general the Latin American countries have tried to solve their balance of payments problems through reduction of imports and exchange payments, by means of quotas, import prohibitions, higher tariffs, exchange taxes, penalty import rates and curtailment of exchange allotments for transfer of profits and capital and for travel. Rarely have steps been taken to facilitate exports. On the contrary, there are numerous instances of the use in Latin America of export taxes, restrictive export monopolies, export permit systems and export prohibitions at the very time when exchange is scarce and balance of payments problems are acute." [16]

At mid-century the region could no longer count on earning significant sums of dollars from its trade with Europe; indeed, individual European countries were hoping to earn dollars on their trade with Latin America. Fortunately, the volume of dollar bonds outstanding had been sharply reduced and the burden of fixed charges on it was relatively small. New government borrowing was being accomplished through the agencies in Washington at reduced costs. And while earnings of private direct investments loomed large in the balance of payments, they were in considerable measure related to the volume of exports so that any significant bulge in remittance of earnings was likely to stem from a rise in the volume of exports. Increased participation of the Latin American countries in ocean shipping was reducing the drain on exchange resources for transportation of exports and imports. If there was to be continuity on a rising scale in its industrialization and diversification, however, the region needed to maintain and expand the volume of its exports, it needed to encourage existing investors to plow back their earnings, and it needed to find sources of capital willing and able to assume the risks and to provide the technological com-

---

[16] John S. DeBeers, "Some Aspects of Latin America's Trade and Balance of Payments," *American Economic Review*, Papers and Proceedings, May, 1949, p. 395.

petence for fields most likely to create enlarged purchasing power abroad. It could, with more serious cultivation of the tourist trade, look for an expanding volume of dollar earnings from the travel expenditures of foreigners. The travel expenditures in Latin America by residents of the United States in 1949 amounted to about one-tenth of the foreign purchasing power yielded by American imports from Latin America. As Table 64 shows, more than one-fourth of American travel expenditures abroad were being made in Latin America, but the competition for the tourist traffic was keen and the Latin Americans had characteristically been slow to cultivate the field intensively.[17]

TABLE 64

Travel Expenditures by Residents of United States 1920-1949

(millions of dollars)

	In Mexico		In West Indies and Central America	
	Amount	% of total spent in world	Amount	% of total spent in world
1920	$ 6	3.1%	$19	10.0%
1929	36	7.5	37	7.7
1933	33	16.6	19	9.5
1937	44	12.6	35	10.1
1946	125	27.3	35	7.7
1949	135	19.4	57	8.2

Source: F. P. Sasscer, "American Expenditures for Foreign Travel in 1949," *Survey of Current Business*, March, 1950, p. 18.

Trade Among the Latin American Countries. Before the second world war, trade among the Latin American countries was relatively unimportant. About 9% of Latin America's imports in 1938 came from within the region. The trade was largely concentrated in the Plate and Brazil which accounted for 75% of this intra-Latin American trade. There was

---

[17] Persons living or visiting adjacent to the international boundary (persons who cross frequently to use facilities in the border towns) accounted for 48% of the tourist dollar expenditures in Mexico.

an important movement of wheat from Argentina to Brazil, trade in oil for the petroleum-deficit regions, export of Brazilian coffee to the Plate, West Coast use of Peruvian sugar, movement of foodstuffs from the east coast of South America to food-importing countries on the West Coast. Manufactured goods did not figure significantly in the traffic.

The disruption of normal trade channels during the war threw the countries back on their own resources to a larger extent. Countries which had been promoting industries such as Mexico, Chile, Brazil and Argentina found their manufactured goods in demand in the less-industrialized countries.[18] The market for textiles, for instance, was largely free from the competition of the traditionally more efficient competitors. And there was greater reliance on raw materials and foodstuffs available from within the region. By 1943 one-fourth of Latin America's imports came from within Latin America. But most of the gains were not permanent. As manufactured goods became available from the more industrialized areas, the competition proved too much for most of the Latin American competitors. Mexican textiles, for instance, suffered quickly and heavily once the older sources of supply became available. By 1948 Latin America was taking only about one-ninth of its imports from within the region, close to the pre-war figures; trade of the Plate and Brazil continued to be the leading factor.

As the steel mills and other ambitious industrial ventures appeared in Brazil, Chile and Mexico, there was much talk of the possibility of enlarging trade within the region. This, especially as an answer to critics who felt that the individual countries might not themselves be able to support plants of economic size. It was notable, however, that the individual Latin American countries were no more easily resigned to dependence on other Latin American countries for their im-

---

[18] Some of the countries enjoyed a short-lived boom in exports to areas like South Africa also. There was even a trickle of manufactured goods into the United States! Brazilian and Argentine textiles became known in South Africa but not favorably enough nor at sufficiently competitive prices to carve out a significant permanent place in the market.

ports than to dependence on Europe or the United States. The availability of a great low-cost grain producer (Argentina) did not prevent Brazil from pressing for domestic production of a larger proportion of its breadstuffs regardless of cost. Chile squirmed under the need to import sugar, despite the proximity of sugar-exporting Peru. And the spirit of "good-neighborliness" did not reach to the point where countries might be willing to pay more for their manufactured goods than they needed to pay the more efficient exporters of Europe and the United States. There was a brisk traffic in intra-Latin American barter arrangements in the late 1940's but the motivation was the need to dispose of certain goods and the unavailability of alternative sources of supply rather than a serious interest in integration of the region's economic effort.

Terms of Trade.[19] From time to time, individual countries profited from fortuitous shifts in the terms of trade, as for instance in the autumn of 1949 when the spectacular rise in

---

[19] Variations in the terms of trade measure changes in the quantity of imports which can be obtained in exchange for a given quantity of exports. A favorable change in the terms of trade can make it possible for an under-developed country to obtain its previous amount of imports for a reduced amount of exports and to utilize the domestic resources thus set free for developmental purposes; or to use the extra imports obtained for the previous amount of exports for purposes of development. But it should be remembered that a favorable change in the terms does not automatically further economic development. The rise in export prices may be due to limitation of supplies to such an extent that total export yields are reduced rather than increased, so that the total imports that can be obtained after the "favorable" change in terms of trade are less rather than more. Again, where the "favorable" change in terms results from a natural or deliberate restriction in supply of exports, the reduced volume of foreign trade may force domestic measures into less productive employment than exports were even at the previous lower price level. Again, the benefits of improvement in terms of trade may be wasted in the form of under-employment or unemployment and fail to quicken the pace of economic development. Finally, it is possible that the improvement in the terms of trade may accrue largely to foreign companies operating in the country. See United Nations Department of Economic Affairs, *Relative Prices of Exports and Imports of Under-Developed Countries* (Lake Success, 1949), pp. 121-127.

the price of coffee promised a quarter to a half billion dollars in additional revenue from coffee exports at a time when the price of many imported goods was falling. While the Latin American countries were increasingly disposed to use such windfalls as far as possible for developmental requirements rather than to permit them to be dissipated in luxury imports, they felt they could not plan developmental policy with any assurance of increasingly favorable terms of trade.

In 1950 the International Monetary Fund published a Staff Paper which suggested that the terms of trade of Latin America in 1946 on a 1938 basis had been 108.[20] (Export price index in terms of dollars 219, import price index 202). Eliminating intra-Latin American trade, a figure of 110 was reached for the terms of trade with the outside world.[21] As Table 65 shows, the findings for individual countries differ widely. Using a second method (see Table 66), the terms of trade for the period 1925 to 1948 were calculated, showing deterioration in the terms of trade from 1929 to 1938, the gain from 1938 to 1946, the more rapid gain from 1946 to 1948.[22] Late in 1948 wholesale prices of farm products suffered the first significant price downturn since the beginning of the second world war, repeated the familiar pattern of decline from inflationary peaks by falling earlier and farther than non-farm prices. While the sharp change in the export position of grains and fats and oils was seriously affecting countries like Argentina, mineral prices in 1949 sagged also to disturb the balance of payments position of countries like Chile. On the other hand, in the large group of coffee-exporting countries, the terrific boost in coffee prices

---

[20] J. Ahumada and A. Nataf, "Terms of Trade in Latin American Countries," *International Monetary Fund Staff Papers*, February, 1950 (Washington, 1950), pp. 123-135.

[21] 1938 was a year of unusually low raw-material prices and cannot be considered as a "normal" prewar year.

[22] The second method yielded an estimate of 130 for the terms of trade in 1946, compared with a figure of 110 by the previously cited calculation. The figure of 130 was considered too high because it was based in an import price index that apparently under-estimated seriously the increase in Latin American import prices.

TABLE 65

Indices of Terms of Trade of Selected Latin American Countries 1946

(1938 = 100)

	Export Prices	Import Prices	Terms of Trade
Brazil	277	200	138
Argentina	258	215	120
Ecuador	268	227	118
Mexico	192	169	114
Costa Rica	195	175	111
Guatemala	195	175	111
Colombia	200	190	105
Cuba	233	234	100
Venezuela	160	168	95
Nicaragua	178	190	93
Peru	195	217	90
Chile	163	198	82
Bolivia	193	237	81
Latin America	219	202	108

Source: J. Ahumada and A. Nataf, "Terms of Trade in Latin American Countries," *International Monetary Fund Staff Papers*, February 1950 (Washington, 1950), p. 131.

more than cancelled out weaknesses in minor sectors of their export lists.

TABLE 66

Terms of Trade for Latin America

(1938 = 100)

	Index of Export Prices	Index of Import Prices	Terms of Trade
1925	192	142	135
1929	164	126	130
1933	87	82	106
1935	107	93	115
1936	115	96	120
1937	131	102	128
1938	100	100	100
1946	200	153	130
1947	281	183	153
1948 (10 mo.)	293	195	150

Source: Ahumada and Nataf, *op. cit.*, p. 135.

Balance of Payments Problems: A Latin American View-point. At this point it is worthwhile to cite a Latin American viewpoint on the relation of balance of payment problems to economic development as expressed by Javier Marquez, a highly-skilled Mexican economist.[23] Marquez starts out by noting that "balance of payments disequilibria in Latin America have come to be, to a large extent, a result of the efforts to accelerate the pace of economic development. The attempt to minimize the influence of the ups and downs of economic activity in the major industrial countries on the economies of the individual Latin American republics also brings about autonomous disequilibria in their balance of payments." Recognition of the fact that the Latin American countries depend on economic trends in the large industrial countries, that they are influenced but do not influence, results in establishment of these bases of policy: (a) lack of confidence in the likelihood that the more advanced economies can maintain conditions of prosperity; (b) ability to reduce the impact of depression in the more advanced regions by diversification in Latin America; (c) "since the price of exported primary products shows a persistent tendency to fall more than the price of imported manufactured goods, with the consequent deterioration of the terms of trade," diversification through industrialization is suggested, with accompanying social advantages and a higher standard of living than primary activities promise; (d) the behavior of large industrial concerns in the major economies is potentially harmful to sound independent economic development. To these bases are added the force of nationalism.

Marquez then notes that implementation of developmental policy on these bases understandably is increasingly proceeding under governmental auspices. "To carry on their not always well-defined programs, the governments have had recourse to all kinds of policies, and all of them have had as a consequence: (a) an upward pressure on the money supply;

---

[23] Javier Marquez, "Notes on Balance of Payments Problems in Relation to Economic Development in Latin America," *Inter-American Economic Affairs*, September, 1947, pp. 104-117.

(b) an upward pressure on imports; and (c) a downward pressure on exports." This seems to provide the basic balance of payments problem—the short-run equilibrium of the balance of payments sacrificed to a long-run increase in the standard of living and to the security afforded by greater independence from foreign sources of supply. While the Latin American governments in their drive for development are supplying the basic facilities needed before production can rise substantially (irrigation, education, sanitation, labor training, housing, road construction), the supply of goods fails to keep pace with incomes. "The natural outlets of increased income are imports and prices. Imports rise because they are needed for industrialization itself and because higher incomes require more goods than domestic industry can provide. Prices of domestic goods increase because incomes are higher, because population becomes more concentrated in big towns, thus creating increased demand, and because transportation charges, marketing costs, and the rate of profits are high. Price increases on the other hand will obviously exert a downward pressure on exports." Marquez is not disturbed by the fact that development programs by increasing money incomes and prices may raise costs, diminish the possibilities of exporting and consequently reduce the receipts of foreign exchange which are needed for development. He feels that the significance of exports to the economies is such that they are likely to be protected against all contingencies [24] and that "increased costs are more likely to influence the development of the industry concerned, that is, future investments in it, than present production and exports."

Marquez agrees that with an improved fiscal system, with efficient, flexible and progressive income taxes, many Latin American countries could put themselves in a better position to achieve development without endangering their balance of payments to the extent that it is currently being endangered.

---

[24] He cites the protection given Venezuelan coffee and cacao by subsidies to exporters, the likelihood that exemptions from taxes and export duties would be tried, and finally if all means of promoting exports fail, depreciation.

But he warns that "a strong fiscal system is compatible with economic development along capitalistic lines only when the taxpayer is psychologically prepared for it," and he suggests that in many Latin American countries they are not so prepared. He points out that many people in Latin America believe that private enterprise will not carry economic development through the right or more desirable channels and that the pace of development under private auspices would be too slow. Finally, on the all important question of balancing objectives—rapidity of development to a higher standard of living, and security—he declares flatly: "No doubt there is a lot of demagogy in the popular support of industrialization and diversification programs or tendencies in Latin America. Such demagogy is superfluous, for the advantages of industry over primary activities and the insurance-through-diversification theory constitute sufficiently sound bases for these tendencies. . . . The country . . . will prefer to pay an insurance premium, in the form of higher prices, for domestically produced goods previously imported so that it will not be so badly off when its customer stops buying the commodity which it sells."

The Situation in 1950. At mid-century it was common among the Latin American countries for the value of exports to run one-sixth to one-third of gross national product. Three commodities comprised about half of the value of exports of the region. Latin American participation in world trade was larger than its share of world production, running about 9% of world exports in 1937, 13.4% in 1946, 12.3% in 1947, but the Latin Americans were quite correct in emphasizing that instead of exercising significant influence on the level of business activity the world over, they were largely at the mercy of policy-decisions in foreign markets over which they had no control. Increasingly the level of business activity in the United States had come to be of decisive importance to Latin American foreign trade and through trade to the Latin American economies generally. While debate continued on the question whether insurance against excessive dependence upon foreign markets could be achieved without excessively re-

tarding progress toward the goal of a higher productivity, the Latin Americans were quite generally committed to the policy that the insurance was worth whatever it might cost.

In the utilization of their foreign-exchange resources, progress was being made toward concentration of an increasing proportion upon development requirements. In the prewar period, even in the more-industrialized bloc of countries (Argentina, Brazil, Chile and Mexico) about half of imports had consisted of consumers goods, one-quarter or less capital goods, one-quarter fuel and raw materials for industry; in the less advanced countries the proportion of consumers goods had been much greater. Moreover, a large proportion of consumers goods had consisted of luxuries for the small but powerful section of the population in which a large part of purchasing power was concentrated. The relative unavailability of capital goods during the war, and the low level of inventories and the great pent-up demand for consumers goods in the immediate post-war period, interfered with greater diversion of exchange resources to developmental requirements. But in 1950 official policy was clearly outlined of directing a larger and larger proportion of exchange-resources into the acquisition of capital equipment destined to reduce further the "minimum requirements" for foreign consumers goods and to increase the extent to which exports were processed before shipment overseas.[25]

If the ambitious plans for development were to be realized, however, it was likely that requirements from overseas would exceed the gain in resources that could be achieved from more skillful mobilization of resources currently accruing from exports. For many export commodities pressure on exportable surpluses was likely to arise from the rapid increase in population and, if it materialized, from improvement in the standard of living. Foreign-controlled enterprises were accounting for one-third or more of the value of exports and

---

[25] The tendency to export in more highly processed form could be seen in exports of oil instead of oilseeds, flour instead of wheat, clean wool instead of unwashed wool, refined metals or concentrates instead of ores.

had in recent years accounted for a larger proportion of the increase in volume of exports. For some policy-makers this suggested the desirability of replacing foreign enterprises with local activity as a means of increasing the yield to the local economy. For others it suggested that encouragement of more foreign enterprise might be the key to expanding the foreign-exchange resources. Vitally important in this decision was the concept of the role of the government. Let us next examine the role of the government.

SUPPLEMENTARY READING

United States Department of Commerce, *The Balance of International Payments of the United States 1946-48* (Washington, 1950), pp. 182-188.

United States Department of Commerce, *International Transactions of the United States During the War 1940-1945* (Washington, 1948), pp. 131-144.

B. C. Swerling, *International Control of Sugar, 1918-41* (Stanford University Press, Commodity Policy Studies No. 7, Stanford, 1949), pp. 1-69.

International Monetary Fund, *Balance of Payments Yearbook 1938, 1946, 1947* (Washington, 1949), pp. 57-67, 86-93, 108-115, 122-137, 154-163, 169-171, 207-208, 250-259, 272-276, 288-293, 374-381.

United States Tariff Commission, *The Foreign Trade of Latin America, Part I* (Washington, 1942), pp. 16-57.

Russell Baker and Dwight Hightower, "The Western Hemisphere Trade Corporation: A Problem in the Law of Sales," *Tulane Law Review*, December, 1947, pp. 229-263.

David L. Grove and Gerald M. Alter, "Latin America's Postwar Inflation and Balance of Payments Problems," *Federal Reserve Bulletin*, November, 1948.

United Nations Department of Economic Affairs, *Economic Survey of Latin American 1948* (Lake Success, 1949), pp. 183-234.

Chapter 14

The Role of the Government:

Public Finance, Banking and

Economic Planning

The frequent use of the term "policy-maker" up to this point may have created the impression that centralized decision-making plays the determining role in guiding the economic activities of the Latin American countries. It is true that the role of the government has broadened steadily in recent years. In 1950 the governments were accounting for more than one-fourth of the economic activity of the Latin American countries but this did not measure adequately the influence of the governments. Government expenditures commonly ran 15 to 25 per cent of the national incomes of individual countries and were tending to advance more rapidly than national incomes. Long before they had fulfilled the ordinarily-accepted functions of government such as creation of elementary public health facilities, schools, flood control, water supply and the like, the governments were expanding steadily into the more controversial spheres of activity—steel mills, international aviation lines, petroleum exploration and exploitation, motion-picture production, chemical manufacturing.

In industry, governments intervened sometimes because existing entities could not continue and yet the services could not be dispensed with, as in the case of some of the transportation ventures; sometimes because private capital appraised the market potential of an industry as not warranting investment; sometimes for reason of international prestige; some-

456

times to create monuments to a particular administration; sometimes in nationalistic protest against the alternative of foreign participation; sometimes because they alone could mobilize sufficient capital. But rarely if ever did they intervene from a popular belief that government ownership and operation was an economically superior method, that the State could do it better.

In the field of labor-management relations, the governments intervened directly not only in industrial conflicts but also in the internal affairs of trade unions. In finance, a mounting structure of government-controlled banking institutions was increasingly influencing the relative speed with which development could take place in particular lines as well as the policies under which the borrowing entities were to conduct the activity. In foreign trade, governments increasingly dictated what goods could be imported, and in so doing determined not only what industries might flourish within the country but also the extent to which the consumer was to profit from pressure for greater efficiency and productivity. In the field of formal planning, the governments had broken out in a rash of "planning" activity of various sorts, whose importance was frequently puffed up to ridiculous proportions for political purposes at home and out of ignorance abroad. Thus, the simultaneous publication of a heterogeneous collection of projects and proposals, many of which had happily been gathering dust in government files for years and even decades, became for political purposes in Argentina a "plan" for economic development, and became for a friendly professor at one of our great universities another demonstration of the ascendancy of planning which must quickly be brought to the attention of "less well informed" Americans whose ignorance "derived from smugness regarding the strength and resilience of capitalism!" Nevertheless, although the lack of substance in much of the paper work and the immense gap between programming on paper and implementation into reality were frequently obscured by the wave of exuberant announcements concerning establishment of new government coordinating agencies, it could not be denied that the Latin American governments were increasingly undertaking responsibility for designing a framework for economic develop-ment.

National Economic Budgets or Plans. The task of detailed planning of the economy within a national economic budget or plan whose execution would involve centralized decision-making in minute detail seemed far beyond the capacity of the Latin American governments, however. Such planning and implementation requires a strong government, a competent administrative staff, and an incorrupt group of administrators. All of these were generally lacking in Latin America.

Ambitious governments were undertaking to formulate the desire for economic development and to implement it into action. But while they might be able to bear down on individual segments of the economy, and while they might be able to enforce measures such as import controls the more readily because the objections of the groups hurt were compensated by the advantages accruing to other elements who wanted protection, the governments lacked the strength to enforce the measures that a detailed economic budget required.[1]

The civil service was characteristically over-staffed, standards were low although they were improving in some countries, government personnel generally lacked the training and the comprehension of the larger issues involved and could not be counted upon to act effectively.

Corruption was deep in the tradition of government administration in Latin America. If the people were permitting the governments to formulate programs and to translate them into action, they were not doing it from any deep-seated conviction of the superiority of State action over that of alternative social institutions or from confidence in the likelihood that

---

[1] Marquez points out, on a relatively narrow sphere of policy—the case for basic development in times of prosperity and the anti-cyclical development program—that "the expediency factor is all important . . . the actual authority of governments over economic life is limited . . .governments do not feel strong enough to impose exchange restrictions in times of prosperity . . ." *Op. cit.,* p. 117.

the government services were sufficiently incorruptible to act squarely in the public interest. It was the inability to perceive or to comprehend any alternative holding out the probability of such early improvement as that which the politician readily *promised* that occasioned acceptance of the State effort. Indeed, the lack of the popular enthusiasm for the job which might have produced a willingness to bear hardships and tolerate mistakes and accept the time-consuming requirements, was one of the great handicaps that every Latin American government suffered in its developmental activity. With the prevailing political instability, itself partly deriving from the lack of economic development, governments were not permitted the "luxury" of seeking out "best" methods. They had to produce results or a plausible substitute therefor, and were thus likely to choose those policies promising the earliest demonstration of something accomplished.

Most of the Latin American governments at one time or another have consisted of strong dictatorships. While the ordinary "strong-man" might make a show of strength against an individual group in the community, or exploit a particular section for his personal advantage, while he might even interest himself in broad development if he were confidently digging in for a long stay, he too did not dare the detailed decision-making for the entire economy which a national economic plan required. Whatever his strength he retreated from the idea of imposing priorities, ordering the use of specific capital and land and energies in specified manners, rationing. And the training of an effective disciplined incorrupt "priesthood" to administer such a plan appeared to most Latin American dictators, even the "benevolent" ones, as a suggestion for "doing it the hard way." It was easier to run the government by coercion and corruption.

Guidance by the Body of Inconsistent Economic Policies. Thus, the main lines of government guidance of economic activity derive and are likely long to derive not from systematic national plans with centralized decision-making in detail at the core, but rather from the varied body of economic policies which the governments adopt in the continuous process of responding to the pressure of particular groups in the community, of aping other governments, of compromising social and economic objectives, of reflecting shifts in political power as in the case of the shift from landowners to industrialists which in many countries has made the one group more vulnerable to independent government decision-making while the other gained in its ability to dictate policies affecting its activities.

From the viewpoint of development, the difficulty is the inconsistency of these policies. (a) An objective of greater productivity is defined. But the national aspirations for industry regardless of cost cause excessive protection to be given to politically powerful industrialists, with corresponding discouragement of efficiency. Nationalism sometimes combines with the fear of superior productivity of foreign enterprise to shut out such investment. Agricultural reform in some instances poses a fundamental conflict in that it may require sacrifice of productivity to achieve "land for the landless." (b) An objective of greater equality in the distribution of income is defined, looking to creation of mass purchasing power and greater productivity for a healthier better-educated working class. But political pressures have slowed the use of the progressive income tax. And the policy of encouraging industry has reinforced the inequality in distribution by creating immense concentrations of income for a handful of industrialists paralleling the inequality that originally stemmed from the landowners' control of the economy and the government. (c) An objective of provision of a wider network of basic government services is defined. But the governments refuse to reorganize so as to remove the dead weight of unproductive over-staffed government offices. They are unwilling or through the power of the military in unstable political situations unable to reduce the burden of the military expenditures which may run one-quarter of total government expenditures and which increase steadily without relation to the potential need for such military machines. Unable to finance necessary services by curtailing the misuse of tax funds, governments must turn to raising more money. They cannot raise what they need from the lower income brackets which are already burdened with a regressive tax system and an incredibly low standard of living, and political barriers stand in the way of raising the money from those who can better afford to pay. The governments recognize the need to boost the national income if the people are to have the services. But other policies stand in the way of such a rise in national income. Thus the vicious circle takes its vicious course. (d) The need for foreign capital is recognized, and preference for investments that promise to boost foreign purchasing power as rapidly as possible is indicated. But the political usefulness of condemnation of foreign enterprise has been so great that it has become politically difficult to recognize openly the contribution which foreign capital can make. (e) An objective of greater insurance against recurring collapse of foreign markets is defined. But it turns out that policies providing that insurance favor particular interests in the community so that the governments soon find themselves buying more insurance than they can afford. Result: an insurance-poor country permanently, or at best one with development definitely slowed. (f) An objective of greater productivity per man to permit higher wages and broadened purchasing power is defined. But instead of encouraging the growth of a free labor movement whose efforts would be concentrated on bargaining for higher wages with their stimulus to management to increase productivity, the governments have focused on enactment of a mass of social and welfare legislation which in its complexity of administration, contribution to inflexibility in industry and origin apart from any relationship with the problem of productivity, only tends to slow down the attainment of greater productivity and accelerated development.

The inconsistencies in policies are especially damaging for the Latin American countries because their needs are so great and their economies still so unproductive as to leave little or no slack for errors. No pronunciamento heralding a new "plan" can be a substitute for the systematic reconciliation of economic policies that must precede effective guidance of economic activity by the governments.

Public Finance: Expenditures. Some years ago a gifted

British observer given to exaggeration to drive home her points commented that in Latin America "government is the goal of every ambitious individualist. Government employment is the refuge of everyone incapable of earning a living in any other fashion. Political power means the certainty of a fortune. It is far more profitable than agriculture or industry. Naturally, there are in South America, as in every other country, eminent and honest statesmen who attempt, Canute-like, to stem the tide of corruption, but generally with as little prospect of success as the Danish monarch faced by the English Channel. . . . Graft is a habit rendered sacred by custom and success. State employment ensures political adherence, so economy on any big scale is impossible. . . . Municipal, state and federal payrolls are crowded with names representing sinecures." [2]

The first significant fact to note about public expenditures in Latin America is this inflation in administrative personnel and the failure to establish suitable standards of performance. Since perhaps 8 to 12 per cent of the gainfully employed in Latin America are involved in these public posts, the effect on the productivity of the economy is obvious. Public administration is costly. And there is great inflexibility. At the height of a financial crisis in Costa Rica in the late 1940's, for instance, a Finance Minister reviewing the possibilities of curtailing expenditures noted that he must draw the line at cutting down on government personnel because he doubted that these employees could find employment in any other line of work. It is especially important for us in our consideration of developmental problems to note this aspect of the institutional background of the expanding role of government. If over-staffing cannot be avoided, if the standards of the civil service cannot be lifted, if the employment rolls cannot be systematically combed for excess staff, each proposal for further intervention of the State in economic activity carries with it an initial handicap of serious proportions.

A second damaging characteristic is the heavy outlay for

---

[2] Rosita Forbes, *Eight Republics in Search of a Future* (Cassell and Company, London, 1933), p. 6.

military establishments. In an area unlikely to be a directly significant military factor in any world conflict and one in which international machinery for prevention of conflict within the area is expected to function reasonably well, it is unfortunate that military expenditures should absorb 4 to 5 per cent of the national income. It is true that some of the outlay is attributed to the requirements for maintaining internal political stability, but since internal requirements must be related to the amount of force that can be mobilized by the opposition, a point is early reached beyond which increases in the military establishment yield constantly diminishing returns in terms of stability. The height of absurdity from the viewpoint of its aspirations for economic development was reached in Argentina in the late 1940's. Argentina had successfully avoided participation in the first and second world wars and was not counted upon for significant military contributions in any future war among the great powers. It could not wage war against any other major Latin American power without being confronted with the hopelessly superior bulk of the North American military establishment. And it was unlikely to be able to use its armed forces in its relations with the less important neighboring countries. Yet, while its vast developmental hopes were bogging down for lack of financing—external and internal, the country devoted more than 40% of the public expenditures, perhaps 8 to 10 per cent of the national income, to the military establishment.

Under the terms of the Lend-Lease Act of March 11, 1941, $493 million of defense aid had been provided the other Latin American countries. In the course of the transfer of $141 million of aircraft and aeronautical material, $70 million of tanks and other vehicles, $65 million of ordnance and ordnance stores, $98 million of ships and $119 million of other defense materials and services, many Latin American countries got their first taste of relatively modern equipment on a substantial scale and the general stimulus to expansion was not lost when the flow in this fashion was discontinued.[3] It might be pointed out, also, that since most of the countries lack production facilities for mdoern military equipment, the excessive proportion of public expenditures devoted to the military is reflected in a drain on foreign exchange resources as well as on internal financial capacity.

Analysis of individual budgets shows the importance of these major barriers to productive use of the funds paid in to the Treasuries. In the late 1940's the largest categories of Brazilian expenditures were: military establishment including internal policing 30 to 35 per cent, transportation and public works 15 to 20 per cent, public debt service 10 per cent, education and health 10 per cent, agriculture and mining 5 per cent. About half of the budgeted expenditures were for personnel, one-fifth for maintenance of public services (largely materials), one-fifth for growth in the national estate (buildings, transportation facilities, industrial enterprises), one-tenth for public debt. Receipts of the more than eighty autonomous entities which functioned largely outside the regular budget had come to exceed half of the revenues in the regular budget.[4] In Cuba in 1949-50 the military establishment absorbed more than one-fifth of budgeted expenditures, education and health and other social services about one-third, public works about 10%, agriculture less than 5%. Colombia in 1950 budgeted about one-fifth for the military

---

[3] Lend-lease for Latin America was handled under special agreements with the individual countries. Provisions for repayment, in part, varied among the countries. Some of the assistance was limited to expediting deliveries on cash purchases. Of the $493 million in defense aid under the program, Brazil accounted for $361 million, Mexico $39 million, Chile $23 million, Peru $19 million, Uruguay $7 million, Colombia $8 million, Ecuador $8 million, Cuba $7 million, other countries $20 million.

[4] These entities outside the regular budget include such varied organizations as the Bank of Brazil, some of the railways, social insurance funds, Merchant Marine Commission, National Highway Fund, commodity-control entities for sugar, salt, pine and other commodities. Their form of organization varied: some were mixed corporations with private capital participation, others were wholly government-controlled, some merely regulatory boards. Their forms of financing varied too: some were supported by special taxes not included in the regular budget, some were self-supporting, some received regular subsidies from the Treasury, some depended on commercial operating revenue largely. While their autonomous form of organization aimed at greater flexibility and administrative efficiency, there was an accompanying dis-

establishment, 15% for public debt service, 20% for public works, 13% for education, health and other social services, about 5% for agriculture, mining and industry. Uruguay in 1949 devoted about 30% to public works, 10 to 15% to public debt service. Mexico in the late 1940's was devoting about 25% of of its expenditures to public works, less than one-fifth to the military, more than one-fifth to education and health activities. The high degree of government intervention in the Argentine economy in the late 1940's may be seen in estimates that government budgeted expenditures were at least one-fourth to one-third of the national income, and the expenditures of the autonomous entities amounted to perhaps 60% of those in the regular budget.

Public Finance: Revenues. The Latin American tax systems have been regressive—leaning heavily upon consumption taxes, holding the burden of income taxes to relatively low rates on the upper brackets, allowing savings to escape in large measure. From the standpoint of development policy, some Latin American economists have argued that this is unavoidable, because shifts in the direction of a more progressive system would slow down the already inadequate capital formation, boost the rate of consumption. Others argue that the initial effect might be upon the currently high level of luxury consumption rather than on the volume of investment and thus the disadvantage less marked. Still others point out that serious question must in any case be raised as to the feasibility of maintaining a rate of savings if the burden falls excessively on current human resources. It is clear that an unsound tax system by contributing to internal instability—political or monetary—may in itself be a basic factor militating against healthy saving and investment. And it is obvious

---

advantage in inadequate review and supervisory activity by the government. The record of the entities reflects the general record of government activity as a whole in Brazil. The same characteristic of excessive personnel and difficulty of enforcing high level standards prevails. In general, the record does not provide an institutional background justifying any great measure of enthusiasm for continuing adventures in direct government intervention in economic activity.

that if the governments are to accept responsibility for providing an expanding body of services, the revenue system must be adjusted to the requirements.

Customs duties and related levies were long the major source of tax revenue in Latin America. They were relatively easy to administer, provided easy collection of large revenues. While they could theoretically have been directed chiefly at luxuries and thus given a more progressive character, in practice they were imposed on mass-consumption goods. The income tax was in many cases accepted only when the decline in revenues from customs duties during the depression compelled it and the burden was increased significantly only when the drop in receipts from import duties during the war occurred. The burden of the income tax tends to be lower than in the United States on high incomes, evasion is much more widespread and is tolerated except in the case of foreign companies, and in many cases the income tax burden on the lower income groups is heavier than in the United States. In the late 1940's, even in the countries using progressive rate structures most vigorously, it was common for the rate progression to stop at the point reached in the United States for incomes of about $11,000 per year. Mexico had a top bracket in which the rate was 30% on income from commerce, industry and agriculture in excess of $100,000; in the United States a person in that bracket would have been struggling to salvage perhaps one-third of his income. A salaried man in Mexico with an income of $8,000 would pay less than 5% tax; in the United States about one-fourth of his salary would have been going to the income-tax collectors. In Venezuela the top bracket was set at 26%, and an income of $400,000 per year paid a surtax of only 9.75%. On the other hand, burdened though he was with various consumption taxes, the Mexican wage-earner with ten children would be liable for income tax on an annual income of $396, would pay 1.3%. In Chile he would be paying 3.5% once past the $400 per year level. Excise taxes were accounting for a heavy share of tax revenues in Latin America, were highly regressive, hitting commodities in common use in the lower income brackets.

It was significant that one of the continuing plaints in

analysis of Latin American economic problems has been the lack of a general land tax which would have stimulated more active use of the great landholdings and the lack of interest in making the land carry its proper share of the cost of government. Yet, the shift of political power from land-owner to industrialist has in many instances only created a new group capable similarly of avoiding the burden of the cost of government, although to a lesser degree.

In Brazil in 1946 tax receipts were divided as follows: income tax 19%, consumption taxes 24%, sales taxes 21%, import duties 8%, rural and urban land taxes 2%, export levies 1%, property transfer taxes 5%, taxes on industries and professions 5%, stamp taxes 8%, others 7%. Import duties had been the chief source of revenue through 1939; the consumption tax had been established in 1907 and expanded in coverage to become a major source of revenue; the income tax had been established in 1923 and had reached a position as a major source despite considerable evasion, relatively low rates, and the difficulty in administration and collection in a predominantly agricultural country.

In Uruguay in 1949 associated levies on imports amounted to about one-fourth of the tax collections; real estate, stamp taxes, inheritance taxes and business levies amounted to 30%; taxes on tobacco, alcoholic drinks, liquid combustibles, etc., about 21%; excess profits tax 17%.[5] Colombia in 1950 budgeted its revenues to be derived 37% from the income tax (defined in Colombia as including the basic income tax, the capital or patrimony tax, the excess profits tax and the surtax), 15% from customs duties, 11% exchange taxes, 4% gasoline tax, 4% stamp taxes. Argentine tax revenues in 1947 were derived one-third from customs and associated levies, one-fourth from the income tax, one-fifth from excise taxes, one-tenth from excess profits levies. Mexican tax revenues in the ordinary budget of 1946 consisted of 23% from income taxes, 15% each from import duties and export duties, 13%

---

[5] In using data on tariff revenues over a period of time to show the decline in the importance of import duties, it should be noted that there has been an expansion in other forms of levies on foreign trade such as foreign-exchange control profits, consular fees, port charges, etc.

stamp duties, 21% taxes on industrial products and services (electricity, sugar, matches, tobacco, alcohol, etc.).

Public Finance: Budgetary Practices. Adding to the damage done by regressive and inadequate tax systems and by poor use of the tax collections have been the unsound budgetary policies and procedures. Careful financing planning has been the exception rather than the rule. "In money matters," wrote the United States Minister in Mexico all too superciliously in 1858, "these people exhibit a puerility and lack of common sense and prudence which is incredible to all but eye-witnesses. . . . One of their peculiarities is to look no further than the day of want in making their pecuniary plans." This was perhaps no more a characteristic peculiar to Latin America than the feature that disturbed his predecessor when he write: "Their necessities are great and their pretensions always very extravigant (sic)." But the attention to the formal requirements of sound practices for the budget has undoubtedly been inadequate in recent years.

In some countries budgets are extended from year to year from inability to arrive politically at a financial plan for the current situation. In others the budget loses importance because of the freedom with which funds can be shifted by the Executive and from the looseness with which both the legislature and the Executive authorize new expenditures, frequently without parallel attention to means of payment. While some of the countries have moved to segregate "public-works capital expenditures" from general budget items, with the dividing line the intention to finance the first by loans and the second by taxation, the unity of the budget more often has been broken by a multiplicity of special funds, special earmarkings of revenues, allocation of taxes to particular expenditures often without consideration of the continuing relationship between needs and prospective revenue. The proliferation of "autonomous entities" has occurred generally without any study of proper organization with respect to the budget, without adequate control and supervision by central budgeting and accounting instrumentalities, and without adequate supervision by the legislative branch of the government.

Public Finance: The Debt. Until the 1930's, the Latin American countries sought to borrow at home and abroad rather indiscriminately. After the collapse of the private capital market for foreign securities, however, there was increasing appreciation of the fact that it is not advisable to borrow abroad for local-currency expenditures. The United States government, which became the only importance source of foreign funds, emphasized in its policy statements that it was opposed to assumption by any country of additional burdens on its balance of payments for funds which were to be spent for local labor and materials.

Unfortunately, in most of the Latin American countries the market for government securities was and is very restricted. (a) Government bonds have to compete with alternative outlets for funds such as real estate mortgages and business investments in which the yields are very high. (b) The funds available for investment are not large. (c) There is frequently a lack of confidence in the government. (d) The technical organization of the local capital market has been neglected. These considerations are reinforced in particular situations by special factors. In Mexico, for instance, Mosk points out:

> Another striking quality of the Mexican investor is his refusal to buy bonds of his government. This has been true since the early days of the Revolution when civil war conditions caused the Mexican government to default on its debts. The credit of the government suffered a severe blow internally as well as externally. As a matter of fact, the loss of government credit for internal borrowing has been more complete than for external borrowing. It was not until 1933 that the Mexican government attempted to launch securities again in the internal market. Since then it has put out a number of bond issues, on which it has scrupulously met its obligations. In addition the government has given its bonds complete tax-exemption privileges. The investing public, however, has steadfastly refused to buy the bonds, and public holdings of government securities have right along been insignificant in amount. Irrational though this attitude may be, nevertheless it is a hard fact which the Mexican government must face.[6]

---

[6] Sanford A. Mosk, "Financing Industrial Development in Mexico," *Inter-American Economic Affairs*, June, 1947, pp. 15-16.

Nor have the private banks in Mexico viewed investment in government bonds with any enthusiasm. Mosk suggests that their attitude is not passive but actively hostile where government bonds are concerned:

> "The explanation for this behavior is found in their deep-seated antipathy to the social program of the Mexican Revolution. For about twenty-five years the bankers have been uneasy about the increased political strength of labor, about the agrarian program, and about nationalization measures such as those in the petroleum and railroad industries. These are only principal reasons—apparently the bankers of Mexico have found many other grounds for being nervous about the government. Whether the reasons are good or bad is beside the point here. The fact is that as a group the bankers of Mexico fundamentally distrust the Mexican government." [7]

Thus in 1946 it was estimated that the Central Bank held about three-fourths of all government bonds, that private banks, other credit institutions, and the insurance companies held about 20 per cent, and individual and other institutional investors about 5 per cent.

When the Abbink Mission studied the Brazilian bond market in 1948-1949, it estimated that at the end of 1947 more than half of the consolidated debt of the Federal Government was held by the general public; that the social-security institutes held 20%, consisting almost entirely of bonds turned over by the government in part payment of its contribution to these organizations; that the banks held 7½%, partly as an element in reserve requirements. It found Federal Government bonds quoted at discounts of 10 to 40 per cent during the previous two years. Attributing the weakness and narrowness of the local capital market for government securities to the preference for real estate and to the reliance on forced subscriptions which had tended to destroy investor confidence and to act as a drag on the market, the Mission recommended a number of measures to improve the technical organization of the bond market, such as: (a) Abandonment of forced subscriptions. (b) Placing of definite maturities on all new

---

[7] *Op. cit.*, pp. 18-19.

public issues. (c) Making of all new issues of the Federal Government general obligations. (d) Prompt payment of interest with a minimum of administrative delay and red tape. (e) An active propaganda campaign to acquaint investors with the merits of investment in government securities. (f) Empowering of the Central Bank, if and when established, to engage in limited open-market support operations intended to broaden the market for government securities and to make them more liquid and therefore more attractive. Nevertheless, the Mission advised the government not to count on individual savers providing a market for its obligations and to look chiefly to institutional investors such as the collective-savings institutions (pension institutes, Federal savings banks, insurance and capitalization companies) and the commercial banks.

Some of the governments have resorted to special devices, such as the payment for public works by handing bonds to the contractors. The main course of action, however, has been to resort to the central banks. While the central banks have usually been protected in their statutes against excessive lending to the governments, in practice it has been almost impossible to resist government pressure when the Treasuries have been hard-pressed for funds. Borrowing from the central banks has been cheap, with government officials participating in the setting of their rates and part of the profits accruing to the governments. Sometimes the central banks have undertaken to develop the market by issuing securities in turn against their government bondholdings, on the theory that their credit is better than that of the government in the eyes of many investors.[8] The reliance on central bank credit has complicated greatly the coordination of fiscal and monetary policies.

Among the important trends in the public debt in recent years have been these: (a) The relative decline in the volume of foreign-held debt as against local debt. (b) The lower

---

[8] It might be noted in this connection that U. S. government officials working on proposed loans to Latin America frequently attach more value to the signature of the Central Bank as debtor than to that of the government.

cost of foreign borrowing in Washington as compared with the bond issues that were floated abroad before 1930. (c) The steady increase in the outstanding debt. (d) The never-ending pressure to increase indebtedness as the politically preferable alternative to systematic revision of the tax structure along sound lines. (e) The steady increase in debt-service requirements in local currency. (f) The drop in debt-service requirements in foreign currencies.

From 1940 to 1949 Uruguay's total funded debt doubled, although the external debt decreased. From 1939 to 1946, while Argentina was largely eliminating its foreign debt, the total government indebtedness rose at least 150% and it continued to mount rapidly thereafter; at the end of 1949 it was estimated that half of the debt was held by the social-security funds. From 1938 to 1946 Peruvian indebtedness doubled, and continued upward thereafter. Brazil's debt rose 225% from 1938 to 1946, but whereas debt service had required some 40% of the budgeted federal expenditures in 1930, it absorbed only 8.8% of the federal budget in 1948.[9]

Fiscal Policy and Monetary Management. In recent years the governments have had at their command an increasing number of well-trained Latin American economists with a special interest in fiscal and monetary policy. In this field as in others, however, severe limitations on independent policy are imposed by the heavy dependence upon foreign trade and its dependence in turn upon the policies of the more advanced countries. Exports and imports function as determinants of national income—exports occasioning an increase in income in the form of wages, profits, etc., without compensating expansion in available goods, imports tending to divert purchasing power from the domestic market. Government efforts to offset the effects of sagging exports by domestic outlays when successful are translated into a boost in imports, a draining away of exchange resources, possibly an eventual depreciation of the currency, with rise in import and export

---

[9] See United Nations Department of Economic Affairs, *Public Debt* 1914-1946 (Lake Success, 1949), pp. 11-14, 27-30, 38-41, 48, 95-97, 154-158.

prices, and broad inflation. Where the drain on exchange is impeded by exchange control the absence of sufficient expansibility of domestic production threatens an early rise in the price of domestic products rather than a boost in volume, rising costs pyramid the difficulties of the exporting industries, with a possible demand for depreciation.

The setting of the problem of monetary management is also defined by the dominant role of international movements of capital and fluctuations in exports and imports in determining the level of economic activity and the money supply. Other elements in the problem are the unavailability or ineffectiveness of traditional central banking weapons in such poorly developed financial markets, and the continuing dependence of the government upon central bank credit which balks effective coordination of fiscal and monetary policies.

It is probable that the more promising sphere of independent policy action will for some time continue to be revision of the tax system, closer scrutiny of government expenditures, specific actions to broaden the market for government securities, and adaptation of the banking system to specific financial requirements of various sections of the community. Some illustrations of the adaptations of the banking system are next considered.

Case Studies: Mexican Banking. Antonio Carrillo Flores has estimated that in the decade 1939-1948 gross investment in Mexico was $3.3 billion, of which about $1.1 billion was devoted to public works.[10] Of the funds allocated to public works, 86% was derived from domestic sources, 14% from foreign loans. Of the amount obtained locally, two-thirds

---

[10] Antonio Carrillo Flores, "Practices, Methods and Problems Involved in the Domestic Financing of Economic Development in Mexico," United Nations Economic and Social Council, *Methods of Increasing Domestic Savings and of Ensuring Their Most Advantageous Use for the Purpose of Economic Development* (General, E/1562, 16 December 1949, Lake Success), p. 184. This section relies heavily on the statistics in this article. For comparison of the investment in private construction and in industry, the Bank of Mexico for the period 1940-1945 estimated the investment in private construction as 1.25 billion pesos and in industry as 1.6 billion pesos.

came from funds provided in the ordinary budgets, one-third from domestic loans. Mexico's problem was to finance the enormous requirements for public works to be undertaken by the government, for industrialization primarily under private enterprise, and for an agriculture where the social objectives tended to clash with the usual conception of sound banking practice. All this in a poorly organized financial market, where individual investors showed an overwhelming preference for investment in urban real estate and construction and mortgages as against industrial securities, where there was a positive aversion to government securities, where hoarding and the holding of funds abroad impaired an already inadequate volume of savings, where the potential investor has been described aptly as a person who "continues to want metallic money that he can keep in his own possession, mortgages on property that he can see with his own eyes, or jewels and precious stones that he can hoard." It is not surprising that in its impatience to provide the public services, accelerate industrialization and preserve the social gains of the agricultural revolution, the Mexican government has come to dominate the financial structure, not only as the authority which provides the laws and rules regulating the capital market but also by its active intervention.

The private banking system has included commercial banks, savings banks, mortgage banks, trust companies, capitalization companies, finance companies, and the rather inefficiently organized operating structure centered around the stock exchanges in Mexico City and Monterrey. At the end of 1948 the commercial banks accounted for almost two-thirds of the resources of the private credit system. There had been an immense expansion in the number of banks, from 102 at the end of 1934 to 121 in 1940 and some 340 in 1948. With legislation emphasizing the maintenance of liquidity, short-term lending was the primary field of activity of the commercial banks; over 90% of the loans were for terms of less than one year, the bulk of them for periods less than six months. Attention was given chiefly to the needs of commerce rather than the requirements of industrial borrowers. The industrial lending tended to be concentrated with a limited number of favored customers, particularly the larger and better-established manufacturing firms, just as before the Revolution the banks had devoted themselves primarily to the needs of the larger landowners. There was general discrimination against the small industrial firm which was accordingly driven to the more costly and less satisfactory financing by money lenders and large commercial houses and which was first and most heavily hit by the periodic need to tighten credit in the money market generally. Although they had authority to make sizable investments in private and government securities, the commercial banks have not done so in practice. In 1948 they held about 7 per cent of the public debt, representing less than 4 per cent of their resources; only one-eighth of their resources was devoted to investments in securities.

The number of savings banks increased from four in 1936 to 81 head offices and 170 branches in 1948. They have been chiefly savings departments of the commercial banks. They have devoted themselves to lending rather than to investment, and have specialized in the more profitable short-term lending rather than long-term lending. They have made no significant contribution to channeling Mexican savings into industry.

The mortgage banks, numbering two in the 1930's and twenty-one in 1948, although in theory able to lend to industrial concerns, have in practice devoted themselves almost exclusively to urban real estate activity, which in 1948 accounted for over 95% of their loans. They function by issuing securities of their own secured by mortgage loans which they themselves had made, and also by guaranteeing mortgage certificates issued by individuals and firms.

The expansion of the finance companies has been a conspicuous development in the past decade in Mexico, although the accomplishments have been distinctly disappointing. There were eight in 1934, 104 in 1948. Many are subsidiaries of the larger commercial banks. They were designed to function as investment banks with primary attention to the promotion of industry; to promote and organize enterprises, to exercise discriminating judgment in encouragement of industries most desirable from the viewpoint of a sound Mexican economy, to participate in other companies for financing purposes, to facilitate the issue and distribution of securities, to expand public interest in industrial securities. In practice they had accomplished little up to the end of the 1940's in creating a market for industrial securities among investors. They had shown little interest in distributing securities to the public, and when they did participate in security-issue it was largely to hold rather than to resell. They issued their own general bonds with such securities as collateral and in this fashion gave the investor a bond which was a direct obligation of the finance company itself, thereby failing to educate the market in acceptance of industrial securities. Of their general bonds, the insurance companies have taken about one-third, the government-controlled central bank has been a large buyer, and individual investors have tended to find them little more attractive than other securities. The finance companies also have yielded to the temptation to allow lending to become a more important function than investment. The banking code fixed six months as the minimum maturity for their loans, with some exceptions. Their record has been one of diverting central bank credit into commercial lending, showing preference for short-term as against long-term credit, and joining in the financing of speculative commercial activity. The volume of activity by private banks other than the commercial, savings and mortgage banks and the finance companies is less important.

Growing steadily in importance has been the corps of government-controlled banks. At the center is the Bank of Mexico. Five of its directors are appointed by the government and 51% of its stock is held by the government. It exercises the general function of a central bank, executing official policy in the monetary and fiscal field. In addition to such activity as attempting to exercise qualitative and quantitative control of credit in order to maximize the effectiveness of available financial resources, it has worked actively to fill individual gaps in the development-financing structure: it has supported the market for the general bonds of the finance companies, bought sizable quantities of the bonds; it stands behind the dominant government vehicle for the supply of investment funds to industry (Nacional Financiera); it has bought the larger part of the government bonds on which the public works program depended substantially; in some cases it has bought the securities of industrial firms; and it has bolstered the agricultural credit system.

Nacional Financiera is the agency assigned the task of organizing the capital market for industrial development. The government owns 51% of the subscribed stock, and while the institution is nominally independent it is in practice an organ of the government. It was originally designed to stimulate investment in government bonds. Upon reorganization in 1941 it undertook the primary task of promoting industrial development. It purchases securities of industrial companies, makes loan to industries, makes loans to finance companies as a sort of central bank for the investment banking community. Its chief source of funds has been the issue of certificates of participation which are backed by designated securities in its portfolio, but which carry fixed rates of interest and a pledge to repurchase at par. Behind the guaranteed rate of return and the repurchase guarantee stands the Bank of Mexico. In 1947 its capital was increased, its status as agent of the federal government reaffirmed, and it was authorized to conduct the negotiation of international loans for capitalization purposes. It was directed to promote industries that would help in improving the balance of payments position, that would maximize the use of local resources, etc. By December 1948 Nacional Financiera was able to report 1,052 million pesos of resources, 126 million investment in securities, 409 million in credits, 305 million in certificates in circulation. It had by that time helped finance 172 industrial enterprises, including 21 in steel and other metal manufacturing fields, 18 in the sugar industry, 14 in textile industry, 11 cement factories, 11 construction companies, 12 printing companies, 10 communications and transportation enterprises, 9 packing and refrigerating plants, 6 electricity generating enterprises, 5 food factories, 4 paper mills. But in the case of Nacional Financiera too the tendency had been to be of less help to the small manufacturer than to the larger enterprises, and the impact on investment habits to remedy the aversion to industrial securities had been inadequate, since the certificates of participation were essentially regarded as issues of what amounted to the investment banking department of the government-controlled central bank.

Other specialized banking agencies of the government include: (a) Banco Hipotecario Urbano y de Obras Públicas, which was set up to finance low-cost housing and public works. It acts as a support agency for the savings and family-housing loan agencies. Its operations range from loans for direct investment to planning and financing cooperation with other government entities. It supplements its capital resources by issuing mortgage bonds, usually of ten-year maturity, which are available to corporate and individual investors. (b) Banco de Comercio Exterior, which was designed to develop foreign trade, particularly the export of agricultural products. Its chief activity has been in organizing small producers of export commodities, short-term loans, discounting commercial paper in connection with export operations. It has been concerned particularly with sisal, bananas, cotton, chicle, wax, nuts. It relies on the central bank heavily for execution of its operations. (c) Banco Nacional de Crédito Ejidal and Banco Nacional de Crédito Agrícola y Ganadero. During the revolutionary period agricultural credit was taken over by the government. The first named bank serves the *ejidos*, the second serves the small landowners and stock farmers. Other elements in the specialized government structure include banks for the motion-picture industry, for the development of cooperatives, for retail trade, etc.

The extreme difficulty of changing the investment habits of a nation has been widely appreciated by Mexican observers and by foreign observers. There has been a tendency, however, to attack policy inconsistencies in evaluating the contribution to developmental policy that has been made by the financial mechanism. One highly-competent American scholar, for instance, has criticized the failure of the Mexican government to curb the alternative outlets for funds which were preferred by individual and institutional investors alike, such as speculation in commodities, commercial lending, urban construction.[11] And the failure to make suitable adjustments upward in the tax burden on those best able to pay helped magnify the problem of placing large government bond issues. The difficulty of mobilizing domestic savings for industrial investment has necessarily made more tempting to the timid official the idea of obtaining financing externally, despite the fact that the continued flow simultaneously of Mexican savings into commercial speculation, urban real estate and commercial transactions might expand the very inflationary process and social tensions against which it is desired to guard. The periodic enthusiasm of foreign private capital markets in the past may have contributed to the Latin American governments' ability to shirk their responsibilities locally, may have provided an "easy way out." Whether a repetition of this foreign atmosphere can be anticipated now that the lending activity is largely confined to Washington remains to be seen. *Unless foreign investors are willing to accept the Latin reluctance to act vigorously in the mobilization of local resources, the alternative for the Latin American government would appear to be acceptance of a slower pace of development.*

Case Studies: Chilean Development and Financing Agencies. In the course of the years the Chilean government has established a series of developmental and financing agencies to meet the requirements of specific industries and specific situations. Policy was largely outlined independently by each agency with a lack of integration that frequently defeated the overall objective of accelerating development. The institutional setup consisted of companies wholly financed by foreign capital, government services incorporated in the civil service and financed directly by the State through such agencies as the Ministry of Highways and Public Works, enterprises wholly owned or directly controlled by the State but administered independently (State Railways, National Electricity Enterprise, the petroleum entity, the iron enterprise), and privately or individually controlled companies.

The government had entered upon the independently administered ventures for a number of reasons: size of invest-

---

[11] Mosk, *op. cit.*, pp. 47-49.

ment beyond the capacity of local enterprise; requirements in foreign exchange necessitating access to foreign capital markets which local investors lacked; excessive risk for the timid local investor; nationalistic refusal to permit foreign capital to participate in certain types of activities. The financing of such ventures was either wholly provided by the State as in the case of the State Railways or it was brought together by organizing limited-liability enterprises in which the State held majority control. The State financing agencies invariably supplied the capital that needed to be borrowed; the commercial banks in some cases provided some very short term capital on current commercial account.

Chile lacked investment banks performing the function of facilitating the establishment of enterprises, taking participation in the financing, helping in the issue and distribution of shares. To a limited extent the commercial banks occasionally performed such services but it was not a characteristic part of their functions. It was more common for private companies to be formed by private interests with their own funds who were prepared to wait for the concern to reach "going-concern" status in anticipation of profits far beyond the normal level. In the absence of investment banking and with the availability of highly remunerative outlets for short-term investment, private investment had not been forthcoming for the major industrial installations that were desired. On exceptional occasions some substantial support had been mobilized for mixed-capital ventures, as in the case of the steel mill when the importance of the venture to other industrial enterprises and the consequent desirability of having a voice in management made commitments advantageous. The securities market was important only for secondary activity, with little interest until securities had gained considerable recognition. Desiderio Garcia in 1949 estimated that savings were approxmately 10% of national income and that undistributed corporate profits constituted the main source of national investment.[12]

To remedy the limitations of such a background for development, the Chilean government had gradually put together a broad structure of agencies consisting of: (a) Ministry of

Highways and Public Works; (b) Nine development agencies whose names help identify their specific functions—Caja de Credíto Agrario, Caja de Crédito Minero, Caja de Colonización Agrícola, Instituto de Fomento de Antofagasta, Instituto de Fomento de Tarapaca, Corporación de Reconstrucción y Auxilio, Caja de la Habitación Popular, and Corporación de Fomento de la Producción; (c) The Mortgage Credit Bank (Caja de Crédito Hipotecario; (d) The welfare institutions including Caja de Empleados Públicos y Periodistas, Caja de Seguro Obrero, and others; (e) National Savings Bank (Caja Nacional de Ahorros).

The Ministry of Highways and Public Works is financed from the national budget, given the responsibility for executing all public works. The development agencies are similarly financed, have a field of activity usually designated in their title, and function largely on credits although they have some income of their own deriving from payments on loans granted by them. The most important development agency is the Corporación de Fomento de la Producción (Fomento Corporation) which has had immense influence, as an example of what developmental entities can do, all over Latin America.

The Fomento Corporation was established in 1939 to draw up a general plan for development of national production, to raise the standard of living, to improve the balance of pay-

---

[12] Desiderio Garcia, "Prevailing Practices, Methods and Problems Involved in Obtaining Domestic Financial Assistance for Economic Development in Chile," United Nations Economic and Social Council, *Methods of Increasing Domestic Savings and of Ensuring Their Most Advantageous Use for the Purpose of Economic Development*, pp. 115-116. Data in this section are in large part taken from this article.

Investment of part of corporate profits was regulated in Law 7747 of 1943 as follows: Profits not exceeding 15% of capital shall be deemed ordinary profits (mining enterprises excluded). Profits exceeding 15%, after deduction of the ordinary and special taxes established in Law 7144, shall be wholly invested in repayment of the firm's own bonds, in expansion of its industrial or commercial activity, or in other enterprises or transactions likely to increase the volume of national production. Failure to comply with such obligation shall necessitate purchase of bonds of the Corporación de Fomento de la Producción to an amount equivalent to the total of the investment not effected. On such bonds the interest was not to be less than 3 or more than 5 per cent per year.

ments position, to seek ways and means of achieving a proper
balance between the development of mining, agriculture, industry and commerce while seeking to satisfy the needs of the
various regions of the country.   In a sense the Corporation
was designed to supply the measure of integration which was
clearly needed in the development activity of the government,
although the lack of technical studies, the period of experimentation required to develop techniques and operational
guides, and the early impact of the second world war on its
activities, all balked achievement of any substantial success in
integration.   The Corporation functions under a flexible authority.   It can perform its work directly, it can enlist the
cooperation of private capital and enterprise in the ways it
deems best, it can participate in financing in a number of
ways.   For instance, it can lend money on terms and collateral
determined by it.   It can invest directly in industrial facilities.   It can experiment with new types of investment or
explore potential sources of production.   It can subscribe
to the capital of new or established undertakings.   It can
render technical assistance.   It is not limited to direct-profit-
yielding outlays.   In practice, it has interested itself in
divergent fields from exploration for petroleum to investment
in expansion of generating capacity for the privately owned
electricity-distributing installations, from the steel mill to
piddling investments in motion-picture production, from assistance to textile mills for acquiring machinery abroad to investment in agricultural mechanization and in irrigation
facilities.   In 1949 it was co-owner of some 60 undertakings.
It was functioning under a policy of selling its shares of enterprises as soon as the undertakings could stand on their
own feet and win the support of private investors, in order
that its funds might serve as a revolving fund for industry.

The tremendous requirements of the Fomento Corporation
have strained the budgetary capacity of the government.   It
was originally contemplated that it might function largely on
government contributions derived from the tax on copper,
but this proved inadequate for requirements and also a rather
unstable basis for activity by a corporation whose work needs
to be carried forward on a steady permanent basis.   For-

tunately, the Corporation has enjoyed an unusual asset in the form of personnel who quickly adapted themselves to the mechanism for borrowing in Washington. Up to the end of 1948 the Fomento Corporation had borrowed $102 million in Washington, used $47 million. The contribution of the Chilean government from 1939 to 1948 was 2.4 billion pesos, and other income 1.6 billion pesos.

No satisfactory study of the operations of the Fomento Corporation has yet been written. The problem of the priorities adopted by the Corporation has been widely debated in Chile. The heavy participation in electric power generation won broad support but the organization of the steel mill project and the planning for a group of derivative and associated industries were criticized by many who felt that higher priorities should have been given to agricultural development. In the agricultural field the Corporation had stepped up the importation of farm machinery, operated a fee service for medium and small farms for soil preparation, planting and harvesting, encouraged improvement of livestock, engaged in experimental sugar beet production; it stimulated irrigation work by loans to individuals and secured large foreign loans for major irrigation projects. Compared with the steel venture, the scale of such activities was piddling. Again, in the field of forestry and fisheries, technical studies were financed, some aid was given to existing saw mills, reforestation encouraged and attention given to the problem of rationalizing the timber industry, but here too the priorities tended to be low. In part, the character of Export-Import Bank financing contributed to the concentration on certain projects. The approach to the Bank in Washington tends to be more successful when concentrated on well-planned individual projects that can be related directly to ultimate savings in foreign exchange rather than when it is designed to support a variety of small ventures. And the political feasibility within Chile of supporting major "show-case" operations cannot be disputed.

One point should be kept in mind. Discussion of the Fomento Corporation frequently leaves the impression that it is so organized as to be able to provide over-all economic direction. In reality the Corporation functions in terms of specific fields of development and the Chilean government up to 1950 had lacked the institutional structure which might have integrated the Corporation's plans with fiscal and monetary policy being enunciated elsewhere in the governmental structure.

The welfare institutions are financed by contributions from employers, the government, and the particular group of workers involved. The President of Chile is empowered to "direct and integrate the investment policy of the various welfare funds." In practice a small part of the funds has been invested in securities and the remainder has been used to grant long-term loans to members for the purchase of real estate and construction of homes. The Mortgage Credit Bank was established "to facilitate loans on mortgages, preference being given to loans contributing to the development of agricultural production and construction," and functions by issuance of mortgage bonds. The National Savings Bank was sponsored by the government to encourage thrift and provide a safe remunerative outlet for the savings of persons of modest means. It is the only banking institution legally authorized to receive savings deposits. It is authorized also to carry out transactions normally executed by commercial banks. Its investment policy is closely restricted by legislation governing the Bank. While provision is made for investment of up to 50% of its available funds in readily marketable first-class securities, provided that the securities are listed on the Santiago or Valparaiso stock exchanges, in practice this makes it impossible for the Bank to support new enterprises since their securities are not readily marketable nor listed. Emphasis on maintenance of liquidity characterizes the regulations regarding lending policy.

The private banking system is not geared to developmental financing. The commercial banks cannot legally grant medium or long-term loans. Although the custom of granting overdrafts "up to a certain sum" sometimes permits a debtor to enjoy the equivalent of a medium-term loan, the basic regulation restricts loans to terms not exceeding one year. In practice, preference is given to commercial transactions which are most remunerative. The regulations governing the insurance companies accentuate the prevailing preference for real estate investment by providing that the accumulated funds "corresponding to the technical reserves, capital, and corporate reserves" be employed up to a limit of 60 per cent in revenue-producing urban real property. In addition to this proportion, the companies are encouraged also to invest in mortgage bonds. The specification of "revenue-producing" in practice largely restricts the companies to commercial construction in the capital, to the prejudice of low-cost housing and buildings for industrial development.

In Chile, as in many other Latin American countries, the difficulty of initiating fiscal reforms and of altering deeply-entrenched investment habits tempted government officials to find an easier way out in the form of foreign loans. Even the principle of restricting loans to foreign-currency requirements, which had seemed so sound when enunciated in the creditor country, was under fire by 1950.[13]

Case Studies: Policy-Relationships among Brazilian Government Entities. The easy proliferation of government entities —financial, developmental, welfare, and others—outside the regular budget not only has been occurring without adequate command of organizational problems but also poses serious questions of policy relationships. The case of the National Steel Company (Companhia Siderúrgica Nacional) is pertinent. The National Steel Company was incorporated in 1941 with a capital of $25 million, which was subsequently raised until it reached $62.5 million. The capital was raised in Brazil by issuing preferred and common stock. Brazilian governmental and semi-governmental institutions subscribed the whole issue of preferred stock. The common stock was sold to both private investors and the government. In addition, a loan of $45 million, guaranteed by the Brazilian Treasury, was negotiated at the Export-Import Bank in Washington, and loans totalling $65 million were obtained in Brazil, chiefly from the government. At the end of 1949 the Company's

---

[13] Desiderio Garcia, *op. cit.*, p. 143, suggested for instance that Washington should consider financing complete projects and thus enabling the local government to avoid having to finance local-currency outlays which had tended to hamper anti-inflationary activity.

properties included the steel mill, a modern town which it owned and operated, railway yards, sewage system, airport, coal and manganese properties, coal washery, and five coal transports. Its steel ingot production had been 244,000 tons in 1948, about half of the total produced in Brazil, and the volume and proportion had expanded in 1949. Its net profits were at a pace in excess of $6 million per year, it was current on its loans, and its preferred and common shareholders were getting dividends at the rate of 6 per cent per year. In the use of limited local financial resources and limited foreign borrowing capacity the steel mill had been given top priority. In terms of national pride the political decision to build the mill had proved itself. But what were the related policy questions?

(a) The selling prices for most of the Company's products were substantially higher than imported steel. Late in 1949, for instance, its rails were quoted 45% above the imported product, tinplate 65% above, steel sheets 17% above. This despite duties, freight and insurance charges on the imported goods. Because the government was able to give the local steel mills a virtual monopoly of the market through operation of an import licensing system, prices could be maintained at such levels. Despite the higher selling prices, the mill was earning less per ton than foreign mills. Despite the rapid progress of industry in the 1940's, there had been no such spectacular rise in the consumption pattern for steel as had characterized other manufacturing industries—a 50 to 60 per cent increase in steel compared with postwar consumption of automobiles, refrigerators and other manufactured products of iron and steel of 150 per cent over prewar on the average. It is true that before 1946 when Brazilian production had been limited to the output of about 25 charcoal furnaces averaging 40 tons per day each, domestic production had been only 30% of Brazilian consumption. In 1948 local production, thanks in large part to the National Steel plant as well as to other local expansion, accounted for 69% of consumption. Was policy success measured in terms of greater self-sufficiency regardless of cost?

(b) The National Steel plant had been given priority in

meeting the requirements of other government entities. Was the plant to be subsidized at the expense of other government entities, as for instance, the transportation companies whose deficits already hung heavily over the government budget? In forecasting manufacturing costs relative to foreign competition, it was commonly asserted that Brazilian wages were favorable to low-cost steel production, railway freight charges were somewhat lower than those in the United States, these factors and the richness and easy workability and low cost of the ore might compensate for the high cost of limestone and metallurgical coke. Were the low railway charges of a rail system producing heavy deficits another form of subsidy for the mill? Or, was it desirable that the steel mill should stand at the core of the industrial structure, permitted to run up deficits in order to sell steel and buy rail service at rates that would enable the transport system to pay its own way? A group of associated industries was being encouraged into existence by control of imports and the availability of the basic materials of the National Steel plant. The chemical industry was for the first time being supplied with a variety of raw materials formerly available only through importation. Was a high-cost structure in the industries purchasing from the National Steel plant to be encouraged, or was industry to be encouraged by the steel mill's meeting of import prices and even under-selling them, with consequent acceptance of heavy deficits?

(c) The mill was admittedly over-capitalized, with a plant investment per ingot ton produced of $558 in 1949. In 1947 data had been distorted by operation at only 54% of capacity, in 1948 at 67% of capacity. But in 1949 the mill had functioned at 85% of capacity. One official answer was the formulation of a program to expand capacity from 360,000 tons of steel ingots to 540,000 tons and from 250,000 tons of rolled products to 375,000 tons. By borrowing another $25 million, the program stated, a fifty per cent increase in capacity could be obtained with only a fourteen per cent rise in investment, and consequent reduction of the investment per ton. To hold production at this volume, however, the full protection of the local market would be needed regardless of price, and in addition export would have to be promoted. Were exports to be promoted by accepting "unessentials" from other countries despite the clash with policy governing control of imports? Were exports to be billed at high prices by allowing foreign producers of certain products also uncompetitive in world markets to ship their goods into Brazil at non-competitive levels, and if so, how did this benefit the price structure at which the Brazilian consumer bought his merchandise?

(d) Profits in the industry within Brazil were high, and likely to be higher than those yielded by the National Steel mill. Were prices internally to be fixed so as to permit competition of the less productive unit at the cost of producing excessive profits for some producers, whom incidentally it was not feasible to tax adequately for political reasons? If the National Steel enterprise were to find eventually that it could produce cheaper than some local units, was it prepared to run out of business these competitors, or would that prove politically impossible?

(e) The National Steel mill in the spring of 1950 was employing about 9,500 persons, of which 7,000 were in the steel mill operations and the others in the various auxiliary services in the community. The mill had experienced no difficulty in obtaining sufficient workers although it had found it necessary to train most of the men for the skill-requiring posts. At the higher levels local specialists were being trained to replace gradually the foreign technicians. Already more than 98% of the workers were Brazilians. There had been no serious labor troubles up to that time, and absenteeism had been held at about 8%. Was the enterprise willing to step out front as a "model" employer whether or not this jeopardized the labor-cost advantage in the cost comparisons with foreign producers or other local producers?

(f) Would this entity and others emerging under government aegis in the industrial domain be factors in preserving a policy of low tax burdens on business?

All this *not* by way of discounting the importance of the steel mill project which marked the first real step toward the establishment of a heavy industry in Brazil nor of challenging the fact that it was there to stay and to expand. Rather, by way of suggesting that entities of this kind were increasing the urgency of the need for systematic reconciliation of all public policies that might bear on development.

Concluding Comment. In 1950 there was still a tendency in Latin America to emphasize structure rather than policy. It was easier to decree a "national economic coordinating council" than it was to implement a systematic evaluation of conflicting policies directed at the central problem of development. It was easier to multiply the number of agencies — public corporations outside the budget and government bureaus inside the budget—than it was to attack the congenital infirmaties—the toll levied by the bureaucracy and the military. It was easier to set up an administrative machine to attempt to impose a welfare floor for labor than it was to attack directly the cause of maldistribution and to expand productivity to support higher returns to labor. "Blue-printing the economy" was a phrase calculated to titillate politically, but the sensation wore off quickly in the absence of both the statistical apparatus and the technical staff for planning and the willingness to undertake serious modifications in the relative position of the economic classes.

The Latin American countries were suffering essentially from a greater readiness to accept the results of economic development than the requirements for such development. They were ready to accept the welfare standards of mid-twentieth century advanced countries before they had expanded their productivity so as to be able to afford them—and in the process of importing advanced social legislation they frequently found themselves confronted with the unsatisfactory alternatives of either not enforcing the laws effectively or enforcing the legislation and finding that it impedes the process of industrialization and development generally. They could import the advanced medical techniques without the background in which they made their impact on population trends in the advanced countries—and in the process find that their populations were increasing at an even faster pace, imposing additional strains thereby on the effort to raise per capita standards of welfare. They could develop a taste for the consumers goods of the advanced countries—and in the process place additional strains on the financing available for the development process. They could easily ape the advanced countries in setting up structures for government planning — only to find they lack the technical means to utilize them effectively and even to find that with the Latin American institutional background of government activity such structures might even serve to slow development. They could exploit politically the achievement of freeing themselves from the "burden" of foreign financial participation—and in the process find that they had in so doing fixed definite limitations on the pace of development. For the Latin American countries, the role of the government properly consisted in a contribution to maximum mobilization of capital—domestic and foreign—for the development process, to the fullest possible utilization of technological advances, to establishment of priorities that would comprehend the importance of the external economies in economic production.

SUPPLEMENTARY READING

Herman Finer, *The Chilean Development Corporation* (International Labour Office, Montreal, 1947), pp. 1-84.

United Nations Department of Economic Affairs, *Economic Development in Selected Countries* (Lake Success, 1947) : Argentina, pp. 18-49; Bolivia, pp. 49-61; Brazil, pp. 62-92; Chile, pp. 93-116; Peru, pp. 117-131; Venezuela, pp. 132-149.

Robert Triffin, "Central Banking and Monetary Management in Latin America," *Economic Problems of Latin America,* Edited by Seymour E. Harris (McGraw-Hill, 1944), pp. 93-116.

United Nations, *Mission to Haiti* (Lake Success, 1949), pp. 275-320.

Sanford A. Mosk. "Financing Industrial Development in Mexico," *Inter-American Economic Affairs,* June, 1947, pp. 5-50.

United Nations Economic and Social Council, Department of Economic Affairs, Fiscal Division, *Mexico: Public Finance Data 1938-1948*, E/CN. 8/ 31/ Annex 71 (Lake Success, 1948) ; *Chile: Public Finance Data 1937-1948; Argentina: Public Finance Data 1938-1947*.

Report of the Joint Brazil-United States Technical Commission (Washington, 1949), pp. 132-169, 83-87.

Chapter 15

The Role of the Government: Social Legislation and Labor Organization

In 1950 the bulk of the industrial and commercial workers in Latin America were protected by systems of compulsory contributory insurance against the long-term risks of income-loss resulting from old-age, non-occupational disablement or chronic illness, and death of the family breadwinner. There was protection against sickness in the form of medical service and cash benefits to replace partly the wage loss from short-term illness. Workmen's compensation systems were in general application to provide cash benefits and medical service for persons suffering work-connected injuries or illness. A start had been made on family-allowance programs and on unemployment insurance. When the United States Federal Security Agency reviewed social security legislation throughout the world in 1949, it reported that 12 out of the 20 Latin American countries including those with the major population concentrations had old-age and invalidity insurance programs, 11 had survivors insurance programs, 9 had health and maternity insurance programs, 17 had workmen's compensation systems. (See Table 67).

There had been a rapid development of protection against long hours, low wages, unsatisfactory working conditions, in the form of minimum-wage systems, adoption of the eight-hour day and special pay for overtime, vacations with pay, profit-sharing plans, regulations prescribing minimum conditions of work. The labor codes which had been adopted by eight of the twenty countries by 1940 showed the characteristic lines of the early legislation: all provided for the eight-hour day as a maximum, seven out of eight established mini-

492

TABLE 67

Social Security Programs in 1949

Type of Program	Argentina	Bolivia	Brazil	Chile	Colombia	Costa Rica	Cuba	Dominican	Ecuador	El Salvador	Guatemala	Haiti	Honduras	Mexico	Nicaragua	Panama	Paraguay	Peru	Uruguay	Venezuela
Countries with compulsory contributory insurance:																				
Old-Age insurance	x		x	x		x	x	x	x					x		x	x	x	x	
Invalidity insurance	x		x	x		x	x	x	x					x		x	x	x	x	
Survivors insurance	x		x	x		x	x	x	x					x			x	x	x	
Countries with national pension or assistance programs supplementing insurance:																				
Old-age	x																		x	
Invalidity																			x	
Survivors																				
Countries having health and maternity insurance:		x	x	x	x	x		x	x		x			x				x	x	x
Countries having workmen's compensation:	x		x	x	x	x	x	x	x					x	x	x	x	x	x	x
Countries having unemployment insurance programs (compulsory insurance):				x															x	
Countries having family allowance programs:			x	x															x	

Source: Federal Security Agency, *Social Security Legislation Throughout the World* (Washington, 1949), pp. 2-5. Data are generally for early 1949.

mum wages for one or more groups, seven provided for annual paid vacations, seven provided for premium pay for overtime, five established Saturday half-holidays, seven recognized specifically the right to organize, all made specific provisions regarding the labor of women and children, six restricted the proportion of the labor force that could be of non-national origin.[1] Where codes had not been adopted the growing volume of labor legislation was generally directed at similar objectives. From 1940 to 1950 the adoption of a "floor" for wages gained favor throughout the area, and special attention was paid to greater security in the job through restrictions on the employer's right to dismiss employees and through establishment of severance pay requirements that were frequently staggering in their proportions and implications.

Ratification of the minimum international standards formulated by the International Labour Conference had not been uniform throughout the area, but the record of the major countries compared not unfavorably with that of the advanced industrial nations elsewhere in the world, as Table 68 indicates. Estimates of trade union membership were notoriously unsatisfactory, ranging in 1950 from 5 million to 8 or 9 million, but it was recognized that the industrial labor force had largely been organized.[2]

Judging alone by the external manifestations, it could be said that Latin America had early grasped the social and

---

[1] Codes had been adopted by Cuba (1940), Bolivia (1939), Ecuador (1938), Venezuela (1928, 1936), Haiti (1934), Mexico (1931), Chile (1931), Guatemala (1926). In eight other countries (Argentina, Brazil Colombia, Honduras, Nicaragua, Panama, Uruguay, Peru) codes had been prepared by 1940 and presented to the legislative bodies without success. Progressive labor legislation was not limited to countries with labor codes, however. Uruguay, for instance, had adopted the eight-hour day in 1915, to be followed eventually by general adoption. See Eugene Davis Owen, "Recent Latin American Labor Codes," *The Inter-American Quarterly*, January, 1941, pp. 68-79.

[2] Claims of union membership are usually far above the number of "dues-paying members in good standing." The unions use exaggerated figures to impress potential membership, rival unions, employers and the government with their importance. The employers and unfriendly governments have sometimes welcomed the use of exaggerated claims as evidence of "how dangerous these unions are."

TABLE 68

Ratifications of International Labor Conventions

(March 1, 1950)

Argentina	16	Australia	15
Brazil	13	Belgium	38
Chile	35	Canada	12
Colombia	25	Denmark	20
Cuba	26	France	49
Dominican Republic	5	Germany	17
Guatemala	1	Italy	26
Mexico	32	Japan	14
Nicaragua	30	Netherlands	29
Peru	11	Switzerland	18
Uruguay	30	United Kingdom	41
Venezuela	19	United States	6

Source: International Labour Office, *Industry and Labour*, 1 April 1950.

human implications of industrialization, had determined that social justice was not to be sacrificed in the process of expanding productivity. The implications of this decision with respect to developmental policy needed to be fully probed, however. And there were qualifications arising out of the gap between legislative enactments and practical enforcement that could not be ignored.

Inconsistency of Objectives. A thoughtful labor leader in reviewing the many examples of advanced social and labor legislation—for instance, the right of railway workers in Argentina and Uruguay to retire at 55 at actuarially questionable rates, the eligibility for pensions amounting to 75% of their wages of Colombian railroad and river transportation workers, severance pay amounting to many months wages in a number of countries, one month of vacation with pay for every eleven months of employment in Cuba, vesting of a life-long right to a job after a given number of years of employment in Brazil—has remarked that "while this seemingly enlightened attitude toward workers undoubtedly contributes to their sense of security, it has not resulted in an appreciable betterment of their standard of living. In fact, being keyed to a wage norm so low that it guarantees only the barest kind of existence, it has led to a standardization of misery." [3] For him the basic problem is the low purchasing power of the worker, such as is shown in Table 69, and as a labor leader he sees the problem in terms of the tactics of the unions. In the United States the workers aimed first at achievement of a high level of wages—a "saving wage"—and then sought social security and welfare legislation to supplement it. In Latin America they have won, or rather been given, a mass of social legislation while wages remain at a level that does not permit any significant expansion of mass purchasing power.

An equally thoughtful employer, head of the Chilean association of manufacturers in 1944, sees the problem as involving "excessive badly studied social legislation which pretends to a miracle beyond the economic capacity of the country by creating wealth through higher returns to labor and lower production. . . . We have dictated and continue to consider the issuance of innumerable laws which pretend to assure protection in all cases of emergency, accidents, old age, invalidism, sickness, dismissal, retirement, etc. We have so increased the cost of production and the cost of living in favor of the trappings that we have neither the time nor the money to solve the fundamentals." For him the inflexibility and the continuing charges against current production introduced by the mass of legislation seem to doom the economy to a high-cost structure in which the low output of the worker is a permanent obstruction to advance to higher wages and higher purchasing power.

Examining the situation with a broader viewpoint the economist emerges also dissatisfied. The basis for a rising standard of living is the investment of the surplus from current production in the form of capital goods. In the United States priority was accorded the accumulation of capital, and the broad concern with social security developed after investment in capital equipment out of current production had made

---

[3] Serafino Romualdi, " Labor and Democracy in Latin America," *Foreign Affairs*, April, 1947, p. 481.

TABLE 69

The Worker's Ability to Buy Essential Goods
(As of December 31, 1946)

| Country | Type of Worker | Amount of Labor Necessary to Buy: | | |
		A Shirt	A Pair of Shoes	A Suit of Clothes
Colombia	Textile worker	1½ days	3 days	1 month
Brazil	Commercial worker	1 day	3 days	2 weeks
Chile	Metal worker	15 hours	20 hours	150 hours
Paraguay	Skilled worker	2 days	4 days	1 month
Peru	Unskilled industrial worker	2 days	2½ days	22 days
Mexico	Unskilled worker	3 days	7 days	1 month
Cuba	Industrial worker	1 day	2 days	1 week
Venezuela	Skilled industrial worker	6 hours	2 days	12 days
United States of America	Manufacturing worker	2 hours 12 minutes	5 hours 54 minutes	37½ hours
	Miner	1 hour 36 minutes	4 hours 18 minutes	27½ hours
	Steel worker	1 hour 54 minutes	5 hours 24 minutes	34 hours
	Retail worker	2 hours 42 minutes	7 hours 24 minutes	46½ hours

Source: Serafino Romualdi, "Labor and Democracy in Latin America," *Foreign Affairs*, April 1947, p. 478.

497

possible the tremendous growth in industry which assured
sufficient expansion of production at sufficiently low cost to
permit devoting an increasing amount to the requirements of
social security. The risk in Latin America is that achievement of the measure of social security immediately sought
may be incompatible with the expansion of capital accumulation that is the key to a higher standard of living. It is in
fact even conceivable that the former objective might absorb
the current inadequate surplus and thus not only defeat acceleration of the developmental process but also slow it down
further.

Qualifications in Practice. It is true that the standards of
application fall far short of standards of legislation. It has
been remarked with ample justification that "the activity of
legislative bodies in Latin America is often in inverse proportion to the ability to put the legislation into effect." Many of
the countries have rushed into legislation, largely on the basis
of foreign models, without local experience or adaptation to
local conditions. The absence of a non-political independent
civil service has imposed obstacles to satisfactory enforcement; the development of experience both in legislation and
in enforcement of labor laws would in any event require time
and attention. The large area and sparse population have
frequently made effective enforcement impossible since it is
prohibitively expensive to send inspectors into remote communities to see that the law is enforced. In many instances
the legislation has been intended as a nationalistic measure
against foreign companies and accordingly enforcement
against locally-controlled concerns who were blanketed under
the legislation to avoid charges of unconstitutional discrimination has been deliberately weak. In other cases the strong
political factor has made evasion easy.

More significant, perhaps, from a policy standpoint has
been the difference in treatment as between agriculture and
other fields of activity. Farm labor has been less effectively
organized than industrial and commercial labor. Enforcement of labor legislation in the rural areas was less effective.
And local control of agriculture by interests long powerful

politically has helped in the exclusion of farm labor from much of the benefits of social legislation, except in countries where foreign ownership of plantations made agriculture a suitable target for nationalistic legislation.

In the old-age, invalidity and survivors insurance programs, Argentina, Brazil, Ecuador, Mexico, Paraguay are among the countries excluding agricultural workers; Chilean legislation covers agricultural workers, Cuba covers sugar and tobacco cultivation, Peru includes tenant and share farmers on small holdings cultivating rice or cotton, Uruguay has a special non-contributory pension system for the farms with some special taxes used as the employer contribution. In the health and maternity insurance programs, Brazil, Ecuador, Cuba, Mexico, Venezuela, Paraguay are among those excluding farm workers; Argentina excludes all farm workers except women harvesting fruit, cotton, grapes and sugar cane; Chile includes agricultural workers, Peru includes tenant and share farmers on small holdings devoted to rice or cotton cultivation.

The link with developmental policy comes most prominently in the combination of privileged treatment for industrial labor and heavy protection for local manufacturing industries. And, it might be added, in the tendency of organized labor to support the protection of local manufacturing from foreign competition. In an area where more than two-thirds of the population is directly dependent upon farming and where broadening of the market for local industry hangs in large measure on bringing its goods within the purchasing reach of the mass of rural workers, the governments have created a privileged urban labor force, working in factories which—poorly equipped and often built on an unsatisfactory resource base—are protected from foreign competition and inadequately stimulated to produce efficiently. Under these conditions, the translation of the process of industrialization into benefits for the rural population is at best a slow operation, the creation of a substantial national market on a mass basis remote.

It is true that the combination of social legislation and employment opportunities in the initial stage of industrialization has proved an attraction for rural workers, and that this has forced attention in a number of countries to improvement of conditions of labor on the farms in order to hold the labor force. In Brazil, for instance, in 1950 a former Minister of Justice told the Brazilian Rural Society that he had decided that the only way to keep men on the farms was to write a labor contract under which they would get the annual paid vacations and the weekly day off with pay that legislation guaranteed them in the cities. And British stockholders of the Cambuhy enterprises in Brazil (producing coffee and cotton) were similarly told that the drain of labor to the cities had forced the company to provide better housing and "amenities of all kinds" in order to keep adequate supplies of labor on the farms.[4] Conceivably the agricultural populations may become sufficiently articulate and may eventually substitute rural leaders for the leadership which has heretofore been offered from the cities, to the end that legislative consideration paralleling that given urban labor may be given to the rural workers.

It would be unfortunate if the end product of industrialization were to be merely a shift from unsatisfactory control of the economy by large landowners to equally unsatisfactory control by a small industrial group living off government favors and sharing, when politics compel, with its own labor force the gains from parasitical practices at the expense of

---

[4] The same factor would also be expected to stimulate mechanization. The Chairman of the Cambuhy Estates in a recent report noted that in the past Brazilian workers had been paid only for the days they worked on the fazendas, but recent legislation had given them 20 working days annual holiday, paid Sundays, Bank holidays, etc., so that they were now paid a daily wage for 365 days while they worked 285 days. This had prompted additional interest in mechanization, but since coffee picking could not be done effectively by machine and since labor must be kept available for that function, it proved more profitable to keep the same labor doing hoeing and cultivation the balance of the year although some mechanization might be possible in the other functions.

In Argentina in 1949 a decree was issued to provide an increase of 100% in basic wages of farm labor in an attempt to halt the movement to the cities.

the mass of rural workers. In this connection the strong political flavor of trade union organization in Latin America must be noted.

Labor Organization. Romualdi suggests that "perhaps the chief reason for the retarded condition of the Latin American labor movement is that none of these countries has enjoyed a sufficiently continuous period of political freedom to permit the growth of labor unions." Writing in 1947, he noted:

> In Mexico, Colombia and Argentina, for example, labor has achieved freedom only during the past generation. Although several countries, notably Cuba and Uruguay, accorded freedom to labor earlier, the growth of trade unions has been interrupted by governmental repression. In some countries, including Costa Rica, Peru and Venezuela, the labor movement is less than a decade old, while in a number of others, such as Haiti, the Dominican Republic and Ecuador, governments are just beginning to allow workers to organize freely. Brazil has permitted the existence of trade unions for almost 15 years—but under absolute government control.[5]

The trade unions, largely a twentieth century development in the area, have engaged in political action and relied on the power-potential of intimate relations with the governments rather than on the type of trade union efforts such as development of a system of independent collective bargaining between employer and employee which were in the past commonly associated with the labor movement in the United States. Union leadership has tended to be mediocre, frequently bogged down in differences in theory, usually oriented strongly toward political action. Union leaders sought the friendship of politicians in order to win and maintain the right to organize, and they have gambled on acceptance of extensive government intervention in labor conflicts and in enforcement of labor agreements on the theory (a) that they might exercise sufficient strength to keep "friendly governments" in power and (b) that if they lacked that strength, they were unlikely to be able to resist the actions of "unfriendly governments" whether government intervention was

---

[5] *Op. cit.*, pp. 478-479.

or was not written into the law regarding industrial conflict. The governments in turn have acted to strengthen unions which they regarded as politically friendly and to bear down heavily on unions that might be inclined to challenge them. The self-sustaining independent labor union movement in Latin America remains the exception rather than the rule.

Mexico furnishes an extreme case of the relationship of government and trade union and of the development of labor and social legislation. In 1917 Mexico lacked a trade union movement of significant proportions; there were perhaps 25,000 to 40,000 workers organized in unions. There had been more than a decade of increasingly active labor legislation, but the workers had not participated significantly in the passage of the laws. Mexico was then overwhelmingly agricultural, it had little industry, and native capital was notably unimportant in mining, industry and commerce. Under these conditions, there was nevertheless written into the constitution of 1917 a great mass of labor and social law, much of it borrowed from abroad without attempt to relate it to local conditions. The labor and social clauses were a vehicle by which the government gained leverage against foreign capital; since they did not hit directly at any prominent local interest, this was a politically acceptable procedure. In addition, the constitution boldly adopted the trade union as a vehicle of State control over the economy. The status of the trade union was defined to give it special rights and privileges, the government assured it status in industrial relations and defined the range of its activities. At one stroke labor was handed detailed protection with respect to hours of labor, minimum wages, labor of women and children, participation in profits, the right to organize, security in the job (regulation of discharges, compensation for unjustified removal), conditions of work, assumption by the employer of responsibility for accidents. The union became the legal vehicle to protect the dominant collective rights of the group, its collective labor contract governed relationships with the employer as law, and Boards of Conciliation and Arbitration were provided with judicial supervision over the execution of contracts, the determination of the legality of strikes, etc. Since these

Boards were made up of representatives of labor, the employer and the State, the State became the decisive authority. In bolstering the position of labor, the government had strengthened itself against the influence of foreign interests in the economy, projected a powerful instrumentality in the form of the trade union to offset the existing strength of foreign capital and the emerging strength of locally controlled industry, but at the same time it had maintained its control over the instrumentality. The union was another vehicle of growing central control of the economy, to be used as the government saw fit.

In Venezuela the dictator Gómez had resisted the establishment of any independent labor organization. But within a decade after his death a progressive government (Acción Democrática) was installed which counted on labor support, and was ready to encourage labor organization. But the organizations were not free and independent. Perhaps three-fourths of the estimated 200,000 to 300,000 members of organized labor joined unions affiliated with the National Confederation of Venezuelan Workers which was entirely controlled by Acción Democrática. When a farmers federation was organized, it too was under the government leadership. The alignment of labor and government was mutually profitable: labor support gave the government a more solid basis, and a "friendly government" could help in winning concessions from employers without strikes and in winning strikes when they became necessary. And the less successful record of the communist-dominated unions of the period seemed to point to the necessity to be under the wing of "friendly governments." But it should also be noted that the early return of a military regime quickly pointed out the weaknesses of a strictly political trade union movement.

The origins of the modern labor movement in Brazil are commonly considered to be in local organizations of printing trade and transportation workers in the 1890's. By the first decade of the twentieth century the textile workers and some other groups were establishing syndicates. It is characteristic of the labor movement up to 1930 that these local unions were described and considered themselves as "movements of resistence." Spanish anarcho-syndicalism was a dominant influence. Support for the revolution of 1930 came in part from working-class dissatisfaction with the attitude of previous administrations which tended to regard labor organizations as proper subjects for police control. The number of syndicates expanded rapidly after the revolution. There was no unified labor movement, however. The movement was highly splintered, and it was common for syndical leaders to use their positions for political exploitation as intermediaries between the government and the workers. From 1937 to 1945 the syndical movement succumbed completely to the purposes of the government and as an arm of the State lost all its force and vitality—current and potential. A large volume of labor and social legislation was promulgated, but independent constructive labor leadership was discouraged. With the coming of the new government, hopes revived for a greater measure of syndical liberty and autonomy. But the desire to suppress left-wing leadership quickly involved the administration in harsh suppression of strikes and disputes, constraining of organizational forms, personal persecution of labor leaders, countering of the drive toward central unionization by authorizing other centralist activities more subject to government influence and control. Brazilian legislation provides for associations of employees to be subject to approval by the Ministry of Labor and for the organization of national federations to require the approval of the President of Brazil. In the late 1940's when membership of some one thousand unions was estimated at half a million members, supervision by the government was tight, partly to prevent financial abuses, partly to prevent communist domination, partly to avoid the rise of any strong independent force that might challenge the administration. In 1947 the government reported that it had "intervened" in 143 out of 944 syndicates in order "to eliminate extremist elements."

The characteristic elaborate body of social legislation without parallel development of independent trade unions is present in Brazil. Important labor legislation dates from provision for accident compensation in 1919. By the time that the labor laws were consolidated under decree-law of May 1, 1943, there was provision among other things for: minimum wages; inspection to ensure health and safety; a normal working day of eight hours, with additional two hours overtime permissible under contract at 20% pay increase; special protection for women and children; 15 days annual vacation with pay for every employee; weekly rest of 24 hours; two-thirds of the employees of an establishment must be Brazilians who must get two-thirds of the payroll; workers dismissed without lawful cause must receive a month's pay for each year of work, and after ten years employment an employee shall not be dismissed except on account of serious offense or *force majeure* as duly established by competent authority. In 1946 the constitution provided among other things that establishments employing more than 100 persons shall maintain free primary schools for their employees and for children of the employees. In 1949 provision was made that except for essential services work is prohibited on civil holidays and up to seven days of religious holidays under local custom, but that labor must be paid for these days. The social security system is a vast sprawling network of institutes and funds under which some 15 million persons are covered; excluded are the rural workers, domestic servants and some types of urban workers. The Twentieth Century Fund reported in 1949 that the charges growing out of social legislation amount to 20 to 26 per cent of an employer's payroll, not including payment for weekly rest days or for public holidays which involves about 22.8% additional and constitutes in effect a flat wage increase.[6]

In Argentina in 1949 the best estimates put the average social security benefit burden at 60 per cent of the basic payroll. By that time there had been a wholesale usurpation by the government of ordinary trade-union functions, in the course of which the unions had surrendered their autonomy in return for some long overdue reforms. By the time the second world war began, the Argentine labor movement had

---

[6] Wythe, Wight, Midkiff, *op. cit.*, 243. A typical breakdown is given as follows: work accident insurance 3%, social services 2%, annual holidays 5.26%, social security monthly contribution 5% and other items 2.06%, apprentice schools 1%, sick pay 0.22%, severance 0.22%, other items 0.49%.

already enjoyed several decades of active expansion. There had been a labor federation in the 1880's, slow growth up to the first world war, emergence of many important unions in the following decade and a half. The General Confederation of Labor was one of the more stable and better disciplined labor organizations in Latin America. By 1940 it had some 300,000 members, while another 170,000 Argentine workers belonged to other central union organizations. But the farm workers were unorganized and largely neglected in national legislation, the urban workers were not at all satisfied with the pace at which union leadership torn by factionalism and theoretical debate worked its miracles, the pension funds were alleged to be actuarially unsound, and the unions themselves were vulnerable to recurring declarations of a "state of siege" under cover of which union organizers could be arrested, officials detained, unions "intervened," meetings prohibited, funds confiscated, police interference justified. When Waldo Frank met with prominent union leaders in Buenos Aires in 1942 to discuss the "demoralized state of the country" and the state of siege which was gradually restricting liberties and obviously moving Argentina toward a vicious dictatorship, he asked them: "Why not smash the state of siege with a general strike?" And he learned that "only thirty-five per cent of labor in Buenos Aires was organized; in the provinces, far less. Certain industries like oil and sugar were not organized at all. The trade unions were torn by factions, sectionalism, politics. Many out of jealousy or fear truckled with the Government. The workers as a whole lacked confidence in themselves. They feared that an attempt at concerted action might bring the dictatorship out into the open." But, asked Waldo Frank, "don't the workers realize that the Government is afraid of them?" "No," the union leaders replied.[7]

The military men who took over the government in 1943 were quick to sense the potential usefulness of organized labor and the mass of unorganized farm workers as a political in-

---

[7] Waldo Frank, *South American Journey* (Duell, Sloan and Pearce, 1943), pp. 209-210.

strument. Perón was willing to gamble that the workers would surrender the autonomy of their unions in return for immediate material gains and that the unorganized workers would respond faithfully to a show of interest in their problems. The Labor Ministry was made a vehicle for political organization. In the nineteen months preceding Perón's election to the Presidency in 1946 almost one hundred decrees poured out to expand labor and social assistance. Agricultural workers were offered a minimum wage and improved conditions of work. Questionable pension funds were put into the hands of the government and the government credit pledged as assurance of eventual payment of pensions. Minimum wage standards were established and raised, annual bonus of one month's wage was generously promulgated, emergency wage increases were decreed, a national employment service was set up, the power of dismissal was limited, provision was made for medical care, paid vacations were ordered, family assistance plans were initiated. The worker was made to feel important—someone to be catered to, someone that the government was glad to cater to. A New York reporter remarked that "not only has the worker been given an extra month's pay but also he has received the protection of all sorts of laws for industrial security and job-severance benefits; every corner news-stand sells the text of the laws; the worker who carries one in his pocket feels for the first time in his life that he holds a whiphand over his employer."

But the unions succumbed—some by bribery, some by force, some out of sheer confusion and inability to grasp the cost ultimately of surrender to the iron discipline of the government. The devices varied. When union leadership failed to submit to the government, interventors were appointed with complete power over the affairs of the union; the elected officials were stripped of control over power and treasury, sometimes removed from office by the interventors; sometimes elections were held and repeated until an administration satisfactorily subservient to the government was voted in. Other unions accepted special concessions for their workers in return for their independence. Others were broken by withholding the *personería gremial*, which was the legal recognition required for any union to carry on its functions; the list of unions that were refused the *personería gremial* included some of the oldest and most responsible unions in Argentina.[8] In some cases the police power was used to seize the premises of unions that balked at government control and to place under arrest union leaders who resisted "reason and persuasion." Strikes by unions that refused to go along with the government were doomed to prompt declaration that the activity was illegal while government-controlled units rode to success on the knowledge that employers were not in a position easily to resist. In a number of cases the government made generous contributions out of the public treasury to unions that were loyal to its purposes.

When a delegation of representatives of the American Federation of Labor and Railway Brotherhoods arrived in Buenos Aires in 1947 to investigate, upon invitation, labor conditions and to determine the degree of independence from government domination of the Argentine labor movement, it found that "any attempt to discuss trade-union principles on the basis of the traditional American concepts of free and independent action evoked no responsive note whatever in those labor circles within the government's sphere of influence, which comprises by now the majority of the General Confederation of Labor. Some of the leaders with whom we talked indicated that the notion that organized labor should make its gains through independent action rather than from governmental handouts was ridiculous and certainly roundabout. They seemed thoroughly convinced that the best and simplest

---

[8] This recognition was necessary in order to represent union members before the Department of Labor, the Pension Administration and other government agencies; to participate in collective discussions with employers for negotiation of agreements and to assure enforcement of existing regulations and agreements; to participate in political activities decided upon by meetings of the members; to collaborate with other organizations. The government in some cases was willing to disregard enforcement of labor laws for unions which lacked this recognition and was quick to point out to members that in the case of unions which went along with the government they were even allowed to have their own liaison men inside the Department of Labor to provide a channel of authority from government to the union.

method was to sit at Perón's banquet table and wait until the good things were passed around." The once-powerful and relatively independent Confederation had been converted into a political arm of the government which could not elect its officers independently of the government, could not determine its policies independently of the government, could not carry on collective bargaining with employers independently of the direction of the government, could not administer its own internal affairs. Before the decade closed, however, the decline in labor productivity, the high degree of absenteeism, the apparently unlimited expectations of the workers, had become extremely embarrassing to the government which found, however, that any slowdown in the pace of paternalistic activity threatened to revive labor interest in the price it had paid for political cover.

Status of Social Security Programs. The political value of social security programs and labor legislation has been recognized alike by dictatorships and by the more democratic regimes in Latin America. Even a tight little dictatorship like that of the Dominican Republic in the 1940's instituted a social security system, promulgated some labor laws including provision for the eight-hour day and forty-eight hour week with premium pay for overtime. The growth of the programs may be seen in a review of legislative developments from 1939 to 1949.

In 1939 when the United States Department of Labor undertook a survey of social insurance in Latin America it found 31 insurance systems covering various segments of the population of 11 countries.[9] Argentina in 1919 had brought railroad workers and employees under an old-age, invalidity and survivors insurance program, added public utility employees and workers in 1921, bank employees in 1929, set up maternity benefits for workers in industry and commerce in 1934. Bolivia provided for insurance of bank employees in 1926 (without contribution by the government), for journalists,

---

[9] Anice L. Whitney, "Social Insurance in Latin America," *Labor Conditions in Latin America* (From *Monthly Labor Review*, September, 1939, U. S. Department of Labor), p. 2.

railway, streetcar, and printing establishment workers and employees in 1938. Brazil insured public utility employees and workers and miners in legislation dating from 1931 and 1932, maritime workers in 1933, bank employees, commercial employees, stevedores, transport and warehouse employees and workers in 1934, industrial employees dating from 1936. Chile was a leader in the development of a social security program. Its comprehensive system of insurance dates from 1924, with steady extension thereafter. It blanketed in all persons dependent on wages or salaries, including wage-earners, independent workers, domestic workers and even agricultural workers. The usual distinction between "workers" and "white-collar employees" here resulted in a separate labor code and a separately administered social insurance system for the latter, whose status has suffered from relative over-crowding to take advantage of the "respectability" of white-collar occupations and from ineffective organization. Colombian legislation was limited to old-age insurance for railway and street-car employees and workers in 1932. Ecuador's bank and railway workers were insured in 1928 and a broad plan for industry and commerce dates from 1935. Panama insured commercial and industrial employees for old-age benefits in 1931. Paraguay covered railroad employees in 1926. Peruvian legislation covering commercial and industrial employees and wage-earners and home workers dates from 1935. Uruguay was one of the great leaders in labor and social legislation; coverage for industry, commerce and public utilities dates from 1919, insurance of bank employees from 1925. The Cuban system covered maritime wage-earners and employees in 1927, gave limited coverage to railway workers in 1929, covered bank employees in 1938 and journalists in 1935. (Table 70 summarizes the situation in 1939).

Legislative developments came rapidly in the period 1939 to 1949. Argentina provided old-age, invalidity and survivors insurance for persons in commerce in 1944, extended it to industry in 1946. Bolivia amended its workmen's compensation law substantially in 1942, created a miners' welfare fund financed from tin export taxes in 1947, enacted a general social insurance law in 1949. Brazil provided family allow-

TABLE 70
Latin American Systems of Social Insurance, 1939

Country, groups covered, and date of original law	Old age	Invalidity (general)	Disability arising from duty	Survivors	Death or funeral	Sickness	Maternity	Employees	Employers	Government
Number of systems	28	23	10	26	14	11	8	29	31	19
Argentina:										
Railway employees and workers, 1919	X	X	X	X				X	X	X
Public-utility employees and workers, 1921	X	X	X	X				X	X	
Bank employees, 1929	X	X	X	X				X	X	
Industry and commerce, 1934							X	X	X	X
Journalists, Province of Cordoba, 1938	X	X	X	X				X	X	X
Bolivia:										
Bank employees, 1926	X		X	X				X	X	
Journalists, 1938	X	X		X	X			X	X	X
Railway and streetcar employees and workers, 1938	X	X		X				X	X	
Printing workers and employees, 1938	X	X		X				X	X	X
Brazil:										
Public-utility employees and workers and miners, 1931 and 1932	X	X		X		X		X	X	X
Maritime workers, 1933	X	X		X	X	X	X	X	X	X
Bank employees, 1934	X	X		X	X	X		X	X	X
Commercial employees, 1934	X	X		X	X	X	X	X	X	X
Stevedores, 1934	X	X		X	X	X		X	X	X
Transport and loading and warehouse workers and employees, 1934 and 1938	X	X		X	X	X	X	X	X	X
Industrial employees, 1936		X		X	X	X	X	X	X	X
Chile:										
Wage earners, independent workers, domestic workers, and agricultural workers, 1924; preventive medicine, 1938	X	X		X	X	X	X	X	X	X
Mercantile marine officers, 1937	X	X		X	X	X		X	X	
Colombia: Railway and streetcar employees and workers, 1932	X								X	
Cuba:										
Maritime wage earners and employees, 1927	X	X		X				X	X	X
Railway and street-railway workers and employees, 1929	X		X					X	X	
Industrial and commercial workers, 1934							X	X	X	
Bank employees, 1938	X	X		X				X	X	
Journalists, 1935	X	X	X	X	X			X	X	X
Ecuador:										
Bank and railway employees, 1928	X		X	X	X			X	X	
Industry and commerce, 1935	X	X	X	X	X	X		X	X	X
Panama: Commercial and industrial employees, 1931	X								X	
Paraguay: Railroad employees, 1926	X	X	X	X				X	X	
Peru: Commercial and industrial employees and wage earners and home workers, 1936	X	X		X	X	X	X	X	X	X
Uruguay:										
General industry, commerce, and public utilities, 1919	X	X		X				X	X	X
Bank employees, 1925	X			X	X			X	X	X

Source: Anice L. Whitney, "Social Insurance in Latin America," *Labor Conditions in Latin America* (From *Monthly Labor Review*, September, 1939, U. S. Department of Labor), p. 5.

ances for large families in 1941, revised its workmen's compensation law in 1944, provided for unification of social security in 1945 (although it was not made operative), boosted pensions in 1945, provided medical care in commerce in 1945. Colombia provided benefits for employment injuries and general illness in 1945, enacted a compulsory old-age, invalidity and survivors insurance law in 1946 which was to be operative for health insurance in 1949. Costa Rica passed general social insurance laws in 1941 and 1942, made health insurance operative in 1942, amended its workmen's compensation law in 1943, set up old-age, invalidity and survivors insurance for salaried and administrative employees in 1946. Cuba provided old-age, invalidity and survivors insurance for sugar workers in 1943, for tobacco workers in 1946, for various other occupational groups from 1939-1948; it amended a maternity insurance program in 1944. The Dominican Republic provided for health and old-age, invalidity and survivors insurance in 1947, amending the law in 1949. Ecuador replaced former legislation with a comprehensive social insurance law in 1942. El Salvador created a national council to plan a general social insurance law in 1948. Guatemala passed a comprehensive insurance measure in 1946. Haiti set up an agency to introduce social insurance. Mexico enacted a comprehensive social insurance law for health, old-age, invalidity and survivors insurance and workmen's compensation in 1942, liberalized the benefits and increased the contributions in 1949. Nicaragua amended its workmen's compensation program in 1945. Panama passed social insurance legislation in 1941 and 1943, amended its workmen's compensation provisions in 1947. Paraguay passed a comprehensive social insurance law in 1943, becoming operative as to workmen's compensation and medical benefits for sickness and maternity in 1944. Peru expanded medical benefits in 1941, increased workmen's compensation benefits in 1948, extended social insurance to salaried employees in 1948. Uruguay provided for family allowances in 1943, set up special insurance provisions for agricultural workers in 1943, extended old-age, invalidity and survivors insurance to domestic servants in 1943, adopted unemployment insurance for the meat-packing industry in 1944 and for the wool and hide industry in 1945. Venezuela provided a comprehensive social insurance law in 1940, made it operative in certain areas by regulation of 1944 concerning health insurance and workmen's compensation, provided special protection for employment injuries for persons not covered by social insurance in 1945. Table 71 shows the organization of financing for certain types of social insurance coverage in 1949.

The Role of the Government. The tendency of the Latin American governments to specify the conditions under which trade unions can develop and function and the tendency to force by law larger returns from the job and greater economic security away from the job were in 1950 part of the larger policy of broadening the range of responsibilities assumed by the government and of undertaking guidance of the economy. The inter-relationship of policies came into focus on the central issue of increasing productivity. In many of the countries the government control of the labor movement was being challenged from the extreme Left. This served some governments as reason for demanding even tighter supervision of union activity, prompted many to recognize the feasibility of legislative concessions to labor so as to lessen the attraction of the extreme Left.

In an earlier period the government had faced an easier problem, because labor legislation and social legislation could be used as defense against foreign capital without disturbing any significant local interest. Increasingly, however, concessions to labor involved a choice between the local employer and the local labor force. If productivity did not rise, the concessions to labor threatened to be at the expense of local employers and at the expense of the vitally needed growth in capital accumulation, with consequent pressure from employers to resist labor's demands whatever the accompanying effect in terms of stimulating labor to more vigorous independent organizational activity. If productivity did rise, the purchasing power of the worker could be expanded without interfering with other elements or with the expansion in capital equipment. If productivity failed to rise, and govern-

TABLE 71

Source of Funds for Certain Coverage under Old-Age, Invalidity, and Survivors Insurance Programs, January 1949

Country	Coverage	Source of Funds		
		Insured	Employer	Government
Argentina:	Industry and commerce	8% of earnings	11% of payroll and ⅛% of gross sales or 3% additional payroll tax	5% sales tax on certain items plus use of general revenues if need
Brazil:	Industry and commerce	5% of earnings	Same	Same
Chile:	Wage-earners, self-employed, farm workers	2% of earnings, 3% in mining areas, 4.5% for self-employed	5% of wages paid, 6% in mining areas	1½% of wages
Costa Rica:	Salaried employees	2.5% of earnings	Same	Same
Cuba:	Sugar	3% of earnings	3% of wages and salaries	Specified taxes
	Tobacco	4% of earnings	4% of wages and salaries	Certain taxes
Dominican:	Industry and commerce	2.5% of earnings	5% of earnings	1.5% of taxable wages and salaries
Ecuador:	Industry and commerce	5% of earnings	7% wages and salaries paid	Taxes equal to 2% of earnings
Mexico:	Basic law	1.5% of earnings	3% of payroll	1.5% of earnings
Panama:	Wage-earners and salaried employees	4% of earnings	4% payroll	1.3% of earnings of insured
Paraguay:	Industry and commerce	2% of earnings	5% of wages and salaries paid	1.5% of covered wages and salaries
Peru:	Wage-earners, home workers, certain tenant and share farmers	1.5% of wages	3.5% of wages paid	1.0% of wages
Uruguay:	Industry, commerce and public utilities	5% of earnings	9% of wages and salaries paid	Taxes including 3% sales tax

Source: Federal Security Agency, *Social Security Legislation Throughout the World* (Washington, 1949), pp. 6-58.
Note that a maximum of earnings for contributions is usually specified.

ments sought a compromise by setting off the industrial community—employer *and* employee—against the less easily organized and less articulate extractive industries, they threatened to slow down development in the latter, with consequent restriction of the volume of exports on which depended the flow of imported capital equipment. If productivity did not rise and governments still counted on the political vulnerability of foreign capital, they already had indications that they were legislating themselves into a stoppage of that capital flow with serious effect on both the desired expansion of exports and the desired raising of production for local use. If they adopted the latter course they had already been informed in the major capital market, the United States, that this might prejudice the volume of government-to-government lending on which depended creation of the broad background —power, transportation, investment in labor's education and health and skills—without which the desired gains in productivity were unlikely to be achieved at any early date.

It was unfortunate that the acceptance of a larger role in guiding the economies had not been accompanied in Latin America by the necessary improvement in the political machinery, in the administrative apparatus. Without parallel advance in the efficiency of government and in the integrity and skill of the bureaucracy, the central challenge of so reconciling divergent policies as to contribute effectively to an expansion in productivity imposed a task of awesome proportion.

SUPPLEMENTARY READING

Ernesto Galarza, "Argentine Labor under Perón," *Inter-American Reports*, No. 2, March, 1948, pp. 3-15.

John Coe, "Recent Labor Developments in Mexico and the Caribbean," *Inter-American Economic Affairs*, March, 1948, pp. 55-70.

Royal Institute of International Affairs, *The Republics of South America* (Oxford University Press, London, 1937), pp. 204-226.

Carl H. Farman, "Social Security in Latin America, 1945-47," *Social Security Bulletin*, September, 1947, pp. 18-26.

Frank Tannenbaum, *Mexico—The Struggle for Peace and Bread* (Alfred A. Knopf, New York, 1950), pp. 113-121.

Report of the Delegation to Argentina (The American Federation of Labor and Railway Labor Executives Association, 1947).

Chapter 16

The United States and the Inter-American System

The policies of the United States are of tremendous importance to developmental activity in the other American republics. The volume of its imports is the key determinant of external purchasing power of the larger part of the Latin American countries. Maintenance of a high level of prosperity in the United States is a basic condition of Latin American well-being. The United States is the chief, almost the only important, capital market which the Latin Americans can hope to tap for significant volumes of investment funds. The ability to draw freely on the technological knowledge, on the "know-how," of the United States is recognized as a primary requisite for rapid improvement in productivity and the standard of living.

The sympathies of the government and of the people of the United States have long been deeply engaged by the desirability of accelerating the economic development of Latin America. Until the 1930's, direct interest had been expressed largely through non-governmental channels. The American investor moved into Latin America to bring technological advances, to bring "know-how" and to promote development by "show-how." Latin American governments and private interests drew on the private capital market and mobilized technical competence through commercial channels. In the 1930's the United States government moved to fill the gap left by the virtual closing of the private capital market to Latin American governments, it worked vigorously to reduce tariffs and broaden the market for Latin American exports through the reciprocal trade program, it obtained legislative sanction for increased loans of technicians to Latin American countries, and it labored constantly to strengthen the Inter-American System through successive conferences and through development of Inter-American instrumentalities to promote regional cooperation. The increasing tendency to place developmental cooperation on a government-to-government basis necessitated a choice between the multilateral and the bilateral approach. The architects of the Good-Neighbor Policy had believed that it might be possible to make as much progress under the multilateral approach in the economic field as in the political and security fields. By 1950, however, a body of experience had accumulated to raise some question as to this conclusion.

During the second world war a number of central problems arose in the economic field: (a) Supplying the minimum essential requirements of the Latin American countries from the United States—which started as a financial problem when it was uncertain whether the Latin American countries would be able to withstand the disruption of normal trade channels and evolved into a problem of distribution of short-supply commodities so as to minimize the strain on the United States war effort by reducing United States exports to the minimum essential requirements of the individual countries. (b) Maximizing the production and flow of strategic materials from the other American republics. (c) A series of measures taken directly to counter enemy interest in the hemisphere—preclusive buying, control over re-exports, foreign funds control, replacement of Axis airlines, liquidation of German and Italian and Japanese industrial and commercial assets, employment of Axis shipping immobilized in hemisphere ports. For this task the Inter-American System provided broad policy statements out of the conferences and a structure for discussion which included the Inter-American Financial and Economic Advisory Committee. To the Committee any country could bring its proposals for joint action, and the United States faithfully sought to create the impression that the Inter-American structure was proving a major operating factor in the solution of wartime economic problems. But in practice, the success of the Inter-American war effort can be measured in terms of the success of the bilateral activity. An

Assistant Secretary of State was to say later that "the huge complicated problem of economic development does not lend itself to solution through the mere holding of conferences nor the passing of resolutions." The huge complicated and even more urgent problems of the war lent themselves even less to the multilateral devices. It was a bilateral effort that mobilized larger quantities of strategic materials, stimulated by *quid pro quos* reached in friendly and sometimes not so friendly bargaining. The flow of short-supply items from the United States was a bilateral operation. The liquidation of Nazi assets—a very uneven process throughout the hemisphere in both speed and scope—came from exertion of pressure on a bilateral basis.

The limitations of the multilateral system can be seen in some of the tragic failures of the period—the inability to mobilize Argentine support for the war effort, and the inability to mobilize sufficient energy and in some cases integrity on the part of the Latin American countries to achieve a proper disposition of the proceeds of Axis-asset liquidation. These failures came out of the weakness of the multilateral arrangements and out of the unwillingness or inability of the United States to press firmly in bilateral negotiations lest the fiction of impregnable solidarity be weakened. Thus, the Executive branch of the government continued to assure the Congress that the Inter-American System was producing a method of pooling the proceeds of Axis-asset liquidation to be allocated eventually on the basis of respective claims, with the remaining assets thrown into the general fund for reparations. The System produced nothing, partly because it would have necessitated obligations on the part of certain nations, partly because the United States was unable to offer an inducement on a bilateral basis after general policy statements had been enunciated. The United States eventually closed the book quietly—defeated. Again, Axis firms grew stronger and more aggressive in Argentina, our Latin American neighbors thought too little of their multilateral obligations or objectives to stop the growing flow of re-exports to the Argentine, the United States hesitated to stop the import of non-essentials from the Argentine, refused to challenge the neutrals in their deliveries to Argentina, and itself maintained a flow of essentials. In a sense it was a prisoner of its belief in the effectiveness of the multilateral Inter-American approach. Finally, it is significant that shortly after the war the State Department was forced to report to the Congress that despite its continued efforts and the network of resolutions binding the American Republics, the German organization in only nine of the countries had been broken up and that in some of the others it remained nearly intact.

The experience with the institutional structure for development has been similar. In 1940 the Inter-American Development Commission was established. The author of the motion that brought the Commission into being has written that "we were primarily concerned with (a) the heavy drain on the Latin American economy resulting from its unfavorable interchanges with the United States and (b) the dangerous dependence of the United States on extra-continental sources of supply for vital strategic materials; but the ultimate goal of the plan was a general readjustment of continental economies to make them complementary and, if need be, self-sufficient." [1] When officials of the Commission sat down to map its activity, however, they found that the Commission had been conceived without any real concept of operating function, with a vague objective of promoting development and the woolliest sort of suggestions as to how that might be accomplished. In the United States government, officials immediately went to work to hatch out some piddling projects that might produce the fiction of work in progress. It publicized the fact that some technical data regarding production of tapioca starch had been furnished to Brazil, that American department stores had been urged to import Latin American handicraft articles. But as the Commission threatened to become a major embarrassment to all concerned, someone was blessed with an inspiration. Why wouldn't it be a grand idea to create a local commission in each of the American Re-

---

[1] Carlos Davila, *We of the Americas* (Ziff-Davis Publishing Company, Chicago, 1949), p. 33.

publics? This would at least take the heat off the Commission as far as finding function was concerned. The organizational task absorbed a year, but when it had been completed the absence of function again became embarrassing. Now the Commission entered upon its war effort, which it has itself summarized as including conspicuously: collaboration with the U. S. Board of Economic Warfare, preparation of bulletins explaining war measures, rendering of assistance to local groups in coping with wartime regulations and restrictions in Washington, establishing of a merchandising advisory service. In most of the efforts enumerated the Commission failed to figure as a major element and in none was there much substance. Since such duplication of effort proved no answer to the central problem of function, the Commission set about again to find something to do. This time it came up with the idea of holding a conference of the local commissions—with the obvious merit of taking months in preparation for the conference and months to recover from it. The Conference was held in May 1944, yielded the usual crop of resolutions, and more pertinently decided that if the Commission were to enter the already well-populated area of helping with technical surveys, the much-needed function might there be found.

The nature of surveys being that no one ever rejects the idea and few consent to take the constructive action as recommended, the Commission was able to make technical services available to more than half the American republics. It published a number of studies, reported that it was servicing many phone calls and mail inquiries. It had been operating largely on funds furnished by the United States Government. By June 1948 the Commission dared report that thus far "its activities have been handicapped by limited funds and limited organization" and recommended that its functions (sic) be assumed by a new Commission on Development to be created by the Inter-American Economic and Social Council which had meanwhile come into existence. The search for a function had failed. The original sponsor said that "the usual inertias, as well as the deadly hand of anti-Pan American economics, did their work." [2] But experienced American observers were inclined to see in the failure a misconception of the role that could be undertaken by an inter-governmental body in the field of economic development.

Meanwhile the Inter-American Economic and Social Council had been created at the Inter-American Conference on Problems of War and Peace at Mexico City in 1945 to work toward strengthening economic relations among the American Republics. The Council was launched with the full lyrical range of the good neighbors' rhetoric. "None of the inter-American institutions," thought the Chairman, "has responsibilities comparable with those entrusted to this Council." The Council would be, said another delegate, a laboratory of ideas and principles to serve the aspirations of the people of this hemisphere. But errors were immediately made. The American republics chose to give membership on the Council a diplomatic rather than a technical character and they provided inadequate staff. These errors were compounded when the Council proceeded to misinterpret the character of the economic situation confronting the American republics. At Mexico City, it had been thought that the urgent problems of the next period would be readjustments in the external economic relationships deriving from reorganization to a peace-time basis. In actual practice, the challenge of the period turned out to be the intensification of the internal problems which many of the countries had refused to face courageously during the war. Instead of a damaging curtailment of procurement activity, instead of a pincers movement in export-import prices, exports rose to an all-time high. The period turned out to be one in which the individual republics were given by the external situation the flexibility to achieve the adjustment to peace safely and soundly. The real problem of the times was coping with inflationary tendencies, the failure to control government expenditures, the failure to take adequate action on tax systems, the failure of price controls. But the Council went blithely on its way emphasizing in its every meeting that it was dealing with an emergency requiring international action when what was

---

[2] Davila, *op. cit.*, p. 35.

needed was vigorous internal action. The fact of the matter was that the international structure could not in any event have been of much assistance in the situation.

Not to have foreseen this turn in events was excusable. But the deliberate refusal to operate with an understanding of the facts once they became known was not. Meanwhile, with its woolly instructions and its failure to concentrate activity instead of ranging over the lyrical aspirations and hopes of mankind, the Council botched successive opportunities for constructive contributions. The Marshall Plan offered a major opportunity for constructive activity, but the Council hesitated to recommend to the Latin American republics that they join the United States in the effort to bolster the European economies by effective contributions. Hampered by the limitations of agreement for agreement's sake, the Council botched the preparations for the Bogotá Conference by producing an inadequate basic document from which grew the unsatisfactory economic agreement of Bogotá. And the Council even missed the opportunity to tighten the definition of its field of activity, once and for all, when it permitted the United Nations to invade its area, apparently with the thought that two agencies accomplishing nothing were no worse than one accomplishing nothing. Carlos Davila has written caustically and correctly that approval of the creation of a United Nations Economic Commission for Latin America was "an easy way of doing nothing for Latin America. Where Inter-American economic problems were concerned, commissions and committees are the only things that have *not* been lacking." [3] Significantly the Ad Hoc Committee that passed on the desirability of setting up the United Nations Economic Commission for Latin America was impressed with the fact that creation of the Commission *could not impede* the program of the specialized agencies. In other words, a proliferation of agencies on the theory that "at least they can do no harm." The experience with the Commission by 1950 furnished ample support for those who had felt that the United Nations effort was an unnecessary duplication of regional

---

[3] Davila, *op. cit.*, p. 79.

machinery that itself had not yet shaken down into an acceptable function.

In 1950 the Inter-American Economic and Social Council
assembled in Extraordinary Session to consider a number of
problems in the realm of developmental policy. The Economic
Agreement of Bogotá had not yet gained acceptance, the proposed Buenos Aires Economic Conference to pass on the vital
issues of Inter-American economic cooperation had been successively postponed largely at the instance of the United
States, and the part that the Inter-American system was to
play in expansion of cooperation in technical assistance programs was not yet clear. The difficulty of getting agreement
on a multilateral basis on matters of operating importance
was again underlined when the delegates concluded that they
were unable to reach an acceptable basis for the economic
agreement. The only basis would have been one at such a
low common denominator as to be useless. This prompted
the unusually frank delegate of the United States to conclude
that the role of multilateral activity may well be partly to
show that "some types of problems, particularly in the economic field, can perhaps best be dealt with bilaterally, according
to the needs and conditions of particular countries." [4] The
proposal for an economic conference in Buenos Aires was
rejected, again with a remark by the American delegate that
"there has been some tendency to attribute many of the
economic ills of the hemisphere to the delay in holding that
Conference . . . and to blame the United States because the
Conference has not yet been held, but it is an incontrover-
tible fact that the huge complicated problem of economic
development does not lend itself to solution through the mere
holding of conferences nor the passing of resolutions." The
Session closed on that note, with a small positive accomplishment in a decision to proceed with a minor cooperative technical assistance program. At least from the viewpoint of the
United States, the position seemed to have been established
that the area of multilateral activity is distinctly limited and

---

[4] Edward G. Miller, Jr., Assistant Secretary of State, Department of
State Press Release No. 336, April 10, 1950.

that the solution to the central problems facing the Americas in the sphere of economic development did not seem likely to be found in simple proliferation of structure or increase in the pace of conference-holding and resolution-passing.

In bilateral activity, the United States was proceeding in 1950 with negotiation of treaties with individual countries seeking to establish "rules of the game" for investment of capital by private investors. Through its Export-Import Bank it was making capital available for fields in which private investment was unlikely to flow. And it was co-operating with the International Bank for Reconstruction and Development in the financing of Latin American projects, although the exact relationship of the two institutions was still not clear in the minds of U. S. officials. Private capital was moving into Latin America as rapidly as it could find a suitable climate of investment. "Know-how" in many fields was a commercial product merchandized by American private firms. In addition, the United States government was co-operating actively to enable Latin America to draw on our technical competence in the fields of public health, agriculture, education, sanitation, geology and other fields. Among the variety of devices for cooperation were the detail of government specialists from agencies like the Department of Agriculture for specific assignments, cooperation in jointly-financed institutions such as the Inter-American Institute of Agricultural Sciences, study and exchange programs, and U. S.-sponsored agencies like the Institute of Inter-American Affairs. The latter was a successful device that merits fuller discussion.

During the second world war President Roosevelt established the Office of the Coordinator of Inter-American Affairs, with Nelson Rockefeller as its head. Rockefeller brought in a group of fresh imaginative people, free of the resolution-consciousness and rhetoric-intoxication which had caused the State Department to bog down rather badly. To this group it was clear that the challenge was to give the Good-Neighbor Policy content, to reach the people instead of the chancelleries, to reach the people in a way that the financing of a highway for a President's personal profit or the uneconomic diversion of scarce materials to build a gambling casino for politically influential officials (both of which had been tried, incidentally) could never hope to do. After many false starts ranging from poorly-conceived ballet tours to hastily improvised advertising campaigns that backfired, the group hit on the idea of a program of cooperative health and education services in the other American republics. In the uninspired language of the Budget Bureau, the purpose of the program was "to aid and improve the health and general welfare of the people of the Western Hemisphere in collaboration with their governments." But in practical terms, the program represented the first significant success in finding a mass-basis for the Good-Neighbor Policy, in implementing the policy so as to give it direct meaning and appeal for the masses in Latin America.

The technique was new, the difficulty of executing a program multiplied in proportion to the number of countries involved, and a war period added its own special difficulties. The program was carried out under cooperative agreements signed with the individual Latin American governments. Operations were carried out under a system which brought the Latin American government in as a partner in the enterprise by setting up a department within the appropriate ministry of the country in which the program was to operate. The work to be executed by this unit or "servicio" was determined in advance, with specific projects outlined. Commonly both governments contributed to the financing from the start, with the United States contribution on a sliding scale, so that at termination of agreements the share financed by the local government had increased sufficiently so that the project could be continued in the event that United States financing had to be suspended. The average venture undertaken by the cooperative services showed satisfactory results, the weaker ones were gradually eliminated or corrected, and a number achieved outstanding results. A highly competent unbiased investigator was able to report to the State Department in 1947 that "the operations are reaching the masses. . . . Politically significant effects have quickly occurred. In the great majority of the large number of cases tested, the individuals interrogated recognized the fact of United States participation in the projects they knew, and there is a large body of satisfactory visual evidence that the publicity has generally been adequate in this important aspect of the effectiveness of the programs as a vehicle of good will." [5]   It was then estimated that the program had benefited directly some 25 million people.   The Congress in 1949, reviewing the record of the period 1942-1948 when the United States government had devoted about 3/100 of 1 per cent of its expenditures to this program, found the program so successful that it voted an extension of the life of the supervising agency—the Institute of Inter-American Affairs—to 1955.   The Institute was then active in 16 Latin American countries and was conducting 25 work programs, of which 4 were in the field of agriculture, 7 in education, 14 in health and sanitation. When, in 1950, debate began on the so-called Point IV program for aiding the under-developed areas of the world, the technique of joint control of funds, joint planning, joint staffing and joint execution, was recognized as basic to any world-wide extension. [6]

Still another type of cooperation was that provided through the U. S. Department of Agriculture.   This program of cooperation with 15 countries was in its tenth year in 1949.   It aimed at increasing agricultural efficiency and improving living standards as well as increasing production of certain crops in which the United States was particularly interested such as rubber, rotenone crops, tropical woods, essential oils, certain fibers, cacao, cinchona.   In some of the countries the United States has helped to establish and maintain cooperative stations for research and education, at which is pooled the technical competence of the cooperating countries.   More than 300 research and demonstrational projects were current in 1950.   Other cooperation took the form of training for local leadership; from 1942 to 1949 about 300 "in-service"

---

[5] House of Representatives, Hearings before the Subcommittee of the Committee on Appropriations, "Government Corporation Appropriation Bill for 1948," Part I, p. 394.

[6] See *History of the Office of the Coordinator of Inter-American Affairs* (Washington, 1947), pp. 231-244.

trainees came to the United States from Latin America to work in the Department of Agriculture or in the State universities.[7]

Nor was the cooperative effort to bring higher levels of technical competence to Latin America confined to governmental activity. In 1943 the Rockefeller Foundation initiated a program at the invitation of the Mexican Government which had two objectives: (a) to improve agriculture through research leading to the production of more high-quality food crops; and (b) to train Mexicans in several fields of agricultural science for future leadership in the solution of Mexico's agricultural problems. The program was set up jointly with four chief divisions—soil science, plant breeding, plant pathology, and entomology—to work on improvement of basic food plants, higher production through soil improvement, protection from pests and diseases. By 1950 it had resulted in the development of improved corn varieties and hybrids which were being rapidly accepted and contributing greatly to production; new rust resistant varieties of wheat, well adapted to Mexican conditions, had permitted for the first time the summer production of wheat on a commercial scale; superior selections of beans were being increased for distribution; green mature crops, either in rotation or interplanted with corn, sorghums and wheat, were being used for soil improvement; and soybeans and sorghums were being tested, further selected, and increased.

Still another type of venture was the International Basic Economy Corporation which had been organized on a commercial basis by the Rockefeller interests to search out economic bottlenecks in agricultural and industrial production in Venezuela, Brazil and eventually other Latin American countries. To produce more and better corn in Brazil, a hybrid-seed corn company was established and on the basis of an excellent hybrid cross already developed by two Brazilian

---

[7] See P. V. Cardon, "The World's Potential in Food and Agriculture," a paper read before the joint meeting of the American Statistical Association, American Farm Economic Association, Population Association of America and American Economic Association in New York, December 27, 1949.

researchers, seed was offered for sale which often yielded twice as much as local varieties. In Venezuela the Corporation worked on growing of corn under tropical conditions, with such problems as weeds that grow at almost visible speed, a husk that is not adapted to ordinary husking equipment, etc. Another venture in Brazil was the farm-service company to provide on a fee basis such services as stump pulling, cultivating, terracing and harvesting. As has been the case with all American investment history, the technological advances introduced in such ventures inevitably filter into the framework of general knowledge which governs the production activity of the nations.[8]

In the case of technical assistance, as in other phases of cooperation from abroad, there was an inclination sometimes to fail to appreciate that the effectiveness of external assistance depended largely on the individual country's willingness to push vigorously toward the objective. Actually in an area where the governments were spending some $6 billion per year, the amount of assistance projected for foreign technical aid had not been particularly significant. The real problem was to persuade the governments to recognize the priority which technological progress must assume in their thinking and in their budgeting. Recognition of this priority had to go beyond the budget into the governmental machinery to permit effectiveness of operation without political interference. Otherwise, agricultural extension work, public health activity, educational reform, were all likely to deteriorate into bureaucratic political operations, which no amount of continuing outside assistance was likely to be able to make fully effective. There was already in fact ample experience with such machinery as that of agricultural extension services which, politically controlled, had ended up with excessive distances from farm to government center—not physically, but

---

[8] In addition to the International Basic Economy Corporation, the Rockefeller interests also supported a non-profit venture called the American International Association for Economic and Social Development which collaborated with Latin American governments on diet, farm techniques and other educational programs. See "Nelson Rockefeller's I.B.E.C.", *Fortune*, February, 1950, pp. 81-83, 158-162.

mentally and staffwise. "Know-how" by "show-how" had definite limitations on the extent to which the process can be telescoped in time, whether it be industrial technique or elementary education or good farming practices. And in this field, as in the others we have discussed, the pace with which development could proceed was one which the Latin American countries would individually largely determine for themselves.

*   *   *

A competent Minister of Economy in Chile not long ago reminded the Chileans that "when don Pedro de Valdivia was leaving Peru to undertake the conquest of Chile, the Cuzco Indians kept repeating: 'The gold, master, is farther south. The gold, master, is farther south.' But there was no gold. Or more correctly, there was no gold until the gallant Castillians resigned themselves to extracting it with their own hands, alternating their armed vigil with mining."

In recent years there has persisted the thought that "the gold, the gold lies up north," that the road to development consists of developing costless access in some fashion to the body of technical competence and industrial capital in foreign countries, that it ought to be possible to find some structure or some system by which great advances in productivity can be achieved without systematic revision and studied reconciliation of the economic policies which have kept the Latin American economies at low levels of efficiency. But the course of rapid development is at best a rough one. Whatever the circumstances of international relations which may serve to expand or modify the degree of economic assistance along that road, the fundamental policy-decisions, the fundamental priority of objectives, are those which can be determined only by each individual country. On those decisions will depend the pace of development.

SUPPLEMENTARY READING

Henry C. Wallich, "Some Aspects of Latin American Economic Relations with the United States," *Foreign Economic Policy for the United States* (Edited by Seymour E. Harris, Harvard University Press, Cambridge, 1948), pp. 155-168.

Acierto, "A Marshall Plan for Latin America," *Inter-American Economic Affairs,* September, 1947, pp. 3-20.

Institute of Inter-American Studies, "Institute Memorandum on the Latin American Policy of the United States," *Inter-American Economic Affairs,* Autumn, 1949, pp. 81-94.

The Brookings Institution, *Major Problems of United States Foreign Policy 1948-49* (The Brookings Institution, Washington, 1948), "The Problem of Economic Assistance to Latin America," pp. 161-184.

Gordon Barrows, "Foreign Policy in a Vacuum: The Study Guide of the Brookings Institution," *Inter-American Economic Affairs,* Winter, 1948, pp. 31-42.

John Hickey, "The Cooperative Services and the Good Neighbor Policy," *Inter-American Economic Affairs,* Winter, 1948, pp. 83-93.

Simon G. Hanson, "Case Study in Futility: United Nations Economic Commission for Latin America," *Inter-American Economic Affairs,* Autumn, 1948, pp. 81-99.

A. Edward Stuntz, *To Make the People Strong* (The Macmillan Company, New York, 1948), pp. 62-155.

Institute Reports on Inter-American Policy, March, 1949, "Economic Cooperation with Latin America—The Record of the United States 1946-1948," pp. 1-8.

Simon G. Hanson, "The Economic Work of the Inter-American Agencies," *Inter-American Economic Affairs,* Spring, 1949, pp. 74-83.